SPORT, PHYSICAL ACTIVITY, AND THE LAW

Neil J. Dougherty, EdD
Rutgers University

David Auxter, EdD
Research Institute for Independent Living, Edgewater, MD

Alan S. Goldberger, JD
Goldberger & Goldberger Counsellors at Law
Clifton, NJ

Gregg S. Heinzmann, EdM
Rutgers University

With Canadian applications by
Hilary A. Findlay, PhD, LLB
Durocher Simpson Barristers and Solicitors, Edmonton, Alberta

Human Kinetics Publishers

Library of Congress Cataloging-in-Publication Data

Sport, physical activity, and the law / Neil J. Dougherty . . . [et
  al.].
       p.   cm.
     Includes index.
     ISBN 0-87322-512-0
     1. Sports--Law and legislation--United States.   I. Dougherty,
   Neil J.
   KF3989.S65   1994
   344.73'099--dc20
   [347.30499]   93-21763
                                                          CIP

ISBN: 0-87322-512-0

Acquisitions Editor: Rick Frey, PhD; **Developmental Editor**: Rodd Whelpley; **Assistant Editors**: Dawn
Roselund, Moyra Knight, Julie Lancaster; **Photo Editor**: Valerie Hall; **Copyeditor**: Nancy Talanian; **Proof-
readers**: Pam Johnson, Anne Byler; **Indexer**: Theresa Schaefer; **Production Director**: Ernie Noa; **Typesetter
and Text Layout**: Yvonne Winsor; **Text Design**: Keith Blomberg; **Cover Design**: Jack Davis; **Illustrations**:
Andy Nelson; **Printer**: Braun-Brumfield, Inc.

Printed in the United States of America

10   9   8   7   6   5   4   3   2   1

Human Kinetics Publishers
Box 5076, Champaign, IL 61825-5076
1-800-747-4457

Canada: Human Kinetics Publishers, Box 24040, Windsor, ON N8Y 4Y9
1-800-465-7301 (in Canada only)

Europe: Human Kinetics Publishers (Europe) Ltd., P.O. Box IW14
Leeds LS16 6TR, England
0532-781708

Australia: Human Kinetics Publishers, P.O. Box 80, Kingswood 5062
South Australia
618-374-0433

New Zealand: Human Kinetics Publishers, P.O. Box 105-231, Auckland 1
(09) 309-2259

CONTENTS

PREFACE

It is virtually impossible to exist within organized society without having one's actions affected, and to some degree controlled, by elements of law. The laws of a society dictate the rights and responsibilities of individuals as well as procedures for redress when the actions or inactions of others infringe upon those rights.

Although sport, as an institution, and the individuals who deliver and participate in programs of sport and physical activity are subject to the same legal principles as the rest of society, historically the nature of the activity and the attitudes of those involved created a subculture where the authority of the coach was unquestioned and the rights of participants depended primarily on the coach's desires and decisions. Questions concerning eligibility to participate and disqualifying conditions or circumstances have been a matter of local or league preference. Injuries were considered part of the game and, although unfortunate, certainly not subject to litigation. In all matters of team discipline and control, the decision of the coach was final. His word was, in effect, law.

No longer is this true. Recent case law and the growing legal sensitivity of the populace has pulled sport from its self-protecting cocoon squarely into the mainstream of legal practice. Issues such as the right to participate and compensation for injuries are frequently the subject of formal legal proceedings. Coaches, administrators, game officials, and even other players are the target of legal action based on their alleged commissions or omissions.

These developments make it essential that all persons involved with creating and delivering programs of amateur sport and physical activity clearly understand the fundamental legal principles that most directly affect their actions and activities. *Sport, Physical Activity, and the Law* has been developed to meet this need. (Because legal considerations in professional sport are vastly different from those of amateur sport and physical activity, and because the legal aspects of professional sport affect relatively few practitioners, we have elected not to address professional sports in this text. An effective treatment of this topic requires a volume of its own.)

This text provides the legal knowledge practitioners need to function effectively. We've taken great care to present accurate, legally sound information in language that is clear, simple, and concise. To address the issue of gender inclusiveness in pronouns, we have randomly assigned feminine and masculine pronouns throughout the text in circumstances where the particular referent is not identified. Of course, the concepts discussed are not intended to appear gender-specific.

The text begins, as you might expect, with an introduction, "Part I: Law, Legal Systems, and Research" which lays the necessary foundation for the four sections that follow. "Part II: Who May Participate?" focuses on the legal requirements for fair and equitable opportunities for all people. It provides background, fundamental principles, and practical guidelines to help you determine who may or may not participate in sport and physical activity and under what circumstances. "Part III: Rights of the Participant" addresses issues of freedom of speech and expression as well as individual rights regarding due process and search and seizure.

"Part IV: Who Is in Charge?" identifies the current status and legal significance of certification, licensure, and legal immunity for professionals and volunteers who deliver programs of sport and physical activity. This section also discusses the rights of sport governing bodies and the legal parameters of their interaction with the various public and private institutions and groups that comprise their membership. Finally, "Part V: Responsibility for Safe Participation" addresses the fundamental obligation to provide a reasonably safe program and environment for all participants. Principles of risk management, safety, and legal liability are examined as they apply to coaches, teachers, program leaders, officials, and athletes themselves.

The common organizational pattern of the chapters facilitates study and review. First we present a brief scenario to illustrate the nature of the topic at hand. This is followed by a list of objectives that articulates the key elements of the chapter. As important new terms are introduced, they appear in bold print. Many chapters contain management sections that show the sport administrator how to turn the legal concepts and requirements discussed into proactive tools that build better programs. At the end of each chapter is an index of the chapter's key terms.

Following the text discussion in each chapter are several case studies that demonstrate real-world applications of the legal concepts addressed. The cases have been presented in a simple narrative form rather than a formal legal reporting style. Although all are based on actual situations, not all have been adjudicated and reported at the appellate level. Case studies based on lower court decisions are identified and for the most part use fictitious names and places. We chose this format, as opposed to the more common reporting of appellate decisions only, to maximize readability and interest for readers and to allow us to base cases on matters adjudicated in the lower courts (or in some instances settled before trial). This practice lets students develop a better understanding of the day-to-day application of legal principles than if examples were limited to the relatively rare instances in which formal legal precedent has been established.

The case studies are followed by a brief summary of the chapter concepts, a list of the key terms, and several questions to aid in review and self-evaluation. Finally, we give suggested additional readings for those who want to explore further the material presented. The text also features Canadian applications for each part, which address the major differences in how the concepts discussed would be treated under Canadian law.

We have written this book to help current and future practitioners and administrators develop safe and legally sound sport and physical activity programs. It is not intended to substitute for the advice of an attorney when it is called for, nor can it necessarily forestall lawsuits—no text can make such claims. But we are convinced that the principles and guidelines in *Sport, Physical Activity, and the Law* can form a foundation for a program that complies with both the letter and spirit of the law regarding safety and individual rights, which in turn minimizes the likelihood of lawsuits and maximizes the likelihood of winning any that may occur. Even more important, participants in such programs will be given maximum opportunities and options in a safe and effectively regulated environment.

ACKNOWLEDGMENTS

Throughout the development and completion of this text, the authors were fortunate enough to have the help of a number of persons without whom the project would not have succeeded.

We are particularly grateful to Thomas M. Egan, Margaret Dougherty, Carole Goldberger, Barbara Brandis, and Douglas M. Lehman, Esq. for their advice and assistance with regard to content and editing. We would also like to thank our typists, Ann-Marie Charleston and Jan Houtman, for their efficiency and tolerance throughout our many drafts and revisions.

Finally, we would be remiss if we did not acknowledge the outstanding support provided by Rick Frey, Rodd Whelpley, and the entire Human Kinetics family. They were cooperative and supportive while continually challenging us to create a book of which we could all be proud.

PHOTO CREDITS

PART I

LAW, LEGAL SYSTEMS, AND RESEARCH

The body of law that pertains to physical activity and sport is not an entity unto itself but, rather, is a small component of the complex and constantly evolving legal system. Moreover, the legal ramifications of the actions of athletes and sports organizations cut across many areas of the law. For example, an athlete who feels she has been denied her legal rights by an association that refuses to allow her to compete may assert legal theories embracing concepts of contract, constitutional, labor, tort, and even antitrust law in challenging the disputed action. Sport law, therefore, must focus on such topics as contracts, torts, and constitutional law, and professionals in the field of sport and physical activity must be able to understand and apply basic concepts of law throughout the course of their day-to-day activities.

To this end, chapter 1 sets forth the basic concepts necessary to understand the law and to apply it to sport-specific situations such as those addressed in Parts II through V. The chapter emphasizes the practical benefits of law as an effective tool in the management process.

Chapter 2 outlines the basic tools necessary to conduct legal research. It describes the commonly accepted sources of legal information and explains how to access them and how to assure the timeliness and accuracy of researched information.

Careful study of chapters 1 and 2 will help you develop the concepts and skills you need to understand and apply the principles of law in sport or any other form of human interaction.

CHAPTER 1

OVERVIEW OF THE LAW AND THE LEGAL SYSTEM

Ladies and gentlemen of the jury: We are here today because a young athlete has suffered severe and permanent injury as a result of her coach's failure to exercise the degree of care that she owed to the members of her team. The coach was negligent. Because of this negligence, Margaret Quinn has been made to suffer physical and mental discomfort, extensive medical bills, and severe and permanent disability. Only you can compensate Margaret Quinn for the needless damage that she has suffered as a result of the unprofessional and improper actions of her coach, Jean Sharp.

—Opening statement to the jury by the attorney for the plaintiff

How does a successful, highly regarded coach land in a courtroom, being labeled by the plaintiff's attorney as negligent and responsible for the injuries suffered by one of her athletes? Although the scenario presented is fictitious, it represents an ever-increasing occurrence in the field of sport and physical activity. More and more, people are turning to the courts as a means of correcting or seeking compensation for wrongs which they claim to have suffered because of the actions of others.

Our society has reached a level of complexity whereby much of our day-to-day function is controlled by law. The legal process is designed to protect the rights of every person. In so doing it establishes the limits of individual rights and responsibilities not only for those who participate in sport but for leaders and administrators as well. Therefore, thorough understanding and application of the law as it applies to sport and physical activity have become essential components of the planning and delivery of all activities.

LEARNING OBJECTIVES

The student will be able to

1. distinguish between matters that are normally subject to criminal laws and those that are normally subject to civil laws;
2. name and explain the steps in the process of a civil suit;
3. describe the nature and application of the primary forms of pretrial discovery; and
4. recognize the value of the law as a managerial tool.

DEFINITION OF LAW

Reduced to simple terms, law is a system of principles or rules that are established and enforced to regulate human behavior. This regulation is accomplished by establishing obligations and rights and by imposing a system for redress that allows penalties to be imposed for violations. Elements of law can be found in virtually every aspect of American society. This is certainly no less true in the field of sport and physical activity, where issues such as who may participate, who may assume leadership roles, and the rights and responsibilities of each are often prescribed by law.

The written pronouncements of the law are preceded historically by the development of the **common law**, a somewhat amorphous framework of principles and strictures dating back to ancient times and refined and preserved by the courts of England. Common law, the root of the American legal system, was derived from custom and usage rather than rules set forth for the conduct of various societies by the legislative arms of government. Concepts of common law have been discussed, refined, defined, codified, and sometimes nullified by courts, legislatures, and Congress throughout the history of those institutions. Thus, the vast tentacles of the common law, together with official pronouncements of federal, state, regional, and local governmental organizations, both legislative and administrative, all comprise *the law*.

SOURCES OF REGULATION AND CONTROL IN SPORT AND PHYSICAL ACTIVITY

Just as in sport there are rules that govern how a game is played, there are rules that govern how sport and physical activity programs are managed and run. However, unlike sports where all the rules are set forth in a single rulebook, regulations concerning the provision and administration of sport and activity programs come from a number of sources including federal, state, and local laws, and league and organizational rules.

Law

The United States functions under both federal and state judicial systems. Many of our day-to-day activities fall within the bounds of federal, state, and local law. Laws affecting discrimination against individuals because of sex, race, or handicapping condition, for instance, have been enacted at the federal level and in every state.

The question of whether federal or state law would take precedence in any given situation is fairly clear-cut. Federal law takes precedence unless the requirements of the state are stricter. The state law takes precedence if it is more restrictive than, and not in conflict with the intent of, the federal law. Federal law, for instance, excludes contact sports from the prohibitions against sex discrimination. However, a state law that requires all sports, whether contact or not, to be accessible to both sexes would take precedence because it would be seen as a more restrictive interpretation of the legal equality of the sexes. Indeed, some states have enacted legislation to that end.

The same principles apply to laws enacted at the local level. That is, the laws enacted by a given municipality may not contravene those of the state or federal governments. It is important, therefore, to be aware of applicable state and local laws as well as federal laws.

Laws are divided into two major categories: criminal laws and civil laws. **Criminal laws** regulate public conduct and are enforced by the government body that enacted them. Violations of criminal laws result in action by the government aimed at imposing some form of **punishment**. Criminal acts are classified according to their level of severity. **Felonies** are the most heinous crimes and include murder, rape, assault, and robbery. Such offenses are punishable by monetary fines, imprisonment in a state or federal penitentiary, and, in extreme cases, capital punishment. **Misdemeanors** are lesser criminal offenses such as driving while under the influence of alcohol, disorderly conduct, and vandalism. Persons found guilty of misdemeanors may be subject to short-term imprisonment, fines, or both.

The overwhelming majority of legal actions involving sport and physical activity focus on alleged violations of civil law. **Civil laws** regulate interactions between individuals or groups. A civil action may be brought when one person feels wronged by another. The purpose of the civil action or lawsuit is to seek compensation for or to right an alleged wrong. Unlike criminal cases, civil suits seldom result in punishment beyond normal recompense for damages and the correction of the alleged wrong.

Legal precedent constitutes a major element in establishing the day-to-day application of the law. This concept is embodied in the legal doctrine of *stare decisis*, which literally means "to stand by the decision." In practice this means that courts called upon to adjudicate disputes customarily consider case **precedent** (that is, they will consider how other courts have ruled on similar cases) as well as existing statutes. When a court issues a decision, it establishes a precedent that ordinarily guides the subsequent actions of all courts of equal or lower stature within its jurisdiction on cases in which the facts and circumstances are essentially similar to the previously decided case.

Administrative Regulations

Much of the day-to-day operation of governmental organizations is controlled by **administrative regulations**. Various governmental agencies have the authority to develop and enforce policies, rules, and regulations for activities under their control. These have the force of law and therefore play important roles in the organization and management of many sport and physical activity programs. For example, the New Jersey Administrative Code contains guidelines established by New Jersey's state department of education regarding the educational qualifications of coaches employed by public schools. The athletic programs of every New Jersey public school district must honor these regulations.

League and Organizational Rules

Virtually all sport and physical activity programs establish rules and regulations regarding competition, organizational structure, and the conduct of their members. Generally speaking, all members of a given group are bound by its rules and regulations. However, when such rules are believed to conflict with existing law, or when the organization takes actions that conflict with its own rules, the aggrieved party can seek redress through the courts. Chapter 11 describes the complex nature of these interactions in detail.

THE BUSINESS OF THE COURTS

Most civil cases brought against programs of physical education or sport involve an alleged tort. A **tort** is a legal wrong for which one may, under certain circumstances, seek compensation through the courts. A person who believes that he has suffered an injury or a loss because of the actions of another, or because of that person's failure to act in a prescribed manner, has the following three legal or quasi-legal options to choose from:

1. Do nothing. Many people are unwilling to get involved with the legal system, are unaware of their rights, or are unsure of the validity of their complaints. These and numerous other personal factors lead some individuals simply to accept a situation rather than to pursue any legal remedy.

2. Attempt to obtain satisfaction without professional aid. Depending upon the nature of the grievance, an individual could contact school or program administrators or insurers and set forth the elements of his complaint. Then the officers of the organization or their insurers would either offer to correct or compensate for the problem or would deny such support depending upon their assessment of the circumstances and of the potential legal outcome if the **grievant** (the individual seeking compensation for an alleged loss) chose to pursue the matter through the courts.

3. Seek the services of an attorney who, upon reviewing the matter, would either refuse the case or agree to represent the client, in which case they would probably agree to pursue one of the following options:

   a. The attorney could agree to act as the grievant's official representative in attempting to negotiate a settlement with the organization and/or its insurer without instituting a lawsuit.

   b. The attorney could agree to institute legal action, or litigation.

If the attorney decides to seek compensation through the court system, she would file a complaint or petition in the appropriate court. A **complaint** is a formal document that initiates a civil suit. The complaint would enumerate the basic legal theories and facts put forth by the injured party (the **plaintiff**).

The complaint would also state the damages or other form of relief the plaintiff seeks from the **defendant** (the individual against whom the complaint is filed). Figure 1.1 (pages 7-9) shows portions of a sample complaint. After a complaint has been filed and served on the defendants, their attorneys normally file an answer. The **answer** normally denies all or some of the allegations made in the complaint and puts forth legal arguments on behalf of the defendants. Figure 1.2 (pages 10-11) is an example of an abbreviated answer to a complaint filed by a plaintiff.

Jones, Smith & Brown, P.A.
9 South Avenue
Point Pleasant, New Jersey 08742
ATTORNEYS FOR PLAINTIFF

PLAINTIFF(S))	SUPERIOR COURT OF NEW JERSEY
MARGARET QUINN)	LAW DIVISION: OCEAN COUNTY
v.)	DOCKET NO.: OCN-L-3200-90
)	Civil Action
DEFENDANT(S))	AMENDED COMPLAINT
JEAN SHARP AND CITY OF)	AND
WELDON, BOARD OF)	DEMAND FOR TRIAL BY JURY
EDUCATION, a public)	
entity of the State of)	
New Jersey)	

The Plaintiff, Margaret Quinn, residing at 12 Banks Street, in the City of Weldon, County of Ocean, and State of New Jersey, by way of Complaint against the Defendants, says:

FIRST COUNT

1. On or about February 9, 1992, Plaintiff, MARGARET QUINN, was a high school student enrolled in Weldon High School, located at 121 St. Johns Avenue, Weldon, New Jersey, and a member of the Weldon High School Girls' Track and Field Team.

2. On or about February 9, 1992, and at all times hereinafter relevant, the Defendant, JEAN SHARP, was an employee of the Defendant, CITY OF WELDON, BOARD OF EDUCATION, and was specifically employed as a physical education teacher and coach at said Weldon High School.

3. On or about February 9, 1992, and at all times hereinafter relevant, the Defendants, JEAN SHARP and CITY OF WELDON, BOARD OF EDUCATION, were directly responsible for the instruction, control, and supervision of students enrolled at Weldon High School, including, but not limited to, members of the Weldon High School Girls' Track and Field Team, of which Plaintiff was a member.

(continued)

Figure 1.1 Complaint of the plaintiff.

4. On or about February 9, 1992, and at all times hereinafter relevant, the duties, obligations, and responsibilities of the Defendants included, among other things, the proper, reasonable, and careful supervision of all students involved in organized practices of any and all athletic teams conducted upon school premises, including the Weldon High School Girls' Track and Field Team, and the protection of said students from injuries while involved in said practice sessions.

5. On February 9, 1992, Plaintiff, MARGARET QUINN, was a student properly and lawfully enrolled in Weldon High School, and a proper and lawful member of the Weldon High School Girls' Track and Field Team, involved in team practice.

6. On February 9, 1992, while the Plaintiff was present and in attendance in the aforesaid team practice, she was injured as a direct and proximate result of the negligence of the Defendants, JEAN SHARP and CITY OF WELDON, BOARD OF EDUCATION, in failing to properly supervise and control the aforesaid practice session of the Weldon High School Girls' Track and Field Team.

7. As a direct and proximate result of the aforesaid negligence of the Defendants, the Plaintiff, MARGARET QUINN, was caused to sustain, and did sustain, serious, severe, and permanent personal injury; she did and has continued to experience great pain and suffering; she has and will continue to be obliged to seek medical treatment as a result of her injuries; she has and will continue to incur medical expenses substantially in excess of $1,000.00; she has and will continue to be unable to engage in her routine activities and affairs; and she has otherwise been damaged.

8. On or about March 14, 1992, Plaintiff filed a notice of claim on Defendant, CITY OF WELDON, BOARD OF EDUCATION, in accordance with NJSA 59:8-9. Six months have elapsed since the filing of said notice of claim, and no disposition of this case has yet been made as to Defendant, CITY OF WELDON, BOARD OF EDUCATION.

WHEREFORE, the Plaintiff, MARGARET QUINN, demands judgment against the Defendants, JEAN SHARP and CITY OF WELDON, BOARD OF EDUCATION, jointly, severally, or in the alternative, in the amount of her damages, together with interest and cost of suit.

SECOND COUNT

1. Plaintiff, MARGARET QUINN, repeats and realleges all the allegations contained in the First Count of the Complaint and incorporates the same herein by reference.

2. The Defendant, CITY OF WELDON, BOARD OF EDUCATION, is liable for the negligence of its public employee, Defendant JEAN SHARP, in accordance with the doctrine of respondeat superior and pursuant to NJSA 59:2-2 of the New Jersey Tort Claims Act, NJSA 59:1-1 et seq.

Figure 1.1 *(continued)*

WHEREFORE, the Plaintiff, MARGARET QUINN, demands judgment against the Defendant, CITY OF WELDON, BOARD OF EDUCATION, a public entity of the State of New Jersey, in the amount of her damages, together with interest and cost of suit.

DEMAND FOR TRIAL BY JURY

Plaintiff hereby demands a trial by jury as to all issues.

CERTIFICATION

The undersigned hereby certifies that the matter in controversy is not the subject of any other action presently pending in any court or of any pending arbitration proceedings and that no other actions or arbitration proceedings are presently contemplated.

The undersigned further certifies that there are no other parties of which she is presently aware who should be joined in the action.

NOTICE OF TRIAL COUNSEL

Please take notice that NANCY R. JONES, ESQ., is hereby designated as trial counsel in the above-captioned matter for the firm of Jones, Smith & Brown, pursuant to Rule 4:25 et seq.

> JONES, SMITH & BROWN, P.A.
> Attorneys for Plaintiff
>
> By: _____
> Nancy R. Jones

DATED: October 23, 1992

Figure 1.1 *(continued)*

LLOYD JAMES, ESQ.
85 Livingston Avenue
Tidewater, New Jersey 08745
Attorneys for Defendants, JEAN SHARP AND CITY OF WELDON,
BOARD OF EDUCATION

	SUPERIOR COURT OF NEW JERSEY
	LAW DIVISION: OCEAN COUNTY
	Docket No.: OCN-L-3200-90

MARGARET QUINN,   :
    Plaintiff,   :   Civil Action
          v.   :
JEAN SHARP and CITY OF   : ANSWER, SEPARATE DEFENSES,
WELDON, BOARD OF EDUCATION, : DEMAND FOR STATEMENT OF
a public entity of the   : DAMAGES AND JURY DEMAND
State of New Jersey,   :
    Defendants.   :

The Defendants, JEAN SHARP and CITY OF WELDON, BOARD OF EDUCATION, by way of Answer to the Complaint of the Plaintiff, say that:

FIRST COUNT

The Defendants, JEAN SHARP and CITY OF WELDON, BOARD OF EDUCATION, deny the allegations contained in Paragraphs 6 and 7 of the First Count of the Complaint.

SECOND COUNT

The Defendants, JEAN SHARP and CITY OF WELDON, BOARD OF EDUCATION, repeat their answers to all allegations contained in all paragraphs of the First Count of the Complaint as though set forth at length herein and makes them their answer to paragraph 1 of the Second Count.

FIRST SEPARATE DEFENSE

These Defendants were guilty of no negligence that was the proximate cause of the injuries and damages alleged.

SECOND SEPARATE DEFENSE

Any injuries or damages allegedly sustained by the Plaintiff were the result of the contributory negligence of said Plaintiff.

(continued)

Figure 1.2 Answer to the complaint of the plaintiff.

THIRD SEPARATE DEFENSE

Any injuries or damages allegedly sustained by the Plaintiff were the result of the sole negligence of a third party or parties over whom this Defendant had no control.

FOURTH SEPARATE DEFENSE

The Plaintiff is barred by contributory negligence, which negligence was greater than that of these Defendants.

FIFTH SEPARATE DEFENSE

The Plaintiff is not entitled to recover for pain and suffering, pursuant to NJSA 59:9-2(d).

SIXTH SEPARATE DEFENSE

Any amount the Plaintiff may recover shall be reduced in proportion to the amount of negligence attributable to the Plaintiff.

DEMAND FOR STATEMENT OF DAMAGES

Please take notice that the defendants, JEAN SHARP and CITY OF WELDON, BOARD OF EDUCATION, request within the time provided by the Rules of the Court that the Plaintiff serve a written statement of the amount of damages claimed in the within action.

JURY DEMAND

The Defendants, JEAN SHARP and CITY OF WELDON, BOARD OF EDUCATION, hereby demand a jury trial on all triable issues.

CERTIFICATION

I hereby certify that the within Answer has been served and filed in accordance with the provisions of the Rules of the Court.

LLOYD JAMES, ESQ.
Attorney for Defendants,
JEAN SHARP and CITY OF WELDON,
BOARD OF EDUCATION

Dated: December 12, 1992   By: _____

                                            Lloyd James, Esq.

Figure 1.2 *(continued)*

After these initial pleadings have been filed, the case moves into what is commonly called the discovery phase of the proceedings. The **process of discovery** encompasses the period between the commencement of the lawsuit and the commencement of the trial. During this time the attorneys exercise a number of legal options to find and develop all the pertinent facts that bear upon the case. The primary forms of pretrial discovery are interrogatories, depositions, and requests for production of physical evidence.

Interrogatories are written questions sent by the attorney representing one party involved in a lawsuit to one of the adversarial parties. These questions must be answered truthfully and under oath. They may be introduced as evidence at the time of trial and should be answered with the advice of an attorney. Figure 1.3 provides examples of questions frequently found on interrogatories.

1. State: (a) your full name, (b) present address, (c) address at the time cause of action arose, (d) date and place of birth, (e) date and place of any marriages or termination of marriages, and if a corporation, (f) date and state of incorporation, (g) names and addresses of officers and registered agent, and (h) whether or not corporation is authorized to do business in New Jersey.

2. State: (a) the date and place on which these interrogatories were answered, (b) whether you were ever convicted of a crime, and, if so, (c) the nature of the offense and (d) the date and place of conviction.

3. State: (a) the names and addresses of all insurance or surety companies that insure or guarantee any possible liability on your part for occurrences set forth in the pleadings; (b) which of said insurers or sureties have primary, excess, or concurrent coverages; (c) the policy or bond limits with respect to each category of coverage; and (d) the carrier's names, policy numbers, and coverages for each insurance policy owned by you or any relative residing in your household at the time of the said occurrences.

4. With respect to all expert witnesses, including treating physicians and experts who have conducted an examination, inspection, or investigation, or who have been consulted with respect to the facts of the instant litigation, whether or not said expert is expected to testify: (a) state such expert's name, address, and area of expertise; (b) state date and place of examination, inspection, investigation, or consultation; (c) state what or who was inspected or examined; (d) state names of experts expected to testify at trial; and (e) annex a true copy of all written reports rendered to you; or (f) if no written report has been submitted, supply a summary of any oral reports rendered to you or the essence of such testimony as is anticipated will be given by said experts.

5. Set forth the names, addresses, and all alleged knowledge of all persons having knowledge of relevant facts: (a) respecting the cause of action, (b) surrounding the happening of the occurrence set forth in the pleadings, (c) as to the damages claimed, (d) who were eye-witnesses to said occurrences.

(continued)

Figure 1.3 Examples of questions found on interrogatories.

6. State with regard to the track practice during which Margaret Quinn was injured on February 9, 1992: (a) the number of athletes on the team, (b) the names of the athletes on the team, and (c) the present addresses of the athletes on the team, and (d) the identities of any other persons who might have been present at said practice, listing names and current addresses if known.

7. Please state the view of the Weldon Board of Education as to how the incident that gave rise to the cause of action of this suit occurred.

8. Was any accident report, to either the Weldon High School Authorities or to any municipal or law enforcement authority, made with reference to the incident that is the subject of the complaint? If so: (a) state name and address of the person making the report; (b) state name and address of the person to whom the report was made; and (c) attach a copy of each such report to these answers.

9. Was Jean Sharp the only coach or supervisory person in charge of the track and field team on February 9, 1992? If not, state the names and addresses of the other persons in charge on that date.

Figure 1.3   *(continued)*

A **deposition** is pretrial testimony of a witness that is taken in response to a legal order. Attorneys for all parties are usually present at a deposition, and a court stenographer is present to administer oaths of truthfulness to the witnesses and to make a verbatim recording of the testimony. As with interrogatories, the transcript of a deposition may be used as evidence at the trial. This procedure serves a dual function: It allows the discovery of a great deal of factual information about the case; and, no less importantly, it allows the attorneys to assess the manner in which witnesses conduct and present themselves under the pressure of adversarial questioning.

The wide availability of videotape equipment has led to its increasing use in the judicial process. Sometimes, for instance, the attorneys for all parties to a suit agree to videotape the testimony of a witness prior to trial. The procedure is conducted under oath, with all parties having the opportunity to question the witness. The videotape can then be shown to the jury at the trial. This is particularly useful when circumstances beyond reasonable control would prevent a key witness from appearing at the trial.

During the process of discovery, attorneys for each side also make requests for various types of physical evidence to be produced. It is not uncommon, for instance, for attorneys or their representatives to examine equipment that was being worn or used at the time of an injury, or written items such as lesson plans, accident reports, attendance records, and medical records.

Although the pretrial process itself is conducted by the attorneys for each party according to clearly prescribed procedures, its eventual outcome can be greatly affected by factors within the defendant teacher's or coach's control. The completeness and availability of written materials such as lesson plans, diagnostic test scores, accident reports, or documents used in employer screening and evaluation can provide persuasive evidence of the propriety of one's actions. Moreover, the confidence, poise, and professionalism one displays during depositions can greatly influence both the likelihood and the nature of one's appearance before a jury at the time of trial. Simply put, a plaintiff's attorney would not be anxious for a jury to listen at length to a poised professional who displays thorough subject matter knowledge, honest concern for the athletes in her care, and a clear understanding of the nature and the reasoning behind the actions that are at issue.

Once all the pertinent facts have been disclosed and each side has had the opportunity to assess the relative strengths and weaknesses of its case, a pretrial conference is usually scheduled. At this conference, the attorneys attempt to reach agreement on certain undisputed facts such as the date, time, and location of the incident in question.

By this time, each side will have had an opportunity to establish a dollar figure that they feel would satisfactorily conclude the litigation; therefore, pretrial conferences frequently include negotiations leading to **settlement**. During these negotiations, the judge frequently acts as an arbiter and tries to facilitate an equitable settlement to avoid the relatively costly and time-consuming process of trial. It is important to recognize that the overwhelming majority of civil cases are settled prior to the conclusion of a trial. Such settlements are financial agreements between the parties involved and carry no connotation of guilt or innocence. Both parties simply agree that the advantages of accepting the negotiated financial agreement in order to end the legal process outweigh the advantages of continuing. However, if no such agreement can be reached, the case normally proceeds to trial.

At the trial, the plaintiff is required to prove the elements of his case by the greater weight of evidence. Both parties present **physical evidence** such as incident reports, lesson plans, the equipment involved in the incident, and game films as well as testimony from the witnesses who appear in court. **Fact witnesses** are called to testify concerning what they saw, felt, or heard. **Expert witnesses**, on the other hand, are persons who, as a result of training and experience, have greater knowledge in a given field than the general populace. Expert witnesses are frequently asked to testify on the professional standards that apply to the incident in question and the degree to which the actions of the defendant complied with those standards.

It is not necessary for the jury in a civil case to return a unanimous verdict. Normally the agreement of any five of the six voting jurors constitutes an acceptable majority.

A party to a civil suit who is not satisfied with the outcome of the trial has the right to file an initial **appeal** to the appellate court of the state. Subsequent appeals are granted at the discretion of the higher courts only in cases in which the interests at stake or the disputed issues of law are considered significant enough to warrant their determination.

It is important for people involved in developing or delivering physical activity programs to recognize the possibility that they may be sued. They should prepare themselves for such an occurrence by developing a thorough background in the law as it applies to their day-to-day activities. They must then translate this knowledge into action by planning and documenting their activities in a manner that minimizes the risk of lawsuits and maximizes the likelihood of successfully defending themselves in any that may arise.

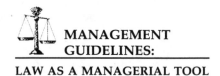

MANAGEMENT GUIDELINES:

LAW AS A MANAGERIAL TOOL

The impact of law on physical activity and sport is without question a major concern for teachers, coaches, and administrators. It would, however, be a serious professional error to view the law only as a source of problems or additional paperwork. Although ignorance or breach of applicable law can create problems, and effective documentation to prepare for or to avoid the possibility of a lawsuit will likely require at least a qualitative change in your usual level of paperwork, there are real advantages to be gained from applying the law effectively.

The law is in fact a kind of managerial tool. Like any tool, its value depends upon the skill and efficiency with which you use it. The more you know about the day-to-day application of the law, the easier it will be for you to apply it and the less likely you will be to misuse it. Moreover, like any other skilled person, you will begin to find ways in which elements of law can be creatively applied to become positive forces in program development and improvement.

For instance, consider the plight of an athletic director to whom a coach has presented a request for the purchase of new equipment, which the coach claims is necessary in order to meet acceptable safety standards for the sport. Can the director really afford to deny the request and risk the potential liability of an injury attributable to substandard equipment? Although the answer to this question would vary based upon the level of risk, the nature of the program, and many other factors, clearly the legal ramifications of the decision can be used as a persuasive point of argument.

One of the most readily observable examples of the benefits of creatively applying law can be seen in programs that have sought to guarantee equal opportunities to individuals regardless of gender. Although some individuals view the prohibitions against gender-biased programming as a major problem, others have seized upon it as a virtually unassailable argument for developing and improving their programs. They have implemented elective programs of physical education, reduced class sizes, individualized the instructional content, and instituted skill-referenced ability grouping and many other procedures that maximize the instructional potential and interest while reducing the difficulty of coping with heter-ogeneous class groups. As a result, they have been able to redesign or modify their programs in ways that have enhanced opportunities for all students regardless of gender while, at the same time, guaranteeing that no student is denied access without a legally valid reason. Remember: The same legal principles that can be used to condemn poor programs can often be used by the wise professional to develop and improve both programs and personnel.

CHAPTER SUMMARY

Laws are the formal means by which a society regulates the behavior of its members. Violations of civil laws, which regulate the interactions between individuals or groups, represent the majority of cases involving sport and physical activity. People who believe they have been wronged by the actions of others can seek compensation for their losses through the courts. This process, known as **litigation**, is prescribed by law and involves extensive pretrial discovery and negotiations aimed at accomplishing an amicable settlement. If a settlement cannot be reached, the case proceeds through a formal trial and possibly even through a process of appeals.

The more knowledgeable you are about the law and the manner in which it is applied, the better able you will be to work effectively within it and to use it as the productive managerial tool it should be.

KEY TERMS

Administrative regulations (5)
Answer (7)
Appeal (14)
Civil laws (5)
Common law (4)
Complaint (6)
Criminal laws (5)
Defendant (7)
Deposition (13)

Expert witnesses (14)
Fact witnesses (14)
Felonies (5)
Grievant (6)
Interrogatories (12)
Legal precedent (5)
Litigation (15)
Misdemeanors (5)
Physical evidence (14)
Plaintiff (6)
Precedent (5)
Process of discovery (12)
Punishment (5)
Settlement (14)
Stare decisis (5)
Tort (6)

QUESTIONS FOR DISCUSSION

1. Give sport-specific examples of criminal and civil law violations. What are some alternative methods by which one might reasonably seek to remedy each of the cited examples?
2. The process of discovery effectively removes much of the element of surprise from a civil trial. How is this accomplished?
3. Create a situation in which one person feels that she has been harmed by the actions of another. Explain how she would pursue the matter through the process of litigation and appeal. What is the nature of each step in the process, and what alternatives might be possible?
4. Give specific examples of situations in which a knowledgeable or creative professional might use the law as a tool for program improvement. Can you think of positive changes in the nature of particular sports or activities that are largely due to the influence of the legal system?

ADDITIONAL READINGS

Clement, A. (1988). *Law in sport and physical activity*. (chap. 1 & 9). Indianapolis: Benchmark Press.

Keeton, W. (Ed.) (1984). *Prosser and Keeton on the law of torts*. St. Paul: West.

Van der Smissen, B. (1990). Legal aspects overview. In *Legal liability and risk management for public and private entities*. Cincinnati: Anderson.

CHAPTER 2

INTRODUCTION TO LEGAL RESEARCH

For practitioners in sport and physical activity, the single most valuable resource for approaching the law is a good attorney. When you are faced with a lawsuit or must interpret the nuances of federal or state statutes, there is no substitute for the skill, training, and experience of a practicing attorney. Advice of counsel sought prior to embarking on a course of action can help prevent many lawsuits from developing and can lay the foundation for winning a case if litigation ensues.

Nevertheless, familiarizing yourself with the law and staying abreast of the ever-changing application of the law governing sport and physical activity will help you assist and interact with the attorney. This chapter, therefore, explains how to research the law and access legal resources.

LEARNING OBJECTIVES

The student will be able to

1. provide references to appropriate case or statutory law to support or refute the point addressed when given a legal problem;
2. describe the technique for guaranteeing the currency of legal opinions;
3. retrieve applicable case law when given a key number reference; and
4. utilize the major research tools available to find statutes, regulations, and reported cases to support class assignments.

THE COMPLEXITY OF LEGAL RESEARCH

The law, to paraphrase the great jurist, Oliver Wendell Holmes, is the prophecies of what the courts will do. How, then, can you go about finding out what the courts have done? In addition to approximately 4 million reported cases in the United States to date, volumes of state and federal statutes, administrative codes, government agency regulations, rulings, and opinions all proliferate at a great rate.

The decisions of judges in the United States who have interpreted, shaped, and defined the law were first reported in 1658 (Jacobstein & Mersky, 1990). Decisions that find their way into the **reporters**, the bound volumes that line the stacks of law libraries, are published in the chronological sequence in which they are released by the court or the official reporter for publication.

To be sure, the decisions made by judges across America far outnumber published opinions. Nevertheless, approximately 65,000 cases find their way into U.S. law books every year (Jacobstein & Mersky, 1990). In addition,

the 50 state legislatures and Congress together churn out approximately 50,000 pages of new or amended statutes each year. Federal, state, and administrative agencies produce a similar volume of rules, regulations, and commentary annually.

To complicate matters further, what may be "the law" for one purpose may not apply for another purpose. For example, a basketball referee may be an "independent contractor" for purposes of worker's compensation law but an "employee" for purposes of tort liability to a third party. In addition, what may be "the law" in one jurisdiction, or in one politically determined division of a jurisdiction, may not be the law 50 yards away in another jurisdiction or subdivision.

Finally, law is, to be sure, transitory. Today's law may be overturned tomorrow. Legislatures can and do repeal entire statutes, phrases, or exceptions. Immunities may be created by statute and then taken away. Judges declare statutes or regulations unconstitutional; appellate judges reverse their rulings; and legislatures and Congress respond with still more enactments. Thus, legal research is in many ways an ongoing process.

FINDING THE LAW

Where, then, do we find the law? In all legal research of any kind, heed the maxim: A problem well stated is half solved. In other words, it is necessary to define as precisely as possible the issue to be researched and the facts that comprise the problem. Without all the facts of the issue being researched, it is impossible to find a satisfactory answer to the question, What is the law that applies to the particular situation? Once the facts have been identified, what next?

Everybody remembers from high school those social studies lessons that taught us "how a bill becomes a law." Visions of little cartoonlike figures carting around a "bill" and toting it from the House of Representatives to the Senate to the President are fixed in every good student's mind! For those involved in the law of any activity, the business of how to go about finding that little bill that became a law that went into the law books is another matter.

Topical indexes to various subjects in the law are found in **legal digests**, about which more is forthcoming. But first, a word about the U.S. and State governments: Legislation enacted by Congress and by state legislatures deals with many issues in sport and physical activity.

Statutes passed by state legislatures are typically published as *slip laws* in booklet form and not generally or readily available to the public. When enough of these laws are assembled, a larger publication called *session laws* supersedes the slip law pamphlets and this version becomes the official statement of what the legislature has done.

Finally, the text of the session laws is republished as part of the **statutory code** of a particular state. At this point, grammatical errors are corrected, repealed provisions are deleted from text, cross-references are interposed and the new law is integrated into the numbering system established by the existing codification of the state's statutes.

Federal Laws

Acts of Congress are arranged according to subject matter in **statutory codes** and officially published under the title *United States Code*. The official *United States Code*, published by the United States Government, is also published in two commercially available annotated editions: The *United States Code Service* (USCS) and the *United States Code Annotated* (USCA). These two editions are the best sources to use when researching federal law. This is because they contain descriptive word indexes and **annotations**—brief capsules of cases interpreting the section and

containing **citations**—so the whole case can be read.

State Laws

Like federal law, state statutes are typically arranged according to subject matter and published in fully annotated and indexed editions. Annotations in both federal and state statutes are important because the final wording of that "bill that becomes a law" is often the result of political compromise over phraseology that can leave everyone wondering about the meaning of a law. They also frequently contain references to other legal resources and reference books that discuss the statutes being researched.

Administrative Codes

Finally, federal and state **administrative codes** contain rules and regulations promulgated by government agencies whose authority is derived from the legislative bodies that created them. Many of these codes are quite lengthy and are of value only to attorneys who appear before these agencies. Nevertheless, administrative codes are primary resources in the law, and the agencies who promulgate them have the authority to see that their regulations are carried out. An example of such an agency on the federal level would be the Equal Employment Opportunity Commission (EEOC). Therefore, it is important to determine if your legal situation is regulated by administrative rules and regulations.

FINDING COURT DECISIONS

After you have found citations to **reported cases** in legal digests and annotations to statutes, then what? How, and why, do some lawsuits ripen into reported cases while others languish in anonymity, never to be analyzed and digested for posterity? The answer is to be found in the internal mechanisms of our court systems and the procedures by which the decisions of courts are announced.

When a court is called upon to decide a case, that decision is communicated by the judge to the parties and the public in one of several possible ways. The method of communicating a court's decision differs according to the locality, the type of court (administrative agency tribunal, trial, or appellate), the preferences of individual judges, the type of controversy presented to the court, and the local rule or custom. The judge may

- announce the court or administrative law decision from the bench without issuing a written decision;
- issue a written decision merely to inform the parties to the lawsuit of the judge's decision; or
- issue a written decision that articulates the facts and how the law applies to those facts so that it may serve as an instructive model for other judges and courts faced with similar legal controversies.

Although opinions of **trial courts** are not binding as **precedent**, or authority for decisions, on other courts, they often serve as guiding lights to courts considering the same or similar fact patterns. A trial court is usually the first court to decide a lawsuit. Testimony and presentation of other evidence are customarily considered by this court, with or without a jury. **Appellate courts**, courts that consider appeals from rulings of trial courts and lower appellate courts (see chapter 2 for further information), render decisions that are binding upon lower courts within the same jurisdiction.

Nevertheless, a judicial opinion, whether on the trial court or appellate level, is only as good as the judicial officer who renders it. In theory, a judicial opinion contains an accurate discussion of appropriate facts, a clear statement of the legal principles involved, an accurate analysis of the existing decisions that bear upon the case, and a well-reasoned conclusion of law upon which other courts and attorneys can rely. In practice, because judges are only human, the quality of judicial writing varies widely. Further, not every written opinion is reported in the national reporter system.

In the federal court system, there are three types of written decisions:

1. Summary orders
2. Memorandum opinions
3. Full-dress opinions

Summary orders generally state the decision without delving into legal reasoning or analysis of prior authorities. These orders are usually not written for publication.

Memorandum opinions are somewhat more detailed than summary orders and may be published, although publication is not required.

Full-dress opinions contain detailed analyses of facts and legal principles to be articulated and developed from those facts. Legal authorities are cited. Full-dress opinions are generally reserved for those cases that raise either significant or novel issues of law. Due to the nature of our judicial system, **appellate decisions**—decisions of courts that hear appeals from the rulings of trial courts—are afforded more weight than trial decisions because they have **precedential value** for lower courts in their jurisdiction.

There are various rules and regulations in all federal circuits for deciding whether or not an opinion should be published. One such rule provides that

an opinion, memorandum, or other statement explaining the basis for this Court's action in issuing an order or judgment shall be published if it meets one or more of the following criteria:

1. With regard to a substantial issue it resolves, it is a case of first impression or the first case to present the issue in this Court;
2. It alters, modifies, or significantly clarifies a rule of law previously announced by the Court;
3. It calls attention to an existing rule of law that appears to have been generally overlooked;
4. It criticizes or questions existing law;
5. It resolves an apparent conflict in decisions within the circuit [one of 12 Federal jurisdictions in the United States] or creates a conflict with another circuit;
6. It reverses a published agency or District Court decision, or affirms a decision of a District Court upon grounds different from those set forth in the District Court's published opinion; or
7. It warrants publication in light of other factors that give it general public interest. (D.C. Circuit Rule 14[b])

Once an opinion is published, it is ripe for interpretation by the following groups:

- The parties to the lawsuit, one or more of whom may challenge the opinion by appealing to a higher court, where an attorney for each side will assert arguments as to why the opinion is erroneous and should be reversed, or why the opinion is correct and should be upheld
- The legal commentators who analyze and reanalyze the significance of opinions on issues that significantly affect a large number of people
- The class of individuals or institutions affected by the opinion who will, in most cases, glean their information from reports in the media or other secondary sources

READING AND UNDERSTANDING LEGAL OPINIONS

The best way to research legal opinions is to go right to the source and read them for yourself. To do so, you mush know the various parts of an opinion. Typically the parts are presented in the following order:

- Names of the parties to the lawsuit
- Name of the court
- Date of the decision
- Brief summary of the case
- *Headnotes* reciting the various points mentioned in the case (see page 24)
- Names of the attorneys for the parties and the judge writing the opinion
- Opinion of the court

When you are reviewing the opinion of the court, you should be able to distinguish between its two parts: the dictum and the holding of the case. The **holding** is the precise statement of the law enunciated by the court in making the decision. The holding therefore includes the facts vital to the decision and states the scope of the decision. By contrast, the **dictum** discusses additional items the court found to be significant, but it is not necessarily intended to formulate law on the topic being discussed.

To compare the holding and the dictum, let's look at a case known as *Christian Brothers Institute of New Jersey*. In that case, the plaintiff, who operated a Catholic high school, sued an interscholastic league and all member schools after the league had denied several applications for membership. A complaint was originally filed with the New Jersey Division on Civil Rights. That action was settled by written agreement, with the league agreeing to open its membership rolls to private high schools and to entertain the plaintiff's future application if a vacancy for a team occurred in the league. While the agreement was being negotiated, a vacancy did occur and still another public high school was chosen for membership over the school operated by the plaintiff. Thereafter, the plaintiff filed a second complaint in the Superior Court of New Jersey, charging violation of its constitutional rights and the New Jersey Law Against Discrimination. The issue, then, was whether or not the agreement entered into between plaintiffs and defendants would bar the plaintiffs from having the matter decided by the Superior Court.

The holding of the court was as follows:

Plaintiff's election to pursue its grievance before the Division on Civil Rights operated to waive its right to pursue, in state court, other avenues of relief for the same grievance except through the appellate process.

Such election, however, did not prevent plaintiff from obtaining judicial determination of its constitutional claims. (*Christian Brothers Institute of New Jersey v. No. N.J. Interscholastic League*, 86 N.J. 409, 1981)

The court said, by way of dictum, that

the proper procedure was to raise these claims before the Appellate Division upon appeal from the adverse decision of the Division on Civil Rights.

While we hold that the trial court should have refused to hear this matter, it is also necessary to make some comment upon the court's findings of discrimination and violation of the equal protection guarantees. . . . It is clear that a rational basis can exist for an interscholastic league's decision to limit membership to public schools. . . . and that such a limitation does not result *per se* in a denial of equal protection under the Federal Constitution. . . . In any event, under the Conciliation Agreement, Defendant League has

agreed to open its membership to non-public high schools so that the classification issue . . . is not a viable concern in this case. (86 N.J. 409, 1981, p. 418)

Thus, the holding of a case consists of only those facts that bear directly upon the court's decision and the decision based on those facts. Therefore, in researching a case for its value as *precedent*, look at the holding—that is, the court's answer to the questions presented to it by the parties. Keep in mind that due to the adversarial nature of the U.S. legal system, courts confine their answers to the questions presented to them by the parties. Questions that parties to lawsuits could have raised in their litigation but chose not to may not be answered by the court and, if they are, would be part of the dictum, not the holding.

LOCATING AND REFERENCING LEGAL OPINIONS

The publication of written opinions and decisions of courts in the United States is dominated by the country's largest private law book publisher, the West Publishing Company of St. Paul, Minnesota. Case reports from the 50 states and the federal court system are part of the West National Reporter System, which is linked according to subject matter by the West Key Number System, Headnote Analysis System, and American Digest System. All of these materials are duplicated by electronic research systems such as Westlaw, which are now widely used by attorneys and legal scholars.

For over 100 years, the National Reporter System has published the decisions of state courts primarily in series of volumes that group cases by geographical region. These reporters are known as the Atlantic, Northeastern, Northwestern, Pacific, Southwestern, Southeastern, and Southern Reporters.

West also publishes opinions of state courts around the country as the *official* court reporter. Examples are *New Jersey Reports* and *New York Supplement*.

Decisions of federal courts are published in the **Federal Reporter** (now in its second edition and containing decisions of Federal Circuit Courts of Appeals) and the **Federal Supplement**, which contains decisions of Federal District Courts at the trial level. The federal judicial system is divided into 11 circuits and the District of Columbia's circuit court that are each made up of a number of federal district courts. Each state has one or more federal districts: For example, Delaware has one; Missouri has two; Texas has four.

For purposes of *stare decisis*, the decision of an appellate court in the Ninth Circuit is not binding on an appellate court in the Third Circuit, or vice versa. Nevertheless, well-reasoned and cogent opinions from courts in different circuits are often cited by attorneys and found persuasive by courts in other circuits.

American Digest System

West's system of state, federal, regional, and national **digests** enables researchers to review cases standing for various principles in the law throughout the country. The digests contain brief summaries of various points of law in the decisions. They are laid out according to the key number system described in the next section.

West publishes a digest of United States Supreme Court decisions called the *Supreme Court Reporter*. These decisions are also published in a number of "unofficial" services.

On a national basis, there is the massive *West Decennial Digest* system, which digests, according to the publisher, all federal cases decided since 1896 in 10-year increments. These digests are also tied to the key number system.

Key Number System

The **key number system** works by assigning a consistent number to a principle of law throughout the U.S. court system, regardless of the jurisdiction or court. The key number system divides the body of legal knowledge into seven major categories and then divides each of those categories into about 450 specific legal topics. The seven major categories in the digest system are

1. persons,
2. property,
3. contracts,
4. torts,
5. crimes,
6. remedies, and
7. government.

The ever-increasing and evolving listing of the several hundred topics treated under one of the seven major categories is found in the front of the West digest volumes.

Theoretically, if you were to look up the key number for a specific legal concept in all the digests that have been published, you would find, hopefully, all reported cases on that principle of law. In practice, however, the key number system, like all indexing retrieval systems, is only as good as the person who did the indexing. Therefore, the alert student will not rely solely on the key number system to uncover all relevant authorities. Here are some examples of digest entries with key numbers:

1. Monopolies 12 (6)

Actions of the amateur basketball association in refusing to reinstate former professional basketball player's amateur status were exempt from the federal antitrust laws where monolithic control exerted by the association over its amateur sport was a direct result of congressional intent expressed in the Amateur Sports

Act and the association could not be authorized under the Act unless it maintained exactly that degree of control over its sport that was alleged as an antitrust violation. Sherman Anti-Trust Act, Section 1, 15 U.S.C.A. Section 1; 36 U.S.C.A. Sections 371-382b, 391-396, 391(a), (b) (4, 12), 393 (1, 7).

2. Constitutional Law 298.5

The amateur basketball association is a private rather than governmental actor and thus was not subject to the due process standards in refusing to reinstate professional basketball player's amateur status, even though it undertook to be the exclusive licensing authority for its sport and Congress, under the Amateur Sports Act, had bestowed on the association exclusive powers as a national governing body under the United States Olympic Committee. U.S.C.A. Const. Amend. 5; 36 U.S.C.A. Sections 371-383, 391-396. (*Behagan v. Amateur Basketball Association of the United States*, 1989)

Legal research, then, usually begins with a perusal of one or more of the resource digests that classify court opinions by locality (state or region), by forum (the type of tribunal deciding the lawsuit, such as Federal District Courts or a particular state's appellate court), or by subject matter within a particular jurisdiction. The information assembled in these digests is generally in the form of short vignettes of case opinions arranged by subject matter under either a topical index or the key number system. Cases that deal with more than one point of law (as most do) are cited under each appropriate topic or key number section.

The logical starting point for researching a point of law in the digests is the index, or the **descriptive word index** as it is called in most digests. For example, a case involving a state high school interscholastic athletic association may be digested under the general topic of "Schools." You may then find a principle of law under "Constitutional Law." A procedural point relating to the action of the judge may be listed under "Appeal and Error," and so on.

With a little practice, you can become proficient in smoking out the right descriptive words necessary to identify the focus of legal research. Often you'll find that a single case dealing with the general subject matter will cause the research to grow exponentially, as additional cases are cited, each with its own points of law and key numbers. Further research of the cases cited can help you narrow your focus.

Once you have determined the key numbers that most accurately describe the point of law you are researching, you can use the same numbers to find cases in any digest that uses the key number system, regardless of locality or forum.

Headnote Analysis System

A word of caution, however, is in order: Every law student is warned—and you are too—that **headnotes**, the short summary written by the digest editor summarizing the point of law for which the case stands should not, *under any circumstances*, be relied on without reading the actual decision. The editor may be thinking something different from what the judge was when she wrote her summary; nor do all editors accurately digest each point of law articulated in each decision in the United States. Many a researcher has been led astray by headnotes that appeared to indicate that an issue had been decided one way when, in fact, the opposite was true. As one handbook states, "The authority is what the court said in the body of the decision, not what the editors of West say the court said" (Bledsoe, Johnson-Freese, & Slaughter, 1985, p. 7).

Finding Cases in Case Reporters

The citation method used to identify cases is quite simple. Citations first list the names of the parties to the lawsuit that resulted in the decision. Usually the plaintiff's name is listed, followed by the abbreviation "v." or "vs." (meaning "versus"), and followed in turn by the name of the defendant or defendants and a series of numbers and letters. The first number tells you which volume in the set of reporters contains the decision. Next is an abbreviation of the title of the reporter, followed by the page number. Often the year in which the case was decided is provided as well.

For example,

University Interscholastic League v. North Dallas Chamber of Commerce Soccer Association, 693 S.W.2d 513 (1985)

is the citation of the lawsuit brought by the University Interscholastic League against the North Dallas Chamber of Commerce Soccer Association, which was decided in 1985 and reported in Volume 693 of West's *Southwestern Reporter Series*, 2nd edition, beginning on page 513.

Cases that are reported in more than one reporter have multiple citations. For example, the University Interscholastic League case could also be found at

251 Tex. Civ. App. 432.

In addition, if a case was appealed, and the decision of the Appellate Court was reported, the citation would indicate that fact. For example,

Ennis v. Bridger, 41 F. Supp. 672, 674 (MD Pa. 1941), *aff'd.*, 129 F.2d 1019 (C.C.A 3 1942)

means that this case was reported in Volume 41 of the reporter known as *Federal Supplement* (which contains decisions of the United States District Courts, the federal trial courts) on pages 672 and 674 and was decided in the United States District Court for the Middle District of Pennsylvania in 1941. It was subsequently appealed to the Third Circuit Court of Appeals, which decided the case in 1942, and was reported in Volume 129 of the *Federal Reporter*, 2nd edition (which contains the reported decisions of the Federal Circuit Courts of Appeals), starting on page 1019. The abbreviation *aff'd.* means that the decision that was reported in the first citation was *affirmed*. If a decision is modified or reversed, the abbreviations *mod.* or *rev'd.* are used.

Often in appellate courts, one or more judges on the panel hearing the case write **separate opinions**. These opinions can be in the form of **concurring opinions**, which state that the judges agree with the result reached by the court, but for different reasons than the majority of the judges who decided the case, and the concurring judges wish to state their reasoning. There are also **dissenting opinions**, in which judges on the panel hearing the case disagree so strongly with the result that they feel compelled to render their views of the law as applied to the facts.

ENSURING UP-TO-DATE RESEARCH

In legal research, if you want to be the best and the brightest, you'd better be able to find the latest. That is to say, a court's decision that has since been overturned by a higher court in the jurisdiction is no longer of precedential value, and therefore is no longer the law. For this reason, your legal research project will not be complete until you Shepardize the relevant court decisions.

The process known as Shepardizing is named for the original publisher of *Shepard's Citations Volumes*, Frank Shepard, who started printing lists of cases that cited Illinois decisions in 1873. The service is now a division of publishing giant McGraw-Hill. **Shepardizing** is accomplished by consulting the appropriate volume of *Shepard's Citation Volumes*, which reveal any case opinions that cite, overturn, comment on, or otherwise make reference to that case. The volumes list the reported cases from each official reporter in the West system in numerical order. Under each case is a list of cases that cite the opinion being researched. Similar volumes of Shepard's are published for many other legal authorities. The same information is also available on computer-assisted legal research systems. (For more information, see *How to Use Shepard's Citations*, 1976.)

Shepard's uses superscript code letters and symbols next to some citations to indicate whether the cited case reverses, mentions in dissent, modifies, or speaks to a particular point of law dealt with in that opinion. These codes also indicate whether the citation is the same case reproduced in a different set of reporters.

Shepard's also refers to headnote numbers assigned to the particular point of law to help researchers find the section of the opinion that is dealt with in the later case. This is especially helpful when Shepardizing a lengthy opinion that contains many points of law unrelated to the topic being researched. For example, a 27-page opinion dealing with the denial of an athlete's due process rights may contain statements of legal principles regarding contract rights, legal theories of awarding damages, and procedural errors of lower courts in admitting evidence. Only some of these areas may be of interest in any given research project. Therefore, you can save much time and effort by consulting only those cases cited in *Shepard's* that are denoted by the appropriate headnote number.

ADDITIONAL RESOURCES

Rounding out the legal research tools are **treatises**, which are similar to textbooks that cover particular areas of the law. Treatises may be restricted to the treatment of one or several legal topics within a particular jurisdiction or may be national in scope. Newsletters and various periodicals that cover issues in sport and physical activity can also be useful resources. Consult a law librarian to find out which publications are currently available.

Other resources include **restatements**: topical treatments of various areas of law that are not jurisdiction specific, the aim of which is to "restate" common law principles in an ongoing fashion. (Restatements currently available that are most likely to be of interest to students of the law of sport and physical activity are contracts, torts, agency, and property.) The restatements are published by the nonprofit American Law Institute and are widely quoted by courts, especially in cases for which no clear case law precedent exists.

Just as the rules of any sport largely depend upon definitions, so does the law. Therefore, law dictionaries and legal encyclopedias are vital to the success of any legal research project. West's *Black's Law Dictionary* is recommended from among the dozen or more law dictionaries and thesauri currently available. Black's advantage is that many of its definitions are *annotated* with key notes that guide the researcher to cases that illustrate the legal term. Therefore, do not underestimate the value of a good law dictionary.

The biggest and best legal encyclopedia is clearly West Publishing Company's 153-volume *Corpus Juris Secundum* (CJS). CJS has both a detailed table of contents before each major topic and a multivolume comprehensive index that makes it easy to use. It also cross-references topics to the key number system. Although the breadth of treatment of the topics in CJS may seem too detailed for nonlawyers, keep in mind that the authors attempt to render all aspects of American law within its pages. Therefore, comprehensively speaking, CJS can help you perform exhaustive research in a particular area of American law.

CHAPTER SUMMARY

When researching a legal topic, the first step is to assemble all the facts of the situation and define the legal concepts involved as precisely as possible. The law that relates to an issue may be found in one or more of the following: case reports, state or federal statutory codes, or in administrative codes, which contain the rules and regulations of certain government agencies.

In order to find reported cases whose precedent-setting decisions help describe the application of the law to a set of facts, look in West's state, federal, regional, and national digests or annotated statutes to review cases in which the legal issue in question has been tested. The logical place to start looking for cases would be in the digest's descriptive word index. Knowing the concept on which the case is based will lead you, via the index, to the page upon which short vignettes of relevant case opinions are arranged. It is important to know that principles of law are assigned a West key number. Looking up the key number of a specific concept in all published digests would, in theory, lead you to most published opinions on the precise topic you are researching. Therefore, you may use the key number associated with the first relevant court opinion you find in the digest to find other relevant opinions. Key number topics are divided into seven major categories and a listing of the topics treated under any one of the seven major categories is found in the front of the West digest volumes.

Because headnotes (the short summaries written by a digest's editor that summarize the point of law for which the case stands) are only as good as the editor who writes them, you will want to read actual decisions from the reporters of the National Reporter System. The National Reporter System publishes the decisions of state courts in a series of volumes that group cases by geographical region. Decisions of federal courts are published in the *Federal Reporter* and in the *Federal Supplement*. The citation of any case will give you the name of the reporter in which the case decision may be read and the page number on which the case appears. The citation will also show multiple listings for cases and whether or not the decision of the court was appealed. When reading a reported case, it is important to be able to recognize and distinguish the case's holding from the dictum.

To ensure up-to-date research, you should "Shepardize" your findings by consulting *Shephard's Citation Volumes*, which reveal case opinions that cite, overturn, comment on, or otherwise make reference to the decision of the case you are researching. Finally, legal research can be rounded out by consulting other resources such as treatises, restatements, legal encyclopedias, or a good law dictionary.

KEY TERMS

Administrative codes (19)
Annotations (19)
Appellate courts (20)
Appellate decisions (20)
Citations (19)
Concurring opinions (25)
Descriptive word index (24)
Dictum (21)
Digests (23)
Dissenting opinions (25)
Federal Reporter (23)
Federal Supplement (23)
Full-dress opinions (20)
Headnotes (24)
Holding (21)
Key number system (23)
Legal digests (19)

QUESTIONS FOR DISCUSSION

1. Outline the steps necessary to formulate an answer to a legal research problem.
2. List the steps necessary to determine if a reported case is binding precedent in a particular jurisdiction.
3. What is the difference between the dictum and the holding of a case?
4. Describe the advantages and disadvantages of the key number system for looking up law.

REFERENCES

Behagen v. Amateur Basketball Association of the United States of America, 884 F.2d 524 (10th Cir. 1989).

Bledsoe, R.L., Johnson-Freese, J., & Slaughter, D.B. (1985). *Legal research handbook*. Dubuque, IA: Kendall/Hunt.

Christian Brothers Institute of New Jersey v. No. N.J. Interscholastic League, 86 N.J. 409 (1981).

Ennis v. Bridger, 41 F. Supp. 672, 674 (M.D. Pa. 1941), *aff'd*, 129 F.2d 1019 (C.C.A. 3 1942).

How to use Shepard's citations. (1976). Colorado Springs: Shepard's/McGraw-Hill.

Jacobstein, J.M., & Mersky, R.M. (1990). *Legal research illustrated* (5th ed.). Westbury, NY: The Foundation Press.

Sobel, S.A. (Ed.) (1991). *Judicial writing manual*. Federal Judicial Center.

University Interscholastic League v. North Dallas Chamber of Commerce Soccer Association, 693 S.W. 2d 513 (Tex. Ct. App. 1985).

ADDITIONAL READINGS

Bledsoe, R.L., Johnson-Freese, J., & Slaughter, D.B. (1985). *Legal research handbook*. Dubuque, IA: Kendall/Hunt.

Cohen, M.L., & Berring, R.C. (1983). *How to find the law* (8th ed.). St. Paul: West.

Corbin, J. (1989). *Find the law in the library*. Chicago: American Library Association.

How to use Shepard's citations. (1976). Colorado Springs: Shepard's/McGraw-Hill.

Jacobstein, J.M., & Mersky, R.M. (1990). *Legal research illustrated* (5th ed.). Westbury, NY: The Foundation Press.

Kunz, C.L., Schmedermann, D.A., Erlinder, C.P., Downs, M.P., Bateson, A.L., Greene, C.M., & Millard, K.D. (1989). *The process of legal research* (2nd ed.). Boston: Little, Brown.

LAW, LEGAL SYSTEMS, AND RESEARCH

THE LEGAL SYSTEM

The Canadian legal system is derived from two main sources of law: common law and statute law. These two sources are discussed in the following sections.

Common Law

Common law, or case law, represents the accumulation of court decisions over hundreds of years. From these hundreds of thousands of accumulated decisions, a body of judicial principles has evolved that give our current judiciary direction and substance in its decision making. Canadian common law has its roots in British case law but is slowly developing a flavor of its own.

The reasoning of a decision in a case, known as its *ratio decidendi*, may serve as a precedent for future courts to follow when deciding cases with similar sets of facts. Such decisions are known as precedents. Black's Law Dictionary defines **precedent** as "an adjudged case or decision of a court, considered as furnishing an example or an authority for an identical or similar case . . ." (Black, 1979, p. 1059). The use of precedent is a fundamental principle, or doctrine, of the common law.

In practice, however, not every court must follow every decision of every other court. As Figure CA1.1 shows, essentially a lower court must follow the decisions of any higher court in its jurisdiction. Therefore, the Provincial Court of Ontario is bound to decide cases in a manner consistent with its county or district court, supreme court (trial and appellate division), and the Supreme Court of Canada. Although lower courts are not obliged to follow the decisions of higher courts from other jurisdictions, such decisions have varying degrees of influence on the lower courts depending on the jurisdiction in which the higher courts are located. For example, a decision from a court within Canada would have greater influence than a decision from a U.S. court. A decision from a British court may have greater impact than one from a U.S. court because the British court comes from the same common law tradition as the Canadian courts. However, U.S. decisions are starting to have greater weight in the Canadian courts because of geography, common elements of culture, and other factors. This whole hierarchical application of the doctrine of precedence is known as the doctrine of *stare decisis* and is the second major doctrine within the Canadian legal system.

As a result of the operation of the doctrines of precedent and *stare decisis*, a body of case

29

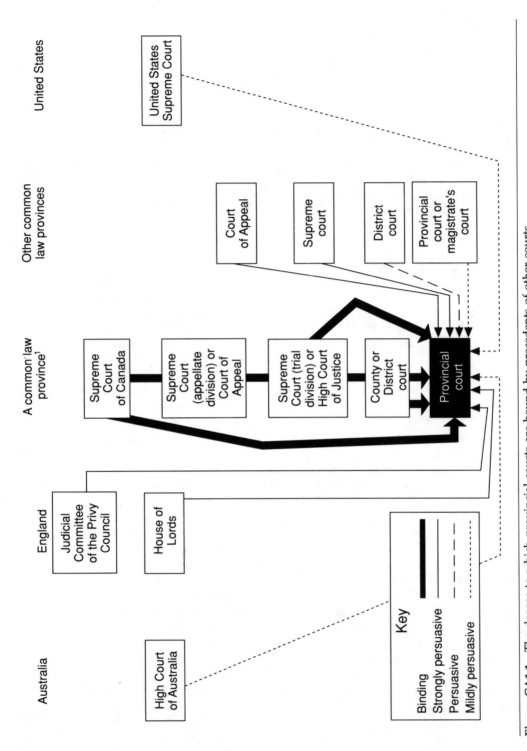

Figure CA1.1 The degree to which provincial courts are bound by precedents of other courts. [1]Ontario, for example, prior to the 1990 changes in its court structure. See Bill 2, An Act to Amend the Courts of Justice Act, 1984. *Note.* From *The Canadian Legal System* (p. 221) by Gerald L. Gall (Ed.), 1983, Toronto: Carswell Legal Publications. Copyright 1983 by the Carswell Company Limited. Reprinted by permission.

law has developed to guide judges hearing cases. As new fact situations arise and new cases are decided, the existing principles are broadened, exceptions are developed, and the case law is expanded.

The Canadian legal system in all provinces except Quebec is characterized as a common law system. Quebec follows the civil law system in which the courts look to a civil code to determine a given principle and then apply the facts of a particular case to that principle. Thus, whereas the common law system extracts existing principles of law from decisions of previous cases, the civil law system draws guiding judicial principles from an established code.

Statute Law

The second main source of Canadian law is statute law. Canada adopted the British parliamentary system of governance under which parliament is sovereign. Parliament can make or repeal any law, provided that it does so within the limitations set out in the Constitution Act of 1967. The federal parliament can enact federal law, any provincial legislature can enact provincial law, and either has the authority to repeal or modify any principles set out in the case law. Many of the present federal and provincial statutes incorporate the case law either wholly or in part; other statutes explicitly overrule case law.

Thus Canadian statute law is a combination of provincial and federal legislation. The domain of authority for each level of government, whether provincial or federal, is set out in the Constitution Act of 1967. Section 91 of the Act stipulates specific areas of authority designated to the provinces. Section 92 defines specific areas of federal authority and also provides that all residual or unnamed areas come under the authority of the federal government. So, for example, education is within the domain of the provinces, whereas

criminal issues, as set out under Canada's criminal code, is a federal matter.

Other sources of law play much less prominent roles within Canada's legal system. Custom or convention can be a guide within Canada's legal system. Custom refers to a long-established practice that has the explicit consent of the majority of the population. Custom often acquires the force of law where no statute or case law exists to set a precedent. A good example of this is in the area of international sport. Although there is no international law regarding sport per se, the rules and regulations of the International Olympic Committee have generally been accepted by countries as being the "law of international sport" (Nafziger, 1988, p. 35).

Evolving Nature of the Law

Although the sources of Canadian law are ancient, the law should never be considered stagnant. In fact, the very nature of the common law ensures that it will continue to evolve. Furthermore, the law must remain contemporary to fulfill the two basic functions of the legal system: to provide some order and regulation to the affairs of all "persons" (this includes individuals, corporations, governments) and to act as a standard of conduct or morality. As Gall (1990) notes,

> when one . . . reads a reported decision of a court of law, one is reading the judgment rendered by the court with respect to the facts by opposing litigants, but also a judgment that must be regarded realistically as reflecting the judge's notion as to what constitutes public policy, the existing state of morality and the political and economic conditions of the day. (Gall, p. 5)

In other words, the law can guide us by telling us what is expected of us as individuals within our society and as professionals in our places of work. It is therefore a valuable resource to be used to govern our behavior and against which our behavior is judged.

ANATOMY OF A LAWSUIT

The rules of court of each province set out how a lawsuit will proceed. The process begins with the filing of pleadings, or statements of the alleged offenses, by the complaining party (the **plaintiff**) and the filing of the defense or renunciation by the opposing party (the **defendant**), and ends with a trial. Very few lawsuits proceed through the entire process to trial; typically a settlement is reached somewhere along the way.

Once the pleadings have been filed with the court and served on all the parties involved, the **discovery** process begins. The main purpose of the discovery is to allow both sides to "lay their cards on the table." The discovery should ensure that there are no surprises at trial. In fact, any party who attempts to withhold evidence or to surprise the other side at trial may be severely penalized. During discoveries, counsel for each party is permitted to ask the opposing party questions about the material facts of the incident. All of this is done under oath and in the presence of a court reporter. Once discoveries are completed and pertinent documents and materials have been exchanged, the trial is set.

The discovery process can last a long time, often months. Through discovery, each side learns the strength of the other party's arguments, sees its evidence, and has an opportunity to evaluate their relative positions in the lawsuit and quite often to decide which party is at fault. Therefore it is common for parties to a lawsuit to settle the issues between them after the discoveries are complete, without a trial.

The other part of a typical lawsuit is the amount or quantum of damages being asked should the defendant either admit to fault or be found responsible for the incident at trial. The parties may even be able to come to agreement on this issue after the discoveries, but if not, the quantum of damages then becomes a triable issue for the court to decide.

If the matter does proceed to trial, the plaintiff decides whether to have the matter heard before both a judge and a jury or by a judge alone. Once in the trial, the plaintiff presents its case first. In civil cases the plaintiff must prove "on a balance of probabilities" that its injuries and damages are a result of the actions of the defendant. In a criminal case the level of proof is much more stringent, and the accused must be proven guilty "beyond a reasonable doubt." The plaintiff's counsel presents its witnesses to the court, asking each witness questions that will draw out the points advantageous to the plaintiff's case. The defense counsel has an opportunity to cross-examine each witness in an attempt to weaken the plaintiff's case. After all witnesses for the plaintiff have been presented, the plaintiff then closes its case, and the defense has an opportunity to present its case to the court, using witnesses, in the same manner.

After both sides have presented their witnesses to the court, counsel for the defense and then the plaintiff are permitted to make their final summary statements to the court. It is then up to the judge (or judge and jury) to make a decision.

In a trial, each side typically uses experts to strengthen its case. These experts may be either medical personnel or professionals who can inform the court of the common standards in situations similar to the case before the court or people who are able to reconstruct an accident for the court.

If the plaintiff is successful in convincing the court that the defendant is liable or responsible for the plaintiff's injuries, then the defendant will be required to pay **damages** to the plaintiff. The principle behind the awarding of damages is to attempt to return the plaintiff to a position that he or she would have been had the accident not occurred or, if the nature of the injuries is too severe, to compensate the plaintiff for the loss suffered. The courts are more interested in the effect of the injuries on the individual than in the severity of the injury, although the more severe injuries typically have greater consequences. Usually the court will look at the following factors:

1. The physical injury itself and the pain and suffering associated with it up to the time of trial
2. Disability and loss of amenities before trial
3. Loss of earnings before trial
4. Expenses incurred before trial
5. Pain and suffering expected to be experienced in the future, either temporarily or permanently
6. Loss of amenities after trial
7. Loss of life expectancy
8. Loss of earnings to be suffered after the trial and in the foreseeable future
9. Cost of future care and other expenses (Wright, Linden, & Klar, 1990, pp. 20-24)

The amount of damages can vary tremendously from one case and from one jurisdiction to another. U.S. courts are notorious for their high awards, and Canadian awards are slowly creeping higher and higher. However, they remain for the most part smaller than U.S. awards. Among the factors affecting Canadian settlements that may well have a bearing on the different quantum awarded between Canada and the United States are the various provincial court rules that are intended to encourage reasonable settlement. For example, such rules often stipulate that if a defendant offers a settlement to the plaintiff that the plaintiff rejects and that ultimately turns out to be greater than that granted by the court at the conclusion of the trial, then the settlement the plaintiff receives will be reduced by an amount of court-awarded costs, which can be substantial. Alternatively, if the defendant offers a settlement that is lower than that ordered by the court, then the defendant may be forced to pay court-awarded costs as well as the final settlement.

Usually court-ordered costs do not include legal fees but are financial awards that help defray the cost of either defending or prosecuting an action. Typically, they are set out in the rules of court for each province and vary according to the amount of the judgment.

KEY TERMS

Damages (32)
Defendant (32)
Discovery (32)
Plaintiff (32)
Precedent (29)
Ratio decidendi (29)
Stare decisis (29)

REFERENCES

Black, M.C. (1979). *Black's law dictionary* (5th ed.). St. Paul, MN: West Publishing Co.

Constitution Act of 1967, Enacted as Schedule B to the Canada Act, 1982, (U.K.) c. 11.

Gall, G. (1990). *The Canadian legal system* (3rd ed.). Toronto: Carswell Legal Publications.

Nafziger, J.A. (1988). *International sports law.* New York: Transnational Publishers.

Wright, C., Linden, A., & Klar, L. (1990). *Canadian tort law: Cases, notes and materials* (9th ed.). Toronto: Butterworths.

PART II

WHO MAY PARTICIPATE?

Considered logically, sport is a test of skill and strategy and should be relatively immune to the problems of arbitrary bias and discrimination. After all, the winner of a contest is determined by the fastest time or highest score, not by skin color or gender. However, sport is also a reflection of the society in which it takes place. As a result, although prejudicial behavior has seldom affected the outcome of a given sporting event, historically it has greatly affected the opportunity to participate in many forms of sport and physical activity. It is perhaps equally reflective of the nature of American society that the initiative for eliminating discriminatory practices in sport came not from the leadership of the athletic community but from the actions of the legislature and the courts.

Part II examines the legal standards that determine who may participate in sport and physical activity programs. The order of the chapters reflects the chronology of legal interest in the three types of discrimination within the athletic community: segregation, sexual discrimination, and exclusion based on disabling conditions.

Although the legal issues affecting equal opportunity are quite complex and, at least with regard to women and handicapped individuals, are still being tested in the courts, you would be well advised to keep in mind a simple answer to the title question, Who may participate?—**Everyone**.

CHAPTER 3

SEGREGATION BY RACE, COLOR, AND CREED

B efore the 1950s, it was rare that blacks participated in integrated intercollegiate and professional athletics such as basketball and football.
After this period, black athletes began to outnumber whites in football,
basketball, and track at major universities. But because of questionable academic practices concerning incoming athletes, the National Collegiate Athletic Association (NCAA) enacted a requirement in 1983 that prospective
athletes in member schools attain a certain minimum score on college-apti-
tude tests to be eligible to participate in competitive sports in their first year
of college.

Opponents of the new proposition argued that black athletes would be
adversely affected by it; intensive study revealed that 51% of black male
freshmen and 60% of black female freshmen would be disqualified from
athletic competition in their first year of college. Reports from the Big Eight
Athletic Conference put the figure as high as 80%. Some claimed that the

motive for cut-off scores was to reduce the number of black faces in college athletics and certain professional sports.

Two legal questions arise from these circumstances: Is a test score from which one admittedly cannot predict academic achievement a legitimate screening tool for excluding more blacks from sport participation than non-blacks? And does the NCAA, who sanctions the test, have the right to promote these allegedly discriminatory practices?

LEARNING OBJECTIVES

The student will be able to

1. recognize the relevant entitlements of the Civil Rights Act of 1965 as they apply to the conduct of programs of sport and physical activity;
2. describe how civil rights programs are monitored and the consequences of non-compliance;
3. explain the difference between de jure and de facto segregation;
4. list the legal responsibilities of sport governing bodies with respect to discrimination practices;
5. understand the obligation of managers of public accommodations for conducting business in a nondiscriminatory manner; and
6. recognize fundamental principles for reducing potential litigation due to allegedly discriminatory practices in sport and physical activity.

DISCRIMINATORY PRACTICES IN SPORT: A PERSPECTIVE

Sport, being just a part of the larger context of American society, has not been immune from some of its ills. Professional baseball, considered the national pastime by some, serves as a cogent example of America's history of institutionalized racial discrimination.

In the early years before the game was an established "legitimate" business enterprise, baseball was a relatively tolerant sport. In 1872 Bud Fowler, a second baseman from Cooperstown, New York, took the field for a team from New Castle, Pennsylvania, to become the game's first black professional player. Although the foremost league in the nineteenth century, the National League, had no black players, as many as two dozen blacks played on otherwise all-white professional teams on other circuits from 1872 until 1887, when International League officials banned future contracts with black players "in response to player protests" (Tygiel, 1984, p. 12).

By 1895, integrated professional baseball had ended. The major leagues developed, gaining so much notoriety and financial success that many people felt that the major and minor leagues represented the only professional baseball in the United States. The Negro Leagues, formed after 1920, took a back seat to the all-white game, with black players earning, on average, less than half what their white counterparts earned (Tygiel, 1984, p. 20).

Segregation has historically affected collegiate athletics as well. This is not surprising considering that here the issue of discrimination was compounded by racially discriminatory practices in educational opportunity. Although some predominantly white colleges admitted black students from their early beginnings, and some (such as Amherst, Harvard, and Tufts) granted them access to some or all of their varsity teams, in the early part of this century most black collegiate athletes played for teams representing predominantly black institutions. These colleges and universities, such as Grambling, Howard, Stillman, and Arkansas A&M, seldom competed against "major" collegiate programs (Edwards, 1970, pp. 1-11). Athletes who were involved in athletics at high-profile universities were few. For example, between 1817 and World War II only 12 blacks represented the University of Michigan on its sports teams (Behee, 1974, p. 12).

World War II, which was in part a struggle against Nazi racism, "caused Americans to re-evaluate their racial attitudes" (Tygiel, 1984, p. 37). Shortly thereafter, on April 15, 1947, Jackie Robinson became the first black man to play major-league baseball in the twentieth century. Robinson, UCLA's first four-sport letterman, also represents the growing integration of "major" collegiate athletics of that time. The courage of black athletes like Robinson, and the legislation resulting from the civil rights movement of the 1950s and 1960s, helped continue the breakdown of barriers for minority athletes, as is evidenced by the fact that between World War II and 1972 the University of Michigan awarded letters to 159 black athletes (Behee, 1974, p. 12).

CIVIL RIGHTS ACT OF 1964

The **Civil Rights Act of 1964** has significantly affected institutions of sport and physical activity in the U.S., including intercollegiate and interscholastic athletics, school physical education programs, community recreation programs, and private health spas and fitness centers. Three parts of the Act apply directly to the conduct of sport and physical activity: **Title II** prohibits discrimination in places of public accommodation, **Title VI** prohibits discrimination in federally funded programs, and **Title VII** prohibits discrimination in employment. In all the parts, discrimination is

based on race, color, or national origin. The entitlements of these aspects of the legislation are monitored either by the federal government or in private action by individuals who are aggrieved. When private action is taken, discrimination can result in punitive damages. Violations of the Civil Rights Act by government entities that receive federal financial assistance may end their assistance. The types of programs subject to the civil rights laws, the monitoring mechanisms, and the consequences of noncompliance are described in the following sections and are highlighted in Table 3.1.

Title II

Title II of the Civil Rights Act of 1964 outlawed racial discrimination in most places of **public accommodation**. In sport, these include sport centers, fitness centers, health spas, and community recreational facilities. Although the law has not completely ended this kind of discrimination, public sport facilities and community programs have for the most part abandoned discriminatory policies. Among the sport organizations that have been affected by Title II are racquetball and tennis clubs, golf courses, after-school sport programs, and YMCAs and YWCAs. Discrimination practices related to Title II are monitored through information of noncompliance received by an office of civil rights.

Title VI

Title VI of the Civil Rights Act of 1964 prohibits discrimination in programs and activities that receive federal financial assistance. Because schools and community recreation programs receive substantial federal assistance, Title VI covers a considerable portion of instructional and recreational activity in sport and physical activity. More specifically,

Table 3.1   Analysis of the Civil Rights Act of 1964: Implications for Conducting Sport and Physical Activity

	Purpose	Who affected	Compliance
Title II	Makes discrimination unlawful in public accommodations	Physical fitness centers, health spas, municipal recreation programs, sport programs, sport competitions	Private action; Office of Civil Rights
Title VI	Makes discrimination unlawful in organizations that receive federal financial assistance	Municipal recreation programs, public schools, colleges and universities, physical activity and sport programs	Office of Civil Rights
Title VII	Makes discrimination in employment unlawful	Sport and physical activity organizations that employ more than 25 people	Equal Employment Opportunity Commission

Title VI applies to interscholastic and intercollegiate athletics, intramurals, and physical education instruction in schools, colleges, and universities, and to those community recreation programs that receive federal financial aid.

Title VI is enforced by the federal government through the **Office of Civil Rights (OCR)**. An OCR complaint is filed by a plaintiff. OCR investigates and then writes a decision informing the parties of the outcome of the complaint. If OCR decides that a program is discriminatory, and the program fails to comply with the OCR decision, the discriminatory program may have its federal funding withheld.

Title VII

Title VII of the Civil Rights Act of 1964 prohibits employment discrimination. It affects all employers with 25 or more employees and employment agencies that regularly obtain employees for an employer covered by Title VII.

Title VII outlaws employment practices that fail to employ or refuse employment or that place discriminatory conditions upon the employment of an individual based on the individual's race, color, religion, or sex. Sports programs and other organizations that conduct physical activity and that have more than 25 employees must comply with Title VII. For a fuller discussion of Title VII, see chapter 10.

DE JURE AND DE FACTO SEGREGATION

When individuals began contesting segregated schools in the 1950s, at least two types of segregation prompted their claims of discrimination: de jure segregation and de facto segregation.

De Jure Segregation

De jure segregation is intentional racial segregation and is clearly prohibited by law. The landmark litigation of de jure segregation in U.S. public schools is *Brown v. Board of Education* (1954). That case ruled separate-but-equal educational practices, which had been established as permissible by *Plessy v. Ferguson* (1896), as unconstitutional. Subsequent court decisions to remedy de jure segregation were directed toward integrating public facilities and accommodations.

The unconstitutionality of de jure segregation on the basis of race, color, or creed has been well accepted by U.S. society for many years. Even though the enforcement of civil rights involves complex combinations of state and federal civil rights agencies, case law reveals little room for discrimination or exclusion from physical activity, competitive sports, or extracurricular physical activity in the schools based on race. Furthermore, there is little legal evidence of racial segregation in community-based athletic programs sponsored by governmental agencies or in for-profit sports facilities and enterprises that are public accommodations. The growth and improvement of civil rights in these areas has indeed been impressive.

De Facto Segregation

The elimination of de jure segregation does not necessarily mean that racial minorities have equal opportunities with nonminorities in the community at large. Differences in housing and economic patterns can result in **de facto segregation**. Furthermore, racial minorities have historically been excluded from participation in some sport forms and environments in our society. Thus, the opportunities of minority groups in the inner city to participate in community-based sports and to use sport facilities may be substantially different from the opportunities of the nonminorities of the suburbs. Unfortunately, many such situations are beyond legal remedy.

De facto segregation can exist in a number of environments in sports, such as physical education classes in public schools and universities, municipal recreation sport programs, and private for-profit sports clubs that are places of public accommodation.

De Jure and De Facto Segregation in Public School Physical Activity

Racial discrimination in physical activity and sport in the public schools is a function of the racial balance after legal remedies have been applied to achieve equality. Thus, de facto segregation in the schools results from housing patterns and practice, which in turn usually reflect the socioeconomic conditions of the families of the children. Wealthy children tend to be white and to go to better schools with more and better program opportunities.

Educational institutions have at least three types of physical activity and sport programs in which differences in racial balance may occur

1. Physical activity instruction programs in which virtually all students must participate
2. Interscholastic and intercollegiate athletic programs in which competent individuals may choose to participate
3. Intramural programs that attempt to maximize participation for all and club sports, usually organized by students and composed of individuals interested in playing a sport

In the case of public schools, the physical activity instruction programs, for the most part, are representative of the population of the school and thus reflect the racial balance of the neighborhood. Courts have taken corrective action to remedy segregation in public schools through school boards to balance the racial distribution in a given district. On the other hand, intramural and interscholastic programs may reflect a different racial balance than the school physical education class or the school at large because they are based on interest. Thus, socioeconomic forces may cause students to follow interests they have developed as a result of their social environments. Race may very well be a factor in their choices of activities.

Sport clubs formed in public schools and colleges may be more racially imbalanced than intramural and athletic programs. Often these clubs are formed without school sponsorship and supplement interscholastic and intercollegiate programs. Examples of these sports are riflery, golf, fencing, skiing, synchronized swimming, skating, and ice hockey. All of these sports require financial outlays for expensive equipment and access to facilities. They may also require instruction that is not equally available to all portions of the population. Their membership therefore tends to be skewed toward higher socioeconomic groups. Some schools seek to mitigate such bias by requiring all sport clubs to provide beginner-level instruction free of charge or for a nominal fee (see Figure 3.1). Such policies open access to anyone with an interest in learning more about the sport.

DE FACTO SEGREGATION IN THE COMMUNITY

Community recreation programs often fall under the jurisdiction of civil rights regulations because they are sponsored by the government. Other sport facilities and agencies that are private and for profit may be considered public accommodations; therefore, they are also barred by Title II regulations from discriminating based on race, color, or creed.

However, community recreation programs such as Boys Clubs, YMCAs, YWCAs, and community-based school programs often reflect the racial balance that is present in the

Figure 3.1   Some sport clubs attempt to overcome de facto segregation by providing low-cost beginner's instruction.

local community. Therefore, de facto segregation may result from racial imbalances in the housing patterns of the neighborhoods surrounding the community recreational facilities. Similarly, community baseball, basketball, and football leagues usually reflect the racial balance of neighborhood housing patterns and therefore may also result in de facto segregation.

Nevertheless, legal remediation for such de facto segregation is unlikely. In fact, in a landmark decision regarding de facto segregation (*Rodriguez v. San Antonio*, 1973), the Supreme Court indicated that the Constitution does not require equal financial allocations of funds among school districts and that disparity among school districts based on the economic status of residents is therefore constitutional.

RACIAL BALANCE AMONG SPECIFIC SPORTS

The degree of racial balance varies according to the sport. For instance, minorities in the inner city may participate in basketball at levels that are at least comparable to those of nonminorities. Inner-city playgrounds are as likely as suburban playgrounds to have baskets. The availability of facilities provides opportunities for racial minorities to participate in basketball at the same level as do nonminorities of the suburbs. Opportunities for minorities and nonminorities to participate in other sports such as baseball, football, wrestling, and boxing differ only slightly.

There are, however, some sports in which socioeconomic conditions may constrain the participation of racial minorities. These sports include tennis, golf, horseback riding, fencing, sailing, crew, and to some degree bicycling. These sports require considerable economic outlays for equipment and access to playing facilities. As a result, these facilities are not available in most inner-city neighborhoods, and these sports are more commonly engaged in by persons of higher socioeconomic levels. Therefore, a person's socioeconomic status may help determine whether or not the individual has an equal opportunity to participate in these sports.

This lack of opportunity for participation due to socioeconomic conditions may lead to a form of de facto segregation in certain sports. However, case law that treats racial segregation and discrimination based on the type of sport is scarce because de facto segregation is largely beyond the reach of legal remedy and because many of the segregated sports are outside of the jurisdiction of federal, state, and local governments. Thus, historical social forces may still perpetuate racial segregation in some sports.

DISCRIMINATION IN MUNICIPAL FACILITIES

In applying the theory of law to the Civil Rights Act, it is critical to distinguish between governmental and nongovernmental action. The equal protection clause of the 14th Amendment protects individuals from governmental action. Thus, in order to be covered by constitutional protection, a plaintiff seeking to contest discrimination must demonstrate that it is the government that has caused or allowed the discrimination. Purely private disputes do not ordinarily raise constitutional protection issues.

However, the boundaries separating the acts of government from acts of the individual are not always clear in a society like that of North America, where government plays a large role in many daily activities. When acts of a private entity are the subject of argument, the relationship between the state and private entity may be such that private action may be treated as that of the state itself. Therefore, civil rights litigation that involves the schools, community recreation programs, health spas, physical fitness centers, Little League, and athletic associations must consider how much the government figures into the alleged costs of discrimination.

ENFORCEMENT OF CIVIL RIGHTS LAWS

Title VI of the Civil Rights Act of 1964 gives the federal government the authority to withdraw federal funds from programs and activities that discriminate on the basis of race, color, or creed. One of the main issues in implementing these regulations was whether enforcement should be applied to an entire institution or only to those specific programs within an institution that receive federal funding. This interpretation of the law was critical to physical education and sport programs in that many of these programs operate without direct federal funding but may indirectly receive federal funds that are administered within the institutions. Tracing federal funds to determine whether or not any given program is free of them is a complex task.

The federal regulations were initially interpreted to apply institutionwide but were reversed between 1984 and 1988 in favor of limiting their application to specific programs. Subsequent legislation has clarified the issue and restored the institutionwide application of the Civil Rights Act.

PRIVATE RACIAL DISCRIMINATION

It is well established that racial segregation in public facilities is unacceptable. On the other hand, censure for private discrimination is less certain. Courts have been reluctant to impose discrimination remedies on private citizens. However, private discrimination may be barred by a combination of constitutional and statutory law. Administrative enforcement of these laws is another matter that depends upon the complex relationship between the state and federal civil rights laws (Frakt and Rankin, 1982).

Title II of the Civil Rights Act prohibits discrimination in most places of accommodation that are open to the public. The principal exception to this is that it shall not apply to a **private club** or to other establishments that are not, in fact, open to the public. A central issue that has come before the courts is the distinction between a private club and a public accommodation. Standards used to distinguish between private clubs and public accommodations follow.

A club is considered private and therefore not subject to Title II if and only if

1. it is not involved in interstate commerce, for example, has no nonresident members, and its facility uses no materials or products that are from out of state;
2. genuine selectivity and privacy of membership is based on some reasonable criteria (for example, the individual resides in a specific area, or if the individual owns property in a specific community); and
3. there is a plan or purpose for exclusiveness.

Privately owned commercial health clubs, sport training camps, and other commercial sport enterprises that are designed for profit, that advertise, and that often involve interstate commerce may find it difficult to meet the standards of a private club and may instead be viewed as places of public accommodation. If they are, then they come under the jurisdiction of the federal government based on Title II of the Civil Rights Act of 1964.

For example, a Supreme Court decision involved the issue of distinguishing between a public accommodation and a private club. In that case, a private athletic club in a park was theoretically in the hands of "private trustees" who had taken over the facility from the city to meet the desires of a benefactor who had left the park for use of "whites only" (*Evans v. Newton*, 1966). Under their management, blacks who attempted to use the park were rebuffed. The ruling of this case was that black people could not be excluded. Justice Douglas wrote that, because of the service rendered, the facility was municipal in nature. He reasoned as follows:

It is open to every white person, there being no selective element other than race. Golf clubs, social centers, luncheon clubs and other like organizations in the private sector are often racially oriented. A park, on the other hand, is more like a fire department or police department that traditionally serves the community. The predominant character and purpose of this park is municipal. (*Evans v. Newton*, 1966)

DISCRIMINATION AND ATHLETIC GOVERNING BODIES

Athletic governing bodies for high schools, colleges, and professional sports, such as the National Collegiate Athletic Association (NCAA) and the National Football League (NFL) have not, for the most part, been held to as high a standard with regard to racial discrimination as government entities have. Historically, athletic governing bodies have been viewed by some courts as private and their discriminatory practices therefore outside the legal system. However, recent developments in both statutory and case law indicate that this may not be the case.

In most cases involving athletic governing bodies, courts have taken the view that member institutions pay dues in the form of government monies. The monies paid to associations are raised in part through government taxes that fund member institutions. Furthermore, government-sponsored facilities are provided for contests. Therefore some courts have concluded that the athletic governing bodies are so imbued with a governmental character as to be subject to the limitations placed upon state action, including those that protect constitutional equal rights.

In *Parish v. NCAA* (1975), the findings of the court were that the NCAA performed a "traditional governmental function by taking upon itself the role of coordinator and overseer of college athletics." Thus, the NCAA and many other athletic governing bodies such as state athletic associations may be subject to federal antidiscrimination activities. Based on the governmental function of the NCAA, the NCAA may be linked with discriminatory practices as a proxy for the state for imposing academic standards on member institutions that may result in disproportional exclusion of black athletes from athletic programs. Chapter 11 describes the relationship between state and athletic governing bodies in more detail.

Many high schools impose academic requirements that athletes must meet to be eligible to participate in interscholastic sports. These requirements may exclude greater numbers of blacks than nonblacks. There is a paucity of case law on the exclusion of athletes from competition in high schools based on academic criteria that translate into racial discrimination. This legal issue remains unresolved.

Yasser (1983) indicates that there has been a shift in the nature of discrimination from one of open hostility to more subtle modern manifestations. He concludes that the success of black athletes to gain equal access to sports opportunities will depend largely on the willingness of the court to find that the subtle modern forms of discrimination are to be treated as the constitutional equivalents of outright racial discrimination.

PROVING DISCRIMINATION

The Lansdowne club case (*U.S. v. Lansdowne Swim Club*, 1989), in which a supposedly private club was alleged to have been guilty of discrimination, revealed the limits of evidence for proving discrimination. In this case the government brought action against a swim club that had allegedly violated Title II of the Civil Rights Act of 1964. The court held that the swim club was a place of public accommodation, not a private club that was exempt from Title II.

Although the government won the Lansdowne case, there was a revelation of what was acceptable evidence for proving discrimination. The court failed to provide weight to the following evidence of discriminatory practices:

1. Statistical evidence that indicated that 379 nonblack families were admitted to the club without a single rejection, but that 5 out of 6 black or part-black families were rejected for membership (This was 10 to 15 times more than the legal statistical standard deviation for assessing discriminatory practices.)
2. Evidence that showed that the club had a discriminatory regulation
3. Evidence that black Boy Scouts were never involved in or attended lifesaving instruction at the club
4. Testimony that purported that an officer of the swim club would not allow a black girl who was the guest of a club member to use the pool
5. Evidence that the swim club's board failed to adopt a resolution that no family would be denied membership solely on the basis of race
6. Evidence that club members failed to implement a written recommendation from a religious organization requesting that the board take action against future discrimination
7. Evidence that the swim club did not approve proposed changes in membership procedures for potential discriminatory procedures
8. Evidence that a swim club official made a statement that the club was "only segregated because no black people had ever applied"
9. Evidence of racist comments by swim club members

10. Evidence of swim club's rejection of a recommendation that it invite qualified people of any race or religion to apply for membership

The fundamental reason that the case was awarded to the plaintiffs was that Lansdowne Swim Club was a place of public accommodation under Title II of the Civil Rights Act. The entire facility was a place of entertainment effecting interstate commerce. The club's diving board was manufactured in a foreign state, and out-of-state residents used the facility.

MANAGEMENT GUIDELINES:

ENSURING INTEGRATION

Remedies for de jure segregation are largely outside the scope of the public schools and community officials; they rest with the courts. However, positive steps may be taken to counter to some degree the effects of de facto segregation. Recruiting minorities by offering various programs to bring them in as new members can help minimize social segregation. The environments in which positive action in minority recruitment may be explored are

1. public school physical education intramural and athletic programs,
2. college intramural and club programs,
3. community government-sponsored recreation programs,
4. private for-profit physical activity or sports enterprises that are places of public accommodation, and
5. sport governing bodies.

There is a management process that can be used to minimize the potential for racial discriminatory practices in municipal facilities of public accommodation. This process includes the following steps:

1. Look at the racial make-up of participants to determine if there are effects of racial discrimination.
2. If yes, develop policies of nondiscriminatory practices.
3. Implement a plan of affirmative action to achieve better racial balance.
4. Monitor the racial balance of the participants.

In addition, the following principles should be considered in the development and implementation of programs of sport and physical activity.

1. Public school sport and physical activity instruction and intramural programs at all levels should be designed to promote integrated racial participation. For example, design integrated programs that include the following:

   a. Teach lifetime sport skills such as tennis, golf, swimming, and dancing that will provide all students with the necessary prerequisite skills to choose among a broad variety of different activities.
   b. Encourage minority and nonminority groups to participate in broad-based, integrated intramural activities by removing barriers such as transportation schedules that prevent participation in after-school activity and by providing programs that raise interracial awareness and require cooperative efforts among the races to achieve team goals.
   c. Take affirmative initiatives to publicize and encourage minority students to participate in intramural and club activities.
   d. Conduct surveys to determine the status of participation of minorities in intramural and club activities for subsequent initiatives.

2. Government-sponsored sport and physical activity recreation programs should conform to nondiscriminatory racial practices. For example, program administrators should do the following:

   a. Conduct recreational activities of physical activity and sport to the greatest extent possible in geographical locations that are accessible to both minority and nonminority persons.
   b. Take affirmative measures to encourage minorities to acquire and utilize sport skills that traditionally have a nonminority orientation.

3. Public accommodations that promote physical activity and sport should conform to nondiscriminatory racial practices. Administrators should take affirmative measures to solicit minority participation and to make sure that enrollment policies and procedures do not discourage minorities from participating at the sport facilities.

4. Clubs seeking private status should conform to the exemption clause of Title II, which requires them to meet the standards of genuine selectivity, should not perform functions of a public accommodation, and should refrain from engaging in interstate commerce.

CASE STUDIES

Case 3.1   **Government Discrimination**

The Jackson City municipal government closed swimming pools in predominantly black neighborhoods, thus allegedly eliminating the opportunity for most black residents to swim under sanitary and economically feasible conditions. The plaintiffs complained that closing the municipal swimming pools in question was tantamount to denying blacks the opportunity to swim.

The court at that time ruled to close the pools and sided with the municipal government. The rationale of the court was that the other swimming pools were integrated and could be operated on a safe and economic basis. Therefore, the municipal government was considered justified in closing the swimming pools in black neighborhoods.

Although the city council affirmed that the other pools were open to integration, the actual outcome of the decision was not racial segregation in swimming, but a de facto denial of opportunity for blacks to participate in swimming. This was the case because geographical constraints drastically limited their opportunities to participate.

However, if this case were tried today, the outcome might be different. There is a tendency now for courts to draw inference from all relevant facts in determining whether or not discriminatory practices actually exist. They also examine the motives of municipalities that lead to discriminatory practices.

[Adapted from *Palmer v. Thompson*, 403 U.S. 217 (1971)]

Case 3.2

Municipal Accommodation or Private Club
Little Hunting Park was a community composed primarily of white citizens. The community had a private athletic facility in which the residents of the community gathered and engaged in athletic activities. The Sullivans, a black family, purchased a home in Little Hunting Park. Because of the close proximity of the athletic facility and the opportunity for athletic activity, Mr. and Mrs. Sullivan applied for membership. The application was denied. Mr. and Mrs. Sullivan initiated legal action against Little Hunting Park to gain access to the athletic facility and won.

This case helped define the differences between municipal accommodations and private clubs. Domains of the community that are used by the community, even if they are privately owned, may be ruled municipal accommodations. When a set of facts leads to this conclusion, then the municipality must by law follow nondiscriminatory practices.

Furthermore, the court found that Little Hunting Park had no plan or purpose of exclusiveness because it was open to every white person within the geographic area. Each case that has looked into private discrimination by a club subsequently has defined a little better the characteristics of private clubs that are and are not subject to antidiscrimination laws.

[Adapted from *Sullivan v. Little Hunting Park*, 396 U.S. 229 (1969)]

CHAPTER SUMMARY

It is well accepted in our society that public school physical activity and sport programs, government-sponsored community recreation programs, and public accommodations should not discriminate on the basis of race. Furthermore, private sport clubs that wish to exclude members based on race are required to meet all the qualifications of a private club. This is difficult.

The bases of nondiscriminatory federal legislation are found in Titles II, VI, and VII of the Civil Rights Act of 1964. This legislation prohibits racial discrimination in public schools, places of public accommodation, and community recreation programs that receive federal financial assistance. If racial discrimination is found, federal funding can be withheld through Title VI. In general, enforcement mechanisms are government oversight and private action that can be taken by individuals who have been discriminated against by organizations and agencies that violate civil rights laws. However, intentional discrimination is difficult to prove in the courts.

KEY TERMS

Civil Rights Act of 1964 (39)
De facto segregation (41)
De jure segregation (40)
Office of Civil Rights (40)
Private club (44)
Public accommodation (39)
Title II of the Civil Rights Act (39)
Title VI of the Civil Rights Act (39)
Title VII of the Civil Rights Act (39)

QUESTIONS FOR DISCUSSION

1. There is considerable disparity between the ratios of black and nonblack professional baseball, football, and basketball players and blacks and nonblacks in managerial and front-office positions. The ratio of blacks is higher among players and much lower among managers. Should this disparity in the ratio between black players and black front-office personnel in professional sports be of concern? If so, what should be done?

2. The NCAA's cutoff of SAT scores as a condition for participation of first-year university students in intercollegiate athletic programs disqualifies 80% of the blacks in the Big Eight Conference and may therefore be discriminatory. Should the condition be rescinded? Why, or why not?

3. You are the manager of a suburban commercial physical fitness center with a white clientele. Three nonwhites apply for and are granted membership. You subsequently learn that some of your current members will withdraw from the club if more nonwhites are granted membership. What would you do if a black person asked to join the physical fitness center? Why?

4. You are the manager of a private club that has never had a black person as a member. If a black person applied for membership, what would you do? Why?

5. You coach a predominantly black interscholastic basketball team in a predominantly white school. Persons in the community are requesting that the composition of your team be more racially balanced. What would you do? Why?

6. You are an administrator at a school that is racially balanced, but most participants in after-school intramural sport activities are white children. Would you take action to remedy this imbalance? If so, what would you do? If not, why?

REFERENCES

Behee, J. (1974). *Hail to the victors! Black athletes at the University of Michigan.* Ann Arbor: Ulrich's Books.

Brown v. Board of Education, 347 U.S. 483 (1954).

Civil Rights Act of 1964. 78 STAT. 241

Edwards, H. (1970). *The revolt of the black athlete.* New York: Macmillan.

Evans v. Newton, 382 U.S. 296 (1966).

Frakt, T., & Rankin, J. (1982). *The law of parks and recreation*. Salt Lake City: Brighton.

Palmer v. Thompson, 403 U.S. 217 (1971).

Parish v. National Collegiate Athletic Association, 506 F.2d 1028 (1975).

Plessy v. Ferguson, 16 SCT 1183 (1896).

Rodriguez v. San Antonio, 93 SCT 1278 (1973).

Sullivan v. Little Hunting Park, 396 U.S. 229 (1969).

Tygiel, J. (1984). *Baseball's great experiment: Jackie Robinson and his legacy*. New York: Vintage Books.

U.S. v. Lansdowne Swim Club, 713 Supp. 785 (E.D.Pa. 1989).

Yasser, R. (1983). The black athletes' equal protection case against the NCAA's new academic standards. *Gonzaga Law Reviews, 19*, 83-103.

ADDITIONAL READINGS

Frakt, T., & Rankin, J. (1982). *The law of parks and recreation*. Salt Lake City: Brighton.

Low, A.W., & Clift, V.A. (1981). *Encyclopedia of black America*. New York: DeCap Press.

Yasser, R. (1983). The black athletes' equal protection case against the NCAA's new academic standards. *Gonzaga Law Reviews*, **19**, 83-103.

CHAPTER 4

DISCRIMINATION BASED ON GENDER AND SEXUAL ORIENTATION

K aren O'Connor was an extraordinarily gifted basketball player who had played the game with boys since she was 7 years old. She participated in Arlington Heights YMCA and youth basketball leagues; together her teams had won 97 games and lost only 17. She was often the team's high scorer and had received many awards.

Karen wanted to play with boys at the high school interscholastic level so that she would be able to compete at her level of ability and develop her skills further. She was not allowed to try out for the team. Arlington Heights had a girls' interscholastic basketball team, so the issue was not exclusion from participation but accommodation of her interest and abilities. Only the boys' team could provide her with suitable levels of play. The question can be asked: Should Karen O'Connor be allowed to participate on the male interscholastic high school basketball team? (*O'Connor, K. v. Board of Education of School District No. 23*, 1981).

LEARNING OBJECTIVES

The student will be able to

1. enumerate and explain the legal entitlements of women for participation in sport and physical activity;
2. recognize the responsibilities of managers of public accommodations to conduct programs of physical activity and sports that do not discriminate based on gender or sexual orientation;
3. apply the elements of the Title IX regulations to sport and physical activity;
4. enumerate and discuss issues of discriminatory practice that may confront athletic governing bodies; and
5. discuss the legal implications of discrimination based on sexual orientation for the conduct of physical activity and sport programs.

TITLE IX

The **equal protection** clause of the 14th Amendment to the U.S. Constitution was the principle judicial forum for addressing gender discrimination during the 1960s and 1970s. During the late 1970s, the Educational Amendment of 1972 to the Civil Rights Act of 1964, known as **Title IX** (P.L. 92-318, 86 Stat. 373), became the legal remedy for gender discrimination. It states that "no person in the United States shall, based on sex, be excluded from participation in, be denied the benefits of, or be subjected to discrimination under any education program or activity receiving federal financial assistance" (20 U.S.C. 1681[a][1] 1972).

Through Title IX, Congress sought to assure athletic equality for females. But Title IX did not remove the problem of gender discrimination from constitutional concerns. It merely created an administrative remedy that can—subject to federal review—be used to enforce the prohibition of gender discrimination in educational programs that receive federal financial assistance. However, state equal rights amendments may also be used to seek remedies against gender discrimination in physical activity and sport.

In brief, when conducting educational programs, Title IX requires that there be equal treatment and opportunity for both sexes. The principle exemptions are in the sports of wrestling, boxing, rugby, ice hockey, football, basketball, and other sports involving body contact.

Title IX addresses instructional programs, interscholastic and intercollegiate athletics, and intramurals. It applies to all educational levels from preschool to postgraduate education. Administrative structures that may be subject to Title IX regulations are public schools, colleges and universities, some public accommodations in the community, and athletic governing boards such as the National Collegiate Athletic Association (NCAA) and high school interscholastic athletic associations.

Community agencies and certain parts of the private sector must comply with antisex discrimination regulations that may be enacted by state and local governing bodies. These laws do not supersede Title IX regulation unless they are more stringent. (See discussion of legal procedures in chapter 1.) For example, a provision of Washington state's equal rights amendment is more stringent than Title IX because it permits female students to participate in all contact sports including football (*Darien v. Gould*, 1975). If a state's law contains a broader or more stringent interpretation of the rights of women, it takes precedence over Title IX. People who conduct physical activity and sport programs should know and carefully observe the regulations of their specific state.

Title IX is enforced by the U.S. Office of Civil Rights, which can terminate federal financial assistance for violations of the provisions of Title IX and can impose a damages remedy to further enforce this legislation. For example, Christine Franklin filed action against Andrew Hill, a male teacher and coach, for alleged continued sexual harassment. The U.S. Supreme Court held that a damage remedy is available for an action brought to enforce Title IX.

The rationale for the decision was that federal courts have the power to award any appropriate relief in a cognizable cause of action brought pursuant to a federal statute (*Cannon v. University of Chicago*, 1979).

However, Title IX damages were to be limited to back pay and prospective relief. In this case, both suggested remedies were inadequate in that they would provide Franklin no back pay because she was a student when the alleged discrimination occurred, and no prospective relief because she no longer attends school in the respondent system and because Hill, the teacher-coach, no longer teaches there. Thus, no relief was granted in this case (*Franklin v. Gwennett County Public School*, 1992).

PHYSICAL EDUCATION INSTRUCTION

Title IX specifically addressed physical education instruction in the public schools, where gender inequities can result in disparities in both the allocation of resources and the formats of instruction. The sections that follow discuss the management of equitable physical education programs with respect to gender.

Comparable Instruction Facilities and Resources

The facilities and resources allocated to male and female physical education programs should be equitable. Here are some guidelines for actively administering programs that are free of gender bias.

1. A school that has one gymnasium or one pool must give members of both sexes opportunities to use it on a nondiscriminatory basis.
2. Schedules for prime-time, right-after-school practices and games should accommodate both female and male teams equally. For instance, practice schedules for females and males in the gymnasium should alternate so that both have equal opportunity to practice after school (for example, 4 p.m. to 6 p.m.) rather than after dinner.
3. Locker rooms, toilets, and practice and competitive facilities for female and male teams should be comparable. For example, if males have a weight-training facility, females should have the same opportunity for weight training.
4. Equipment and supplies should be provided equally to female and male athletic teams. These could be checked by keeping and comparing inventories of what has been supplied to both teams.
5. Physical education and athletic staff must be assigned without regard to gender. This means that available qualified men may be assigned to women's athletics and physical education, and available qualified women may be assigned to men's athletics and physical education.

6. Office space that is comparable in size and location must be provided to staff without regard to gender.
7. The physical education graduation requirements must be the same for males and females. A committee representative of the administration should review all course descriptions, curriculum guides, and related materials developed for physical education and athletics to ensure that there is gender fairness.

Proportionate Equality

Title IX enforcement is directed at the provision of equal opportunity rather than equality. In allocating financial resources for men's and women's programs, regulations do not require equal amounts of revenues for each program. Instead, they require **proportionate equality**: Monies are to be allocated according to the proportion of participation between men and women in a particular program. For instance, if 35% of the participants in a track and field program are female and 65% are male, then financial resources would be allocated to females and males in the same proportion (35% to females and 65% to males) if the monies are allocated from *tax dollars*. However, if a sport program such as football generates *revenues*, these revenues can be used for the specific program (*Blair v. Washington State University*, 1987).

Using different formulas for determining proportion and different methods of counting may result in issues for determining the respective shares of financial resources for each program because perception of equity may differ. However, acknowledged unequal funding based upon male/female participation ratios is acceptable only if both sexes have equal opportunities to participate.

Class Organization

In order for physical activity instruction to be nondiscriminatory, it should be organized so that it provides equitable benefits to both females and males. In addition, quantitative measures of fairness should be applied to detect subtle discriminatory practices. Measurements that may show disparity include the following:

- More school-sanctioned sport activities for males than for females
- Disparities in length and continuity of athletic seasons, with more advantageous seasons provided for males
- Disparities in times and places of instruction and practice, with more prime-time practices given to male sport programs

Disproportion in Classes

A basic principle of Title IX is that individuals who are offered educational programs of physical activity should have equal access to them regardless of gender. For example, segregation can exist in the physical education classes of public schools if there is a disproportionate ratio of females to males in classes. Title IX regulations clearly indicate, however, that a disproportionate number of individuals of one gender in educational classes does not, in and of itself, constitute discrimination on the basis of gender. If 80% or more of the participating students are of one gender, that school needs to assure itself that such disproportion does not reflect grouping or tracking procedures that lead to gender discrimination.

The key issue is the manner in which the disproportionate representation occurred. For instance, in the case of an elective program, if a modern dance class consisted primarily of women and a weight training class was largely men, this would not, in and of itself, be a violation. If, on the other hand, there is bias in the enrollment procedure, or if the class were not an elective but instead reflected the manner in which the administration chose to place the students by gender, then there would appear to be a violation of the principle of Title IX.

Standards for Grouping

Title IX regulations do not prohibit grouping of students in physical education classes and activities by ability, provided that objective standards of individual performance are developed and applied without regard for gender. Grouping of students is permitted, provided that the students are grouped by objective standards of ability. Coeducational or integrated programs are preferred to cope with the discriminatory effects of grouping.

When grouping students for instructional or competitive purposes, certain factors such as size, strength, and physical maturity must be considered. Clearly, grouping to equate competition and to minimize the risk of disparate power and strength of individuals is a desirable goal.

It is worth noting that grouping by body size and other physical characteristics varies greatly as a function of age. There is less difference between males and females in the early elementary-school grades than after puberty. But at puberty, males begin to grow stronger and more powerful than females. Even so, during the early adolescent period following puberty, individual differences within gender are at least as broad as those between sexes. Thus, discrepancies between all participants widen greatly at this age and require particular care and attention (see Figure 4.1).

Standards of performance used for classifying, grouping, inclusion, or exclusion from activities must be applied in a nondiscriminatory manner. If the standards being used discriminate or limit the opportunities and benefits for people of one gender, do not eliminate the standards but replace them with standards that do not have biased effects.

Two actions can be taken to remedy the adverse effects of a standard that limits one gender's opportunities to benefit from physical activity and sport programs. First, the standards may be used to measure improvement, and second, two separate standards can be developed. Either of these two remedies can be used to ensure that the standards used do not cause females to miss opportunities for acquiring program benefits.

Integration of Sexes

Title IX regulations encourage integration of female and male students in public school programs and activities. They apply to physical education and to sport activities, including extracurricular activities such as intramural sports. These programs can be designed to remedy the historical exclusion of females from intramural and interscholastic sports and physical education programs based on biased notions of inferior physical capabilities. Integrated or coeducational activities help assure that female opportunities are equal to those of males.

The requirements of Title IX dictate that all physical activity classes be integrated except during periods when contact sports and sex education are being covered. To facilitate this procedure, a school system or community should publish a guide that specifies how coeducational curricula are to be integrated. On the other hand, if there are separate programs, each with its own standards, the guide should also spell out which standards apply.

The regulations regarding separation of students are often unclear. They allow students to be separated for three weeks out of a semester; for example, for an instructional basketball unit. However, when the basketball unit ends, the separation cannot continue if the new unit involves a noncontact activity.

Figure 4.1   Boys and girls in the early elementary-school grades vary little in body size and strength. At this age, physical activity programs such as Little League baseball can be safely run in a coeducational setting.

But instructional programs can and should for the most part be conducted coeducationally. For example, when teaching basketball, provide a coeducational unit in which students learn and practice skills without bodily contact. The individual skill development in basketball and many other sports has little to do with competitive disadvantage due to physical maturity and strength.

The regulations of Title IX exert a minimum of intrusion in the actual conduct of physical activity programs at the local level. For example, they do not require any specific activities within a physical education program, nor do they specify any particular process for assigning or selecting students for physical education courses or classes. These procedures for administering the programs are left up to the local educational districts. The only principle that applies to Title IX is a standard of fairness based on gender.

ATHLETICS

Most schools provide a variety of extracurricular activities, including interscholastic sports. These programs should be administered in a nondiscriminatory manner to the greatest extent possible, following the same nondiscriminatory principles that apply for allocation of resources for the instructional physical activity program. Here are some practical examples of nondiscriminatory principles for conducting extracurricular activities:

1. Female and male athletic teams should receive comparable publicity.
2. Medical and training facilities should be made equally available to female and male teams.
3. Housing and services, when provided on trips away from school, should not give female or male students preferential treatment.
4. Awards for athletic achievements should be comparable for both genders. (Letters for boys and pins for girls are unacceptable.)
5. Sports banquets and honor assemblies should be provided to both females and males equitably.
6. Dollar-for-dollar expenditures are not required for female and male athletic programs. However, the type of services provided to male and female teams should be equitable. (Failure to provide necessary funds for female teams may constitute noncompliance with Title IX regulations.)
7. Rules that govern male and female clothing and behavior should be equitable.

Female athletic teams must receive as much coaching as male athletic teams. A disproportionate amount of coaching, such as three coaches for 60 male students and one coach for a 40-student female team, would result in less individual attention for the female athletes than for the male athletes.

Accommodation for Differing Context and Equal Outcomes

There is a difference between attaining equal opportunity and attaining equal benefits and equal treatment for both sexes. Identical benefits and treatment are not required as long as the overall results of the sport competition and physical activity programs are essentially equal. Thus, in the absence of sport-by-sport equality, schools may still be in compliance if they can show that, even though the context of the sport is different and will result in a different outcome, the program as a whole is equitable. For instance, females in high school, as a rule, do not participate in football, but they may have the opportunity to participate in field hockey during the fall football season, and possibly in volleyball as well. If the school offered no fall sport activities for females, and males had a football program, this discrepancy in sport participation between the sexes could be rectified if in other sport seasons of the school year females had greater opportunities than males. Thus, although sport opportunities are not the same, a school may be in compliance if its overall sport and physical activity opportunities are equally available.

Separate Teams

In providing equal access to extracurricular activities, schools must decide whether it is more desirable to provide separate teams for the males and females or to have a single team that is open equally to both genders. If the local educational agency has discriminated in the past or has limited athletic opportunities for students of one gender, then it must take affirmative action to inform members of the disadvantaged gender of the availability of equal opportunities. It should also provide support and training to enable the students of that gender to participate in the extracurricular activity.

School districts may operate or sponsor separate athletic teams for members of each gender if selection for such teams is based upon competitive skill or if the activity involves a contact sport. If the school district sponsors only one team, members of both genders must be allowed to try out for the team unless the sport is a contact sport.

Separate teams in noncontact sports may be warranted if the following conditions exist:

1. Opportunities for members of the excluded gender have historically been limited.
2. There is sufficient interest and ability to sustain a team and a reasonable expectation of interscholastic or intercollegiate competition.
3. Members of the excluded gender do not possess sufficient skill to be selected for an integrated team or to compete actively if selected.

School districts should assess the equality of their male and female competitive sports programs. If the programs are unequal, the district should ideally provide separate teams or, if this is not appropriate, permit competition in coeducational activity. In either case, the programs should be monitored to assure gender equity.

PROGRAM MANAGEMENT AND GENDER DISCRIMINATION ISSUES

To conduct programs of sport and physical activity in the community and in the schools, you need to be familiar with case law on gender discrimination. You should also understand how those laws are enforced. People who operate community private sports facilities or who conduct physical activity programs for government entities should also know the law as it pertains to the administration and organization of physical activity programs.

Gender Discrimination Scheduling

The requirement for equal programs has caused some providers to schedule some male and female athletic sports activities at different times during the year. For instance, women's volleyball may be scheduled in the fall and men's volleyball in the winter. These measures may be necessary if facilities for sports such as swimming, basketball, volleyball and tennis are limited (see Case 4.6).

Discrimination in Rules of a Game

Inequalities in benefits between the sexes may occur if the rules for the same sport are different for men than they are for women, as they were in Case 4.7. Such differences may result in economic and social disparities between males and females.

This was the case in states where males and females played the game of basketball under different rules. It was alleged that the two games were different and that females were denied the opportunity to transfer their skills to traditional basketball settings. They were, in effect, learning skills that were not useful. On the other hand, males were learning skills that were useful and could be transferred to other basketball settings.

Though courts have been sympathetic to arguments of discriminatory practices against females on this issue, they have refrained from intrusion in the administration of sport programs by athletic associations. They judge that those who play, coach, and administer interscholastic sports, not the federal courts, should decide.

Equality for Males

There has been litigation that has addressed potential discriminatory practices against males as a result of rules for participation in sports developed by athletic governing bodies. For the most part, the courts have held that practices that excluded males from female sports were acceptable (see Cases 4.9 and 4.10).

Although the law requires that females have opportunities to try out for male teams during prepubescent years and for noncontact sports teams during and after puberty, the rights of males to try out for female teams is less clear. Cases of gender discrimination against males have used the equal protection clause of the U.S. Constitution, state equal rights statutes, and state constitutions in litigation. Legal outcomes have varied based on the constitutions and statutes used, on whether or not there was overall discrimination against males at a given school, and on the degree to which a specific school district has eliminated practices that discriminated against females.

Peculiarities of Colleges

There are administrative differences between the conduct of interscholastic and intercollegiate athletics. Intercollegiate programs can be more complex than interscholastic programs because they can use scholarships as an economic incentive to attract more skilled players and because of the considerable amount of resources and facilities that were originally targeted to men's athletic programs such as basketball, football, and other revenue-producing sports.

Equity in scholarships for males and females has been an issue in the administration of intercollegiate athletic programs funded by legislative appropriations. The law requires equity of scholarships per capita. For example, if $100,000 in scholarships is available, and 60% of the applicants are males, then 60% or $60,000 should go to males and $40,000 to females.

However, when a single sport generates revenues from gate admissions, media rights, or conference revenues, these funds may be used to augment scholarships for that specific sport program. In major university sport programs such as basketball, gate admissions and media rights account for millions of dollars that may be targeted for those specific programs. Therefore, disparity in funds for scholarships at such colleges and universities is permissible.

The NCAA, in challenging the application of Title IX to intercollegiate athletics, raised the issue of the standing of athletic governing bodies such as the NCAA and member institutions for challenging Title IX regulations. In *NCAA v. Califano* (1980), the NCAA alleged that the Department of Health, Education, and Welfare exceeded its authority and that some of its regulations created a gender-based quota system that violated Title IX. They were concerned that such regulations would adversely affect the NCAA and its members.

The court held that the NCAA could not litigate in its own right to challenge the Title IX regulations but could challenge the Title IX regulations as a representative of its members. The court also ruled that the alleged injuries the NCAA would suffer if Title IX regulations were enforced were much too speculative.

Title IX Enforcement

The procedures for terminating federal financial assistance under Title IX include the following:

1. Notice of intended termination of financial assistance
2. A hearing
3. An opportunity for voluntary compliance

The **Office of Civil Rights (OCR)** has two methods of enforcing Title IX: One is through a compliance review process; the other is through complaints. In the **compliance review**, the OCR periodically selects government entities at random and investigates their compliance with Title IX. Private parties may also file **complaints** with the OCR or may sue the government entity directly without relying on government administrative mechanisms.

The OCR has 90 days in which to conduct an investigation and 90 additional days thereafter to reach a voluntary compliance agreement with a government entity that is in violation. If a voluntary compliance agreement cannot be reached within that time, the OCR begins the formal administrative process leading to termination of federal financial aid.

Discrimination and Federal Financial Assistance

One main issue in the implementation of Title IX regulations has been whether enforcement should be applied on an institutionwide basis or only to specific programs that receive federal funds. **Institutionwide compliance** means that if a single sport or other program at a college or university discriminates on the basis of gender, federal financial assistance will be withheld from all programs at the college or university. **Program-specific compliance** means that federal funds will be withheld only from the specific program of a college or university in which the discrimination occurs; funds to other programs will not be interrupted. The courts have not been entirely consistent in this area.

The interpretation of Title IX by the U.S. Department of Education during the 1970s was that compliance required an institution to conform on an institutionwide basis. However, a court determined in 1981 that Title IX is not applicable in cases where an institution receives federal assistance, but the program itself does not. The court declared that benefits conferred on the athletic program are outside the scope of Title IX protection (*Bennett v. West Texas State University*, 1981).

In 1984, Grove City, a private church-related college, had received no federal funds for educational programs because its president's failure to sign a routine Civil Rights Title IX compliance form had triggered the withdrawal of federal monies from the college's Basic Educational Opportunity Grants program, which had previously been available to Grove City College students (*Grove City College v. Bell*, 1984). In this case, the Supreme Court raised the institutionwide versus the program-specific issue and resolved it differently.

The central issue in this case was the definition of the word "program." The Department of Education argued for an institutionwide definition of "program," while Grove City argued for program-specific enforcement.

Another issue in the decision was direct versus indirect funding. Grove City had not received funds directly. Its students, however, were beneficiaries of federal financial assistance.

The Supreme Court ruled that receipt of Basic Educational Opportunity Grants was sufficient to make the institution a "recipient" of federal assistance. But on the second question of program-specific or institutionwide enforcement of Title IX, the court ruled that enforcement was limited to the specific program that received the funding.

A key point that contributed to the Supreme Court's Grove City decision for programs of athletics was that many of those programs were funded through gate receipts and outside donations and may not have needed federal funding. Subsequent to this decision, it was no longer possible to interpret "program" as inferring all elements within an institution. Very soon after the Grove City decision, Congress attempted to overturn the court's interpretation of "program." Subsequently, numerous female student athletes at Temple University brought an action against the university. They claimed that the university offered them unequal opportunities to compete in intercollegiate athletics and provided disparate funding and allocation of financial aid to male and female student athletes that favored the males. The court ruled that a college that receives financial aid from the state or federal government invokes Title IX on an institutionwide basis (*Haffer v. Temple University*, 1987). This originally was the interpretation by the U.S. Department of Education. However, the Supreme Court rejected that interpretation in a later case.

It was not until passage of the **Civil Rights Restoration Act of 1988** that the Supreme Court decision on civil rights enforcement as program-specific was overturned and prior institutionwide interpretations of federal regulations reinstated. Interpretation of civil rights enforcement during the period between 1984 (Grove City) and the 1988 enactment of the Civil Rights Restoration Act was unique. It is important that you be aware of the difference in enforcement of civil rights when comparing that period with the current period.

Two additional comments can be made regarding the Grove City case.

1. Though the case did not involve sports programs, the NCAA contributed to the college's defense because the case would set precedent for subsequent cases involving schools with self-supporting athletic programs.
2. The case shows that the Supreme Court's interpretation of federal legislation may differ from what the legislature originally intended.

Government Gender Discrimination

Gender discrimination is not legally permissible unless it ensures safety and prevents harm to the individual or furthers a governmental interest. Therefore, gender discrimination in government-sponsored programs is not generally allowed. Considerable litigation has also revolved around government involvement in gender discrimination and has reinforced the requirement that there be no gender discrimination when municipalities are involved in the provision of facilities to private organizations such as the Little League.

For instance, if Little League facilities are laid out and maintained by a municipality to the specifications and for the primary benefits of the league, or if a quasi-private organization with a sympathetic relationship to the city, such as the Little League, is carrying out a government function, the government involvement is sufficient so that there can be no gender discrimination (*Fortin v. Darlington Little League*, 1975).

Private Sex Discrimination

Federal law has limited application to private gender discrimination in sport. Several states have framed laws that prohibit gender discrimination in places of public accommodation. Those civil rights laws vary in their interpretations of the scope of facilities covered by private club exemptions but have usually been interpreted as not including gender as a protected class (Frakt & Rankin, 1982).

Athletic Governing Bodies

Administrative structures of traditional athletic governing bodies may promote policy inequities that limit female participation. Member schools may then be held accountable for discriminatory practices under Title IX. Where inequities are shown to exist, however, both the governing body and the member schools are to be held accountable under appropriate laws.

Athletic governing bodies have frequently been challenged on the grounds of gender discrimination. The courts have examined state athletic governing bodies to determine whether females are given the same opportunities to participate in *established* athletic programs.

Some of the issues being resolved in the courts that relate to enforcement of civil rights are generation of rules that prevent equal opportunities in sports or that conflict with Title IX regulations. In addition, there is case law that addresses the issue of the legal standing of an athletic governing body to challenge the legal authority of Title IX regulations, such as *NCAA v. Califano* (1980), which is described on page 59.

The issues of gender discrimination that have been brought before the courts because of governing rules by athletic associations have included

1. inequities in resources provided to female and male teams (see Case 4.1);
2. females seeking to try out for male teams when there is no opportunity to participate in sports offered to females (see Cases 4.2, 4.4, 4.5, and 4.8);
3. females who seek membership on all-male teams to experience competition commensurate with their abilities (see Case 4.3);
4. different rules for female and male games that require females to develop nontransferrable skills (see Case 4.7); and
5. association rules that conflict with Title IX (see Case 4.8).

A summary of litigation alleging gender-based discrimination by sports governing bodies appears in Table 4.1.

SEXUAL ORIENTATION

Few groups in our society suffer more from degradation and stigma than gays and lesbians. Persons with homosexual histories are found in every age group, in every social level, and in every conceivable occupation throughout the country.

Federal Legislation

Federal antidiscrimination legislation protects civil rights on the basis of race, color, creed, national origin, gender, and disability but not on the basis of sexual orientation. However, recent passage of state civil rights legislation provides evidence that public consciousness of rights based on sexual orientation is changing. For instance, it took more than 15 years from initiation to pass the Massachusetts Gay Civil Rights Bill of 1989 (Cicchino, Deming, & Nicholson, 1991). The passage reveals the narrow limits of congressional support for protection of civil rights on the basis of sexual orientation.

The U.S. Constitution affirms that all people are entitled to equal protection under the law. Although protection of rights regardless of sexual orientation under the equal protection clause of the 14th Amendment has received theoretical consideration, the courts have been unreceptive in most cases (Ben-Asher, 1990). Although there is no such federal legislation to protect rights on the basis of sexual orientation, the Hate Crimes Statistics Act of 1990 directs the U.S. Department of Justice to collect and publish statistics on the evidence of crime manifested as a result of prejudice against sexual orientation.

State and Local Legislation

In comparison to the relatively narrow and minor gains won in federal legislation, the gay and lesbian communities have gained broader protection from discrimination at the state and local levels. Thirteen states and 87 cities and counties prohibit discrimination in public employment. Massachusetts, Wisconsin, and Hawaii have approved traditional civil rights statutes covering sexual orientation. Similar legislation has been introduced in California,

Table 4.1 Summary of Case Law Against Athletic Governing Bodies

| Litigation against athletic governing bodies for gender-based discrimination | |
Case	Ruling
Yellow Springs Village School District Board of Education v. Ohio High School Athletic Association (1981)	Action against state athletic association because rules conflicted with Title IX
National Organization for Women v. Little League Baseball (1974)	Females physically able to play as equals at middle school level with males
Morris v. Michigan State Board (1973)	Struck down a rule by an athletic association prohibiting female students from competing on the high school tennis team, a noncontact sport
Fortin v. Darlington Little League (1975)	Females allowed to play on Little League baseball teams; physical difference as a justification for exclusion for safety reasons unacceptable; Little League falls under sponsorship of a municipality
Carnes v. Tennessee Secondary School Athletic Association (1976)	Struck down prohibition of an athletic association rule that excluded women from playing varsity baseball
Clinton v. Nagy (1974)	Struck down Cleveland Browns MUNY football league's prohibition of girls from playing because no evidence showed physical incapacity of females to participate
Leffel v. Wisconsin Interscholastic Athletic Association (1978)	Unconstitutional for high school athletic association rule to prohibit coed athletic teams in high schools that do not have separate teams for baseball and tennis
Hoover v. Meiklejohn (1977)	Struck down a Colorado High School Athletic Association rule that prohibited high school women from participating in soccer, a contact sport
Califano v. Webster (1977)	Found separate and exclusive female teams constitutionally permissible; women allowed to have the choice of competing on an open team or a single-gender female team
Gomes v. Rhode Island Interscholastic League (1979)	Constitution permits compensatory benefits to correct past discrimination but does not permit athletic association rules based on archaic stereotypes.
Attorney General v. Massachusetts Interscholastic Athletic Association (1979)	Found that under Massachusetts ERA statutes, males were eligible to participate on female teams
Commonwealth v. Pennsylvania Interscholastic Athletic Association (1975)	Found that for women to develop peak performance levels, they may have to compete with men who play at generally higher levels than women do

Minnesota, New Mexico, New York, Ohio, Oregon, Pennsylvania, Rhode Island, Washington, and Colorado.

Sexual orientation legislation has addressed discriminatory action against sodomy and in housing, credit, and employment. These laws may apply to the use of public accommodations such as community health spas and fitness centers, public recreational facilities such as YMCAs and YWCAs, and community recreation programs. For instance, under the Massachusetts Gay Civil Rights Act, it is illegal for employers in sport and physical activity centers to refuse to hire on the basis of sexual orientation.

Discrimination in public accommodations is also broadly defined as denial of access to "any place . . . which is open to and accepts or solicits the patronage of the general public" (Cicchino, Deming, & Nicholson, 1991). Advertising or publicity about a place of public accommodation that discriminates on the basis of sexual orientation may be unlawful in some communities.

State and local sexual orientation legislation subjects health spas, physical fitness centers, and other government and public recreational facilities in those states and municipalities to laws similar to Title II of the Civil Rights Act of 1964 (see chapter 3). Some states have commissions that enforce sexual orientation laws in these jurisdictions. People who believe they have been victims of discrimination may file complaints with these commissions against their offenders.

GENDER EMPLOYMENT DISCRIMINATION

Title VII of the Civil Rights Act of 1964 makes it unlawful for an employer to discriminate against any individual with respect to compensation, terms, conditions, or privileges of employment because of gender. The first principle for promoting gender equity in physical activity and sport programs involves the selection of personnel with the necessary qualifications to conduct the programs. Coaches and assistants should be hired to keep the ratio of coaching staff to team members approximately the same for female and male teams. Secondly, compensation for the coaches and assistants of the female teams should be commensurate with compensation for the coaches and tutors of male teams. Furthermore, in the area of physical education, the staff should include both females and males and should be assigned to classes without regard to gender.

The Equal Pay Act (1982), prevents employers from discriminating by paying wages to employees of one gender at a rate less than the rate at which they pay wages to employees of the opposite gender for equal work on the job. Standards for assessment of performance of equal work include skill, effort, and responsibility in tasks performed under similar working conditions.

Women coaches at both the high school and college levels have claimed gender discrimination and have brought litigation before federal and state courts. Given the apparent disparity in treatment of athletic personnel based on gender, it is likely that both Title IX and the Equal Pay Act will be utilized to eliminate those disparities. However, the courts have held that the Secretary of Labor should not be put in a position of evaluating jobs and what constitutes a proper differential of unequal work. (For a more detailed discussion of employment practices, see chapter 10.)

MANAGEMENT GUIDELINES:
NONDISCRIMINATION BY GENDER OR SEXUAL ORIENTATION

People who manage sport and physical activity programs should take preventative action to assure that physical activity and athletics are free of discrimination on the basis of gender and sexual orientation. Policy statements should be developed that indicate that all students have a right to participate in physical education, interscholastic and intercollegiate sports, and intramural activities regardless of their gender. These statements should be sent to the appropriate administrators, staff, parents, and students at the beginning of each school year.

Here are some general guidelines that managers can follow to minimize the risk of litigation based on gender discrimination.

- Study state and local laws to determine applicable supplements to federal gender and sexual orientation discrimination laws.

- Monitor programs to determine whether existing practices discriminate on the basis of gender and sexual orientation.
- Have a plan of affirmative action to alleviate gender and sexual orientation discrimination if such practices exist.

Some guidelines for avoiding gender discrimination in public school physical activity and athletics are as follows:

- Provide gender fairness in physical education and interscholastic and intercollegiate athletics at all levels of the curriculum (including the elementary level).
- Accommodate the interests and needs of both sexes by conducting interest surveys.

CASE STUDIES

Case 4.1

Equal Opportunity in Interscholastic Sports

High school girls and their parents brought action against the State Office of Public Instruction in Montana under Title IX. The central issue was equal opportunity for males and females to participate in extracurricular athletics at the high school level. At the time of this case, the plaintiffs alleged that conditions were such that opportunities for girls to participate in high school athletics were grossly restricted compared to opportunities for boys. The court ruled that high school girls did not have equal opportunity to participate in high school interscholastic athletics. Some of the issues that led to this decision were the following:

1. Greater numbers of sports sanctioned and offered by the schools for boys than girls
2. Differences in length and continuity of athletic seasons, providing more advantageous seasons for boys
3. More favorable team support for boys' athletic programs than for girls' activities, which were limited to cheerleading, band appearances, half-time performances, and booster clubs
4. Disparate treatment in the schools' recognition boards, halls of fame, and trophy cases
5. Disparities in the quality of officiating at girls' and boys' athletic events

The court hearing the case of *Ridgeway, K. v. Montana High School Association* set a precedent for enforcement of Title IX regulations. It also applied the regulations in practical settings in high school athletics.

[Adapted from *Ridgeway, K. v. Montana High School Association*, 633 F. Supp. 1564 (D. Mont. 1986)]

Case 4.2

Participation of Females on Male Teams (No Female Teams)

Families of high school female athletes brought an action for all female public high school students in the state of Wisconsin for opportunity equal to that afforded to all males. Sue S. of DePere High School in Wisconsin alleged that she was denied permission to qualify for competition with male students on the high school interscholastic varsity baseball team. The school offered no separate female team for interscholastic competition. Furthermore, under the same litigation, female students at Washington High School claimed that they were denied permission to qualify for competition with male students on the high school's interscholastic varsity tennis team.

In both schools, there were no female teams in comparable sports. School officials excluded the plaintiffs from trying out for the teams based on the provisions of the Wisconsin Interscholastic Athletic Association. The school and the athletic association agreed that exclusion was based on unreasonable risk to the females.

The court found that the exclusion of females from participation in a varsity interscholastic athletic program in a particular sport where such a program is provided for male students violates the equal protection clause of the 14th Amendment. The decision is significant in that it showed that excluding females from all contact sports to protect them from unreasonable risk of injury is not fairly or substantially related to a justifiable government objective. According to the court, the administration's two options for achieving equity of interscholastic athletic programs were to (a) eliminate varsity athletic competition for all students or (b) establish separate female teams for contact sports.

[Adapted from *Leffel v. Wisconsin Interscholastic Athletic Association*, 444 F. Supp. 104 (1982)]

Case 4.3

Female Participation on Male Teams When All-Female Teams Are Available

Cynthia C. of Washington High in Wisconsin desired to participate on a male swim team rather than the female swim team for the purpose of gaining more equitable competition with which to develop her abilities. She alleged that failure to provide such opportunity to maximize her abilities was a violation of the equal protection clause of the 14th Amendment. The court held that there was no intentionally imposed difference in levels of competition on boys' and girls' teams. Such differences arise from abilities of the team members themselves, and relief could not encompass the concept of equal levels of competition.

[Adapted from *Leffel v. Wisconsin Interscholastic Athletic Association*, 444 F. Supp. 1117 (E.D. Wis. 1978)]

Case 4.4

Ability Distinction (Preteen-age)

Allison Fortin, a 10-year-old girl, desired to play baseball in the Pawtucket, Rhode Island, Little League, whose membership was limited to boys. A reason for denial of female participation in Little League baseball at the age of 10 years was the alleged differences in strength and ability between boys and girls. It was reasoned that the difference in physical make-up between boys and girls would jeopardize the safety of the girls.

The judge ruled in favor of Allison Fortin, indicating that the evidence to support the alleged strength and ability distinction between preteen boys and girls was so meager that it could not be accepted. The safety issue was not compelling because the activity was self-regulating in that girls could withdraw from competition. Furthermore, boys who are physically weak, awkward, or disabled had found places on the team, and therefore girls with the same physical characteristics should be permitted to play. The ability distinction between sexes should be applied equally to girls and boys.

Based on the outcome of this case, it is apparent that arbitrary criteria that exclude persons from participating in sports will not be allowed. Physical and psychological differences between male and female athletes at preteen levels are not considered great enough to warrant separating the sexes.

[Adapted from *Fortin v. Darlington Little League*, 514 F.2d 344 (1st Cir. 1975)]

Case 4.5

Ability Distinction in High School

Female high school students brought action challenging the Illinois High School Athletic Association for limiting girls' rights to compete against boys. This court held that physical and psychological differences between male and female athletes were a constitutionally sufficient reason for prohibiting interscholastic athletic competition between high school boys and girls.

Courts that have heard similar cases have ruled differently, based on the ages of the participants. Courts allow valid tests to determine placement for educational and safety purposes but disallow arbitrary, archaic tests or stereotyped biases that exclude females from participation. For instance, girls who cannot catch a baseball cannot be excluded from a team if boys who cannot catch a baseball are not excluded. The relevance of the test for facilitating equitable competition, skill development, or safety is the central issue.

[Adapted from *Bucha v. Illinois High School Athletic Association*, 351 F. Supp. 69 (N.D. Ill. 1972)]

Case 4.6

Equal Opportunity (Scheduling)

Gender discrimination in scheduling high school interscholastic athletics was brought against the State Office of Public Instruction of Montana for alleged gender discrimination in secondary athletic programs under Title IX and the Montana Constitution. The central issue was scheduling high school girls' basketball in the fall and girls' volleyball in the winter. This scheduling was outside national norms. The plaintiffs alleged that this denied the girls equal opportunity.

However, there were practical considerations for scheduling seasons outside the national norms. For example, many schools with limited resources for staff use the same coaches for boys' and girls' basketball programs, and many student athletes, parents, and school supporters favored the existing schedule because it offered wider opportunities for athletes.

The court ruled that scheduling girls' basketball in the fall and girls' volleyball in the winter was acceptable. The schedule substantially contributed to the availability of coaches, officials, and facilities, particularly in smaller high schools.

In this decision the alternative chosen may not have been to maximize equality but may have represented a tradeoff between equality and practicality, because seasons outside of the norm had several disadvantages for the female team members:

1. They restricted competition with teams in other states.
2. They restricted opportunities to be chosen for any All-American teams.
3. They posed disadvantages for recruitment for college scholarships because "letter of intent" dates fell in the middle of the Montana volleyball season.
4. They afforded a lowered psychological experience because team members were aware that they were playing outside the national norm.

[Adapted from *Ridgeway, K. v. Montana High School Association*, 633 F. Supp. 1564 (D. Mont. 1986)]

Case 4.7

Different Rules in the Same Sport
Cheryl Jones was a junior at Northeast High School of Oklahoma City, where she played the position of guard on the girls' basketball team. In Oklahoma, the girls' game was substantially different from the boys' game. The boys' game is full court but the girls' game requires players to stay in one half of the court. Cheryl wanted to play by full-court rules, but she could not because of the rules of the Oklahoma Secondary School Activities Association.

Counsel for the plaintiff argued that the unreasonable distinction between the boys' and girls' rules violated Ms. Jones's equal protection rights and her opportunities to compete in professional and Olympic basketball and reduced her opportunity for a college basketball scholarship. Further, it was argued that the girls' basketball rules caused Cheryl to learn unusable skills and denied her an opportunity to participate in the full strategy of the game.

The court ruled in favor of the Oklahoma Secondary School Activities Association. Although the association's rules were out of step with other states' rules and may not have been in the interest of the high school girls who play basketball in Oklahoma, they did not result in a substantial deprivation of a constitutional right. The court further reasoned that such policy decisions are best left to the judgment of those who play, coach, and administer interscholastic basketball, and not the federal court.

[Adapted from *Jones, C.L. v. Oklahoma Secondary School Activities Association,* 453 F. Supp 150 (1977)]

Case 4.8

Athletic Governing Bodies Conflict With Title IX

The school board of Yellow Springs, Ohio, brought action against the Ohio High School Athletic Association because it prohibited coeducational teams in contact sports. Yellow Springs is a small school composed of 950 students, 220 of whom are in the middle school. It was difficult for such a small school to have both girls' and boys' middle school basketball programs because the school lacked facilities and coaches. School authorities observed that boys and girls of this level have essentially the same athletic skills and had organized coeducational teams for other sports.

But Yellow Springs could not offer a coed basketball team, because the rules of the Ohio High School Athletic Association (OHSAA) prohibit coed teams in interscholastic contact sports such as basketball. The rule was challenged when two Yellow Springs middle school girls tried out for and made the boys' basketball team. Competition on a coeducational team was prohibited by the OHSAA rule. This prevents its member schools from adopting the means Title IX offers for achieving compliance.

The court held that the mandatory separation required by the OHSAA rule conflicts with the permissive rule stated in Title IX. It concluded that schools should give qualified female competitors the opportunity to play on the "male" interscholastic varsity team. This decision sent a clear message that when there is a conflict between Title IX regulations and rules of a state athletic governing body, the federal regulations of Title IX will prevail.

[Adapted from *Yellow Springs Village School District Board of Education v. Ohio High School Athletic Association,* 647 F.2d 651 (6th Cir. 1981)]

Case 4.9

Males on Female Teams

The Massachusetts Interscholastic Athletic Association (MIAA) had a rule that prevented boys from playing on girls' teams, although girls could play on boys' teams if that sport was not offered to girls. The justification of this rule was that the discrimination was not based on gender but on biological differences between males and females. The rule affected virtually all public schools in Massachusetts.

Because there are no boys' softball teams in Massachusetts, two boys were allowed to play on a girls' softball team. In addition, a girls' field hockey team had five senior boys. This provoked the Massachusetts Division of Girls' and Women's Sports to protest to the MIAA. Furthermore, the previously all-female David Hale Fanning Trade School in Worcester had recently admitted 48 boys to a school with a total enrollment of 585. The school could not form teams exclusively for boys, so it allowed boys to play on girls' softball and basketball squads.

The plaintiffs argued that there were increasing numbers of female athletes whose abilities exceed those of most men and, in some cases, approach those of the most talented men. They further indicated that a girl is surely not less exposed to injury as a member of a predominantly male team than as a member of a team that is predominantly female but with some male players. Furthermore, a girl is as entitled as a boy to choose to take a risk subject to the rules of safety and appropriate supervision.

The court held that boys should not be barred from playing on girls' interscholastic teams. Any rule that classifies by gender alone is subject to case examination under the equal protection clause.

[Adapted from *Attorney General v. Massachusetts Interscholastic Athletic Association, Inc.*, 378 Mass. 342 393 N.E.2d. 284 (1979)]

Case 4.10

Males on Female Teams

B.C., a male, was denied an opportunity to participate on the Cumberland Regional High School girls' field hockey team. Litigation was brought against the New Jersey State Interscholastic Athletic Association, which had developed the regulations that prohibited him from playing on the female field hockey team. The issue of this litigation was whether or not such exclusion violated B.C.'s federal equal protection and the New Jersey state laws that prohibit gender discrimination in education.

B.C., the plaintiff, argued that, although there is incidental contact in field hockey, safety and equipment requirements for field hockey were not sufficient grounds for excluding males from female teams. Furthermore, it was argued that stickwork was of greater importance than mere size and speed in field hockey. It was also established that some Cumberland girls were superior to B.C. in certain facets of the sport. Thus, B.C. was excluded solely on the basis of gender. On the other hand, the athletic association argued that the inclusion of males on female field hockey teams would increase the risk of injury, intimidate girls from participation, and reduce opportunities for females to participate in field hockey specifically and sports competition in general.

The court ruled that the equal protection clause of the U.S. Constitution and New Jersey nondiscrimination laws of gender in education had not been violated by the rules of the athletic association. The rationale for the decision was that the athletic association rules were designed to help schools rectify the historical denial of opportunity for females in extracurricular sports activities. Although there were no teams for boys in the same sport, such a position is appropriate until such time as both sexes are afforded overall equal opportunity in athletics. Another reason for the decision was that the prohibition of boys from girls' athletic teams solely on the basis of sex contributes to overall equal opportunity for participation in athletics.

[Adapted from *B.C. v. Board of Education, Cumberland Regional School District and New Jersey State Interscholastic Athletic Association*, 531 A.2d 1059 (N.J. Super. A.D. 1987)]

CHAPTER SUMMARY

Discrimination against females in sport and physical activity, under many conditions, is a violation of Title IX. Title IX extends nondiscriminatory practice based on gender to entities in the educational system that receive federal financial assistance. In addition, athletic governing bodies that were in the past out of sync with federal and state laws regarding discriminatory practices based on gender are promoting rules that affirm nondiscriminatory practices.

Most of the litigation regarding discriminatory practices against females in education have been based on the conduct of interscholastic and intercollegiate athletic programs. There has been little litigation involving instructional physical education programs.

Legal remedies for discrimination based on sexual orientation are scarce at the federal level. However, local municipalities and state governments are beginning to enact legislation that protects gays and lesbians from discrimination.

KEY TERMS

Civil Rights Restoration Act of 1988 (61)
Complaints (60)
Compliance review (60)
Equal protection (52)
Institutionwide compliance (60)
Office of Civil Rights (OCR) (59)
Program-specific compliance (60)
Proportionate equality (54)
Standards of performance (55)
Title IX (52)

QUESTIONS FOR DISCUSSION

1. If you were administering an athletic program and a member of the women's tennis team asked to try out for the men's tennis team, what would your answer be? What facts or issues would contribute most to your decision?

2. If you were a school administrator, and the state athletic association requested that member schools conduct women's volleyball in the winter at the same time as men's volleyball, but you had insufficient facilities for running both programs simultaneously, what would you do? Why?

3. You are the coach of a Little League football team that plays and practices on a junior high school athletic field. Two girls want to try out for the team. You assess them as frail and believe their safety would be in jeopardy. What would you do? Why?

4. You are the athletic director of a women's program. You believe that the resources for your program and for the men's program are not being allocated equally. What would you do? Why?

5. You are an athletic director of a program in which men want to compete in an equitable manner for positions on women's teams. There are teams for men in those sports. Would you permit this? Why or why not? If there were no men's teams, would you permit participation? Why or why not?

6. You are the manager of a health spa, where two members who are avowed

homosexuals made semisexual gestures of love to one another. The gestures were seen by other members, who reported disapproval to you. What would you do and why?

7. You are a school administrator and have received complaints from women's rights organizations that your school's men's and women's sports teams are all staffed by males. What specific steps would you take when the next vacancy occurs for a position as a coach of a women's team? Why?

REFERENCES

Attorney General v. Massachusetts Interscholastic Athletic Association Inc., 378 Mass. 342, 393 N.E.2d 284 (1979).

B.C. v. Board of Education, Cumberland Regional School District and New Jersey State Interscholastic Athletic Association, 531 A.2d 1059 (N.J. Super. A.D. 1987).

Ben-Asher, D.D. (1990, Spring). Legal discrimination against homosexuals in America, and a comparison with more tolerant societies. *New York Law School Journal of Human Rights,* 157-178.

Bennett v. West Texas State University, 525 Supp. 77 (N.D. Tex. 1981)

Blair v. Washington State University, 740, p.2d, 1379 (Wash. 1987).

Bucha v. Illinois High School Athletic Association, 351 F. Supp. 69 (N.D. Ill. 1972).

Califano v. Webster, 430 U.S. 313, 97 S.Ct. 1192, 51 L.Ed. (1977).

Cannon v. University of Chicago, 441 U.S. 677 (1979).

Carnes v. Tennessee Secondary School Athletic Association, 415 F. Supp. 569 (E.D. Tenn. 1976).

Cicchino, P.M., Deming, B.R., & Nicholson, K.M. (1991). Sex, lies, and civil rights: A critical history of the Massachusetts gay civil rights bill. *Harvard Civil Rights-Civil Liberties Law Review,* **26**, 551-631.

Clinton v. Nagy, 411 F. Supp. 1396 (N.D. Ohio 1974).

Commonwealth v. Pennsylvania Interscholastic Athletic Association, 18 Pa. Cmwlth. 45, 334 A.2d 839, 842 (1975).

Darien v. Gould, 85 Wash.2d 859, 540 P.2d (1975).

Educational Amendment of 1972 (P.L. 92-318, 86 Stat. 373), 20 U.S.C. 1681 (a)(1).

Fortin v. Darlington Little League, 514 F.2d 344 (1st Cir. 1975).

Frakt, T. & Rankin, J. (1982). *The law of parks and recreation.* Salt Lake City: Brighton.

Franklin v. Gwennett County Public School (1992). *The United States Law Week,* **60**, 4167-4172.

Gomes, D.M. v. Rhode Island Interscholastic League, 469 F. Supp. 659 (D.R.I. 1979).

Grove City College v. Bell, 104 S.Ct. 1211 (1984).

Haffer v. Temple University, 678 F. Supp 517 (E.D. Pa. 1987).

Hate Crimes Statistics Act of 1990, 104 Stat. 140.

Hoover v. Meiklejohn, 430 F. Supp, 164 (D. Colo. 1977).

Jones, C.L. v. Oklahoma Secondary School Activities Association, 453 F. Supp. 150 (1977).

Leffel v. Wisconsin Interscholastic Athletic Association, 444 F. Supp. 1117 (E.D. Wis. 1978).

Leffel v. Wisconsin Interscholastic Athletic Association, 444 F. Supp. 104 (1982).

Morris v. Michigan State Board of Education, 472 F.2d 1207 (6th Cir. 1973).

National Collegiate Athletic Association v. Califano, 622 F.2d 1382 (1980).

National Organization for Women v. Little League Baseball, Inc., 127 N.J. Super. 522, 318 A.2d 33 (1974).

O'Connor, K. v. Board of Education of School District No. 23, 645 F.2d 578 (7th Cir. 1981).

Ridgeway, K. v. Montana High School Association, 633 F. Supp. 1564 (D. Mont. 1986).

U.S. Congress, Civil Rights Restoration Act of 1988.

Yellow Springs Village School District Board of Education v. Ohio High School Athletic Association, 647 F.2d 651 (6th Cir. 1981).

Schubert, A.F., Schubert, G.W., & Schubert-Madsen, J.C.L. (1991). Changes influenced by litigation in women's inter-collegiate athletics. *Seton Hall Journal of Sport Law*, **1**, 237-268.

Schubert, G.W., Smith, R.K., & Trentadue, J. (1986). *Sports law*. New York: West.

ADDITIONAL READINGS

Frakt, T., & Rankin, J. (1982). *The law of parks and recreation*. Salt Lake City: Brighton.

CHAPTER 5

EXCLUSION BASED ON DISABLING CONDITIONS

Kenny Walker, a defensive tackle for the Denver Broncos, is deaf. Despite Kenny's inability to hear, he was a successful student-athlete in high school and an All-American nominee in football at the University of Nebraska, where he received a college education. Kenny now successfully competes in the National Football League, where hearing to communicate with coaches and other players was once thought to be imperative.

Kenny Walker was allowed to let his abilities outstrip his disabilities partly because his coaching and educational process underwent significant modification. At his high school, and at the University of Nebraska, he received an individualized program with supplemental aids and services, which is an educational entitlement of all persons with disability when in public schools. However, one might ask whether persons with disabilities generally receive coaching and instruction in physical activity and sport to the same extent as Kenny Walker did so that they, too, can develop and express their athletic and physical abilities to the highest degree possible.

LEARNING OBJECTIVES

The student will be able to

1. explain the provisions of the Individuals with Disabilities Education Act, the Americans with Disabilities Act, and the Rehabilitation Act;
2. outline the legal procedure for developing and conducting an Individual Education Program for a person with a disability;
3. explain the importance of least restrictive environment in formulating and conducting the Individual Education Program; and
4. apply appropriate legal principles to minimize risks of litigation in programs of sport and physical activity, both government-sponsored and those of public accommodation such as health spas and commercial physical fitness centers.

DISABILITY LEGISLATION

Three major pieces of legislation for people with disabilities relate to sport and physical activity: the Individuals with Disability Education Act (IDEA), previously the Education for the Handicapped Act P.L. 94-142, 20 U.S.C. 1232; the Rehabilitation Act of 1973 29 U.S.C. 701; and the Americans with Disabilities Act of 1990 (ADA) 42 U.S.C. 12101. The central purpose of legislation for people with disabilities is to provide them equal citizenship and opportunities. The similarities among the three acts are **accessibility** to environments where benefits can be derived, equity of services for those with disabilities

compared to those without, **reasonable accommodation** for the disabling condition so there is equal opportunity to receive benefits of society, and encouragement of societal integration of disabled citizens with nondisabled citizens. The Rehabilitation Act, IDEA, and ADA apply these central purposes to differing contexts. The Rehabilitation Act is general civil rights legislation that applies to social services in the community and the public schools. And the Americans with Disabilities Act focuses on public accommodations in the community; its theme is equal opportunity to enjoy community benefits through public accommodations. The Individuals with Disabilities Education Act applies to educational settings; its implementation requires sophisticated educational procedures, and it is by far the most complex legislation to implement and monitor.

All three acts make provisions regarding education, service compensation for the disability, sport and physical activity, integration, accessibility, federal financial assistance, personnel who conduct programs, and monitoring procedures. Table 5.1 shows similarities and differences of the three acts in each of the common areas reflected in the legislation.

Individuals With Disabilities Education Act

The **Individuals with Disabilities Education Act (IDEA)** of 1990 was designed to provide children with disabilities equal educational opportunity. Two issues guided the framing of the legislation. One is that for disabled children to benefit from education, they must be provided instruction to meet their unique needs. The second is that disabled children should be educated to the greatest extent possible alongside their nondisabled peers.

Table 5.1 Comparison of Features of Disability Legislation

Provisions	Rehabilitation Act of 1973	Individuals with Disabilities Education Act	Americans with Disabilities Act
General	Requires general nondiscriminatory practices in employment, education, health, and social services	Requires nondiscriminatory practices in education with program compensation for disability	Prohibits discrimination in public accommodations
Education	Guarantees educational opportunity to school-age and pre- and postschool-age disabled citizens	Guarantees free appropriate education to pre- and school-age disabled citizens	Requires that school program transition and public accommodation programs for a child complement one another
Service compensation for disability	Requires reasonable accommodation for the disability	Requires an Individual Education Program, supplemental aids and services, and related services	Requires reasonable accommodation for the disability
Sport and physical activity	Prohibits discrimination in physical education and athletics	Explicitly defines physical education, particularly extracurricular sports, and defines a process for conducting physical activities	Requires that public accommodations that provide sport and physical activity make reasonable accommodations to include disabled citizens
Integration	Requires integration to the maximum extent possible	Requires integration in the least restrictive environment and progressive placement in lesser restrictive environments	Requires integration to the maximum extent possible
Accessibility	Requires adaptations to make programs accessible	Requires adaptations to make programs accessible	Requires adaptations to make programs accessible
Federal financial assistance	Provides federal assistance for research, demonstration, and federal monitoring	Provides direct federal assistance to states and funds for research, demonstration, and personnel preparation	Provides financial assistance for monitoring, research, and demonstration
Personnel conducting programs	Sets standards for personnel who conduct programs in which the sport or physical activity is not well defined	Requires that personnel must be qualified to conduct programs of physical activity	Sets standards for personnel who conduct programs in which the physical activity is not well defined
Monitoring	Provides for monitoring by the Office of Civil Rights	Provides for monitoring by the Office of Special Education and Rehabilitation Services, local and state due process mechanisms, and the Office of Civil Rights	Provides for monitoring by the Office of Civil Rights

Another central theme of the IDEA legislation was that of related services. In the event that disabled children could not benefit from programs of physical activity and sport, related services were to be provided to help the children obtain benefits from these portions of their education.

The related service that is most often associated with programs of physical activity is physical therapy. Physical therapy can help a child benefit from physical education if the physical education teacher cannot provide the intended motor skill development. Thus, the mission of IDEA was to provide special education and related services geared to the child's needs (that is, individualized instruction) in the least restrictive environment.

One major problem that disabled citizens experience in society is exclusion from programs in which the nondisabled participate (see Case 5.1). IDEA provides compensatory measures to assure equal opportunity for people with disabilities through individualized instruction and related services. To qualify for these special education services in the public schools, an individual in need must be assessed and found to have a disability.

Under IDEA regulations, there are two criteria for most disabilities. These are

1. a clinical evaluation that establishes the disability associated with a specific condition (for example, hearing or visual impairment or mental retardation); and
2. an assessment of the educational performance of the child in the applied setting to determine whether, in the case of physical education, motor performance is up to normative expectations.

Consider six people who were able to take their academic classes with their peers but who were physically disabled and used wheelchairs. When they participated in physical activity, they needed specially designed instruction in order to benefit from the physical education program. It was argued by the school district that because they were not academically disabled, they did not meet qualifications for disability. This alleviated the need for specially designed physical education programs to meet their individual physical needs. This was a false assumption. For these six people, the clinical label of orthopedically disabled was valid, and their physical performance was adversely affected by their physical disability. Clearly they needed Individual Education Programs in physical education to meet their unique needs.

The criteria for disability under the Rehabilitation Act and ADA are less elaborate than the IDEA criteria. In general, impaired life functions that require some form of accommodation for participation in independent domestic, recreational, or vocational life are considered a disability.

The Rehabilitation Act— Section 504

Section 504 of the Rehabilitation Act of 1973 (P.L. 93-112) states that individuals with disabilities shall not be excluded from, discriminated against, or denied benefits of any program sponsored by a recipient of federal funds. The rules and regulations for administering and implementing Section 504 give attention and emphasis to physical education and athletics, specifically the instructional phase, intramurals, and interscholastic sport programs for school-age children. These aspects of physical activity are also covered by IDEA.

Section 504 extends the principles of the IDEA to community recreation programs and college programs that are provided with federal financial assistance. Compliance of such programs with Section 504 is similar to compliance with Title VI and Title IX of the Civil Rights Act (see chapter 4). Essentially Section

504 requires that people with disabilities receive reasonable accommodation to assure benefits from equally effective treatment received by the nondisabled.

Americans With Disabilities Act

The **Americans with Disabilities Act (ADA)** extends civil rights legislation for disabled citizens by prohibiting discrimination in places of public accommodation. The legislation requires nondiscriminatory practices and bars the use of screening that may exclude disabled persons from the enjoyment provided nondisabled persons in facilities of public accommodation such as health care services, health spas, places of exercise, gymnasiums, and most health and fitness facilities. ADA may require facility managers to modify policies, practices, and procedures to open their facilities to the disabled. Although safe participation in activity is a desirable goal, safety criteria must be based on actual risk and not on speculation, stereotypes, or generalizations about disabilities.

SOME LEGAL ISSUES OF EQUAL EDUCATIONAL OPPORTUNITY

The legislation requiring that disabled citizens have equal educational opportunity, particularly the IDEA, has raised several key issues about the placement and delivery of physical education programs in the public schools for students with disabilities. These issues include

- a new legal definition of physical education;
- exclusion of people with disabilities from physical education programs;
- program accessibility for people with disabilities;

- assurance of benefits through equally effective treatment for students with disabilities;
- creation of an Individual Education Program for each child with a disability, which includes parental participation, provision of related services, and placement in the least restrictive environment;
- provision of separate programs; and
- the hiring of qualified personnel to administer programs for disabled students.

These issues are addressed in the following sections of this chapter.

A New Definition of Physical Education

IDEA set public policy that established physical education as an integral part of special education. In fact, physical education is the only curricular area the IDEA identifies. Its inclusion as an integral part of the act made it necessary for regulatory bodies to define physical education.

Traditional physical education activities include participation in sports, development of physical and motor fitness and other prerequisites for healthful daily living, and recreation in physical activity and sport. These types of activities were already a part of most physical education programs. Federal regulations have established them as the legal physical education curricula for both disabled and nondisabled school-age children.

Federal regulations have defined **physical education** as "the development of physical and motor fitness, fundamental skills and patterns, skills in individual and group games and sports, and aquatics, dance, including intramural and lifetime sports. The term includes special physical education, adapted physical education, movement education and motor development" (20 U.S.C. 1406, 1982). This definition applies to physical education for individuals from preschool ages to the formal age their state has established at which people with disabilities exit schools, commonly 21 years.

There are at least three reasons why it is important that education personnel and parents know this legal definition of physical education. First, it defines the physical education curriculum to which people with disabilities are entitled at federal, state, and local levels. Using the correct definition of physical education is important; office of civil rights complaints have been introduced against schools that had mistakenly defined physical education for children with disabilities as the development of nonspecific gross and fine motor skills and had included it in their special education curricula (Richmond (IN) Community School Corporation, 1987).

Second, the definition sets curriculum outcomes for service providers such as physical educators who deliver the direct services, their local educational agency administrators, officials in state educational agencies, and community sport managers who may be involved in helping people with disabilities use the skills they learn in school to make the transition to adult life in the community. All these people may be responsible for providing these curricular entitlements to persons with disabilities.

Finally, the definition of the physical education curriculum is a management tool for administrators and physical education personnel who must match the physical activity needs of children with disabilities to a broad-based, well-defined curriculum.

Exclusion From Programs

A mission of disability legislation is to assure that all people with disabilities have opportunities to participate in physical activity. At one time it was thought that some children were too disabled to benefit from education. Prior to the passage of disability education legislation, many children who had severe or multiple disabilities or emotional problems were excluded from school.

The Rehabilitation Act and IDEA prohibit excluding students with disabilities from legally required physical activity in public schools. ADA prevents exclusion of disabled citizens from community fitness centers and sport facilities that are public accommodations.

Program Accessibility

Schools and public accommodations of sport and physical activity in communities should operate each program or activity so that, when viewed in its entirety, there is accessibility for individuals with disabilities. No person with a disability who is qualified to be a student in a school may be denied access to any physical activity or sport program in the school's prescribed curriculum or its extracurricular activities that is provided to nondisabled children.

The three pieces of federal disability legislation require schools and sport facilities of public accommodation to make their facilities, when taken as a whole, accessible to individuals with disabling conditions (see Case 5.2). New facilities such as gymnasiums, swimming pools, playgrounds, nature trails, stadiums, or other indoor or outdoor facilities designed for use in physical education instruction, intramural, interscholastic, or intercollegiate sports must be built to meet standards and criteria of accessibility (Steinfeld, 1986). Examples of modifications that may make facilities accessible to people who use wheelchairs are incline ramps, incline slopes to swimming pools, and wider doorways (see Figure 5.1).

IDEA, the Rehabilitation Act, and ADA do not require creation and maintenance of separate facilities; rather, they try to ensure that existing facilities are modified and adapted so that people with and without disabilities have equally effective opportunities for benefits. For instance, to accommodate people with disabling conditions, a swimming area

Figure 5.1 Building facilities such as this one with no steps to the entrance to the pool or locker room make physical activity accessible to all.

may need improved access to the pool, showers, and locker rooms and adjusted schedules to increase access times for practice. A program that has all its gymnasiums located on upper levels and no elevators would not comply because it would be inaccessible to people who use wheelchairs or who have other mobility problems.

Assuring Benefits Through Equally Effective Treatment

The intent of Section 504 of the Rehabilitation Act was to assure that people with disabilities have the same opportunities as the nondisabled. Section 504 rules and regulations therefore require that they be afforded equally effective programs: in other words,

programs that provide equal opportunities to attain the same results, gain the same benefits, or reach the same levels of achievement as peers without disabling conditions.

This does not mean, however, that a benefit or service must produce equal results. It must merely afford equal opportunities to get equal results. This concept is intended to encompass the idea of *equivalent* as opposed to *identical* services. It also acknowledges that, to meet specific needs of individuals with and without disabilities to the same extent, service providers must be prepared to make reasonable accommodations for people with disabilities in some programs.

Reasonable accommodation requirements imply that programs must be made equally effective by adjusting them to compensate for disability. ADA applies reasonable accommodation requirements to public accommodations such as fitness centers. IDEA applies reasonable accommodation requirements to school physical education programs in the form of Individual Education Programs.

The Individual Education Program

IDEA requires school physical education programs to provide **Individual Education Programs (IEPs)** to accommodate the educational needs of children with disabilities (see Case 5.3). Figure 5.2 graphically illustrates the cycle of the IEP process that begins the moment a child is assessed as having a disability and that is periodically reassessed and modified to fit the student's needs.

Each activity of the program should begin at the child's present level of performance and should promote the acquisition of the legally defined physical education skills. Skills should be developed through a series of small steps that lead to the acquisition of objectives and ultimately to the meeting of goals. Aids and supplemental services should be introduced, and the environment should be modified to allow children with disabilities to participate successfully in a setting that is as close as possible to that for nondisabled children.

Supplemental aids and services are used to enable disabled citizens to participate in the same environments with the nondisabled. The Rehabilitation Act and ADA may require that supplemental aids and services be provided as a reasonable accommodation for people with disabilities so they may participate and benefit from a program of physical activity. However, IDEA requires that supplemental aids and services be introduced to allow people with disabilities to be placed in regular physical education classes (see Case

5.5). For many individuals with disabling conditions, adapted aids and services are all the accommodation they need to ensure safe, successful, and satisfying participation in classes with the nondisabled. For example, an adapted aid for the sport of bowling is a bowling ball with a special handle for individuals with cerebral palsy, arthritis, missing fingers, poor coordination, or limited hand and arm strength. Another aid is a bowling ramp that people with cerebral palsy, paraplegia, and quadriplegia can use to deliver the ball. Supplemental services may include personnel, such as an interpreter for a child who is deaf, who help the child benefit from physical education.

Each IEP is evaluated annually by parents and school personnel who make sure the program is implemented. These evaluations can be an effective management tool for the educational system because they oversee the instructional process of the school's IEPs and provide useful feedback, including corrective actions that can help the school better manage instruction. Also, it helps the schools in managing a discussion with parents who must participate in the formulation of educational plans of their children.

Both IDEA and the Rehabilitation Act require individual program goals that directly or indirectly contribute to independent living. An IEP for physical education should contain goals for physical and motor skill development and strategies for participation in individual and team sports.

The Rehabilitation Act requires individual rehabilitation programs similar to the IEPs required by IDEA. However, the act's requirements for individual physical education instruction are less specific than IDEA's requirements for IEPs. The ADA's standard for individualized programs is less specific still: It simply requires reasonable accommodation for opportunity to participate in physical activity in public accommodations.

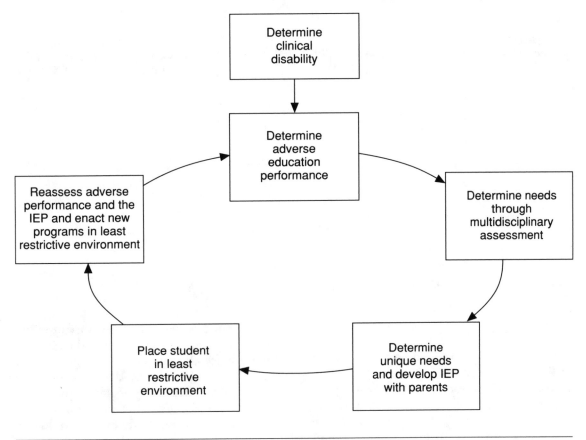

Figure 5.2   The Individual Education Program (IEP) process.

Inappropriate behavior by some disabled individuals in the past have led to their permanent disbarment from sports and physical activity. If behavior management programs had been provided to those people, they may have been able to participate in physical activity and competitive sport programs. Therefore, IEP goals may include social and emotional goals that can be met through behavioral management techniques.

IDEA gives parents the right to be involved in educational decisions affecting their children. This right extends to parents' participation in the development of the IEPs and provides for due process procedures in the event that there is disagreement between parents and local school district personnel.

Parents have followed due process procedures, for example, in school districts that do not provide physical education programs for nondisabled children in all the grades. The question then arose as to whether the school districts were required to provide physical education to their children who have disabilities if the nondisabled do not receive it. An Office of Special Education and Rehabilitation Service's policy statement indicates that if the parents ask for physical education, the school district should provide it (Gustafson, 1979).

ADA does not include provisions for parental participation. The Rehabilitation Act, on the other hand, provides for parental involvement in areas other than the education of children with disabilities.

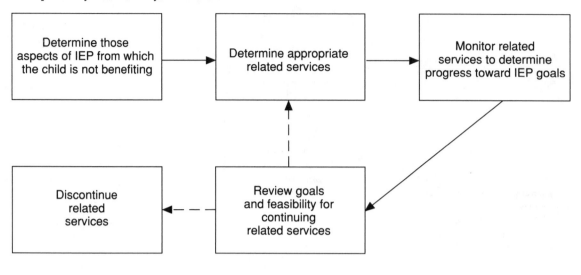

Figure 5.3 Selecting and monitoring related services.

Related Services

IDEA requires that **related services** be part of the IEP for any student with a disability whose skill development does not meet the objectives indicated on a written physical education program. Figure 5.3 shows the process practitioners use to develop and monitor related services.

The related service used in physical education most often is physical therapy. When a judgment is made that the child lacks prerequisite strength or motor functioning in specific muscles and that the development of these prerequisites falls outside the physical education teachers' expertise, the physical therapist is solicited to provide a related service to accomplish outcomes that the physical educator was not able to achieve.

It is imperative that professionals who are administering programs and delivering services know the relationship of a related service to the direct service, in this case physical education. The child's progress toward the goals of the IEP may reveal that he has successfully completed the goals or that he has not benefitted from the related service. In this case, related services may be discontinued due to the lack of progress toward objectives set forth for the student. If a child with a disability needs specially designed physical education and needs physical therapy to benefit from the physical education (a direct service), then physical therapy would be considered an appropriate related service (Long, 1980). However, services requested for physical therapy independent of the prescribed physical education program would be inappropriate.

Neither the Rehabilitation Act nor ADA require that related services have specific educational outcomes. However, under either of these acts, reasonable accommodation to participate and benefit from a program may require a supplemental service or aid.

Least Restrictive Environment and Integration

The **least restrictive environment** is the setting that gives a person with a disability the greatest opportunity to participate with the nondisabled and that minimizes the distinction between participants with and without disabilities. The desired outcome of placement in the least restrictive environment is integration of disabled and nondisabled participants in common physical activity. Therefore, the least restrictive environment for a person with a mild disability would be a regular class with nondisabled children without aids or services. Removal to facilities provided only for the disabled that are outside of the community would be the most restrictive (see Case 5.4).

The least restrictive alternatives for placing students with disabilities in physical education vary widely. Small schools may have fewer alternatives for placement in less restrictive environments than larger schools. Thus, what is an appropriate placement in one school may not be an appropriate placement in another. The resources, size of the school district, and location of the schools may all be relevant factors in placing students with disabilities in physical education.

Placements must reflect individual needs and abilities as expressed in the IEP. Students with disabilities should be moved to special classes only if a regular class cannot meet their needs even if special services and aids are provided. As Figure 5.4 indicates, placement in the least restrictive environment should be made after the IEP has been formulated.

Once the placement has been made, it should be reassessed periodically to determine whether a new environment would be more appropriate for the child. One purpose of special physical education is to give children with disabilities sufficient skills so that they may move to less restrictive environments or to regular classes. Therefore, reevaluation is imperative for an efficient program.

Many school districts provide physical education to all elementary school students in a self-contained classroom; some school districts also follow this practice in special education. As a result, children with disabilities who are taught in self-contained special education classrooms receive their

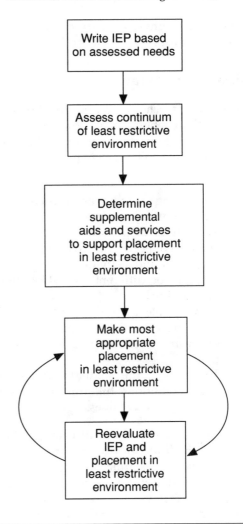

Figure 5.4 Procedures for placing a disabled child in the least restrictive environment for physical activity.

physical education together and are not integrated with nondisabled children. Such arrangements often raise the issue of the child's placement in the least restrictive environment by parents (Bay Arenac (MI) Intermediate School District, 1979).

Modifications can be made in physical activity, equipment, game rules, instructional strategies, and environments to enable students with disabilities to participate in integrated physical activity. Table 5.2 provides examples of such modifications.

Separate Programs

IDEA permits school districts to offer students with disabling conditions programs and activities that are separate or different *only* if all of the following requirements are met.

1. The settings are the least restrictive environment appropriate.
2. The school districts do not deny the students opportunities to participate in programs and activities that are not separate or different for which they are qualified.
3. They enable qualified students with disabling conditions to participate in one or more regular programs and activities.
4. They assign the students with disabling conditions full time to appropriate special facilities.

The Rehabilitation Act requires simply that people with disabilities be integrated with the nondisabled as much as possible. Although ADA does not prescribe integration, it requires that physical activities in places of public accommodation be available to people with disabilities.

Qualified Personnel

IDEA requires that persons who conduct individual physical education programs in the least restrictive environment must be qualified. However, case law to date has not clearly defined the qualifications for teaching physical education to children with disabilities. Case law that establishes such qualifications and standards would help local educational agency administrators set goals and standards for teachers who provide

physical education for students with disabilities. They could then use those standards to assess pupil goals and instructional procedures and to make judgments about the effectiveness of their teachers (see Case 5.6). Inservice and peer teaching training could be provided to raise the level of teachers' skills for teaching students with disabilities.

Neither the Rehabilitation Act nor ADA require that personnel who conduct physical activity programs for people with disabilities be qualified. Therefore, each state or physical activity provider must define its qualifications for personnel.

OPPORTUNITIES FOR THE DISABLED TO PARTICIPATE IN EXTRACURRICULAR ATHLETICS

The Rehabilitation Act and IDEA require that children with disabilities have the same opportunities to participate in extracurricular sports as the nondisabled. ADA provides opportunities for people with disabilities to continue using the sports skills they attained in schools in sport and physical activity programs in places of public accommodation. To comply with the Rehabilitation Act, schools that have intramural athletic activities and interscholastic sports activities for the nondisabled should make the same or similar programs available to people with disabilities. There are many legal implications to be considered in choosing the least restrictive extracurricular athletic programs in which to place children with disabilities. Provisions should be made to separate children with disabilities from nondisabled children during participation only when it is necessary to ensure all students' health and safety. The key principle of providing equal opportunity for participation in intramural and interscholastic activities is that reasonable accommodation should be made that will enable

Table 5.2 Integration Techniques

Modify the activity	Adaption of equipment	Make minor rule changes	Instructional strategies for teachers and coaches	Modify the instructional environment
• Reduce the size of areas of participation such as soccer goals for participants with limited mobility. • Reduce the size of a badminton court by changing boundaries for participants with limited mobility.	• Introduce lighter equipment to facilitate speed of movement for weaker persons. • Provide lighter softball bats, lighter bowling balls, lighter tennis rackets, and lighter archery bows. • Provide bowling balls with handles for those who need them.	• In wrestling, allow people who are blind to use physical contact in takedown. • In volleyball, allow people whose arms or hands are weak to carry rather than hit a volleyball. • In gymnastics, strap the legs of people with paraplegia together to give them greater control of their upper bodies. • In swimming, allow people with disabilities to swim near the edge of the pool and to rest at prescribed distance and time intervals.	• Position yourself so a child who is deaf can read your lips. • Use visual attention-getters to aid children who are hearing-impaired. • Use kinetic and tactile signals to communicate instructions to children who are visually impaired. • Use multisensory communication when instructing people who are mentally retarded. Give simultaneous verbal and visual instructions showing movements to be learned.	• In archery, place pegs in the ground to indicate where children should stand in relation to target. • To enable people who are visually impaired to run or swim, place ropes that indicate running and swimming paths. • In a swimming pool have nonslip bottoms. • Boundaries of play areas for the blind should have different textures to indicate varying surroundings.

students with disabilities to participate in sports activities.

The two ways in which students with disabilities have most often been denied equal opportunity for participation in extracurricular sports competition have been medical disqualification and administrative exclusion in which eligibility standards have been set that screen out students with disabilities. The ADA will likely challenge similar procedures used in sport facilities of public accommodation.

Medical Disqualification

Sport and physical activity providers commonly express fear of liability for giving disabled citizens opportunities to participate in athletics. Although people with disabilities want the same right as the nondisabled to participate and even to risk injury, administrators fear litigation in the event of an injury and therefore assume it is safest to disqualify people with disabilities from participation.

This mistaken assumption was refuted by the New York legislature following the case of *Spitaleri v. Nyquist* (1973), which focused on conditions that excluded students with disabilities from competitive sports. A school physician disqualified Joseph Spitaleri from playing football at the high school level. Salvatore Spitaleri, Joseph's father, pleaded with the school authorities to permit his son to play football. The father agreed to waive the school authorities' responsibility by assuming all the risks of his son's participation in football. Despite the father's petition, the Commissioner of Education of New York upheld the disqualification, and that decision was upheld in turn by the New York Superior Court. Following these rulings, the New York legislature attempted to correct what it believed was an unjust situation by enacting the Spitaleri bill.

The rationale for enacting the bill was that there is a discrepancy between a medical condition as a disqualifier and objective evidence that a student with such a condition may be medically capable of participation. Furthermore, in conflicting evidence from private and school physicians, the State Department of Education favors the decision of the school physician even though the private physician's recommendation may be more reasonable.

The Spitaleri bill required that schools give students with disabilities the opportunity to participate in sports at their parents' discretion. Under the bill, a parent who permits a child to participate in competitive sports over the objections of a school physician thereby releases the physician and the school district from liability for the student's participation in the sport (Tyler, 1985). This example shows that issues relating to the exclusion of disabled citizens are being debated in the legal and educational professions as well as in the courts and that established administrative governmental structures are firmly controlling legal outcomes in cases involving the exclusion of people with disabilities (see Case 5.7).

Although the outcomes of litigation involving attempts to exclude students with disabilities from extracurricular sports participation have been mixed, boards of education have won the majority of such cases. Precedent has been set for the courts to honor the professional opinion of those associated with school boards and other administrative structures, not professionals who support plaintiffs with disabilities (*Kampmeier v. Nyquist*, 1977). Because there is disagreement among courts, lawyers, and medical doctors and professionals on the issue of the "right to risk" of a person with disabilities versus the state's authority to exclude from athletic competition, few guidelines for including disabled citizens, particularly in competitive sports, can be offered to those who conduct sports programs.

Administrative Exclusion by Athletic Governing Bodies

People with disabilities are sometimes excluded from participation in athletics by administrative policies implemented either by local school districts or by athletic associations at the state level (see Cases 5.8 and 5.9). In the case of local school districts, the most common exclusionary rule is an academic requirement. Academic requirements often exclude persons with mental disabilities, who may be less capable academically than the nondisabled.

Another condition that is used to disqualify students with disabilities from athletic competition is the age of the participant. Because nondisabled students usually graduate by the time they reach 19 years of age, state athletic associations often terminate eligibility at that age. Though most states permit students with disabilities who fail courses to remain in school until they reach 21 years of age, they may disqualify them from taking part in extracurricular athletics.

Finally, residence requirements for participation in interscholastic sports have been alleged to discriminate against high school students whose disabling condition causes them to be placed in special residences involuntarily. Through conditions such as these, students with disabilities are denied participation in sports due to circumstances beyond their control.

PRIVATE PHYSICAL ACTIVITY FACILITIES AND PROGRAMS

For-profit commercially operated centers of physical activity that are public accommodations must comply with ADA regulations. In general, ADA requires that public accommodations for sport and physical activity be accessible to the disabled and that policies for membership and participation in activity be nondiscriminatory. In addition, facilities must provide reasonable accommodation to disabled citizens so that they may participate and receive benefits similar to those gained by the nondisabled. A person with a disability should be disqualified from participation strictly for medical reasons and only after the facility manager has held a thorough discussion with the person or a surrogate and the person's doctors.

Sport or physical activity centers that receive direct or indirect federal financial assistance may also be subject to the regulations of the Rehabilitation Act. However, privately owned sport or physical activity centers are seldom subject to IDEA regulations. Such a facility might be responsible for delivering services commensurate with the instructional procedures articulated in IDEA if it enters into an arrangement with a public school district to provide instruction to students with disabilities. It may also be subject to IDEA regulations if it receives students from public school transitional services that give young adults with disabilities opportunities to use the physical skills they learned in school in private facilities where they can achieve goals of independent recreation in the years after secondary school.

PROGRAM MANAGEMENT

Knowing disability case law can help you manage physical activity and sport programs. Some considerations for conducting programs that conform to case law follow.

Monitoring Programs Receiving Financial Assistance

It is sometimes difficult to track federal financial assistance to education programs for people with disabilities because federal monies come from so many sources. For example, many schools have coordinated programs with community recreation agencies. If such an agency receives federal funds for participating in a program for a local school district, that particular physical activity program comes under the jurisdiction of federal regulations for nondiscriminatory sport activity. In one instance, a community recreation gymnastic program that received public school financing was asked to provide an interpreter for a deaf child. The school district argued that the gymnastic program did not have to comply with IDEA regulations because it was not linked to federal financial assistance. However, the hearing officer ruled that the school district, which received Chapter 2 block grant funds from the federal government, cooperatively supported the gymnastics program with the community funds. The gymnastics program therefore fell under federal regulations for conducting the special physical education of a child with a disability. Thus, federal financial assistance that comes to school districts through sources other than IDEA and that is used for the education of students with disabilities is nevertheless subject to IDEA regulations (Northwest Ohio School District, 1987).

Benefits of Knowledge of Disabilities Case Law for School Administrators

School authorities and parents can benefit from knowing the legal ramifications of the Rehabilitation Act, ADA, and IDEA. Those who administer and conduct programs for people with disabilities can apply their knowledge of the law in several ways, such as the following:

1. As a management tool with which to design education for children with disabilities and other children in the schools who are at risk

2. To define the entitlement of people with disabilities to physical activity
3. To design procedures for delivering programs to people with disabilities
4. To select, train, and assign personnel to conduct physical programs for disabled citizens
5. To measure a program's success

There is case law that applies IDEA, the Rehabilitation Act of 1973, and ADA to the conduct of physical education and sport programs for disabled citizens from which lessons can be learned to minimize risk of litigation. These lessons can serve as guidelines for management to use in the provision of equal opportunity for participation, the application of appropriate procedures, the conduct of programs in the least restrictive environment, the accessibility of programs, and the content and procedures used for conducting IEPs.

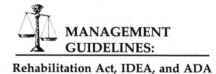

MANAGEMENT GUIDELINES:
Rehabilitation Act, IDEA, and ADA

Here are some principles for minimizing the risk of violating equal opportunity for disabled citizens to participate in physical activity and sport in municipal community recreation programs, public accommodations, and schools.

1. Physical activity and sport environments should be made accessible to people with disabilities.
2. Children with disabilities should be provided with reasonable accommodation to participate in physical activity and sport programs and not be excluded because of administrational convenience.

3. People with disabilities should be medically disqualified only after concerted discussion among the individuals or their surrogates, doctors, school faculty, and facility managers have taken place.

Here are some principles for minimizing risk of violating IDEA regulations in conducting physical education programs for students with disabilities in the public schools.

1. All children whose disabilities adversely affect their physical education performance should have IEPs.
2. Parents should be given opportunities to participate in planning the IEP.
3. Teachers should evaluate children with disabilities to determine whether they are unable to benefit from the regular physical education curriculum.
4. If a child cannot benefit from the IEP, a related service should be considered to help the child benefit from the physical education program.
5. Specific progress, or lack of it, toward preestablished goals and objectives agreed upon by the school and parents should be documented. Technical procedures for selecting objectives appropriate for specific learners should be identified, recorded, and employed. Documents of each child's progress through the IEP should leave a paper trail for studying and evaluating the legality of processes and outcomes of many aspects of the physical education system.

6. Evaluation procedures should be used to determine if the child is making progress on physical education developmental tasks of the IEP. Judgments should be made as to the appropriate placement in the least restrictive environments.

Practical guidelines for conducting physical activity and sports programs in the least restrictive environment follow.

1. To the extent possible, place students with disabilities in the least restrictive environment (for example, regular class).
2. Develop an IEP before placing the child in the least restrictive environment.
3. Be sure that physical education personnel who conduct regular classes and sport competitions are trained to conduct physical activity and sports for people with disabilities.
4. Place children with disabilities on sport teams and programs of physical activity with nondisabled children whenever possible; create separate teams and programs only when necessary.
5. Use supplemental aids and services to enable children with disabilities to remain in regular physical education and sport programs.
6. Give children with disabilities opportunities to participate in intramural athletic competition.
7. Open interscholastic and intercollegiate competition to children with disabilities.

CASE STUDIES

Case 5.1

Equal Opportunity

Betty A.'s parents asked the Elmira School District of New York to allow their daughter to participate in physical education classes. At the age of 6 weeks, Betty had a shunt system surgically implanted in her head to allow her proper cranial development. Although Betty scored above her grade level in several academic assessment scales, the school district denied her the opportunity to receive physical education, which was required for all students attending schools in New York State. The school district cited safety concerns even though there was no current medical data that contraindicated selected physical activity for her. The Office of Civil Rights found that the school district had not conducted the assessment needed to properly develop an IEP for placing the child in physical education class.

IDEA requires a full assessment of the unique physical education needs of each child so that the child can be placed in programs that individualize instruction at the child's present performance level. All children who are well enough to attend school are well enough to engage in physical activity at their ability levels, and must be given equal opportunity to receive physical education.

[Adapted from Elmira City (NY) School District OCR Complaint No. 02-86-1017. (1987). *Education for the Handicapped Law Report*. Alexandria, VA: CRR.]

Case 5.2

Program Accessibility

The high school physical education curriculum of the Monroe-Woodbury Central School District included swimming. However, the pool lacked steps or ladders, and the adjoining locker rooms had steps at the entrance to the showers, narrow toilet stalls without grab bars, and sinks that could not be reached by people in wheelchairs. These conditions excluded students with mobility impairment from the aquatic portion of the physical education curriculum.

The Office of Civil Rights ruled that environmental modifications were to be made so that students who used wheelchairs could participate in swimming activity. Physical activity environments must be made accessible to provide people with disabilities with equal opportunity for physical activity.

[Adapted from Monroe-Woodbury Central School District, Office of Civil Rights, Case No. 07-86-1054. (1987). *Education for the Handicapped Law Report*. Alexandria, VA: CRR.]

Case 5.3

Assessment Process of the IEP

Scott Hollenbeck was a high school student who used a wheelchair and who wanted to compete in track, tennis, and golf at a level that would maximize his abilities in those sports. The hearing officers had ordered that Scott could participate with nondisabled students in golf and tennis but in track only if it were safe. The school district decided that it was not safe for Scott to participate on the track team on an equal basis with the nondisabled. Therefore, Scott and his father, Dr. Gary Hollenbeck, asked the Rochelle Township School District to let Scott compete on an equal level or at the very least provide Scott a stipend to help him locate and compete with other wheelchair track athletes.

The issue then shifted to the process of determining whether or not it was safe for Scott to participate in track with the nondisabled. The investigation revealed that Scott had never been assessed for present levels of abilities by those who conducted the programs nor by an interdisciplinary team. The court ordered procedures to determine his unique needs.

Every child with a disability should undergo a formal assessment process as part of an IEP. Only after the child's needs and present levels of ability have been determined can the IEP goals and objectives be formulated and the benefits be studied.

[Adapted from *Hollenbeck, S. v. Board of Education of Rochelle Township*. (1989). *Education for the Handicapped Law Report*. Alexandria, VA: CRR, *441*, 281-288]

Case 5.4

Least Restrictive Environment (Facilities)

Jane was a 6-year-old girl with moderate mental retardation who was placed in a self-contained special education classroom in the junior high school of the Marsh Valley Joint School District. Jane's parents requested that she be able to participate in meaningful physical education activities appropriate for her age, of which there were few for Jane.

The school district had a high school, junior high school, and several elementary schools. Jane's motor skills were not sufficiently developed for her to participate in regular physical education class even at the elementary school level. Therefore, Jane's parents argued that opportunities for Jane to develop motor and social skills through meaningful interaction in the junior high physical education setting were inappropriate for Jane because she was too young. Because the school district was small and placement options were few, representatives of the school district argued that Jane's placement in the junior high school special education classroom was appropriate.

The Office of Civil Rights ruled that inasmuch as the self-contained classroom at the junior high school was the only self-contained placement in the district, it was the most appropriate placement for the child, and that Jane's level of skill development was not sufficient for her to benefit from physical education in the regular class. Therefore, the placement in the special class housed at the junior high was appropriate.

On occasion, alternatives for placing children with disabilities in the least restrictive environment may be limited due to administrative arrangements in a school district, particularly in rural school districts. Therefore, it is difficult to generalize as to what are the least restrictive physical education and extracurricular sport activities appropriate for children with disabilities. The administrative problems of a specific school district must be taken into consideration.

[Adapted from Marsh Valley (ID) Joint School District, Office of Civil Rights Case No. 10810025. (1981). *Education for the Handicapped Law Report*. Alexandria, VA: CRR, *257*, 272-273]

Case 5.5

Supplemental Services

Amy S., an 8-year-old child who was deaf, attended elementary school in the Northwest School District with the assistance of a sign language interpreter. The school program included an extracurricular course in gymnastics that Amy attended without the supplemental service of an interpreter. Although Amy had benefitted from this program, her parents requested an interpreter for the second session of gymnastics.

The Office of Civil Rights ruled that Amy did not need an interpreter for the gymnastics class because she had successfully participated in and benefited from gymnastics class without an interpreter. The gymnastics teacher had provided sufficient aid to Amy by standing in front of her and articulating clearly with her lips what Amy should do.

This ruling helps clarify the definition of supplemental aids and services. Such aids or services should meet the needs of the individual and should enable the individual to receive benefits that would not be achieved without the aid or service. Thus, the suitability of a supplemental aid or service is measured by its benefits to the individual.

[Adapted from Northwest Ohio School District, Office of Civil Rights, Complaint No. 15-85-1046. (1987). *Education for the Handicapped Law Report*. Alexandria, VA: CRR.]

Case 5.6

Qualified Personnel

Parents of children with disabilities in the Richmond Community School District requested that qualified physical education teachers instruct their children. Certified physical education teachers conducted programs for children with disabilities at the middle and high school levels, but physical education programs at the elementary levels were conducted by special education teachers in self-contained special education classes in segregated schools. The school district argued that special education teachers without professional training in physical education were better able to conduct physical education programs for the children than physical educators who were not trained to teach children with disabilities.

An Office of Civil Rights investigator's opinion was that it was permissible for special education teachers to teach physical education. The elementary school in the district lacked trained physical educators, so regular elementary grade school physical education was conducted by regular classroom teachers. Thus it was reasoned that having special education teachers teach physical education to children with disabilities in self-contained classrooms did not compromise the students' rights for equal opportunities.

The question of who is qualified to teach children with disabilities poses a dilemma that has received little attention in IDEA hearings and OCR complaints. Thus certification of state personnel preparation programs and of professionals trained in these programs awaits resolution in the future.

[Adapted from Richmond (IN) Community School Corporation, Office of Civil Rights, Complaint No. 15-86-1077. (1987). *Education for the Handicapped Law Report*. Alexandria, VA: CRR.]

Case 5.7

Medical Exclusion

John C. had a marked hearing loss of 50% in his left ear and a profound hearing loss in his right ear. A school doctor who examined John C. discouraged him from participating in contact sports and recommended that he be excluded from participation in interscholastic sports. The School Board supported the recommendation, which followed the American Medical Association (AMA) policy for medical disqualifications in sport. The parents pointed out, however, that their son had exceptional athletic talents and had competed successfully in sports without injury for years, and that they gave him approval to play.

The testimony in court in support of John C.'s participation was dramatic. The assistant director of admissions at Gallaudet College, a school for people who are hearing-impaired, in testifying for the plaintiffs, reported that between 1,200 and 1,800 athletes who are deaf had competed in deaf olympics and that 700 had taken part in contact sports. Other witnesses criticized the AMA guidelines as outmoded, exclusionary of people who are hearing-impaired, and in need of revision. But even though the court sympathized with the boy's disappointment and frustration, it believed that the doctor's action was appropriate.

Medical criteria often exclude people with disabilities from participating in intramural athletics and competitive sports, compromising equal opportunity. Medical professionals are uncertain of the circumstances under which it is appropriate for people with disabilities to participate in competitive sports. Judgments must be based on speculation of potential irreversible injury. It is interesting that, since the time of this hearing, the AMA has revised its guidelines and now recommends that the hearing-impaired be allowed to participate in sports that involve physical contact.

[Adapted from *Columbo v. Sewanhaka Central High School Dist. No. 2*, 383 N.Y.S. 2d 518 (N.Y. Sup. Ct. 1976)]

Case 5.8

Exclusion by Governing Bodies

John Doe was an athlete who received psychiatric treatment for an emotional disorder. A case worker decided that John should leave his parents' residence in District A and move to another school district (District B) because of his disability. After his transfer, John learned that he was not eligible to play football that year because of an Interscholastic League rule that prevented participation in varsity competition for one year after a student changed to a school in a district in which the child's parents or guardians did not reside. This policy prevented John from participating in football in his senior year.

This case was referred to the National Federation of Athletic Associations, a governing organization for various state high school athletic associations. The federation refused to recommend eligibility standards pertaining to the wide variety of disabilities that may affect students because complex issues may be involved. Therefore, the federation resolved that each state association should handle its own affairs.

[Adapted from *Doe v. Marshall*, 459 F. Supp. 1190 (S.D. Texas 1978)]

Case 5.9   **Age and Scholastic Exclusion**

Tim Nichols was a student with a severe hearing impairment who started school one year later than his chronological peers. In his senior year he was declared ineligible to participate in varsity basketball because of a state athletic association rule that barred participation of students who have reached their 19th birthday. The state athletic association argued that the rule was designed to prevent older, more experienced athletes from gaining advantage over younger athletes in contact sports. The Office of Civil Rights ruled in favor of the athletic association. The ruling noted, however, that it would be discriminatory to deny interscholastic athletic opportunities to a person who was hearing-impaired and over the age limit if the school district required all students who were hearing-impaired to repeat the first and second grades.

[Adapted from *Nichols v. Farmington Public Schools and Michigan High School Athletic Association*. (1986). *Education for the Handicapped Law Report*. Alexandria, VA: CRR, *558*, 106-108]

CHAPTER SUMMARY

Three pieces of legislation provide equal opportunity in sport and physical activities for people with disabilities. They are the Rehabilitation Act of 1973, which outlaws discriminatory practices against people with disabilities in employment, health, social services, and education; the Americans with Disabilities Act (ADA), which outlaws discrimination against people with disabilities in facilities or public accommodations; and the Individuals with Disabilities Education Act (IDEA), which addresses specific technological practices for providing individual physical education services for the purpose of enabling people with disabilities to enjoy independent, physically active life-styles in the community. Appropriate physical activity and sport services for people with disabilities that conform to IDEA regulations will generally conform to the Rehabilitation Act and the ADA as well. Common elements of all three pieces of legislation are service compensation for disability, equal opportunity, integration, program accessibility, and monitoring by the Office of Civil Rights. Physical education is addressed in depth in IDEA and in more general terms by the Rehabilitation Act. IDEA sets forth the rules for conducting instructional programs in mandatory public school settings. ADA addresses rules for providing opportunities to participate in physical activity in public accommodations.

The three acts vary in their methods of service compensation. IDEA compensates with an Individual Education Program (IEP), related services, and supplemental aids and services in the least restrictive environment. Specific procedures for conducting sport and physical programs presented in the Rehabilitation Act and ADA are less detailed than those set forth in the IDEA regulations. All three pieces of legislation require accessibility to program benefits. However, they vary in the attention they give to the least restrictive environment and to integration of sport and physical activity. Whereas IDEA procedures for placing people in the least restrictive environment are very specific, the Rehabilitation Act places more emphasis on integrated employment and living and the ADA on opportunity for physical activity participation in public accommodations.

KEY TERMS

Accessibility (76)
Americans with Disabilities Act (79)
Individual Education Program (82)
Individuals with Disabilities Education Act (IDEA) (76)
Least restrictive environment (84)
Physical education (79)
Reasonable accommodation (76)
Related services (84)
Section 504 of the Rehabilitation Act of 1973 (78)
Supplemental aids and services (82)

QUESTIONS FOR DISCUSSION

1. You are the athletic director of an interscholastic high school program. An outstanding lineman on your football team has limited vision in one eye and desperately desires to play during his senior year. The school doctor advises against participation, but the player's doctor indicates that it is permissible for the athlete to play. What would you do? Why?

2. You are a school administrator with an excellent intramural program that meets after school. However, children who have physical disabilities, mental retardation, deafness, and blindness do not participate in the sports program, and there are no community sport and physical activity programs for these children. The local chapter of the Association for Retarded Citizens requests that you provide sport and physical activity programs for these children. What is the legal issue? What would you do? Why?

3. You are a school administrator. A child's parents request that you give their child physical therapy instead of physical education. What would you do? Why?

4. Parents of a child who is mildly mentally retarded move into your school district and request that the child be placed in a separate physical education class so that the child can be with other children with similar disabilities. There is no assessment information on the child. What would you tell the parents? Justify your comments based on case law.

5. A child with an emotional disorder who was placed in regular physical education class was disrupting instruction to such an extent that neither the child nor the child's peers could benefit from the instruction. What would you do to remedy this situation? Justify your actions based on legal precedent.

6. A child of early elementary school age who was severely physically disabled was placed in a class with older children with physical disabilities in a junior high school, where all children in the district who required special education were placed. The placement limited the child's opportunities for meaningful interaction with peers of the child's own age. What would you do if the parents requested that the child participate in activities with peers of similar ages? Provide a legal rationale for your decision.

7. As an administrator of a public school, what would you do if the parents of a child with a disability requested an individual physical education program for their child who has been mainstreamed in regular physical education class? Why?

8. If you were a school administrator, and a parent requested an IEP for a 3-year-old child with a disability, which included goals for development in fundamental motor patterns and skills as well as the development of physically fit muscles of the body, would you provide this program? Who would conduct the program? Why?

REFERENCES

Americans with Disabilities Act of 1990, 42 U.S.C. 12101.

Bay Arenac (MI) Intermediate School District. (1979). *Education for the Handicapped Law Reporter.* Washington, D.C.: CRR, *257*, 46-48.

Columbo v. Sewanhaka Central High School Dist. No. 2, 383 N.Y.S. 2d 518 (N.Y. Sup. Ct. 1976).

Doe v. Marshall, 459 F. Supp. 1190 (S.D. Texas 1978).

Elmira City (NY) School District, OCR Complaint No. 02-86-1017. (1987). *Education for the Handicapped Law Report.* Alexandria, VA: CRR.

Gustafson, B. (1979). Fairfax County Public Schools. *Education for the Handicapped Law Reporter.* Alexandria, VA: CRR, *211*, 36.

Hollenbeck, S. v. Board of Education of Rochelle Township. (1989). *Education for the Handicapped Law Report.* Alexandria, VA: CRR, *441*, 281-288.

Individuals with Disabilities Act, 20 U.S.C. 1406 (1982).

Individuals with Disabilities Education Act, 20 U.S.C. 1232.

Kampmeir v. Nyquist, 553 F. 2d 296 (1977).

Long, T.E. (1980). Bureau of education for the handicapped. *Education for the Handicapped Law Report.* Washington, D.C.: CRR, *211*, 167-168.

Marsh Valley (ID) Joint School District, Office of Civil Rights Case No. 10810025 (1981). *Education for the Handicapped Law Report.* Alexandria, VA: CRR, *257*, 272-273.

Monroe-Woodbury Central School District, Office of Civil Rights, Case No. 07-86-1054. (1987). *Education for the Handicapped Law Report.* Alexandria, VA: CRR.

Nichols v. Farmington Public Schools and Michigan High School Athletic Association. (1986). *Education for the Handicapped Law Report.* Alexandria, VA: CRR, *558*, 106-108.

Northwest Ohio School District, Office of Civil Rights, Complaint No. 15-85-1046. (1987). *Education for the Handicapped Law Report.* Alexandria, VA: CRR.

The Rehabilitation Act of 1973 29, U.S.C. 701.

Richmond (IN) Community School Corporation, Office of Civil Rights, Complaint No. 15-86-1077. (1987). *Education for the Handicapped Law Report.* Alexandria, VA: CRR.

Spitaleri v. Nyquist, U.S. 345 N.Y.S. 2d 878 (1973).

Steinfeld, E. (1986). *Specifications for making buildings and facilities accessible to and usable by the physically handicapped.* New York: American National Standards Institute.

Tyler, J. (1985). *New York consolidated law service.* Lawyers Corporation Law Service. Article 89, Section 4409. Albany, NY.

ADDITIONAL READINGS

Appenzeller, H., & Appenzeller, T. (1975). *Athletes and the law.* Charlottesville, VA: Michie.

Frakt, T., & Rankin, J. (1982) *The law of parks and recreation.* Salt Lake City: Brighton.

Herbert, J.D. (1991). The Americans With Disabilities Act. *Fitness Management, 6,* 34-37.

WHO MAY PARTICIPATE?

SOURCES OF CIVIL LIBERTIES

Because the Canadian legal tradition stems from the British common law, it did not initially provide any positive statement or law confirming the civil liberties of the individual. Essentially, civil liberties in Canada did not derive from positive law (actual written and expressed law) but from an absence of such written law or government action (Hogg, 1985, p. 628). In other words, so long as there were no "positive" laws prohibiting a particular act, the individual was free to engage in it. Whatever was left unprohibited formed the basis of one's individual civil liberty. Unfortunately this meant that there was no constitutional protection of those liberties, because parliament could easily pass a law limiting any particular civil liberty or freedom.

When the American colonies were federated in 1787, they enshrined certain guarantees of civil liberties in their Constitution. These guarantees are known as the Bill of Rights. Civil liberties in Canada were not similarly protected by the British North America Act (1867), although in time a number of provinces did pass some legislation protecting limited rights, principally in the areas of employment and rental rights. In 1960, federal human rights legislation was enacted. It is important to recognize, however, that this legislation, known as the Canadian Bill of Rights, was a statute passed by the federal Parliament having application only to the federal government and its domains of authority. Perhaps more importantly, it could easily be repealed or amended by the federal government because it was not enshrined in the Constitution. Changes to the Constitution, unlike either federal or provincial legislation, can only be made in accordance with the constitutional amending formula which generally requires the consent of 7 out of 10 of the provinces.

In 1982, under Prime Minister Trudeau, Canada brought its Constitution home from Britain. At that time the **Charter of Rights and Freedoms** (hereinafter referred to as "the Charter") was adopted and incorporated within the Constitution. As a part of the Constitution, the Charter became applicable to both levels of government, and it now plays a critical role in protecting the civil liberties it guarantees. Also, because it is part of the Constitution, it can be altered only by constitutional amendment.

Since the Charter came into effect, federal and provincial human rights laws that predate it have lost much of their importance; however, they do remain in force and are important to the extent that they are broader in scope than the Charter. Therefore, it is important to look at both the human rights legislation of each province and that of the federal government to determine what specific freedoms and rights are guaranteed.

THE CHARTER OF RIGHTS AND FREEDOMS: TO WHOM DOES IT APPLY?

Section 32 of the Charter defines the scope of the Charter's application. The section expressly provides that the Charter applies to "the parliament and government of Canada" and to "the legislature and government of each province" (Canadian Charter of Rights and Freedoms, 1982, s. 32). The section clearly makes reference to **government action**, but how broadly can government action be defined? The case law has been evolving slowly to the point where a body (such as a government agency or government-funded body) meets the test of government action when, in exercising its power, it has a "direct and definable connection to an act of parliament, the legislatures or their executives, thereby establishing an exercise of governmental power" (*Harrison v. University of British Columbia*, 1988, p. 150).

Clearly school boards, municipalities, and public regulatory bodies come under the scope of the Charter, as do government departments, including Sport Canada. However, amateur athletic associations funded by either federal or provincial levels of government but organized and administered by private individuals and voluntary associations do not come under the Charter. The fact that a private sport organization receives government grants or funding does not mean that it is exercising a governmental function because such funding does not necessarily imply

that Parliament or the legislature has delegated power to the organization. Therefore, provincial and federal sport governing bodies may not fall under the scope of the Charter. (Canadian Applications for Part III explains how government involvement in the affairs of sport is increasing to the point where it may now potentially bring sport governing bodies within the purview of the Charter.) Public school athletic organizations, on the other hand, are considered "arms" of the schools, which in turn receive their power from provincial school legislation. Therefore all school athletic, recreational, intramural, and physical education programs are within the scope of the Charter.

In summary, if a body (that is, a person or organization) does not fit the provisions of Section 32 of the Charter, the actions of that body are not subject to the provisions of the Charter. In those situations, a person looking for legislative protection of certain civil rights must look elsewhere.

Section 15 of the Charter

Section 15 of the Charter contains the guarantee of equality. (Section 15 did not come into force until about three years after the rest of the Charter to give the provinces some time to implement this section within their jurisdictions.) The section states that

(1) Every individual is equal before and under the law and has the right to equal protection and equal benefit of the law without discrimination and, in particular, without discrimination based on race, national or ethnic origin, colour, religion, sex, age, or mental or physical disability.

(2) Subsection (1) does not preclude any law, program or activity that has as its object the amelioration of conditions of disadvantaged individuals or groups including those that are

disadvantaged because of race, national or ethnic origin, colour, religion, sex, age, or mental or physical disability. (Canadian Charter of Rights and Freedoms, 1982, s. 15)

The provisions of equality before and under the law and the right to the equal protection and benefit of the law were inserted into the section to reverse the restrictive interpretations placed on the limited "equality before the law" contained in the Canadian Bill of Rights. Equality before the law as expressed in the Bill of Rights meant only that individuals with similar characteristics would be treated in a similar manner. In other words, as long as the members of a particular group were all treated the same way, albeit more poorly than another group, the law found no discrimination.

Subsection 2 further stipulates that the grounds of discrimination specified in Subsection 1 are not exhaustive. Therefore, grounds other than those enumerated within the section may be accepted by the court.

The meaning of the term discrimination within this section has been the subject of much litigation. The case that best defines what is meant by **discrimination** and how Section 15(1) is to be interpreted is *The Law Society of British Columbia v. Andrews et al.* (1989). In that case, the Supreme Court of Canada said that the words "without discrimination" require more than a mere finding of distinction between the treatment of groups or individuals. It went on to say that those distinctions that are forbidden by the section are those involving prejudice or disadvantage. In other words, the analysis of discrimination must concentrate on the personal characteristics of those claiming to be treated unequally. Issues of stereotyping, historical disadvantage, and prejudice are the main focus of the section, and the impact upon the person affected is the major element

in determining whether or not the act is discriminatory. To quote Madame Justice Wilson of the Supreme Court of Canada in the Andrews case:

Discrimination may be described as a distinction, whether intentional or not but based on grounds relating to personal characteristics of the individual or group, which has the effect of imposing burdens, obligations or disadvantage on such individuals or groups not imposed upon, or which withholds or limits access to opportunities, benefits and advantages available to other members of society. Distinction as based on personal characteristics attributed to an individual solely on the basis of association with a group will rarely escape the charge of discrimination, while those based on an individual's merits and capacities will rarely be so classed. (*The Law Society of British Columbia v. Andrews et al.*, 1989, p. 291)

Thus, a mere distinction is not sufficient to establish discrimination; rather, discrimination under Section 15(1) must have the effect of being "invidious or pejorative" in that it must result from an unreasonable classification or an unjustifiable differentiation.

Relationship Between Section 15 and Section 1 of the Charter

There is a special relationship between Section 15(1) of the Charter and **Section 1 of the Charter**. Section 1 states that "the Canadian Charter of Rights guarantees the rights and freedoms set out in it subject only to reasonable limits prescribed by law as can be demonstrably justified in a free and democratic society" (Canadian Charter of Rights and Freedoms, 1982, s. 1). Section 1 guarantees the rights and freedoms set out in the Charter but makes it clear that such rights and freedoms are not absolute. In other words, Section 1 says that the infringement or breach of a right guaranteed under the Charter may be justified if it is a reasonable limitation in a free and democratic society. The onus of justifying such an infringement of a guaranteed right rests with the party seeking to uphold the limitation. Thus, if an act or provision is found to be discriminatory under Section 15, it may still be upheld under Section 1.

HUMAN RIGHTS LEGISLATION

Most litigation in the area of sport, other than personal injury matters, has come under provincial or federal human rights legislation. This is because most sport activity occurs under the auspices of sport organizations, which have been regarded by the Canadian courts as falling outside the jurisdiction of the Charter.

A distinguishing feature of this legislation—both federal and provincial—is that it establishes a commission before which complaints are heard. Only if members of the commission exceed their jurisdiction by acting unfairly or outside the provisions of the legislation will the courts intervene.

The Canadian Human Rights Act, 1976-77, is similar to other provincial human rights legislation. Section 2 of the Act sets out the prohibited grounds of discrimination, specifically race, national or ethnic origin, color, religion, age, sex, marital status, family status, and disability. Some of the provinces have added additional prohibited grounds such as sexual orientation. The section of the federal legislation used most often to initiate an action for discrimination is Section 5 (or the corresponding provincial section), which states that

it is a discriminatory practice in the provision of goods, services, facilities or accommodation customarily available to the general public

(a) to deny, or to deny any access to, any such goods, service, facility, or accommodation to any individual, or

(b) to differentiate adversely in relation to any individual, on a prohibited ground of discrimination. (Canadian Human Rights Act, s. 5)

The majority of complaints under this section have related to discrimination in the provision of a service (that is, participation in an organization's programs or activities) or in gaining access to facilities. In recent years, there has been considerable litigation about the interpretation of the phrase "customarily available to the general public." Previously a quantitative approach was used, which resulted in a requirement that the "public" include virtually every member of the community. More recent court decisions (for example, *British Columbia Council of Human Rights v. University of British Columbia School of Family and Nutritional Sciences and Janice Berg*, 1993) have recognized that every service has its own public, which may in fact be only a small number of people. The courts now use an approach based not on quantity but on the *relationship* created between the provider and the user of a service. For the purposes of interpreting the section, the issue then becomes, Is this *relationship* a public or private one? Two notable sport cases brought before a human rights commission are *Re Blainey and the Ontario Hockey Association et al.* (1985) and *Cummings v. The Ontario Minor Hockey Association* (1978). These two cases are described in some depth in the following sections because they illustrate the procedural requirements of the human rights legislation and the interaction of the Charter.

Re Blainey and the Ontario Hockey Association et al.

In *Re Blainey*, Justine Blainey, a 12-year-old girl from Ontario, was physically able to compete on an all-boy team that was an affiliate of the Ontario Hockey Association (OHA). To play on the team she needed a Canadian Amateur Hockey Association (CAHA) card, which could be obtained only through the OHA. Pursuant to OHA rules, eligibility was restricted to males. Justine was therefore prohibited from playing on the team of her choice because of her sex. Justine asked the court to find the OHA regulation limiting membership to males contrary to Section 15 of the Charter.

A preliminary matter to be determined was whether or not Section 15 of the Charter was applicable to the OHA, the CAHA, or both. The court held that both were private, non-profit organizations providing a structured amateur program to certain members of the community. Counsel for the plaintiff suggested that, because the two organizations received substantial grants from the federal government and various municipalities, they were exercising a government function. The court held that merely receiving grants does not make an organization a government agency. To hold otherwise would suggest that every charity, business, or organization that receives a government grant is performing a government function and thus is subject to the Charter.

Justine Blainey also asked the court to declare a particular section of the Ontario Human Rights Code (1981) contrary to Section 15 of the Charter. Section 1 of the Ontario Human Rights Code provides that

> every person has a right to equal treatment with respect to services, goods and facilities, without discrimination because of race, ancestry, place of origin, colour, ethnic origin, citizenship, creed, sex, age, marital status, family status or handicap. (Ontario Human Rights Code, 1981, s. 1)

This section provides an absolute prohibition to discrimination. But it was followed by Section 19(2), which stated that

> the right under Section 1 to equal treatment with respect to services and facilities is not infringed where membership in an athletic organization or participation in an athletic activity is restricted to persons of the same sex. [Ontario Human Rights Code, 1981, s. 19(2)]

Therefore, the absolute prohibition from discrimination under Section 1 was not meant to forbid athletic organizations from restricting their membership to one gender.

Any provincial legislation must necessarily come under the influence of the Charter because it is by its very nature government action. Section 52 of the Charter states that the Constitution is the supreme law and that any law that is inconsistent with it will be void to the extent that it is inconsistent. Section 19(2) clearly violated Section 15(1) of the Charter and to that extent was found null and void. However, could it be "saved" under Section 1 of the Charter? (That is, would restricting Justine's right to play, as prescribed by Section 19(2), be considered a "reasonable limit . . . [that could] be justified in a free and democratic society"?) At trial, the court was persuaded that the provisions of Section 19(2) in these circumstances were demonstrably justified based on evidence of physiological differences, the impact to the local minor hockey league for girls in which Justine had been playing, and historical precedent.

The Ontario Court of Appeal upheld the lower court's view that Section 19(2) of the Ontario Human Rights Code was inconsistent with Section 15(1) of the Charter, agreeing that it denied Justine Blainey the right to the equal protection and the equal benefit of the law by reason of her gender. The court then looked to a possible justification under Section 1 to establish that the limit was reasonably and demonstrably justifiable in a free and democratic society. Two main criteria must be satisfied. First, the objective of the discriminatory act must be sufficiently important ("pressing and substantial") to warrant overriding a constitutionally protected right or freedom. Secondly, the means chosen must be rationally connected to the objectives of the limitation and should impair the right or freedom interfered with as little as possible, and the effect of the measures should be proportional to the objectives (*R. v. Oakes*, 1986, p. 227). On this basis, the Court of Appeal overturned the lower court's decision, indicating that the section was discriminatory and neither reasonable nor demonstrably justified "in a free and democratic society."

Cummings v. the Ontario Minor Hockey Association

Gail Cummings, a 10-year-old female hockey player, was selected for the all-star team within the Ontario Minor Hockey Association (OMHA) playoffs. In order to play, Gail needed an OMHA registration certificate, which she was refused. The issue before the court was whether the OMHA was in breach of the Ontario Human Rights Code, 1970 by refusing to accept Gail's registration on the grounds of her gender. Section 2 of the Ontario Human Rights Code, 1970 states that

(1) no person, directly or indirectly, alone or with another, by himself or by the interposition of another, shall,

    (a) deny to any person or class of persons the accommodation, services or facilities available in any place to which the public is customarily admitted; or

    (b) discriminate against any person or class of persons the accommodation, services or facilities available in any place to which the public is customarily admitted;

because of the race, creed, colour, sex, marital status, nationality, ancestry, or place of origin of such persons or class of persons or of any other person or class of persons. (Ontario Human Rights Code, 1970, s. 2)

The section refers to the provision of accommodation, services, or facilities available to the public. In this case, the issue was not the facility where the activity was carried out, but rather the services provided by the organization leasing the facility. The court distinguished between the services which might be provided by the facility (a public arena) and the services provided by the private nonprofit voluntary organization (OMHA). The court determined that while the facility would come under requirements of the Ontario Human Rights Code, 1970 the services of the OMHA did not. Therefore, the court found that the OMHA's refusal to accept Gail's registration was not a breach of Section 2 of the Ontario Human Rights Code.

THE STATUS OF WOMEN'S RIGHTS TO PARTICIPATE IN SPORTS IN CANADA

The two previous cases and a number of similar cases have used Canadian human rights legislation to challenge discrimination based on gender. These have included *Ontario Human Rights Commission v. The Ontario Rural Softball Association* (1979) and *Forbes v. Yarmouth Hockey Association* (1978). Some have been successful, some have not, but by and large, the cases have revolved around technical elements of the legislation and its interpretation.

But despite these challenges, certain indicators in girls' and women's sport show that little has changed over the past decade. John Barnes (1988), in his book *Sports and the Law in Canada*, notes the great disparity between men and women in participation in sport activities, access to facilities and scheduling, budgetary differences, and other areas. These numbers have not changed significantly over the past decade and, far from being just a Canadian situation, the trend is also reflected on the international scene at the Olympic level. Within the Olympic Games there are approximately 165 events for men and only 86 for women, and only 7 of the 90 members of the International Olympic Committee are women (Faulder, 1992).

Apart from opportunities to participate, women are also very much in the minority in sport leadership roles. The most recent data from Sport Canada indicate that women are scarce in coaching, executive, and administrative positions and even as volunteers. Only about 25% of executive directors at the national sport organizations are women, and women account for only about one third of all sport volunteers. As Barnes notes (1988, p. 79), "To effectively promote change, statutory remedies must be coordinated with political initiatives designed to reform the entire social structure of sport."

DISCRIMINATION ON THE BASIS OF NATIONALITY

As with allegations of discrimination on the basis of gender, allegations of discrimination on the basis of nationality can be brought under either Section 15 of the Charter (the discrimination section) or the other federal and provincial human rights legislation discussed at the beginning of this Application. Of course, the difficulty in bringing the complaint under the Charter is that the organization that gave rise to the complaint may not be under the jurisdiction of the Charter. Furthermore, as the two cases described in this Application made clear, it is often difficult for complainants to bring their situations within the strict parameters of the human rights legislation.

DISCRIMINATION ON THE BASIS OF DISABILITY

The primary tools for actions of discrimination on the basis of disability are the human rights statutes, principles of natural justice and procedural fairness, and Section 15 of the Charter of Rights and Freedoms. It should be noted that Section 15(2) of the Charter (see page 100) provides for affirmative action programs in favor of "disadvantaged individuals or groups." Such programs inevitably involve some element of reverse discrimination in the sense that a member of a disadvantaged group will be given preference over a person who is equally or better qualified but is not disadvantaged.

CASE STUDIES

Case CA 2.1 **Discrimination on the Basis of Nationality**
Beattie v. Governors of Acadia University et al. (1976) was decided before the Charter of Rights and Freedoms came into force. It was brought

under the human rights legislation of the province of Nova Scotia. Even if the Charter had been in force at the time, it is not likely to have been applicable given recent case law, which suggests that universities do not exercise a form of government function (*McKinney v. University of Guelph*, 1987, and *Harrison v. University of British Columbia*, 1988). The issue in this case was whether the plaintiffs had a right to play basketball on the Acadia University team under the Nova Scotia Human Rights Act and, if so, whether they had been wrongfully deprived of that right by the university because of their nationality.

The initial decision in this case went against the plaintiffs, and they appealed it. (The party appealing a decision is known as the **appellant**; the other party is known as the **respondent**). The appellants were U.S. citizens and students at Acadia University. They were barred from playing on the university intercollegiate basketball team because of a rule limiting the number of nonresident players to three. The purpose of the rule, according to the respondents, was to maintain well-balanced Canadian teams and to promote the training of basketball players in Canada.

The appellants claimed that the rule discriminated against them because of their race or ethnic or national origin, and that their rights to participate were protected by Sections 3 and 4 of the Nova Scotia Human Rights Act (1969). The relevant sections are as follows:

3. Every individual and every class of individuals has the right

   (a) to obtain admission to and enjoyment of accommodations, services and facilities customarily provided to members of the public;

   (b) to acquire and hold any interest in property;

   (c) to opportunities available for employment; and

   (d) to full membership privileges in any employees' organization, employers' organization, provincial association or business or trade associations,

   regardless of the race, religion, creed, colour or ethnic or national origin of the individual or class of individuals.

4. No person shall

   (a) deny to any individual or class of individuals enjoyment of accommodations, services and facilities to which members of the public have access; or

   (b) discriminate with respect to the manner in which accommodation, services and facilities, to which members of the public have access, are provided to any individual or any class of individuals

   because of the race, religion, creed, colour or ethnic or national origin of the individual or class of individuals. (Nova Scotia Human Rights Act, 1969)

The appellants asked the Court to interpret a denial of opportunity to play basketball on the university team as a denial of "admission to and enjoyment of accommodations, services and facilities" within the meaning of Sections 3 and 4 of the Act. The Court stated that even if it were to accept the denial of such opportunity as a denial of "facilities," the right to enjoyment of facilities is limited under the Act to those "customarily provided to members of the public" or facilities "to which members of the public have access." The Court found that the university did not provide facilities for the public at large, notwithstanding the general perception today that universities are close to being public institutions. Because the appellants could not bring themselves within the terms of the human rights legislation, their case failed.

Note: If this matter were heard today, it likely would be decided differently given the newer "relational" approach to interpreting the Canadian Human Rights Act's phrase "facilities and services available to the public" confirmed by the *Berg* decision (see discussion on page 102).

[*Beattie v. Governors of Acadia University et al.* (1976), 18 N.S.R. (2d) 466, 72 D.L.R. (3d) 718 (C.A.)]

Case CA 2.2

Special Accommodation for Disabled Citizens
McLeod v. Youth Bowling Council of Ontario (1988) involved an 11-year-old girl named Tammy, who had cerebral palsy. Tammy was active in a competitive bowling league, but because of her reduced mobility, she used a ramp assist her father had built, which allowed her to bowl from her wheelchair behind the foul line. Tammy entered a bowling tournament and progressed to the second level of competition. However, the rules of the Youth Bowling Club specified that no mechanical devices could be used to deliver the ball, and Tammy was disqualified.

Tammy brought an application under the Human Rights Code of Ontario to have the disqualification overturned on the basis that the rule used to make the decision discriminated against her because of her physical disability. Based on expert testimony, a board of inquiry found that the ramp assist did not give Tammy any competitive advantage; in fact, it caused a small detriment. Consequently, the effect of the rule was to exclude Tammy from play with her peers because of her disability. The board determined that the rule of the bowling club was discriminatory and found in Tammy's favor.

[*McLeod v. Youth Bowling Council of Ontario* (1988) 9 C.M.R.R. 5371]

Case CA 2.3

Placement of a Student With a Disability
Bales v. School District 23 (1984) concerned the assignment of a student, Aaron Bales, age 8, to a special school for children with moderate disabilities. The case was decided before Section 15 of the Charter came into effect and was argued using provincial human rights legislation, Section 7 of the Charter, and the principles of natural justice and procedural fairness.

Aaron's parents argued that the school board's actions were a breach of the "due process" guarantees under Section 7 of the Charter and also constituted discrimination under the provincial human rights code. The judge responded that, insofar as special education involves discrimination between people with and without disabilities, the distinction is drawn for the purpose of providing disabled citizens with the special services they require. He noted that the segregation was reasonably directed to that objective, even though it exceeded the degree of segregation then considered by experts to be necessary. The judge did not find a breach of Section 7 of the Charter, but if he had, the defendants would have next invoked Section 1 of the Charter to try to justify the breach. Section 1 clearly places the onus on the offending government authority to justify or defend its conduct as a reasonable limit on guaranteed rights once the plaintiff has proven a prima facie case of discrimination against it.

The judge conceded that Aaron's parents had shown that the separate school assignment was less beneficial for their son than mainstreaming. It can be argued that had Section 15 of the Charter been in effect at the time, it may have enabled the parents to meet their onus in showing at least a basic case of discrimination. Had they done so, under Section 1 of the Charter, the onus would then have shifted once again to the government agency to justify or defend its prima facie discriminatory actions as a reasonable limit on the guaranteed right. In other words, the school board would have had to justify the efficacy of its decision with regard to both program content and student classification. In the absence of Section 15, however, the court proceeded on the basis that the school board had in fact acted reasonably and that the burden was on the parents to show otherwise.

Finally, the court analyzed the procedures used to make the classification in terms of the traditional concepts of natural justice and procedural fairness (discussed more fully in the Canadian Applications for Part III). These principles demand that the parents receive full information before decisions are made, and that they have a fair hearing in the decision-making process. Further, each level of the formal appeal process must be independent of the previous level of decision making. It is very important that the parties launching the appeal or complaint be treated fairly and be given an opportunity for full representation. In this case, even though the school board did not fully adhere to the principles of natural justice and procedural fairness, the court was unwilling to find that Aaron Bales had been discriminated against.

[*Bales v. School District 23 (Central Okanagan) Board of School Trustees* (1984), 54 B.C.L.R. 203 (B.C.S.C.)]

KEY TERMS

Appellant (106)
Charter of Rights and Freedoms (99)
Discrimination (101)
Government action (100)
Respondent (106)
Section 1 of the Charter (101)
Section 15 of the Charter (100)
Section 32 of the Charter (100)

REFERENCES

Barnes, J. (1988). *Sports and the law in Canada* (2nd ed.). Toronto: Butterworths.

Bales v. School District 23 (Central Okanagan) Board of School Trustees (1984), 54 B.C.L.R. 203 (B.C.S.C.).

Beattie v. Governors of Acadia University et al. (1976), 18 N.S.R. (2d) 466, 72 D.L.R. (3d) 718 (C.A.).

British Columbia Council of Human Rights v. University of British Columbia School of Family and Nutritional Sciences and Janice Berg. Supreme Court of Canada. May 19, 1993 (1991) 56 B.C.C.R. (2nd) 296, 81 D.L.R. (4th) 497, 1 B.C. A.C. 58, 10 C.H.R.R.

Canadian Bill of Rights. S.C. 1960, c. 44, R.S.C. 1970.

The Canadian Charter of Rights and Freedoms, Part I of the Constitution Act, 1982, being Schedule B of the Canada Act 1982, c. 11 (U.K.).

Canadian Human Rights Act. S.C. 1976-77, c. 33.

Cummings v. The Ontario Minor Hockey Association (1978), 7 R.F.L. (2d) 359 (Ont. H.C.).

Faulder, L. (1992, March 7). Women missing benefit of sport. *Edmonton Journal*, p. 61.

Forbes v. Yarmouth Hockey Association. Unreported N.S. Board of Inquiry (Kimball), October 27, 1978.

Harrison v. The University of British Columbia (1988), 2 W.W.R. 688 (B.C.C.A.).

Hogg, W. (1985). *Constitutional law of Canada* (2nd ed.). Toronto: Carswell.

The Law Society of British Columbia v. Andrews et al. (1989), 34 B.C.L.R. (2d) 273 (S.C.C.).

McKinney v. The University of Guelph (1987), 46 D.L.R. (4th) 193 at 209 (Ont. C.A.).

McLeod v. Youth Bowling Council of Ontario (1988), 9 C.M.R.R. 5371.

Nova Scotia Human Rights Act. S.N.S. 1969, c. 11.

The Ontario Human Rights Code. R.S.O. 1981, c. 53.

The Ontario Human Rights Code. R.S.O. 1970, c. 318 [am. 1972, c. 119 s. 3(1)].

Ontario Human Rights Commission v. The Ontario Rural Softball Association (1979), 260 O.R. (2d) 134, 102 D.L.R. (3d) 303, 10 R.F.L. (2d) 97 (C.A.).

R. v. Oakes (1986), 26 D.L.R. (4th) 200, 53 O.R. (2d) 719n, 24 C.C.C. (3d) 321 (S.C.C.).

Re Blainey and the Ontario Hockey Association et al. (1985), 52 O.R. (2d) 225, 21 D.L.R. (4th) 599 (H.C.); revd. (1986), 54 O.R. (2d) 513, 26 D.L.R. (4th) 728, 10 C.P.R. (3d) 450, 21 C.R.R. 44, 14 O.A.C. 194 (C.A.); leave to appeal to the S.C.C. dismissed, (1986), 58 O.R. (2d) 274n, 72 N.R. 76n, 17 O.A.C. 399n (S.C.C.).

PART III

RIGHTS OF THE PARTICIPANT

Although the Constitution of the United States guarantees certain basic rights to all citizens (the most important of these are found in the first 10 amendments, known as the Bill of Rights, and in the due process and equal protection clauses of the 14th Amendment), athletes historically appear to have been more willing than other student groups or individuals to accept infringements upon their personal rights and freedoms. This may be a function of the team ethic, or it may be the result of a simple desire to satisfy the coach whom they know has ultimate control over who plays and who does not. Regardless of the cause, the fact remains that many coaches have exercised a level of control over the activities of their athletes that exceeds both the norm among teachers and their legal authority.

Coaches or teachers, however, cannot afford to become complacent about individual rights or to assume that their rules and directives will be unquestioningly accepted. Athletes enjoy the same rights and privileges as other students. Moreover, they are becoming increasingly aware of this fact and, thus, more willing to balk when they feel that their rights have been improperly or unreasonably restricted.

Part III addresses the rights of athletes and others who participate in physical activity with regard to freedoms of speech, expression, personal appearance, due process of law, and the currently controversial issues of searches and drug testing.

UPI/BETTMANN

CHAPTER 6

PERSONAL FREEDOM

Bill Thompson, head coach of the Big Town High School football team, had a rule that required all of his athletes to be clean shaven and to keep their hair trimmed above the level of their ears and above their collars in the back. Eric Jones, a starting senior tailback, followed the grooming policy throughout the season. Immediately after the last game of the season, however, he began to grow a beard and to let his hair grow out. By the time of the all-sports awards banquet in the spring, Eric had a full goatee, and his hair extended over the collar of his shirt. Coach Thompson informed Eric that, unless he shaved his beard and cut his hair back to the approved length, he would not be allowed to attend the banquet or to receive the varsity letter he had earned as a member of the football team.

Eric filed suit alleging that the ruling improperly denied him his rights under the 1st and 14th Amendments. Coach Thompson argued that the hair code had been instituted for hygienic reasons and to preserve team discipline and uniformity.

This scenario is particularly interesting because it places a rule that might be judged acceptable during the playing season in a context in which it no longer bears a direct and rational relationship to the sport itself. As a result, the court decided that there was insufficient justification to support restricting the athlete's right to control his own appearance.

LEARNING OBJECTIVES

The student will be able to

1. explain the nature and importance of free speech in the schools and discuss the changes in its application as a result of the Tinker and Fraser decisions;
2. articulate the legal parameters of the interaction between governmental and religious functions; and
3. provide practical guidelines for the development and implementation of rules governing personal appearance.

FIRST AMENDMENT FREEDOMS

The rights of all citizens to freedom of speech and expression are set forth in the **1st Amendment** to the Constitution, which states that Congress shall make no laws that abridge the freedom of speech or of the press or of the right to peaceably assemble. This protects the right not only to express but to see, hear, read, and, in general, be exposed to different opinions and points of view. It also guarantees the right to associate with persons of one's choice and to join or form groups for political, social, economic, or religious reasons. The provisions regarding freedom of assembly protect the right to gather together for the purpose of requesting or otherwise affecting some governmental policy. Assembly rights are often exercised in the form of marches and demonstrations that either support or protest some policy or action.

Though 1st Amendment freedoms are of unquestioned importance, they are not absolute. The government or other individuals in authority may make reasonable rules regarding the **time, place**, and **manner** in which individuals or groups protest, demonstrate, or otherwise share their viewpoints with the public.

The educational setting is a unique source of 1st Amendment problems. When students express themselves, their rights often come into conflict with the rights of others or interfere with the administrative need to preserve reasonable order. A protest in a classroom, for instance, may interfere with the educational rights of those students who do not wish to have their class disrupted or, for that matter, with their right not to hear viewpoints and opinions they find offensive. When such protests occur, the courts are frequently required to weigh the competing interests and to balance the relative give-and-take with regard to individual rights.

FREEDOM OF EXPRESSION IN EDUCATIONAL SETTINGS

In 1965 there was an ongoing heated debate over the issue of U.S. involvement in the Vietnam War. Mary Beth Tinker, her brother John, and three other students in Des Moines, Iowa, decided to wear black armbands to school to express their opposition to the war. Upon learning of this plan, school administrators established a policy that, in order to prevent any possible disturbance, anyone wearing armbands would be asked to remove them. If they refused, they would be suspended until they returned to school without the armbands. Although Mary Beth and her friends were aware of the policy, they wore black armbands to school, refused to remove them, and were suspended. Although some students who saw the armbands argued with Mary Beth and her friends over the Vietnam issue, there was no violence or substantial disruption of the educational process.

Mary Beth and her friends took the issue of the school's policy to court. After a federal judge ruled that the Des Moines armband policy was reasonable, they appealed to the Supreme Court of the United States, arguing that the rules of the school were in conflict with their constitutional rights.

The Supreme Court acknowledged that school administrators must retain authority to control student conduct and can therefore restrict students' rights when there is evidence that the forbidden conduct will "materially and substantially disrupt" the educational process (*Tinker v. Des Moines Independent School District*, 1969). On the other hand, the court emphatically declared that neither students nor teachers give up their constitutionally guaranteed rights to free speech and expression when they enter a school. Effective education for citizenship, they stated, requires that the constitutional freedoms of the individual be protected.

In the eyes of the court, the wearing of a black armband to express disapproval of the American involvement in Vietnam was a form of symbolic speech and was therefore protected by the 1st Amendment. Because the court found no evidence that the wearing of the armbands substantially interfered with either the educational function of the school or with the rights of other students, it held that the prohibition against wearing armbands was unconstitutional. It is also important to note that the court clearly extended the principles of its decision beyond the classroom and

the instructional setting to guarantee the students' right to freedom of expression in all school activities and areas, including "in the cafeteria or on the playing field" (*Tinker v. Des Moines*, 1969).

LIMITATIONS ON THE FREEDOM OF EXPRESSION

For nearly two decades, the Tinker ruling set the pattern for expression within the educational setting. Students were permitted to engage in free speech activities that were nondisruptive, subject to reasonable restrictions with regard to time, place, and manner. Although this continues to be the standard of application, the more recent case of Matthew Fraser (*Bethel School District No. 403 v. Fraser*, 1986) helps clarify the limits of constitutionally protected speech.

In the spring of 1983, Matthew Fraser, a high school senior in Bethel, Washington, gave a speech at a school assembly to nominate a friend for an elected office in the student government. Fraser's speech contained explicit sexual innuendo, which not surprisingly resulted in vocal and "theatrical" responses from some students in the audience. Fraser was suspended from school, and his name was removed from a list of possible commencement speakers.

The District Court and the U.S. Court of Appeals held that Fraser's speech was not disruptive under the standards of Tinker and thus was protected under the 1st Amendment. The Supreme Court, however, reversed the decision. In so doing, it made it clear that disruption is not the only valid cause for restricting student speech. The court recognized the need to balance the freedom to express unpopular or controversial viewpoints with the school's responsibility to teach the "boundaries of socially appropriate behavior" (*Bethel v. Fraser*, 1986). Writing for the majority,

Chief Justice Warren Burger stated that "The process of educating our youth for citizenship in public schools is not confined to books, the curriculum, and the civics class; schools must teach by example the shared values of a civilized order" (*Bethel v. Fraser*, 1986).

To carry out this responsibility, some restrictions on free expression may be seen as necessary and appropriate.

> The schools, as instruments of the state, may determine that the essential lessons of civil, mature conduct cannot be conveyed in a school that tolerates lewd, indecent, or offensive speech or conduct such as that indulged in by this confused boy (*Bethel v. Fraser*, 1986).

The Fraser decision shows clearly that freedom of expression within the educational setting is neither absolute nor unlimited. School officials have discretionary authority to determine what forms of expression are vulgar and offensive in classrooms and assemblies and to take reasonable steps to curtail them. However, this decision should not be interpreted as dismissing the freedom of students to express controversial viewpoints on political, religious, or educational topics or on other matters of public concern. It is more appropriately viewed as a clarification of the existing principles that allow reasonable restrictions as to time, place, and manner of expression.

FREEDOM OF RELIGION

Historically the courts have been unwilling to rule on issues involving the freedom of religious expression because such issues tend to be emotional and controversial. The general governmental policy is held to be one of **benevolent neutrality**: that is, one that permits the free exercise of religious beliefs without official sponsorship or interference. Problems tend to arise, therefore, when official policies or procedures either effectively restrict the exercise of someone's religious beliefs or give the appearance of official support for a particular form of religious expression.

A high school baseball player, for instance, challenged a school board requirement that all athletes receive a tetanus immunization (*Calandra v. State College Area School District*, 1986). Zachary Calandra argued that his religious beliefs prohibited him from receiving immunizations and asked the court to rule the requirement unconstitutional. The court reasoned that participation in interscholastic sports, although unquestionably important, was not of sufficient importance to be seen as a right guaranteed by the government. The court held that, although the immunization rule required Mr. Calandra to choose between interscholastic sports and the full pursuit of his religious beliefs, it did not place an undue burden on his right to the free exercise of religion. One might reasonably speculate that the decision in this case might have been different if the refusal to be immunized disbarred the student from the entire educational program. In such a case, the immunization rule could very probably have been seen as jeopardizing an important governmental benefit to which Mr. Calandra was entitled.

A case that arose in Illinois (*Moody v. Cronin*, 1980) illustrates such a situation. Two students, one male and one female, refused to attend required coeducational physical education classes because attendance would have required them to wear shorts and sleeveless blouses where there was close visual and physical interaction, which would have violated their religious prohibition on immodest attire. The school district argued, on the other hand, that physical education was mandated by the state and that the coeducational setting was necessary to comply with Title IX. The court, in supporting the plaintiffs, indicated in words reminiscent of the Tinker decision that "plaintiffs do not shed their religious freedoms when they enter the public school house door" (*Moody v. Cronin*, 1980). The court refused to dictate whether the school should provide classes segregated by sex or individualized instruction for the plaintiffs or whether it should waive the physical education requirement entirely. It did, however, rule that the school could not direct or force the students to take part in coeducational physical education in contravention of their religious beliefs, nor could they discipline or punish the students for their refusal to do so.

Official actions that are seen as endorsing or encouraging a particular religious belief usually result in a different response. In 1985 a member of a high school marching band in Georgia objected to the practice of having pregame invocations delivered at all home football games. The invocations, he said, frequently began by asking everyone to bow their heads or to join in prayer and frequently specifically invoked the name of Jesus. These invocations, he contended, were in conflict with his own sincere religious beliefs. When extended negotiations failed to bring a satisfactory alteration in the policy, Doug Jager and his parents filed a formal complaint with the courts (*Jager v. Douglas County School District*, 1989).

Although the court recognized that invocations could serve the secular purpose of promoting good sportsmanship, that objective could be accomplished without religious reference. The court also declared that there was no nonreligious justification for allowing a prayer rather than a secular message before football games. The court concluded its findings by reemphasizing the fundamental legal principle that neither the state nor its subdivisions can take actions that are seen as endorsing or advancing religion.

PERSONAL APPEARANCE

Restricting the freedom of individuals to control their personal appearance and imposing dress codes is a relatively common practice in instructional, recreational, and team sport programs. Participants who pursue legal remedies for allegedly improper or excessive restriction of their freedoms in this area most frequently cite the 14th Amendment, claiming that they are in effect being denied protected personal liberties. Some individuals, like the person in Figure 6.1, have also argued that restrictions upon their personal appearance or dress deny them a form of personal expression and therefore violate the provisions of the 1st Amendment. Once again, however, it must be remembered that neither of these forms of constitutional protection is absolute. Individual rights *can* be restricted when there are compelling reasons to do so.

Court decisions in cases involving personal appearance and dress have been mixed. Although the federal district courts in about half of the states have given schools considerable latitude to restrict dress and grooming, many others have taken the opposite viewpoint, opting to view individual decision making with regard to grooming as a constitutional right (see Table 6.1). The United States Supreme Court, on the other hand, has consistently taken the viewpoint that issues of grooming are not of sufficient import to warrant its attention. As a result, the degree of authority that any given coach or teacher can exert over the dress and grooming of athletes and students will continue to vary from district to district.

MANAGEMENT GUIDELINES:

CONSIDERATIONS FOR DEVELOPING RESTRICTIONS ON PERSONAL APPEARANCE

Despite the relative lack of consistency, there are several constants that should be considered carefully when developing and enforcing appearance restrictions.

Figure 6.1 "But Mr. Jones, I'm just exercising my constitutional right to freedom of expression."

1. The more vague or indefinite the rule, the less likely it is to be upheld by the courts. Rules should be stated briefly and explicitly and should minimize the latitude for interpretation and personal discretion. A rule that prohibits hair from extending below a football helmet, for instance, is far less subject to individual interpretation and bias and more easily defensible in court than one that simply prohibits long hair (see Case 6.1).

2. Any and all restrictions imposed must relate directly to the safety of the participants or to the quality of the activity. For instance, regulations that require the removal of jewelry or the use of safety glasses for racquetball would be almost universally accepted, whereas a rule imposed primarily for the sake of conformity might not be.

3. The benefits of the regulations must clearly outweigh the restrictions they impose on the constitutional rights of the participants. A requirement that all bathers must wear clean bathing suits and that prohibits the use of gym shorts or cutoffs in the pool, for instance, would probably be justifiable because the gains in terms of sanitation significantly outweigh the minor loss of individual freedom.

4. A restriction cannot stand unless there is no reasonable alternative that is less restrictive of the constitutional rights of the participant. This is often referred to as the **least restrictive means test** (See Case 6.2). A restriction on long

Table 6.1   Probable Court Rulings on Personal Appearance

States likely to uphold restrictions on grooming and appearance	States that consider personal appearance and grooming a constitutional right
Alabama	Arkansas
Alaska	Connecticut
Arizona	Illinois
California	Indiana
Colorado	Iowa
Delaware	Maine
District of Columbia	Maryland
Florida	Massachusetts
Georgia	Minnesota
Hawaii	Missouri
Idaho	Nebraska
Kansas	New Hampshire
Kentucky	New York
Louisiana	North Carolina
Michigan	North Dakota
Mississippi	Puerto Rico
Montana	Rhode Island
Nevada	South Carolina
New Jersey	South Dakota
New Mexico	Vermont
Ohio	Virginia
Oklahoma	West Virginia
Oregon	Wisconsin
Pennsylvania	
Tennessee	
Texas	
Utah	
Virgin Islands	
Washington	
Wyoming	

Note. Data from *Teachers and the Law* (3rd ed.) (p. 363) by L. Fischer, D. Schimmel, and C. Kelly, 1991, White Plains, NY: Longman.

hair in a swimming pool, for instance, could be shown to relate to sanitation as well as to water resistance. Some form of restriction that would solve these problems would be seen as quite reasonable for a swimming team. But because both of these problems can be overcome by a bathing cap, a requirement that male swimmers shave their heads would probably be seen as placing unnecessary limits on their individual rights and freedoms.

CASE STUDIES

Case 6.1

Vague and Overbroad Rules

The Crosstown High School Athletic Department has a rule that requires all athletes to be neatly dressed and groomed at all times and to maintain standards of modesty and good taste appropriate to their status as highly visible representatives of their educational institution. The rule further states that the athletes must avoid "extreme" styles of dress and grooming.

John Emmett, a baseball player, claims that his beard and mustache are not extreme styles of dress or grooming and thus should be allowable under the code. His coaches and the director of athletics have taken the opposite viewpoint and have suspended John from the baseball team until such time as the "offensive" beard and mustache have been removed. If John decides to pursue this matter to its legal limits, the shortcomings in the Crosstown dress and grooming code virtually guarantee that the code will not be upheld by the courts.

Perhaps the single most glaring fault in the code is its vagueness and overbreadth. The question of exactly what constitutes "extreme" fashion is left almost entirely to the personal discretion of the coach or athletic director. Imagine the difficulty of getting 10 different individuals from 10 different towns to agree on whether or not a beard is "extreme" or, if it is, at what length it becomes so; whether all mustaches are extreme or only those of a certain style; whether tight pants or neon running shorts are immodest; and so forth. The courts will not support a rule that is so broad that reasonable people will almost surely differ over the parameters of its enforcement. If, for instance, the rule had simply prohibited all beards, the guidelines would have been clearly understood by all. Although one might argue the appropriateness of such a regulation, at least the prohibited behavior would be clearly identified and understood.

In addition to clearly defining the standards, a rule must directly relate to some form of compelling interest: that is, it should contribute directly to the proper function and/or improvement of the athletic or academic programs. The guidelines of most adjudicated cases would point to a requirement that the prohibited behavior be directly linked to some reasonably anticipated disruption of the nature and/or spirit of the game. Because it is difficult to envision most beards or mustaches causing undue distraction in a baseball game, interfering with the safety of the player or his opponents, or otherwise disrupting the athletic or educational endeavors at Crosstown High School, it is unlikely that this rule would be upheld by the courts.

Although the courts have generally been reluctant to interfere in matters of dress and grooming, they have consistently struck down rules and regulations that either are overly broad in their application or do not reasonably contribute to the accepted goals of the organization. The desire for conformity for its own sake and in the absence of some more persuasive reason rarely justifies imposing a dress or grooming code that restricts individual freedom.

[Based on *Crossen v. Fatsi*, 309 F. Supp. 114 (D.C. Conn 1970)]

Case 6.2

Least Restrictive Means

A state high school athletic association rule forbids the wearing of hats or other headwear during basketball competition. The stated purpose of this rule is to prevent injuries that might occur if a hat or hair clip were to fall on the court during the course of play and cause a player to slip and fall. Two Jewish schools filed suit, arguing that the rule interfered with the free exercise of their religious beliefs. All male members of their faith, they argued, are required to keep their heads covered at all times, but their yarmulkes were disallowed by the league rule. Further, since members of the league were prohibited from playing against nonmember schools, dropping out of the league would effectively leave the schools without any other opponents.

In its decision, the court ruled that the Jewish athletes did not have a "constitutional right to wear 'yarmulkes' insecurely fastened to the head during athletic competition" (*Menora v. Illinois High School Association*, 1982). Noting that Jewish law required only that the men's heads be covered, and did not specifically require the yarmulke, they directed the schools to propose a more secure form of head covering for their athletes. The court further noted that if a reasonably secure form of headgear was adopted by the schools, and the league did not accept its use, they would reconsider the issue of whether or not the rule violated 1st Amendment guarantees.

This case illustrates the application of the least restrictive means principles discussed with regard to personal appearance. In the interest of safety, it may be reasonable to place certain restrictions on the nature and type of headgear allowable in a basketball contest. The blanket prohibition imposed by the league unnecessarily restricted the exercise of the religious freedom of the Jewish athletes. The court wisely sought to balance the interests of both parties.

[*Menora v. Illinois High School Association*, 683 F.2d 1030 (7th Cir. 1982)]

CHAPTER SUMMARY

The 1969 landmark case of *Tinker v. Des Moines* clearly established the fact that students are not necessarily required to surrender their 1st Amendment freedoms when they enter the schoolhouse. Nearly 20 years later, the Supreme Court made it clear that freedom of expression in the schools is sub-

ject to reasonable restrictions. When a student's freedom of expression comes into conflict with the nature of the educational activity or violates acceptable societal norms, representatives of the school may take reasonable corrective action.

Similarly, the freedom of religious expression is neither absolute nor unlimited. The courts have, however, consistently ruled in favor of the clear separation of governmental affairs and those of the church.

The decisions of the courts with regard to personal appearance, on the other hand, have been more mixed. In general, however, the most enforceable appearance restrictions are clearly stated, relate directly to the safety or quality of the activity, benefit the participants, and meet the least restrictive means test.

KEY TERMS

1st Amendment (114)
Benevolent neutrality (116)
Least restrictive means test (118)
Time, place, and manner (114)

QUESTIONS FOR DISCUSSION

1. Based on the precepts of the Tinker and Bethel cases, create scenarios whereby an athlete's freedom of speech can be subject to reasonable restrictions by a coach. Discuss and modify the limits of these restrictions. How far can coaches go in restricting the expression of their athletes? Consider these issues in the context of a situation in which the coach disagrees strongly with views that an athlete has just shared with representatives of the media.

2. Discuss alternative procedures that might be followed in the Jager case presented on page 117. How might the school fulfill its desire for an opening "invocation" while maintaining the required separation of church and state?

3. Develop sport-specific appearance codes that would meet the criteria for legal enforceability.

REFERENCES

Bethel School District No. 403 v. Fraser, 478 U.S. 675 (1986).

Calandra v. State College Area School District, 512A.2d, 809 (Pa. 1986).

Crossen v. Fatsi, 309 F. Supp. 114 (D.C. Conn. 1970).

Fischer, L., Schimmel, D., & Kelly, C. (1991). *Teachers and the law* (3rd ed.). New York: Longman.

Jager v. Douglas County School District, 862 F.2d 824 (11th Cir. 1989).

Menora v. Illinois High School Association, 683 F.2d 1030 (7th Cir. 1982).

Moody v. Cronin, 484 F. Supp. 270 (C.D. Illinois 1980).

Tinker v. Des Moines Independent School District, 393 U.S. 503 (1969).

ADDITIONAL READINGS

Appenzeller, H. (1985). *Sports and the courts* (pp. 58-67). Charlottesville, VA: Michie.

Fischer, L., Schimmel, D., & Kelly, C. (1991). *Teachers and the law* (3rd ed.). (chap. 9, 10, & 18). White Plains, NY: Longman.

Narol, M.S., & Dedopoulos, S. (1979, November). Beards—Are they a clear and present danger? *Referee,* pp. 36, 51.

CHAPTER 7

DUE PROCESS

During the 1970-71 school year, the Columbus, Ohio, public schools were the scenes of widespread student protest and unrest. Several students who either participated in or were present at demonstrations held on school grounds were suspended: some for documented acts of violence; others, including Dwight Lopez, claimed to have been innocent bystanders at the disturbances. The students were suspended for up to 10 days without hearings and in many cases without having been informed of the charges against them.

A number of these students, through their parents, sued the board of education, claiming that their right to due process had been violated, and the federal district court upheld their contention. The school board appealed to the U.S. Supreme Court, and in a narrow 5-4 decision, the Supreme Court, too, ruled in favor of the students. The court's discussion of several issues with regard to due process helps clarify the interpretation of students' rights under the 5th and 14th Amendments (*Goss v. Lopez*, 1975).

LEARNING OBJECTIVES

The student will be able to

1. explain the nature and meaning of due process of law;
2. discriminate between substantive due process and procedural due process;
3. articulate the due process requirements of situations of minimal and maximal severity; and
4. determine appropriate procedures to guarantee the due process of law, given a theoretical violation of team rules.

DUE PROCESS

Athletes, students, coaches, teachers, teams, and educational institutions continually function within the constraints of a wide variety of rules and regulations. Violation of these rules and regulations often results in the imposition of some sort of punishment or penalty. To the degree that these penalties are perceived as having been unfairly determined or applied, they may be tested in court.

Due process is the concept by which the U.S. Constitution guarantees that the government and institutions acting directly or indirectly on behalf of or under the control of government are bound to utilize procedures to protect and preserve the rights of the individual (see Case 7.1). The legal foundation for individual rights to due process is found in the 5th and 14th Amendments to the Constitution, which provide that no person shall be deprived of life, liberty, or property without the due process of law. The 5th Amendment places these restraints upon the federal government, whereas the 14th Amendment extends the same constraints to situations in which state action is involved.

In applying the principle of due process to the schools, the Supreme Court indicated in the case of *Goss v. Lopez* that, although states are not constitutionally obligated to establish schools, once they do so, students are entitled to attend those schools and to participate fully in their activities. Students' rights to participate cannot be taken away from them without the application of procedures designed to guarantee fairness and impartiality (that is, due process of law).

THE NATURE OF DUE PROCESS

It is important to understand that the due process amendments were developed to prevent arbitrary and unreasonable decisions. As a result, the *focus* of due process litigation tends to be on the manner of determining issues of guilt or innocence and the nature and level of punishment rather than on the more straightforward question of guilt or innocence. In essence, the Constitution guarantees the process, not the outcome. This protection is both substantive and procedural.

Substantive due process addresses the question of whether or not the rule that was violated was fair and reasonable. All rules must have a valid purpose or function. Furthermore, the rule and its application must clearly relate to the accomplishment of that purpose. Additionally, there are clear constitutional due process restrictions that prohibit the imposition of penalties for violating any rule that is so vague that the specific forbidden conduct cannot be consistently determined. Such a rule in effect allows the enforcer to exercise near total personal discretion and thus introduces the elements of bias and inconsistency. "A statute which either forbids or requires the doing of an act in terms so vague that men of common intelligence must necessarily guess at its meaning and differ as to its application, violates the first essential of due process of law" (*Lanzetta v. New Jersey*, 1939).

Procedural due process, on the other hand, allows one to question the decision-making process applied to determine whether a rule has been violated and what penalty, if any, should be imposed. Procedural requirements are flexible and depend upon the balancing of the needs and interests of both parties. Factors considered in the determination of specific procedural requirements include

1. *the severity of the violation.* Although the concepts of fairness and equity apply in theory to all decisions, the courts consistently refuse to trivialize the law with minor issues. Therefore, both the level of due process required and the likelihood of legal intervention increase with the severity of the violation of which the individual is accused.
2. *the severity of the* **sanction** *or punishment imposed.* This, too, is a matter of degree. One would be expected to provide a higher level of due process before removing a player or team from a league than would be required to suspend a player from a single game.
3. *the nature of the procedure used versus the nature of the alternatives proposed.* This is a function of the type of procedures used, the procedures requested by the punished party, and the relative cost of each in terms of both dollars and time. A full-blown adversarial hearing, for instance, is a relatively costly and time-consuming process. Therefore, it would be an inappropriate means of dealing with a simple violation of a minor training rule. The Supreme Court of Nebraska, for instance, in considering a situation of this type stated that

> The courts should refrain from imposing such a burdensome set of requirements on the school administrator that compliance would become too costly and time consuming. The result would be a loss of the effectiveness of a regular disciplinary tool and would result in overwhelming administrative procedures. (*French v. Cornwell*, 1979)

DUE PROCESS REQUIREMENTS

Although due process is a flexible concept that depends upon the specifics of any given situation for its application, it is possible to identify general parameters that define the range of options. **Minimum due process** might include

1. *a statement of the specific violation,* which could take the form of a relatively simple verbal comment from the person in authority: "Mary, you have missed two practices without an excuse."
2. *some notice of what sanctions will be imposed,* which can also be accomplished verbally: "You will not be allowed to play in the next game."
3. *an opportunity for the accused to comment on the action*: At a minimum, the coach could ask Mary if she has any response or could simply pause in a manner indicative of a willingness to accept reasonable comments that Mary might choose to put forth.

Figure 7.1 and Case 7.2 depict situations involving the application of minimum due process.

Maximum due process requirements might include

1. *a written notice of a hearing,* which should indicate the time and place at which the individual will be able to

Figure 7.1 "Mary, I've warned you twice about coming late to practice and I've told you what would happen if you did it again. Unless you can give me a very good reason why I shouldn't, I'm going to bench you for the next game." At the minimum, due process requires a statement of the violation, notice of the intended punishment, and an opportunity to respond.

appear and, in general, to be present while others present charges and facts associated with the matter. This hearing should be conducted by an impartial person or group; that is, persons who are detached from the event in question and have no personal interest in the outcome of the hearing.

2. *a written statement of the charges and the grounds that, if proven, would justify the imposition of sanctions.* This guarantees that the accused person knows what rules have allegedly been violated and by what specific actions or inactions they were violated. This information must be provided well enough in advance of the hearing to allow the accused to prepare a reasoned defense.

3. *the provision of an* **adversarial hearing**, which at the maximal extreme would allow the accused to present evidence and witnesses and to examine the witnesses and evidence used against him. In serious cases, the accused would also be allowed to have the assistance of legal counsel.

4. *a written or taped record of the proceedings.* Although this may not be specifically required in most situations, it provides an excellent resource in the event of further litigation. Copies of the record of the proceedings and the findings should be made available to the accused and retained by the acting agency.

5. *a clearly stated* **right of appeal**. In general, a person should have the right to request that an adverse decision be reviewed or reconsidered. Normally an appeal would be considered at the next higher authority level. A coach's decision therefore might be reviewed by the athletic director or school principal. The theory is that an impartial review will be provided to guarantee that the rights of the accused were not violated and that the procedures used and sanctions applied fit the circumstances.

In the case of *Goss v. Lopez* (1975), discussed at the beginning of this chapter, the Supreme Court decided that students who had been suspended for 10 days or fewer were entitled to due process. Specifically, they should have been offered an oral or written notice of the charges, an explanation of the evidence against them if they denied the charges, and an opportunity to present their side of the story. The court did not give the students the right to be represented by an attorney, the right to cross-examine witnesses, the right to call witnesses, or the right to a hearing before an impartial person.

In arriving at its decision, the court considered the due process interests of **harm, cost,** and **risk of error.** It felt that reputations were harmed and educational opportunities were lost as a result of the suspension. An informal hearing would not place an unreasonable cost burden on the schools and would help reduce the risk of error. The court also stated that in an emergency situation, the students could be sent home immediately and a hearing held at a later time, after the danger or disruption had been removed (*Goss v. Lopez*, 1975).

DUE PROCESS AND STATE ACTION

The 5th and 14th Amendments, which establish the requirements for due process, apply directly to actions of the federal government and of the states. It is therefore clear that disciplinary actions taken by public schools, colleges, and universities will be subject to scrutiny under the appropriate due process legislation.

Far less clear, however, is the degree to which sports governing bodies such as the NCAA or the various organizations that regulate interscholastic sports must function under similar constraints. These organizations are, in the strictest sense of the word, private bodies rather than **state actors.** State actors are those acting under the authority of a governmental entity or that of its agents. On the surface, therefore, it would seem that these bodies would not be bound by the constraints of the 5th and 14th Amendments. A problem arises, however, in that the actions of the ruling bodies are intimately tied to those of their member institutions, which in the majority of cases are state actors and thus are bound by the 5th and 14th Amendments. The legal problems that this entanglement presents are explored in chapter 11.

Until the mid-1980s, the courts ruled fairly consistently that, at least for the purposes of due process, the actions of the interscholastic and intercollegiate athletic associations were so intimately tied to those of the member schools that these private voluntary organizations should be considered state actors. However in 1984, in a case involving the NCAA, the court considerably modified this approach and clearly indicated that simple interaction with the state would no longer be a sufficient basis for imposing a finding of governmental activity (*Arlosoroff v. NCAA*, 1984). Since then, questions regarding the degree to which the association may be acting on behalf of the member schools or fulfilling functions that were actually caused or directed by the member schools have come under consideration (*Graham v. NCAA*, 1986). A similar determination was reached with regard to interscholastic sports in 1988 (*Anderson v. IHSAA*, 1988).

There are other sports organizations (such as officials' organizations and sport-specific coaches' associations) whose members, by virtue of paying dues and otherwise qualifying for membership, are entitled to certain due process rights. Although these groups are not state actors per se, their actions toward their members would nevertheless be held to a reasonable due process standard.

To date, the particular circumstances under which an athletic association will be considered a state actor have not been conclusively defined and articulated. The complexity and variations among the involvements between any given organization and its members further complicate the issue. However, one point should be clearly understood: The best way to avoid legal problems is to treat each situation as though it were subject to due process guidelines. By following appropriate due process procedures and treating all individuals with fairness and impartiality, one can avoid issues of state versus private function.

This is not to say that all rule violations should result in an adversarial hearing, or that coaches must litigate their every decision with regard to punishment. Coaches should, however, apply the principles of due process in a manner appropriate to the severity of the situation, both to protect the rights of their athletes and to reduce their own exposure to legal action.

MANAGEMENT GUIDELINES:

DUE PROCESS

Observing the following general guidelines can help reduce the likelihood of due process complaints and ensure that all alleged infractions of established rules and regulations are treated with consistency and fairness.

1. All rules and regulations should be clearly stated in simple language. If reasonable individuals could interpret or apply the rule differently, then it is too ambiguous.
2. All persons must be presumed to be innocent until there is a reasonable body of proof to the contrary.
3. An admission of guilt removes the possibility of bias or error in the determination of responsibility. Therefore, it fulfills the legal requirement for due process (see Case 7.3).
4. Before disciplinary sanctions are imposed, a reasonable and fair hearing should be provided. In minor offenses

this could take the form of an opportunity to discuss the matter with the person who is imposing the sanctions. In situations in which the effects of the sanctions can be long-term or costly, a formal hearing would be more appropriate.
5. Emergency situations can and should be dealt with immediately. If immediate action must be taken to ensure the safety of persons or property, a hearing must be scheduled as soon after order is restored as practical.
6. Although the formality of the notice should vary according to the severity of the situation, the accused must always be informed of the specific charges leveled against her.
7. Notice of a planned hearing should be given sufficiently in advance to allow the accused to prepare an informed defense.
8. Written records should be maintained for all hearings, which document at a minimum the nature of the offense, specific charges, nature of the proceedings, individuals involved, evidence presented, findings, and sanctions. It is also wise to document even minor infractions and sanctions to provide a record of consistency and fairness with regard to the treatment of different persons and different infractions.

Coaches, teachers, and administrators must recognize the basic principle that all persons have the right to be heard and to present an informed defense before being subjected to enforcement procedures or sanctions. The specific degree of due process required is a function of the particular circumstances involved, the severity of the sanctions imposed, the relative cost of carrying out the due process procedures, and the likelihood and potential effect of an incorrect judgment.

CASE STUDIES

Case 7.1

Due Process in the Private Sector

Edith Slocum paid a U.S.$500 enrollment and membership fee to the Sunnyside Health and Racquet Club. The fee entitled her to 5 years of paid membership and unlimited use of the facilities for that period. Additional payments were required only for instructional programs and court time if desired.

After 1 month of membership, Edith contracted for weekly private racquetball lessons and additional practice time on the courts at a total additional cost of U.S.$30 per week, payable monthly. After she missed her second, third, and fourth payments, Edith's lessons were cancelled and her club membership was revoked without warning or a hearing. She is now seeking guidance as to whether or not her due process rights may have been violated.

This matter is not subject to the constitutional due process requirements because the action did not involve the government or its agents but rather a private commercial enterprise. Although some jurisdictions and some individual contracts impose specific requirements for notice prior to repossession or revocation, these are related to elements of contract law rather than to those of due process.

[Based on legal issues]

Case 7.2

Minimum Due Process

The Needham Township Little League All-Star Team was scheduled to play in the quarterfinals of the state Little League championships. Coach John Barkham told all players to report to the Needham Recreation Center at 3:00 p.m., at which time a bus would transport the team to the game. Three players, Mike Billings, Jeffrey Egan, and Maria Carsey, were not present at the scheduled time of departure. The bus waited 10 minutes and left without them.

The three athletes were being transported to the recreation center by Jeffrey Egan's mother when her car had a flat tire. Mrs. Egan got the tire fixed and arrived at the recreation center at 3:15 p.m. Realizing that the team bus had already departed, she drove the athletes directly to the game.

The three players arrived at the game near the conclusion of the pregame warm-ups. The coach, who was furious at their tardiness, informed them that they would not be allowed to participate with the team. They were to go home with the parent who had brought them rather than return on the bus and have dinner with the team, and they would be suspended from the next game as well. The players were neither asked nor allowed to offer any explanations for their late arrival.

The next morning the parents of all three children came to the office of the director of the Needham Township Recreation Department under whose auspices the team had been organized. They demanded that their children be reinstated, that their travel and dinner expenses be reimbursed, and that the children and Mrs. Egan receive a public apology.

Although this situation would not be of sufficient consequence to justify legal intervention, it is precisely the type of event that the due process provisions of the Constitution are designed to prevent. The coach was understandably tense and preoccupied in the pregame situation. He was annoyed at the apparent failure of three players to comply with the departure guidelines and in no mood to discuss the issue. He simply took the action that most readily came to mind and neither asked for nor allowed any explanations.

The due process procedures are meant to ensure fairness and consistency in situations in which individuals are being accused of violating rules or regulations. Regardless of the severity of the violation, these situations almost invariably involve the emotions of both the accusers and the accused. Worse yet, they are by their very nature unplanned events that seem, at least to the individual in authority, to occur at the most inopportune times. Therefore it is not surprising that, in the absence of careful controls, punishments for these violations can be characterized by snap decisions, inconsistency, and too often bad judgment.

If Coach Barkham had simply allowed his players the opportunity to explain their lateness, he probably would have recognized the folly of penalizing the innocent athletes so severely for the flat tire, especially in light of Mrs. Egan's continuing efforts to get them to the game. Due process procedures are best viewed as the simple, universal requirements for fairness and impartiality to which every individual is entitled. Due process is not a set of rules that apply to deviant circumstances; rather it is, quite simply, the manner in which caring persons treat others.

[Based on a nonadjudicated situation]

Case 7.3

Admission of Guilt Negates Need for Due Process

William Mason was a student athlete at Marwick Regional High School. When William's father found him in an intoxicated state after a Saturday night party, he reported the situation to William's coach.

On the following Monday, the coach held a conference with William and his father. William admitted to having been intoxicated and further admitted that he understood that drinking was a violation of school and team rules. At the conclusion of the meeting, the coach suspended William from competition for a period of 6 weeks but indicated that William would be allowed to practice with the team during the time of his suspension. William received written confirmation of his punishment on the following day. William's father brought suit against the coach, alleging that his son's right to due process had been violated.

The coach handled this situation very well. Faced with an apparently serious violation of an important training rule, he scheduled an informal meeting as soon as possible. The hearing gave William ample opportunity to say anything he wished on his own behalf. Further, he was well aware of both the severity of the situation and the potential punishment.

William had admitted his guilt, removing all possibility of error in deciding his innocence or guilt. Therefore, the coach did not have to weigh conflicting evidence or consider alternative scenarios. The athlete admitted that he understood the rule and that he had knowingly violated it. This, in essence, fulfilled the purpose of the due process requirements.

After assessing penalties according to established policies, the coach confirmed his verbal decision in writing. This action precluded misunderstanding or misinterpretation and provided a written record for comparison to ensure and indicate consistency and fairness in the treatment of all athletes.

[Based on *French v. Cornwell*, 202 Neb. 569, 276 N.W. 2d 216 (1979)]

CHAPTER SUMMARY

Due process is the legal requirement that the government follow fair and impartial procedures before instituting action aimed at depriving individuals of their personal freedom or property. Due process requirements are not intended to prevent governing bodies from punishing those who violate their rules. They are, however, designed to guarantee that such decisions are reached with fairness and impartiality and that punishments, when imposed, befit the nature and severity of the offense. In this regard, due process can be seen as a flexible concept that varies along a continuum from minimum to maximum procedural complexity depending upon the severity of the alleged violation and the potential severity of the punishment that might be applied.

KEY TERMS

Adversarial hearing (126)
Cost (127)
Due process (124)
Harm (127)
Maximum due process (125)
Minimum due process (125)
Procedural due process (125)
Right of appeal (126)
Risk of error (127)
Sanction (125)
State actors (127)
Substantive due process (124)

QUESTIONS FOR DISCUSSION

1. What is due process of law, and what does it entail?
2. Distinguish between substantive due process and procedural due process. Devise sport-specific examples of situations in which each is abridged. Explain what changes could have been made to prevent the due process violations you cite.
3. List the minimum and the maximum requirements of due process. Devise sport-specific circumstances in which each would appear to be most appropriate. Devise other situations that fall somewhere along the theoretical continuum from minimum to maximum due process. Discuss concrete procedures for ensuring fairness and equity within reasonable constraints of time and cost.
4. Assume, for the sake of argument, that William Mason proclaimed his innocence in Case 7.3 rather than pleaded guilty. What procedures should have been followed to ascertain his guilt or innocence and, assuming he was guilty, to determine his punishment?

REFERENCES

Anderson v. Indiana High School Athletic Association, 699 F. Supp. 719 (S.D. Ind. 1988).

Arlosoroff v. National Collegiate Athletic Association, 746 F.2d 1019 (4th Cir. 1984).

French v. Cornwell, 202 Neb. 569, 276 N.W. 2d 216 (1979).

Goss v. Lopez, 419 U.S. 565 (1975).

Graham v. National Collegiate Athletic Association, 804 F.2d 953, 958 (6th Cir. 1986).

Lanzetta v. New Jersey, 306 U.S. 451; 59 Sup Ct 618 (1939).

ADDITIONAL READINGS

Arnold, D.E. (1983). *Legal considerations in the administration of public school physical education and athletic programs* (pp. 246-255). Springfield, IL: Charles C Thomas.

Mallios, H. (1985). Sports, the law and due process. In H. Appenzeller (Ed.), *Sports and law contemporary issues*, (pp. 22-29). Charlottesville, VA: Michie.

Sharp, L.A. (1990). *Sport law*. National Organization on Legal Problems of Education (NOLPE), Monograph 40, pp. 53-60.

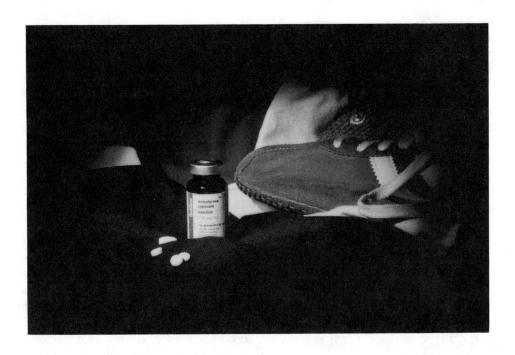

CHAPTER 8

SEARCHES AND DRUG TESTING

A high school freshman referred to as T.L.O. and her friend were smoking in a restroom when a teacher entered. Because smoking was a violation of school rules, the girls were taken to the office of an assistant vice-principal.

When questioned, T.L.O. denied smoking. At the request of the school official, she then opened her purse, which was found to contain a package of cigarettes, rolling papers, marijuana, and an index card suggesting possible involvement in drug sales. After examining the purse and its contents, the assistant vice-principal summoned the police and T.L.O.'s mother.

T.L.O. filed suit, alleging that the search of her pocketbook was conducted without a warrant and therefore violated her constitutional rights. The judge in this case ruled that, although the vice-principal did not have a warrant, his search was conducted on the basis of reasonable suspicion and was reasonable in scope; therefore it did not compromise T.L.O.'s right to privacy (*New Jersey v. T.L.O.*, 1985).

1. explain the differences between the probable cause and reasonable suspicion standards for the institution of a search and to tell when each would apply;
2. develop reasonable guidelines for instituting and conducting a search and for controlling evidence disclosed during the process;
3. explain the primary legal arguments for and against drug testing in athletics; and
4. design a drug testing program that is both effective and legally defensible.

SEARCHES BY SCHOOL AUTHORITIES

The frightening increase in the possession and use of drugs and weapons among America's youth has caused school administrators, teachers, coaches, and league officials to increase their efforts to prevent and punish violations of laws and regulations governing this aspect of personal conduct. Consequently, searches of lockers and other school property and of pocketbooks, bookbags, and even the students themselves have increased in both frequency and thoroughness.

Prior to the 1985 adjudication of the T.L.O. case by the U.S. Supreme Court, searches were for the most part considered to fall within the **in loco parentis** authority of the schools. The in loco parentis doctrine refers to the historically accepted power of the schools to act in the place of the students' parents. In the past, this has given school officials considerable latitude, particularly in matters of discipline and control.

The landmark decision in the matter of *New Jersey v. T.L.O.*, however, has clarified both the role of the school officials and the rights of the students and thus has set guidelines for the justification necessary before a search may be conducted and for the acceptable limits of the search itself. As a result of the T.L.O. decision, school personnel have come to be recognized as **public officials** rather than quasi-parents. Consequently, they are more obligated to operate within the constraints of the antisearch provisions of the 4th Amendment and the due process provisions of the 14th Amendment than previously expected under the in loco parentis doctrine.

Beyond these safeguards on the students' rights, the court recognized the complexity and importance of maintaining effective discipline and a safe school environment. Therefore, it set a less stringent standard for school officials than for other state actors such as police officers. In order to overcome a person's rights under the 4th Amendment, a police officer would have to demonstrate **probable cause** and under most circumstances secure a warrant. This would require proof that the officer had knowledge of facts that indicated that specific evidence of criminal offenses would be uncovered by the search.

School officials, on the other hand, are expected to meet the less restrictive standard of **reasonable suspicion**. This test requires only a reasonable suspicion that the search will reveal evidence that a student is violating or has violated either the law or the rules of the school. The standard of reasonableness involves what the court referred to as a **two-prong test**: The search must be "reasonable in its inception" and "reasonable in scope" (*New Jersey v. T.L.O.*, 1985). Thus, in the T.L.O. case, Justice White, writing for the majority, concluded that, because a teacher had found T.L.O. smoking in a restroom, and the student had subsequently denied the offense, the initial search of her purse was reasonable. White reasoned that finding cigarettes in T.L.O.'s purse "would both corroborate the report that she had been smoking and undermine the credibility of her defense to the charge of smoking" (*New Jersey v. T.L.O.*). When this first search revealed drug paraphernalia plainly visible in the purse, the closer scrutiny that disclosed the marijuana was also considered reasonable in the opinion of the court.

Regardless of the justification that underlies the determination to conduct a search, it must be carried out in a manner that avoids excessive intrusion upon the student's right to privacy. Searching a locker secured by a school-supplied lock, for instance, would be less intrusive than searching a locker secured by a student-supplied lock. Either of these searches would be less intrusive than a search of a student-owned bookbag and less intrusive still than a search of a pocketbook or wallet. At each successive level, the student has a greater expectation of retaining the privacy of the items held, and so the administrator's reasons for the search and the strength of the suspicions that allow the administrator to pinpoint the particular person or object must rise accordingly.

For example, to strengthen their authority to search lockers, it is becoming increasingly common for school and team officials to develop written policies that clearly indicate that lockers are in fact school property. They are therefore subject to the authority and control of designated officials and are not the exclusive private domain of the student or athlete who happens to be assigned to the locker. The school or team then clearly states the premise that it reserves the right to search the lockers for reasons related to discipline and/or safety. Where such policies are fairly applied and given to the students in written form, they successfully overcome most claims of user control over the lockers, and they tend to be accepted as valid by the courts.

Searches of a person constitute a more complex matter. Given sufficient justification, requests that individuals empty their pockets would probably be upheld as reasonable. Even pat-down searches, though certainly more intrusive, could be justified in extreme circumstances. Strip searches, on the other hand, have consistently been found by the courts to violate the students' rights. Such searches would likely be upheld only in the direst of circumstances, under which the wisest course of action would be to turn the matter over to the appropriate law enforcement agency whose officers would conduct a legal search subject to the more stringent criteria of probable cause.

WHEN A SEARCH DISCLOSES EVIDENCE

The administrative concerns for a search do not end, as some might expect, with the physical examination itself. Given the reasoning and justification necessary to conduct the search in the first place, there is every reason to expect that some form of evidence will be disclosed. When the materials found are such that they might be used in a criminal proceeding (for example, illegal substances or weapons), great care must be taken to maintain the **chain of custody**. That is, you must be able to prove exactly who had access to the evidence after it left the student's hands. This is best accomplished by immediately securing the material under lock and key. Further, the number of persons with keys should be held to the absolute minimum (two at most).

If the disclosed evidence is a weapon or an illegal substance, the best and safest course of action is to hand it over to the appropriate law enforcement agency as quickly as possible. Even if no criminal charges are anticipated or desired, the nature of the materials themselves dictates that they be handled carefully by trained individuals. In many jurisdictions, in fact, the failure to deliver a weapon or drugs into the hands of the police could expose the school official to charges of concealing evidence.

The policy of routinely handing all drugs and weapons over to the police also has value beyond the simple question of the chain of custody. It establishes a pattern of consistency with regard to these matters that allows the administrator to counter claims of discrimination in the treatment of individual students or groups.

DRUG TESTING

Societal concerns over drug use have in recent years been reflected in programs of sport. Testing programs designed to detect the use of prohibited substances have been employed at all levels of competition, from the Olympic Games to interscholastic sport programs. These testing programs have resulted in a great deal of publicity and public scrutiny and in some cases litigation.

The justification for any given drug test is usually seen as a function of the potential effects of the drugs for which one is testing and the reasons that underlie the use of the test. For purposes of sport, there are two general categories of prohibited substances: **illegal drugs** such as marijuana and cocaine, which are most commonly associated with recreational drug abuse; and **performance enhancers** such as steroids. Testing is conducted to detect the presence of these substances for one or more of the following three general purposes:

1. To help preserve the health and well-being of the athlete
2. To ensure equitable competition
3. To detect violations of applicable laws and league rules

Legal arguments against drug testing have most commonly focused on alleged violation of the due process and equal protection guarantees provided by the Constitu-

tion. As chapter 7 explains, only federal and state actors in public institutions are generally bound by the requirements of due process; private institutions that are free of governmental control are not.

This issue is not entirely clear cut, however, especially in the case of the National Collegiate Athletic Association (NCAA). Although the NCAA is a private, voluntary organization, many of its member institutions are publicly owned. Prior to 1985 the courts held that the NCAA's intimate involvement with state actors was sufficient to change its otherwise private functions to the category of state action. "State-supported educational institutions and their members and officers play a substantial, although admittedly not pervasive, role in the NCAA's program. State participation in or support of nominally private activity is a well recognized basis for finding state action" (*Parish v. NCAA*, 1975).

This reasoning allowed the courts to impose the same type of due process restrictions on private organizations such as the NCAA as they would impose on its individual member institutions. The courts' reasons for holding the NCAA to the requirements normally imposed on a state actor were as follows:

1. The individual members were state actors.
2. Those individual members were intimately involved in the activities of the NCAA.
3. The NCAA exercised regulatory control over those members much in the same way that a governmental body might.

The courts began to reject this line of reasoning in the *Blum v. Yaretsky* (1982) decision, which indicated a change in the level of involvement necessary for a private entity to be considered as functioning as a state actor. The court held in the Blum decision that mutual involvement with state actors alone would not suffice to support a finding of state action. The decision would rest instead on the degree of control that the private agency exerted over the actions of its public members (*Blum v. Yaretsky*).

In 1984, the federal district court clearly articulated the legal absence of state involvement in the actions of the NCAA:

It is not enough that an institution is highly regulated or subsidized by the state. If the state in its regulatory or subsidizing function does not order or cause the action complained of, and the function is not one traditionally reserved to the state, there is *no state action*. (*Arlosoroff v. NCAA*, 1984)

Therefore it would appear that, at least for the present, the NCAA and similar rule-making bodies are not considered to be state actors and therefore are not restricted by the due process and equal protection requirements of the Constitution. However, individual member institutions that are publicly funded *are* state actors and therefore can and will be individually held to the constitutional requirements of such when they employ drug testing procedures, even if the initial mandate for the testing has come from the rule-making body. Member institutions that are privately funded, on the other hand, would tend not to be faced with the same constraints.

Because drug testing through urinalysis is considered a search in the legal sense, school administrators seeking to employ such a test would be required to justify its use by showing that one of the following three factors was present:

1. The test was given with the written consent of the athlete.
2. The screening met the test of reasonableness: that is, it focused on specific persons with supportive facts (see Case 8.2).
3. The test was conducted subject to a valid search warrant.

Most drug testing in athletics is random and seldom focuses on particular situations in which there are factual reasons to suspect the use of a prohibited substance by a particular individual. Rarely are such tests conducted under the authority of a legally valid search warrant. The key to the constitutional validity of most athlete drug testing programs therefore lies in obtaining the **consent** of the athletes prior to the testing. Forms used to secure and record the voluntary acceptance of athletes should explain the nature of the test and the potential consequences of testing positive. They should also establish the fact that no coercion was used to gain the agreement of the athlete. Although the refusal to sign an NCAA drug testing consent document results in automatic and complete ineligibility, the courts still view the act of signing a drug testing release form as voluntary, because the person who refuses to sign does not get tested and is not disciplined, for example, by being dropped from school or reported to the police.

Similarly, a well-reasoned and carefully applied drug testing program for high school athletes was upheld because the athletic program itself was accepted by the students voluntarily with the understanding that it would place constraints on their behavior both on and off the field. In *Schaill v. Tippecanoe* (1988), the court noted that

interscholastic athletes have diminished expectations of privacy, and have voluntarily chosen to participate in an activity which subjects them to pervasive regulations of off-campus behavior; the school's interest in preserving a drug-free athletic program is substantial, and cannot adequately be furthered by less intrusive measures; the [school district] program adequately limits the discretion of the officials performing the search; and the information sought is intended to be used solely for noncriminal educational and rehabilitative purposes. (*Schaill v. Tippecanoe*, 1988; the Schaill case is discussed at greater length in Case 8.1.)

A similar decision was reached in a case involving intercollegiate athletics wherein the court noted that the denial of eligibility to participate in athletics does not amount to coerced consent to take part in the drug testing program. The NCAA and/or its member institutions, they noted, can and do withhold athletic eligibility for a number of reasons. In the words of the court, "certainly low grades, failure to use protective equipment, or medical reasons could result in the withdrawal of such eligibility" (*O'Halloran v. University of Washington*, 1988).

Although this concept of drug testing as a **voluntary program** has not yet been thoroughly tested in the courts, Steinbrecher has put forth an interesting argument with regard to its applicability (Steinbrecher, 1989). He notes that in the absence of some compelling state interest, it is generally unconstitutional to make the availability of a state-created privilege (such as playing on a school team) dependent upon a requirement that people give up their right to some constitutionally guaranteed protection(s) such as the 4th Amendment protection from unreasonable searches (Steinbrecher, p. 52). It is at least equally conceivable, however, that in the face of strong antidrug sentiment from society as a whole, the courts could consider, as they did in the previously cited Schaill case, that the need for a drug-free athletic program constitutes a compelling state interest.

MANAGEMENT GUIDELINES:
DRUG TESTING PROGRAMS

Certainly, the number of drug testing programs and the frequency of their application

in sport is likely to continue increasing as a result of societal pressures accompanying the increased publicity afforded to the dangers and the pervasiveness of drugs in sport. It is equally probable, therefore, that the frequency of litigation challenging these programs will increase until a definitive legal precedent is established. Although it is too early to articulate definitive guidelines for establishing a testing program, individuals contemplating such a course of action should take the following precautions:

1. Be sure there is a compelling reason to justify the testing with regard to both

   a. the importance of the issue in terms of health, equity of competition, or applicable law, and

   b. the application of the test to the particular group and setting involved. (For example, does the drug problem apply to junior high school basketball players?)

2. Carefully investigate alternative programs and procedures and select the one to be used based on factors of accuracy, cost efficiency, privacy, control of evidence, and the clarity and understandability of the results.

3. Inform all participants of the program in writing. The written documentation should identify testing procedures and should explain what the test is designed to disclose, how the results will be handled and interpreted, and the consequences of positive readings.

4. Provide a well-designed consent form that indicates the athlete's willingness to participate in the testing program.

5. Secure the assistance of legal counsel in the development and implementation of the program.

6. Recognize and accept the fact that the program will trigger a relatively high degree of questioning and criticism from some individuals or groups and

may even result in a court challenge. However, if you are truly committed to safe and equitable competition and to the promotion of a healthy lifestyle, the benefits of the program should significantly outweigh the risks.

CASE STUDIES

Case 8.1

A Justifiable Drug Testing Program

Langhorne High School has instituted a random urinalysis drug testing program for student athletes on all sport teams and cheerleading squads. It is designed to prevent drug and alcohol use, to educate and alert the athletes to the importance and potential dangers of the drug problem, and to maintain an athletic environment that is free of alcohol and drug abuse.

The program follows a carefully articulated and scientifically accurate methodology and includes provisions that guarantee that student athletes who test positive will not be subjected to academic disciplinary procedures or suspended from school. Further, no screenings will be conducted to ascertain whether or not a student is pregnant or uses birth control pills.

Several students indicated that they objected to the required testing as a matter of principle. They brought a lawsuit to test the legality and enforceability of the Langhorne policy.

There is very little case law upon which to base decisions regarding the advisability of a particular drug testing policy. However, this scenario is patterned after the Schaill case mentioned earlier, which was upheld by the courts.

This drug testing program was able to overcome a court test largely because of the thoroughness with which it was justified and the care that had been used to select the testing procedure. The program's case was further buttressed by the fact that it was aimed exclusively at maintaining a drug-free athletic environment. Toward that end it focused only on athletes and their screening and, if necessary, rehabilitation; it did not tie itself needlessly to more complex legal questions of academic discipline. Most importantly, program administrators had kept extensive documentation that demonstrated the impact of drug use on safe and equitable athletic participation.

Not all courts have been supportive of broad-based drug testing, however. In fact, oftentimes the requirement that all persons routinely submit to screening poses serious constitutional problems as seen in Case 8.2.

[Adapted from *Schaill v. Tippecanoe School Corp.*, 864 F. 2d 1309 (7th Cir. 1988)]

Case 8.2

An Unreasonable Drug Testing Policy

A small group of parents in the Pantheon Borough School District formed a coalition to request that the school board increase its efforts to combat drug and alcohol abuse among the students. In response to these demands, the administration began an investigation to determine the extent of substance abuse within the district. Based on a series of interviews with three students who were recovering substance abusers, the high school principal estimated that about one third of the student body used drugs and that over 90% used alcohol. The principal then called other schools that had implemented drug testing programs to obtain further background for developing a program for use in the secondary schools of Pantheon Township.

The school board approved the program, which was designed to implement urinalysis testing for all students in grades 6 through 12 who wished to participate in extracurricular activities. Essentially the students would be routinely tested at the beginning of the fall semester and at random during the course of the school year. Students were given the opportunity to verbally disclose their use of any substances that might lead to a positive response prior to the test. Some preventive measures were implemented to prevent the submission of false samples. After the test results were returned from the laboratory, students who tested positive would be excluded from extracurricular activities until such time as they passed a subsequent urinalysis.

Nick Flanders, a senior at Pantheon High School, decided to challenge the drug testing policy. He refused to submit to the required urinalysis and was immediately excluded from all extracurricular activities. Nick filed a class action suit on behalf of all current and future students who were subject to the Pantheon drug testing policy.

In adjudicating this matter, the court was required to investigate several issues that would be substantially similar in any dispute involving the legality of a search or drug testing procedure or policy. First, to justify action under the search and seizure provisions of the 4th Amendment, Nick was required to show that some form of state action was in fact involved. Because the Pantheon Borough School District was a public school system, the court agreed to investigate the allegations of wrongful search and seizure.

Having agreed to hear the matter, the court was next obligated to determine whether or not an actual search was involved. The courts have consistently ruled that the extensive quantity and variety of information that can be obtained through a urinalysis qualified it as a search within the constraints of the 4th Amendment, so this issue was disposed of quickly and simply.

The second requirement of a 4th Amendment analysis is the determination of whether or not the search in question was both reasonable in its inception and appropriately related to the circumstances that led to its development in the first place. In making this determination, the courts followed the guidelines of the T.L.O. decision (discussed earlier in this chapter), which require a reasonable and an individualized suspicion that the search would disclose evidence of wrongdoing, or, alternatively, evidence that the search was prompted by extraordinary circumstances. Because the Pantheon drug testing program was not based on individualized suspicions, it was Pantheon's responsibility to convince the court that extraordinary circumstances existed that justified the abridgment of student rights that the mandatory urinalysis represented. Reasonable arguments to this effect might include evidence that students involved in extracurricular activities were significantly more likely to be involved in drug use than their less active peers or that drug use by participants in extracurricular activities was substantially interfering with the normal function of the school.

As you might expect, the school board was unable to put forth either of these arguments successfully. Although the Pantheon School District was unquestionably sincere and correct in its belief that its students would benefit from a lifestyle that was free of drug or alcohol abuse, this generalization was by no means sufficient to meet the reasonableness standard required to institute across-the-board testing of all participants in extracurricular activities, especially without evidence of a direct or disturbing relationship either between the participants and drugs or between drugs and the extracurricular programs of the school. The court therefore granted Nick's request for an injunction that prohibited the Pantheon School Board from excluding him or any other student from participation in extracurricular activities based solely on their refusal to submit to urinalysis.

This scenario is based on the case of *Brooks v. East Chambers Consolidated Independent School District* (1989), which is also worthy of review in light of court comment regarding the nature, timing, and procedural laxity of the testing procedure itself. Most notable, however, is the clear limitation on the right to require urine testing or other searches of entire student bodies. This limitation is directly related to the 4th Amendment prohibitions against unlawful search and seizure, which anyone who plans to develop policies for conducting student searches or drug testing must keep in mind. To date, every court that has been asked to consider a policy that required testing an entire student body for drugs has found that policy to be in violation of the provisions of the Constitution.

[Adapted from *Brooks v. East Chambers Consolidated Independent School District*, 730 F. Supp. 759 (S.D. Tex. 1989)]

CHAPTER SUMMARY

The increased incidence of drug and weapons violations among young people in our society has led to increased use of searches and drug testing procedures in many areas of society, including programs of athletics. Searches conducted in school-related settings must meet the reasonable suspicion standard of justification and must be conducted in a manner that avoids undue intrusion on the privacy of the individuals involved and that maintains careful control over any evidence disclosed.

The legal principles governing drug testing are similar in many ways to those affecting searches. In fact, because of the wide variety of personal information disclosed by urine or blood analysis, these techniques are viewed as the legal equivalent of a search. In general, successful drug testing programs must demonstrate compelling justification for the testing, high standards of accuracy, maximal privacy for the testees, well-designed notification of the participants, and a carefully worded consent document.

KEY TERMS

Chain of custody (135)
Consent (137)
Illegal drugs (136)
In loco parentis (134)
Performance enhancers (136)
Probable cause (134)
Public officials (134)
Reasonable suspicion (134)
Two-prong test (134)
Voluntary program (138)

QUESTIONS FOR DISCUSSION

1. Give specific examples of circumstances in which probable cause or reasonable suspicion would be the appropriate standard of justification for a search. What specific evidence might fulfill the standard in each of the cited examples?
2. Develop a written policy, applicable to a local high school, for the conduct of a search and the control of any evidence disclosed.
3. Conduct a debate in class regarding the legal pros and cons of drug testing in sport. Support your arguments with specific reference to applicable laws and case precedent.

4. Redesign the facts of Case 8.2, An Unreasonable Drug Testing Policy, so that the courts would in all probability uphold its validity and application. Develop appropriate written materials in support of the program.

REFERENCES

Arlosoroff v. NCAA, 746 F. 2d 1019 (4th Cir. 1984).

Blum v. Yaretsky, 457 U.S. 991 (1982).

Brooks v. East Chambers Consolidated Independent School District, 730 F. Supp. 759 (S.D. Tex. 1989).

New Jersey v. T.L.O., 469 U.S. 325, 105 S. CT. 733 (1985).

O'Halloran v. University of Washington, 679 F. Supp. 997, 1001 (W.D. Wash. 1988).

Parish v. NCAA, 506 F. 2d 1028 (5th Cir. 1975).

Schaill v. Tippecanoe School Corp., 864 F. 2d 1309 (7th Cir. 1988).

Steinbrecher, J.A. (1989). Constitutional considerations of mandatory drug testing programs for intercollegiate student-athletes. *Quest*, **41**, 46-54.

ADDITIONAL READINGS

Clarke, K.S. (1985). Drug testing in sports. In H. Appenzeller (Ed.), *Sport and law contemporary issues*. Charlottesville, VA: The Michie Co.

Drowatzky, J.N. (1991). Drug testing: Whole loaf, half-loaf or no loaf. *Journal of Legal Aspects of Sport*, **1**, 82-95.

National School Safety Center, Pepperdine University. (1989). *Student searches and the law* (NSSC Resource Paper). Malibu, CA: Author.

Steinbrecher, J.A. (1989). Constitutional considerations of mandatory drug testing programs for intercollegiate student-athletes, *Quest*, **41**, 46-54.

CANADIAN APPLICATIONS FOR PART III

RIGHTS OF THE PARTICIPANT

THE SOURCE OF RIGHTS

Athletes and others in sport have the same rights as every other person in our society. These rights fall into two categories: substantive rights and procedural rights.

Substantive rights refer to essential or fundamental rights, typically those enshrined in a constitution, whereas **procedural rights** refer to the manner in which these substantive rights are granted or withdrawn. Procedural rights also refer to the procedures used to award and withdraw benefits. For example, possession of a driver's license has been described as a privilege or benefit that can only be awarded or taken away in accordance with certain procedures. Likewise, participation in sport is a privilege (as opposed to a right) that also provides opportunities for other benefits such as travel, clothing and equipment, and coaching opportunities. Such benefits can only be granted or withdrawn using fair and judicial procedures.

SUBSTANTIVE RIGHTS

The Canadian Applications for Part II discusses a number of substantive rights, such as the right to equal opportunity and access to programs without discrimination. It notes that such rights arose variously from the Canadian Charter of Rights and Freedoms ("the Charter") and from other provincial and federal human rights legislation.

The Charter is perhaps the most far-ranging source of substantive rights in Canada, entrenching a number of rights and freedoms into the Canadian Constitution. Section 2 of the Charter encompasses the freedoms. It is broken into four subsections, guaranteeing to every person

1. freedom of conscience and religion;
2. freedom of thought, belief, opinion, and expression;
3. freedom of peaceful assembly; and
4. freedom of association.

Section 6 of the Charter refers to the mobility rights of every person to take up residence and to pursue a livelihood in any province. Sections 7 through 14 are concerned with the legal rights or protections generally associated with criminal procedure: for example the right to life, liberty, and security of the person (Section 7); the right to be secure against unreasonable search or seizure (Section 8); and the right to legal counsel (Section 9).

Section 15 sets forth equality rights, specifically equal protection and benefit of the law without discrimination based on race, national or ethnic origin, color, religion, sex, age, or mental or physical disability. This section should perhaps be read in conjunction with Section 28, which guarantees the rights and freedoms referred to in the Charter equally to males and females. Linguistic rights are found in Sections 16 through 23. Multicultural rights and aboriginal rights are addressed in Sections 25 and 27 respectively.

Although the Charter is the most broadly based source of rights and freedoms within Canadian law, there is case law that suggests that its jurisdiction in the field of sport is limited. Specifically, Section 32 of the Charter has been interpreted to limit the Charter's application to matters of "government action." It would thus certainly apply to any institution or program arising from legislative or statutory sources, including programs within the public school system or government-run programs. However, sport organizations are typically voluntary, nonprofit organizations incorporated under provincial societies legislation. Although these organizations are incorporated under statutory authority, they derive their existence not from that legislation but rather from their own constitutions and by-laws. Therefore, they are not automatically considered government action and do not necessarily fall within the scope of the Charter.

It is also clear from case law that simply receiving government funding is not sufficient involvement to constitute "government action" and thus to invoke the jurisdiction of the Charter. But government is also involved in strategic planning, policy development, and personnel management with sport organizations. In fact, an analysis of government involvement in the internal affairs of sport organizations shows a dramatic increase since the early to mid-1980s, when the courts took the position that the Charter had no jurisdiction over these organizations. There is now a strong argument to be made that the Charter could be used to address a number of issues facing sport organizations, including the issue of athletes' rights, although it has not been tested in the courts.

One final source of substantive rights that is often overlooked is the sport organization or club itself. The relationship between the organization and its members (including athletes, coaches, officials, staff, volunteers, and board members) is contractual in nature. The terms of that contract are laid out in the organization's constitution and by-laws, which in turn give the organization its authority to implement policies, procedures, and regulations and to determine the rights of its members.

PROCEDURAL RIGHTS

The procedural rights of athletes and other members of the sport organization can be gleaned from the same sources as the substantive rights discussed in the preceding section. For example, Section 7 of the Charter, which refers to the substantive right to life, liberty, and security of the person, also incorporates the procedural right not to be deprived of those substantive rights without due process of law. Similarly, human rights legislation in Canada provides procedural protection for the individual. The procedural protection of the Charter and the other statutory sources all draw from, or "codify," the common law right to procedural fairness.

It has long been held that the right to procedural fairness applies to members and would-be members of sport organizations. Thus, even if aggrieved persons cannot bring themselves within the jurisdiction of either the Charter or another statutory instrument, they still have the common law right to procedural fairness. The requirement of procedural fairness applies to all organization decisions, whether they have to do with team selection, discipline of club members, procedures for drug testing or training regimes, appeals of decisions, or other matters.

Before the procedural fairness of an action can be determined, it must be clear that the action is authorized and that the person or body making the decision has authorization or jurisdiction to do so. Authorization is found in the constitution or by-laws of the organization, either directly or through delegated reference. For example, does the executive of the organization have the authority to suspend a member from the organization? Perhaps the by-laws state that only the board of directors may do this. Alternatively, the board of directors may have the authority to delegate certain powers and may have delegated this responsibility to a discipline committee.

Having established that the action is authorized and that the parties are acting within the scope of their jurisdiction, you must ask, Is the procedure fair? What is fair is often difficult to determine in particular circumstances. The case law has identified many types of unfair procedures. Indeed, what is fair in one situation may not be fair in another. Much depends on whether the issue at stake involves a right or a benefit and what the possible repercussions of the decision are. For example, the more stringent procedural safeguards of fairness are applied to more closely held rights and those actions or decisions with severe repercussions. The most stringent procedural safeguards can be found in a court of law where a person's freedom, or even life, may be at stake.

There are two basic rules or components of procedural fairness, which themselves comprise many subrules. The first is **the right to a hearing** and the right to be heard, and the second is **the rule against bias**.

The Right to a Hearing

The formality of a hearing will depend on the nature of the issue at stake. However, at the very least, a person must receive notice of a hearing, and the hearing must be fair. Although bodies may establish their own rules, parties appearing before hearing panels must know the full case to be made against them and must be given ample opportunity to present their own case. For example, in a disciplinary hearing the offending party must be given reasonable notice of the hearing and must be fully informed of what rule he has violated and in what way. He must then be given full opportunity to represent his position (or have an advocate act on his behalf). Depending on the formality of the proceedings, this may involve examining and cross-examining witnesses.

As another example, an athlete appealing the decision of a coach not to select her to a particular team must first have a forum to which to appeal. The by-laws of all sport organizations should provide for an appeal procedure, without which the only recourse an aggrieved party would have would be to appeal directly to the courts. The athlete must also know what selection criteria were used to make the team selection. The criteria should have been revealed to the athlete well before the selection procedure took place and should be as objective as possible to avoid allegations of bias or arbitrariness in the selection.

The Rule Against Bias

This second aspect of procedural fairness focuses on the impartiality of those making the decisions. Although impartiality may seem simple in theory, it is often difficult to apply in practice. Bias or a reasonable apprehension of bias may arise due to a **conflict of interest**. Suppose for example that a local coach is appointed to coach a provincial team; one of the coach's duties is to select that team. If some of the coach's own local athletes are among the contenders, then the coach might be more likely to choose local players than to choose many well-qualified players scattered throughout the province. Although common, this situation may well raise a reasonable apprehension of bias. Such a problem can be avoided by using a selection panel and a set of objective, preestablished selection criteria.

Another very serious yet also common example of bias arising from a conflict of interest occurs where one or more persons hearing an appeal had a role in the original decision being appealed. This has the effect of putting them in the untenable position of reviewing their own decision. Therefore, the by-laws of all sport organizations or procedures for implementing the by-laws should be written to prevent such bias from occurring.

JUDICIAL REVIEW

If there has been procedural unfairness, then a person has a right to recourse from such action. Many organizations provide an internal appeal process to hear appeals from such decisions. If the appeal itself is constituted properly and carried out fairly, the courts will not intervene in the decision. If, on the other hand, the unfairness persists through the appeal process, or if there is no appeal process, then the aggrieved party may seek **judicial review** of the matter.

On the whole, the courts are reluctant to become involved in the substance of a decision (for example, to determine whether the selection criteria enabled the organization to select the best possible representative team), but they will review the decision's procedural aspects. If a court determines that the procedure used is fair, the decision will be upheld. If it is determined to be unfair, the original decision will be declared void. In the latter case, the sport organization may revise its procedures to make them fair and then make the decision again using the revised procedures. If it chooses not to revise its procedures, the decision will remain void.

As a general rule, all internal avenues of recourse must be exhausted before an aggrieved party may apply to the court for judicial review. There are two exceptions to this rule, however: first, in cases where the procedures available are so blatantly unfair that further pursuit of recourse within the organization would be futile, and second, where time constraints preclude going through an internal appeal process. This latter situation is very common in the sports world because disputes often arise from decisions to select participants for certain competitive events that might be taking place almost immediately or for which a certain amount of preparation and training is necessary.

SEARCHES AND DRUG TESTING

Since the release of the report of the Commission of Inquiry into the Use of Drugs and Banned Practices Intended to Increase Athletic Performance (Canada, 1990), an inquiry held following the Ben Johnson steroid scandal at the Seoul Olympics in 1988, drug testing in sport has become a high-profile issue. From a legal perspective, there are two important aspects to this issue:

1. the procedures that are used in any drug-testing program, and
2. the legality of the testing itself.

The procedures used in many drug-testing programs are lax. For this reason, procedural requirements are very important in appeals of positive drug tests, and many appeals are won on this basis. The second aspect, legality of drug testing itself, becomes an issue only where the Charter of Rights and Freedoms applies. It is clear that the Charter would apply to school activities and likely that it would also apply to college activities. It is not so clear, however, that the Charter would affect university programs or national and provincial sport organizations. Therefore, in drug testing cases, the argument about the application of the Charter to universities and to provincial and national sport organizations becomes critical.

The Application of the Charter to Institutions Performing Drug Testing

For a discussion of the parties to whom the Charter applies, the reader should refer to the Canadian Applications for Part II. The Supreme Court of Canada has taken an ad hoc approach to determining whether or not the Charter applies to each entity coming before it, focusing on the relationship of each institution to government. The fact that an institution such as a university is created by statute and serves a public purpose does not necessarily imply that it is governed by the Charter. For example, in the case of *McKinney v. University of Guelph* (1990), the Court said that the fact that the institution served a "public purpose" was not sufficient to bring it under the Charter. For example, airlines and railways perform public services but do not form part of the government for the purposes of the application of the Charter.

In *Stoffman v. Vancouver General Hospital* (1990), the Supreme Court stressed the factor of control, distinguishing between ultimate control through statutory authority and routine control of an organization's own affairs through its by-laws (which are not imposed by some legislative authority). Thus, notwithstanding a mandate of public service, the fact that the hospital had control of its own affairs took it outside the scope of the Charter.

It is difficult to predict with any certainty whether or not Charter principles would apply to particular sport bodies. Their application depends on the involvement of government in a body's internal policies, rules, and procedures.

Government involvement has increased substantially since the time 10 years ago when the Courts last heard a Charter case involving a provincial sport organization and determined that the Charter did not apply. In light of the increased government involvement, a different view may now prevail.

If the Charter does not apply to the situation, then a drug-testing program must at least be authorized through the constitution and by-laws of the organization and must be performed in accordance with the principles of fundamental justice. This requirement is discussed more fully in the preceding section entitled "Procedural Rights."

Section 8 of the Charter (Search and Seizure) as a Defense Against Drug Testing

The main section that deals with the legality of drug testing is **Section 8 of the Charter**, which is very similar to the 4th Amendment to the U.S. Constitution, and which states that "everyone has the right to be secure against unreasonable search and seizure" (Canadian Charter of Rights and Freedoms, 1982, s. 8). The decision of the court in *Jackson v. Joyceville Penitentiary* (1990) confirms that the taking of a urine sample (the most common method of drug testing) can be described as a search and seizure, within the scope of Section 8 of the Charter.

Section 8 has been interpreted as providing to all persons a reasonable expectation of privacy (*Hunter v. Southam*, 1984). Indeed, Section 8 is intended to protect three aspects of privacy: spatial privacy, privacy of the person, and informational privacy (*R. v. Dyment*, 1988). Spatial privacy speaks to protection of an individual's property; privacy of the person provides protection against a physical search and its indignity; and privacy of information protects individuals from being compelled to disclose confidential information about themselves. Quite clearly, drug testing could breach all three aspects of an individual's right to a reasonable expectation of privacy.

Under what circumstances may this right be breached? The most obvious is when consent is not freely given. People such as athletes who freely agree to drug testing remove themselves from any Charter issue concerning the legality of such testing, assuming that a procedurally fair process is used in the testing program.

In most cases, the state must establish prior authorization (such as a search warrant) before it can conduct a search of any kind. In instances where a warrant is not obtained, the onus is on the Crown to prove, on a balance of probabilities, that the search was reasonable; in other words, that there were reasonable and probable grounds to conduct a search. Reasonable and probable grounds were defined by the court in *Hunter v. Southam* as follows:

> The State's interest in detecting and preventing crime begins to prevail over the individual's interest in being left alone at the point where *credibly-based probability replaces suspicion* [italics added]. History has confirmed the appropriateness of this requirement of the threshold for subordinating the expectation of privacy to the needs of law enforcement. (*Hunter v. Southam*, 1984, p. 167)

In other words, suspicion of drug use in an athlete is not sufficient: There must be a credibly based probability that an individual has used drugs to justify any search of the person by means of a drug test.

Jackson v. Joyceville Penitentiary (1990) is the sole Canadian decision that considers the constitutionality of mandatory drug testing under Section 8 of the Charter. The Penitentiary Service Regulations (1978) state that,

where a member considers the requirement of a urine sample necessary to detect the presence of an intoxicant in the body of an inmate, he may require that inmate to provide, as soon as possible, such a sample as is necessary to enable a technician to make a proper analysis of the inmate's urine using an approved instrument. [Penitentiary Service Regulations, s. 41.1(1)]

The court determined that the "regulation itself contains no standards, criteria, or circumstances relating to its application, for the guidance of staff or inmates, which would ensure that application is not unreasonable within the meaning of Section 8" (Penitentiary Service Regulations, p. 98). In other words, the regulation gave prison personnel complete discretionary power unconstrained by any objective criteria at all. The court did state that it was unlikely to find objectionable a scheme of random testing or testing of high risk groups, provided it was governed by some criteria or some threshold level of cause to justify the search.

By analogy, it is reasonable to suggest that the state may be barred from intruding into the individual's right to privacy by way of a drug-testing procedure without some threshold level of criteria required of "probable cause" as set out in the *Hunter v. Southam* decision. Assuming that the criteria to establish this probable cause in a drug-testing regime is sufficient, the *Hunter v. Southam* decision suggests that only *random* mandatory drug testing may be at odds with the Charter.

Section 7 of the Charter (Life, Liberty, and Security of the Person) as a Defense Against Drug Testing

The other section that may apply to drug testing is **Section 7 of the Charter**, which states: "Everyone has the right to life, liberty and security of the person and the right not to be deprived thereof except in accordance with the principles of fundamental justice."

As noted at the beginning of this application, Section 7 sets out certain substantive rights—the right to life, liberty, and security of the person—as well as certain procedural rights. However, the section does not provide an absolute guarantee of life, liberty, and security of the person; rather, it qualifies that one can be deprived of these rights only in accordance with the principles of fundamental justice. The issue of drug testing turns entirely on the judicial interpretation of liberty and security of the person. (The right to life is not germane to the issue.) However, should a court decide that a drug-testing regime infringed one of the interests protected by Section 7, the policy would violate Section 7 only if it failed to comply with the principles of fundamental justice. Therefore, the first step in applying Section 7 is to determine whether the drug-testing regime violates an individual's right to liberty and security of the person.

The Right to Liberty

Case law has consistently endorsed a flexible interpretation of the term "liberty" beyond simple freedom from bodily or physical restraint. In *R. v. Morgentaler* (1988), the court included in its interpretation of liberty the right to make fundamental personal decisions without interference from the state and concluded that the provisions of the criminal code on abortion deprived a woman of her liberty interest. In the previously mentioned case of *Jackson v. Joyceville Penitentiary* (1990), the court said that the obligatory urine test to detect the presence of alcohol in the body was a limitation of the individual's fundamental right to liberty. It seems likely, then,

that testing programs that require individuals to provide samples of bodily fluids constitute a deprivation of the liberty interest in Section 7 of the Charter.

Security of the Person

In *Dion and the Queen* (1986), the court determined that requiring inmates of prisons to provide samples of their urine caused them humiliation and constituted intrusions into the security and intimacy of their persons. In another case, the court found that "state interference with bodily integrity and serious state-imposed psychological stress" caused a breach of security of the person (*R. v. Morgentaler*, 1988, p. 56). Therefore, it seems reasonable to suggest that random mandatory drug testing would violate the right to security of the person as well as the right to liberty under Section 7 of the Charter.

Fundamental Justice

As the court noted in its decision in *Jackson v. Joyceville Penitentiary* (1990), even if a drug-testing regime violates one of the substantive interests provided for in Section 7, the drug-testing policy will be found contrary to the Charter only if it is not implemented according to the principles of fundamental justice. In deciding such a matter, the courts will likely scrutinize whether the particular mandatory testing scheme is both arbitrary and infringes on the testees' rights to procedural due process (see prior section entitled "Procedural Rights").

To determine whether a testing program is arbitrary, the court will likely assess whether the testing scheme is irrational and whether it is so unconstitutional that its use opens the door to abuse. This latter flaw was the primary grounds on which the Joyceville Penitentiary's drug and alcohol testing program cited earlier was found to violate Section 7. The court found that because the program had no governing criteria (in other words, prison authorities had complete discretion for compelling inmates to provide urine samples), it was arbitrary and as such violated the tenets of fundamental justice.

The final area of concern to the courts is whether the drug-testing program's procedures are fair. For example, the court will be concerned that testing schemes contain sufficient procedural safeguards, including confirmatory testing (double samples), sufficient notice requirements, and an opportunity to rebut a positive test result.

Section 1 of the Charter as a Justification for Drug Testing

Even if a particular drug-testing policy or regulation infringes on a Charter right under either Section 7 or Section 8, it may nonetheless be upheld under **Section 1 of the Charter**. Section 1 states: "The Canadian Charter of Rights and Freedoms guarantees the rights and freedoms set out in it subject only to such reasonable limits prescribed by law as can be demonstrably justified in a free and democratic society."

The framework for applying Section 1 was basically set out in *R. v. Oakes* (1986). An organization must demonstrate that its regulatory or program objective is sufficiently important to justify the infringement of the right (that is, it must bear on a "pressing and substantial concern") and that the means chosen are reasonable and justified, or appropriate, in terms of the objectives sought.

It is difficult to predict what evidence the Supreme Court of Canada would require to support or establish a pressing and substantial objective. In some cases, it has required a compelling body of evidence; in others, it has simply made assumptions with regard to the significance of the social problem. In any event, the problem must be one in which the safety of the public and other competitors, or associates, is seriously at risk. The Dubin Inquiry (see "Searches and Drug Testing," p. 146) helped

substantiate a problem of banned substance use at the elite level of competitive sport. Whether the same case can be made at the local and provincial levels, at the college and university levels, or at the secondary school level is uncertain.

The second step in examining a drug-testing program under Section 1 involves establishing proportionality between the testing procedures and the overriding state objective. The court will not allow a body to combat even a recognized social problem with methods that are flawed and tenuously related to their overall objectives. The court will examine the accuracy and effectiveness of the testing techniques. It will also consider whether the drug testing constitutes the least restrictive means of achieving the stated objective. For example, McBride (1989) notes that when several student-athletes challenged the Stanford University random mandatory drug-testing program, Stanford University stated as its objective the reduction and eventual elimination of drug use among its student body. In pursuit of this objective, the university instituted random mandatory drug testing among student athletes. In the final analysis it was determined that the preponderance of drug use on campus did not lie within the student-athlete population. Further, evidence showed that the testing did little to alleviate the situation. Educational methods were much more effective and much less intrusive.

The final aspect to be examined by the courts is the sanction to be imposed on those testing positive for drugs. Proportionality must exist between the importance of the objective and the injurious effects of the testing program. In other words, the problem may be remedied much more effectively by counseling and treatment than by suspension or termination of competitive privileges.

In summary, to uphold an otherwise unconstitutional drug-testing program under Section 1 of the Charter, it must be established that drug use among athletes is a pressing and substantial problem, that such testing is a rational or effective method of reducing such use, and that less intrusive methods for achieving the stated objectives of the program do not exist. The Ontario Law Reform Commission in its "Report on Drug and Alcohol Testing in the Workplace" (1992) takes the position that random mandatory drug testing by employers would fail to meet a constitutional challenge under any of the criteria just mentioned. Clearly there are some differences between workplace testing and testing in the sport arena, the main one being that workplace testing is concerned with performance deficits, whereas drug testing in sports is concerned with unnatural enhancement of performance. Nonetheless, like workplace drug testing, random mandatory drug testing (without consent of the athlete) in sport would probably fail a Charter challenge.

CASE STUDIES

Case CA3.1

Procedural Fairness: Bias, Notice of Hearing, and the Right to Make Representation

During the course of a diving meet, three athletes were to be selected to the team. Going into the final dive, the complainant, Depiero, was in first place, thus entitling her to be placed on the team. Her sister had previously been selected to the team. The coach directed the sister not to take the final dive in case it jeopardized the placement of the complainant. Evidence indicated that this was a remote possibility at best. The complainant was selected to the team, but the board of directors of the Canadian Amateur Diving Association refused to uphold the selection, declared the decision invalid, and replaced Depiero with a third diver.

The court held the action of the board to be unfair in both procedure and result. Depiero was the best diver (subject possibly to replacement by her sister). One of the voting board members was in conflict because he was coach of the third diver. Also, Depiero was given no notice of the meeting of the directors at which the decision to drop her from the team was made and was therefore unable to make any representations on her own behalf.

[*Depiero v. Canadian Amateur Diving Association* (1985), 32 A.C.W.S. (2d) 331 (Ont. H.C.)]

Case CA3.2

Procedural Fairness: Violation of Selection Criteria and Bias

The complainant, Brent Garrett, was a weight lifter who had dreamed of going to the 1990 Commonwealth Games in New Zealand. The National Weightlifting Federation had provided each athlete with a list of selection criteria and timelines for selection. Brent met all the criteria. Eventually he received notice of his selection to the national team and was told to report to the final preparation camp shortly before the team left for New Zealand.

Days before leaving for the competition, Mr. Garrett was told that he was no longer on the team. Shortly thereafter he was told that he would have to compete in a "lift-off" with an athlete he had bettered throughout the selection process but who had nevertheless been selected as an alternate to the team. Mr. Garrett participated in the lift-off and tied with the athlete but was still not placed on the team.

By this time it was too close to the competition for Brent to file any appeal of the selection process (if in fact an appeal was available). Instead he applied to the Court for an injunction to stop the alternate from being appointed to the team in his place and to be placed on the team himself.

Documents filed with the court show that the board of the Federation was somewhat confused about the timing of the selection process, but it was clear that Mr. Garrett had received notice of his selection to the team. The board subsequently directed the coach to reinstate Brent on the team. The coach refused. The Court learned that the coach was not only president of the association but was associated with the alternate athlete who had taken Mr. Garrett's place.

Eventually the Court ordered both the Federation and the coach to place Mr. Garrett on the team. Unfortunately, the structure of the selection process to the Canadian Commonwealth Games Team required the Canadian Commonwealth Games Association to make the final selection based on the recommendations of each National Sport Association. Although Brent Garrett's name was finally placed on the recommended list, the Canadian Commonwealth Games Association saw fit to overlook the recommendation and not place Brent on the team. Inasmuch as the Canadian Commonwealth Games Association was not named as a defendant in the lawsuit, there was little more that Mr. Garrett could do.

[*Brent Garrett v. Canadian Weightlifting Federation*, unreported (January 18, 1990), J.D. of Edmonton, Docket No. 9003 01227 (Alta. Q.B.)]

Case CA3.3

Procedural Fairness: Need to Exhaust Internal (Organizational) Remedies
The complainant, Robert Gray, was an international amateur discus thrower and a member of the Canadian Track and Field Association. As an association member, he consented to participate in regularly scheduled and random drug tests. Following one of those tests, Mr. Gray's initial urine sample (or A sample) tested positive for anabolic steroids, and he was immediately barred from further track and field competition. Subsequently, his second or B sample also tested positive. Mr. Gray was offered a hearing, but he declined and sought recourse through the courts instead.

Mr. Gray attacked his suspension on the grounds that it showed a lack of procedural fairness in the process in that he had not been afforded his full rights under Section 7 of the Charter and was suspended before the hearing was held. The Ontario High Court held that the Canadian Track and Field Association had given Mr. Gray the opportunity to be heard but that he had not availed himself of that opportunity. Mr. Gray's failure to exhaust the remedies available to him through the appeal process ruled out any judicial intervention on his behalf. Finally, the Court was of the view that the connection between the Canadian Track and Field Association and the federal government was not sufficient to invoke the Charter, and if they were wrong in that view, they held that there had been no violation of Mr. Gray's Section 7 Charter rights.

This case outlines the major elements that an association or organization should provide to an athlete who is to be disciplined: notice of the infraction and an opportunity to be heard by the disciplinary body. Finally, the association should adhere to its own rules.

[*Gray v. Canadian Track and Field Association* (1986), 39 A.C.W.S. (2d) 483 (Ont. H.C.)]

Case CA3.4

Procedural Fairness: Violation of an Organization's Own Selection Process

The selection criteria originally set for the Canadian ladies national golf team by the Canadian Ladies Golf Association's board of directors called for selection on the basis of the differential average in players' scores in national and international tournaments over the last 2 years. One person arbitrarily changed this process without the board's authorization and brought in a subjective element to team selection.

The Court, responding to a challenge to the team selection under the new criteria, said that the association board had broken its own rules by using a new team selection process without passing a formal resolution authorizing it. The Court ordered the association to disband the team and to either name a team using the original criteria or properly plan a motion changing the criteria.

[*Kane v. Canadian Ladies Golf Association*, unreported (September 18, 1992), Docket No. GS12154, (P.E.I.T.D.)]

Case CA3.5

Procedural Fairness: Violation of By-Laws

Several members of a skating club had their memberships revoked for conduct "injurious to the image of the club and figure skating as an amateur sport." The by-laws of the skating club used those very words as a ground for terminating membership but also required that an explanation for the termination of membership be given to the member. The affected members made an application to the Court asking that the decision to revoke their memberships be held void on the basis that they were not provided with sufficient information about the alleged behavior, contrary to the accepted principles of procedural fairness. An injunction was issued by the Court voiding the termination and restoring membership in the organization. The Court stated that the requirement of the by-laws that an explanation be given was not fulfilled simply by reciting in the notice to the member a ground upon which a membership may be terminated. The organization had in fact violated its own by-laws.

[*Kinnear v. Piper* (1978), 1 A.C.W.S. (2d) 573 (Ont. H.C.)]

Case CA3.6

Procedural Fairness: Breach of Contract

Ms. Maesson, a national volleyball player, had played on the national team previously but did not try out for the 1984-85 year due to sickness in her family. She advised the organization that she might attempt to join the team the following year (1985-86). A letter on behalf of the association confirmed to the athlete that she would be able to try out for the team at any time during the next year.

Shortly thereafter, Ms. Maesson changed her mind and decided to try out for the 1984-85 year, claiming she had the right to try out for the team at any time during the season. The association refused to allow her to try out for the 1984-85 year. She decided to take the matter to court. In interpreting the agreement between the parties, the Court found that, although the athlete might have had a contractual right to try out for the team for the 1985-86 year, she did not have such a right for the 1984-85 year.

[*Maesson v. Canadian Volleyball Association* (1984), 26 A.C.W.S. (2d) 279 (Ont. H.C.)]

Case CA3.7

Procedural Fairness: Full Disclosure, Bias, and Jurisdiction to Act

A number of athletes from the British Columbia Provincial Broomball Team were suspended following an incident of rowdiness on the bus while they were returning home from the Canada Games. The notice of suspension given to each of the affected players did not specifically identify the offensive behavior.

Several of the affected players sought an injunction from the British Columbia court to reverse their suspensions. The Court found that a number of the suspended players had not even been involved in the incident, that no specific conduct had been advanced by the organization to support their assertions of misconduct, that one of the directors voting on the suspensions had been present at the time of the incident and had served as a witness by relaying information to the board in support of the suspension, and finally that there were no existing rules or regulations of the organization that could be relied on in support of the suspensions. In each of these instances the Court found the suspension to breach the Plaintiff's right to procedural fairness, and thus declared the decision of the organization null and void.

[*Omaha v. British Columbia Broomball Society* (1981), 13 A.C.W.S. (2d) 373 (B.C.S.C.)]

Case CA3.8

Procedural Fairness: Limits of Judicial Review

Mr. Stachiw was a softball umpire and a member of the respondent Saskatoon Softball Umpires Association. The executive of the association suspended Stachiw following an allegation that he had been drinking beer at a game he was umpiring. The allegations were supported by a number of sworn statements of witnesses who had been present at the game. Stachiw was given notice of the hearing but did not attend and was subsequently suspended for 1 year. The association s constitution provided that the executive had the right to suspend any member for just cause and that the member had the right to appeal to the executive, whose decision would be final.

Mr. Stachiw appealed the decision and denied drinking the beer. The original witnesses who had sworn the affidavits recanted their testimony, but there was strong evidence that they had done so under duress. The executive took all the evidence into account and did not alter their decision regarding the suspension.

Mr. Stachiw appealed to the Court. The Court ruled that Mr. Stachiw was bound by the rules of the association and that he had been given a reasonable opportunity to refute the allegations made against him. Unless fraud could be proven, the Court would not interfere by reversing a decision that the elected executive had made in accordance with its powers as set out in the association's constitution.

[*Stachiw v. Saskatoon Softball Umpires Association et al.* (1985), 5 W.W.R. 651 (Sask. Q.B.)]

Case CA3.9

Procedural Fairness in Drug Testing

At the 1991 Canadian Foresters' Games held in Brantford, Ontario, the top two placing athletes in each event were required to undergo drug testing. As winner of his events, Jack McCann was selected for participation in a drug-testing procedure. The doping control procedures at the games were conducted under the supervision of the Canadian Federation of Sport Organizations for the Disabled (CFSOD), the games organizers, and representatives of the Sports Medicine Council of Canada/Canadian Anti-Doping Organization (SMCC/CADO). All testing was done in accordance with the *Doping Control Standard Operating Procedures*, a procedures manual of CADO.

In September, Jack McCann was advised that his urine sample had shown evidence of the banned substances stanozolol and metabolites. Upon confirmation of the results, Mr. McCann appealed the finding of the drug tests. According to procedural policy, an arbitration process was established and a hearing scheduled. Evidence was given under oath, and both sides were represented by legal counsel.

The only issue in dispute was the identification of the urine sample. Essentially Mr. McCann alleged that the urine sample that was coded to him on the date of testing, and that eventually tested positive for the steroids, was not in fact his urine sample. The operating procedures make it clear that the SMCC is responsible for the validation of doping control test results, and appeals of positive doping control test results are limited to technical, administrative grounds that may have jeopardized the integrity and ownership of the sample. The arbitrator has no jurisdiction to inquire into the fairness, reliability, or propriety of the testing itself.

All parties agreed that, after his event, Mr. McCann had been escorted to the testing area, where he was required to provide a urine sample.

However, conflicting testimony was given on the volume of the sample provided, coding of the sample, monitoring of the sample, splitting of the sample into two specimens, and the chronology of events during the complete testing procedure.

The arbitrator held in favor of Mr. McCann, stating:

> In my judgment, the Appellant has proved on a balance of probabilities that the integrity of the sample coded to him was jeopardized by the failure of the doping control officials to follow the labelling procedures set out in the SOP [Standard Operating Procedures] such as to impugn the validity of the test results. I also find that the Appellant has demonstrated error in the identification of Urine Sample Code #11696.
>
> [McCann v. The Canadian Anti-Doping Organization, Arbitration Award (May 20, 1992)]

KEY TERMS

Conflict of interest (145)
Judicial review (146)
Procedural rights (143)
Section 1 of the Charter (150)
Section 7 of the Charter (148)
Section 8 of the Charter (147)
Substantive rights (143)
The right to a hearing (145)
The rule against bias (145)

REFERENCES

Brent Garrett v. Canadian Weightlifting Federation, unreported case, January 18, 1990, J.D. of Edmonton, Docket No. 9003 01227 (Alta. Q.B.).

Canada (1990). Commission of Inquiry into the Use of Drugs and Banned Practices Intended to Increase Athletic Performance. Report (Commissioner: The Honourable C.L. Dubin).

The Canadian Charter of Rights and Freedoms, Part I of the Constitution Act, 1982, being Schedule B of the Canada Act 1982, c. 11 (U.K.).

Depiero v. Canadian Amateur Diving Association (1985), 32 A.C.W.S. (2d) 331 (Ont. H.C.).

Dion and the Queen (1986), R.J.Q. 2196, 30 C.C.C. (3d) 108 (Que. S.C.).

Gray v. Canadian Track and Field Association (1986), 39 A.C.W.S. (2d) 483 (Ont. H.C.).

Hunter, Director of Investigation and Research of the Combines Investigation Branch v. Southam Inc. (1984), 2 S.C.R. 145, 11 D.L.R. (4th) 641.

Jackson v. Joyceville Penitentiary (1990), 3 F.C. 55, 75 C.R. (3d) 174 (T.D.).

Kane v. Canadian Ladies Golf Association, unreported case, September 18, 1992, Docket No. GS12154, (P.E.I.T.D.).

Kinnear v. Piper (1978), 1 A.C.W.S. (2d) 573 (Ont. H.C.).

Maesson v. Canadian Volleyball Association (1984), 26 A.C.W.S. (2d) 279 (Ont. H.C.).

McBride, D.H. (1989). The NCAA drug-testing program and the California constitution: Has California expanded the right of privacy? University of San Francisco Law Review, 23, 253-290.

McCann v. The Canadian Anti-Doping Organization, Arbitration Award, May 20, 1992.

McKinney v. University of Guelph (1990), 3 S.C.R. 229, 76 D.L.R. (4th) 545.

Omaha v. British Columbia Broomball Society (1981), 13 A.C.W.S. (2d) 373 (B.C.S.C.).

Ontario Law Reform Commission (1992). Report on drug and alcohol testing in the workplace. Toronto: Author.

Penitentiary Service Regulations, C.R.C. 1978, c. 1251.

R. v. Dyment (1988), 2 S.C.R. 417, 55 D.L.R. (4th) 503.

R. v. Morgentaler (1988), 1 S.C.R. 30, 44 D.L.R. (4th) 385.

R. v. Oakes (1986), 1 S.C.R. 103, 26 D.L.R. (4th) 200.

Stachiw v. Saskatoon Softball Umpires Association et al. (1985), 5 W.W.R. 651 (Sask. Q.B.)

Stoffman v. Vancouver General Hospital (1990), 3 S.C.R. 483, 76 D.L.R. (4th) 700.

PART IV

WHO IS IN CHARGE?

Sport and physical activity cut across a wide range of age and organizational levels. Therefore, the issue of who may act as a teacher or coach and what form of training or credentials may be required to do so is complex and must be determined on the basis of the specific situation.

To understand the requirements for providing instruction or coaching within the public school system, you must first comprehend the overall nature and legal control of education policies in America and then the specific nature of the policies and procedures that govern teacher certification. You should keep in mind that certification requirements, like virtually all other specific education policies, are controlled by individual states. The general concepts discussed here in Part IV, therefore, must be applied within the particular requirements of individual state legislation.

There is currently a great deal of public and legislative interest in the certification of coaches (chapter 9), largely because of the increasing frequency with which coaches and the organizations and groups through which their teams and leagues are administratively controlled have been subjected to costly lawsuits related to individual acts of negligence. Although the occurrence of lawsuits in interscholastic sports is not a new phenomenon, the recent increase in claims against interscholastic coaches and the extension of such suits into the heretofore rarely challenged area of voluntary youth sport coaching has proved a great stimulus to the growing interest and current legislative action regarding the certification of coaches.

The tremendous growth of women's sports has in many cases intensified the problems associated with issues of sex discrimination in sport and physical activity. Chapter 10 discusses issues of fair employment in the area of sport and physical activity that are frequently pondered by the courts. It also offers practical guidelines to help administrators develop and maintain fair hiring and employment practices.

Successful athletes thrive on competition. Competition, to be meaningful, must be regulated in a manner that is consistent not only with the rights of the athlete but with the rights of all involved. Therefore, the role of governing bodies and the avenues of legal redress available to aggrieved participants, the legal limits of authority of governing bodies, and legislation dealing with the regulation of sport and physical activity are all vital topics in the study of the law of sport and physical activity. Chapter 11 describes the major structures that govern sport in North America and the sources and legal limits of their authority.

CHAPTER 9

MECHANISMS FOR CREDENTIALING PRACTITIONERS

R. W. Sears was a science teacher and head softball coach at Allentown High School. During his 8-year tenure, Mr. Sears received outstanding evaluations from administrators, parents, and students, indicating that he was a competent educator and caring role model.

Near the conclusion of the academic year, Mr. Sears applied for the vacant position of assistant football coach. During the summer approximately 6 weeks after he submitted his application, he was informed that he had been denied the position and that the board of education had chosen a recent college graduate to be both a "permanent substitute" and the assistant football coach.

Mr. Sears initiated a lawsuit claiming entitlement to the coaching stipend he would have received had he been hired to coach football during the fall sports season. In defending its decision not to hire Sears, the school board first cited concern over whether or not he possessed the necessary skills and experience to coach high school football. Although Mr. Sears had been a model teacher and outstanding softball coach, he had never played nor coached the sport of football.

The board also maintained that, because of the unique risk associated with football, especially the potential for catastrophic injury, it required that the coach be knowledgeable about the nuances of the sport. Moreover, the increasing number of lawsuits against school districts for injuries to athletes who were instructed by inexperienced coaches compelled them to seek a "qualified" candidate. The newly appointed "permanent substitute" was a former Division I-A college football player who, they claimed, "could better teach the proper fundamentals for safe participation."

Despite the school board's assertion that Mr. Sears was not the best candidate, the judge ruled otherwise, holding that he met the qualifications: "A teacher with a desire to acquire the skills is more 'qualified' than a professional or college athlete who did not teach." The judge also concluded that Mr. Sears had been improperly denied the opportunity to coach, because he was the only certified, in-district applicant at the time the vacancy was announced. As such, he was legally entitled to the position, and no further qualifications needed to be demonstrated. (Adapted from *Chambers v. Board of Education of the Township of Neptune* C. No. 291-85 [commissioner; September 5, 1985])

LEARNING OBJECTIVES

The student will be able to

1. explain the legal distinction between two major credentialing mechanisms: licensure and certification;
2. explain why a hiring authority should be familiar with the legal concept of vicarious liability when selecting individuals to staff their athletic programs; and
3. differentiate between three mechanisms used to credential practitioners in sport and physical activity: licensure, certification, and registration.

TEACHERS

The role of teachers in staffing interscholastic athletic programs is one of major importance. Without the interest and involvement of professional educators, student-athletes would not receive the complete benefits associated with interscholastic athletic participation. Teacher involvement is even more crucial, given that school systems are currently struggling to staff their athletic programs with qualified personnel. Currently less than 30% of interscholastic coaches have formal preparation, and as many as 90% of coaches in any given school district are not trained teachers (Partlow, 1992). Therefore, it is important to understand the bureaucratic system that affects these figures and the mechanism by which teachers come to be "in charge."

Before public education systems were created in the United States, teachers were hired by thousands of local authorities scattered around the nation. Over time, however, the responsibility for issuing teaching certificates was assumed by the 50 state education systems and a few large city school districts such as New York City and Chicago. Presently, teaching certificates are granted to individuals primarily on the basis of their professional preparation. In most states, the minimum educational requirements include a bachelor's degree and passage of an examination (see Table 9.1). Other prerequisites may include citizenship, health, age, and moral requirements such as the signing of a loyalty oath.

The primary objective of the teacher credentialing process is to assure the public that every teacher has met a minimum standard of competence. Each state performs this function differently, but all 50 states approve the content of teacher education programs—**accreditation**. For this purpose, many states adopt standards developed by either of two major agencies that accredit teacher education programs in the U.S.: the National Association of State Directors of Teacher Education and Certification (NASD-TEC) and the National Council for Accreditation of Teacher Education (NCATE).

In the process of granting a teaching certificate, a state has actually issued a license to teach. Many individuals incorrectly use this term interchangeably with certification. In strict legal terms, licensure and certification are discrete concepts. According to *Black's Law Dictionary* (1990), a **license** is "a permit, granted by an appropriate governmental body, generally for a consideration, to a person, firm, or corporation to pursue some occupation or to carry on some business subject to regulation under the police power."

Licensure laws are the most restrictive form of state regulation and are enacted to protect public health, safety, or welfare and to assure the qualifications of new practitioners. According to Shimberg (1985), licensing arose during the latter part of the nineteenth century to "weed out" physicians who had not been properly trained to practice medicine. By the early 1900s, most states had laws for licensing physicians, attorneys, dentists, and pharmacists. In addition, most legislatures established boards made up of practitioners in the licensed occupation to promulgate rules and regulations concerning entry qualifications, examinations, practice standards, and professional ethics.

The distinction, therefore, between licensure and certification is as follows: Licensure restricts the scope of practice so that it is illegal for someone without a license to practice a profession. For example, practicing medicine without a license might invoke criminal or civil penalties. Individuals who are noncertified, however, may offer services to the public, but they may not use the occupational title that is reserved for those who have met predetermined standards and thus are certified. **Certification**, therefore, is less restrictive than licensing in terms of its regulatory effect, yet it also serves to protect the public interest by identifying competent practitioners.

Within the teaching profession, the specific standards for licensure are delegated by state legislatures to state agencies such as state boards of education. For example, in Illinois the superintendent and the state board of education develop regulations in consultation with the state teacher certification board. Other states may delegate the authority differently, but the mechanism for credentialing teachers is basically the same: Under the direction of the state legislature, state boards make regulations and set policy, and state departments of education review credentials and issue teaching certificates.

Although the states function similarly in this regard, specific requirements for licensure vary considerably around the nation. For example, some states give licensure certificates that limit teachers to certain grades or subjects. Other states give broad certificates that allow a person to teach several different grades or subjects. Despite these differences, states have a number of fundamental requirements for individuals who seek teacher certification:

- admission to teacher education programs
- completion of an approved program
- standardized testing
- minimum GPA upon graduation
- performance evaluation
- continuing education

Table 9.1 shows the different requirements for entrance into teacher education programs and for receiving teaching certificates by state.

MANAGEMENT GUIDELINES:
HIRING QUALIFIED TEACHERS

The responsibility for enacting legislation and establishing policy regarding teachers rests with state legislatures and state boards of education, respectively. Under the direction of the state legislature, state school boards establish policy for teacher education and credentialing, and state education departments implement those policies.

Although the mechanism for credentialing teachers is basically a state function, the ultimate responsibility for hiring teachers rests with the local school systems (see Case 9.2). Besides ensuring that teachers are credentialed, schools must make certain that their teachers are qualified, which may mean that their qualifications exceed those required by the state (Appenzeller, 1985). Furthermore, if a local school board decides to impose minimum standards for employment, the requirements must be uniformly applied to all teachers in the district (McCarthy & Cambron, 1981; *Moore v. Board of Education*, 1971).

Because the most qualified teachers are in theory the least likely to be negligent, the challenge for local school districts is to develop and implement both meaningful and relevant in-service training programs for their faculty. Moreover, this training should include instruction in tort liability, because many educators lack adequate knowledge in education law and "have a tendency to practice 'preventive' law after the fact, i.e., management by crisis" (Dunklee & Shoop, 1988).

Many states currently require either continuing education or recertification for teachers.

Local school administrators should contact colleges and universities that offer teacher training programs for assistance in developing in-service programs. They should also contact their state department of education to determine what allowances, if any, are associated with teacher recertification. For example, most states previously accepted only graduate and undergraduate courses. More recently, states have revamped their policies to accommodate school-sponsored workshops and in-service training programs (Partlow, 1992). Finally, higher education administrators who are responsible for developing teacher training programs should ensure that undergraduate professional preparation curricula address the legal responsibilities of teachers (Dunklee & Shoop, 1988).

INTERSCHOLASTIC COACHES

For local school districts, staffing interscholastic athletic programs with qualified individuals is becoming increasingly challenging for a number of reasons. First, the continued expansion of interscholastic athletic programs for girls has increased the number of coaching positions available. Second, fiscal considerations have forced many school districts to eliminate physical education; historically the greatest number of qualified coaches have been physical education teachers. Third, in light of improving teaching salaries, many educators who are eligible to coach feel that coaching stipends are not commensurate with the time demands of the job and choose not to apply. Finally, many coaches are retiring because of factors such as the pressures of winning, year-round programs, lack of family time, lack of appropriate monetary compensation, and inability to handle job-related stress (Schmid, 1988).

In 1986-87, the Joint Committee on Coaching Certification of the National Association

Table 9.1 Requirements for Entrance into Teacher Education and Teacher Certification, 1990

State	Entrance into teacher education		Completion of teacher education/certification					
	Test	Minimum GPA	Test of basic skills	Test of general knowledge	Test of professional knowledge	Test of speciality area	Minimum GPA	Entry year assistance program
Alabama	X	X					X	
Alaska		X						
Arizona	X	X	X		X	X	X	
Arkansas	X	X[b]	X		X			
California	X[a]	X[d]		X[c]		X[c]		
Colorado	X		X		X	X		X
Connecticut	X		X					
Delaware			X		X			
Florida	X	X			X	X		X
Georgia	X	X				X	X	X
Hawaii			X	X	X		X	
Idaho			X	X	X	X	X	
Illinois					X	X		X
Indiana			X	X	X	X		X
Iowa								
Kansas	X	X	X	X	X	X	X	
Kentucky	X	X	X	X	X		X	X[e]
Louisiana	X	X	X	X	X	X	X	X
Maine			X	X	X			
Maryland			X	X	X	X		
Massachusetts								
Michigan		X						
Minnesota			X	X	X	X	X	X
Mississippi	X		X			X		
Missouri	X	X		X	X		X	
Montana			X	X	X	X[f]		
Nebraska			X		X	X		X
Nevada			X		X	X		
New Hampshire			X					
New Jersey	X	X		X[g]		X		

(continued)

Table 9.1 (*continued*)

State	Entrance into teacher education		Completion of teacher education/certification					
	Test	Minimum GPA	Test of basic skills	Test of general knowledge	Test of professional knowledge	Test of speciality area	Minimum GPA	Entry year assistance program
New Mexico	X		X	X	X			
New York			X	X	X			
North Carolina	X				X	X		X
North Dakota							X	X
Ohio						X		
Oklahoma	X	X						
Oregon					X	X	X	X
Pennsylvania			X	X	X	X		
Rhode Island			X	X	X	X		X
South Carolina	X				X	X		X
South Dakota		X						
Tennessee	X		X	X	X	X		X
Texas	X				X	X	X	X
Utah								
Vermont								
Virginia			X	X	X	X		
Washington	X				X[h]	X		X
West Virginia			X		X	X		
Wisconsin								
Wyoming	X	X						

[a]Used for diagnostic purposes; institutional option for use in admission.

[b]Students must rank in top one half of their class.

[c]In lieu of completion of approved subject matter preparation program.

[d]Requirement can be met by minimum GPA, class rank, or minimum college entrance test score.

[e]Effective 1990-91.

[f]To be implemented.

[g]For elementary education certification only.

[h]Effective August 1993.

Note. From *Educational Standards in the 50 States: 1990* by R.J. Coley and M.E. Goertz, 1990, Princeton, NJ: Educational Testing Service. Copyright 1990 by Educational Testing Service. Adapted by permission.

for Girls and Women in Sport (NAGWS) and the National Association for Sport and Physical Education (NASPE) conducted a national survey to assess the existence and nature of requirements for interscholastic coaching certification. The impetus for this survey was concern over the qualifications of individuals being hired to coach and the perceived increase in the number of ''walk-on'' coaches in interscholastic athletics.

In contrast to the mechanism for credentialing teachers (licensure), the type of certification discussed was

> the process by which a nongovernmental agency or association grants recognition to an individual who has met certain predetermined qualifications specified by that agency or association. Such qualifications may include graduation from an accredited or approved training program, acceptable performance on a qualifying examination, and/or completion of some specified amount or type of work experience. (U.S. Department of Health, Education, and Welfare, 1971)

For purposes of the joint committee's survey, a certified coach was defined as ''an individual who has completed a course of study designed specifically to prepare individuals who wish to coach in the schools, and has been authorized to coach by a certifying agency.''

The findings were as follows:

1. Ten states had no required standards governing the hiring of interscholastic coaches.
2. Twenty-five states required all coaches to hold a valid teaching certificate; nine states required all coaches to be employed in some way within the school district.
3. Twelve states did not require either a teaching or coaching certificate to coach; five states did not require assistant coaches to hold a certificate; two states

did not require minor sport coaches to hold a certificate.
4. Five states (Arkansas, Iowa, Minnesota, New York, and Wyoming) required a coaching certificate from some or all of their coaches.
5. Six states with established standards that related only to teacher certification (Alaska, Illinois, Indiana, Oklahoma, Oregon, and Wisconsin) had voluntary coaching certification programs.
6. Thirty-three states indicated that the requirements were the same at the high school level as at other levels such as middle schools; nine states indicated that they were not the same.
7. Twenty-nine states allow exceptions to the requirements; eight states do not. Most of the exceptions relate to the requirement to hold a valid teaching certificate.

Based on these findings, Sisley and Wiese (1987) encourage the physical education profession to consider the current practice of hiring interscholastic coaches in the U.S. They also suggest that professional organizations such as the **American Alliance for Health, Physical Education, Recreation and Dance (AAHPERD)**, state athletic associations, boards of education, and higher education institutions combine efforts to ensure that interscholastic coaches are properly trained to meet their coaching responsibilities. Cohen, 1992 (see *Additional Readings*) describes efforts to develop a national coaching education system.

MANAGEMENT GUIDELINES:

HIRING QUALIFIED INTERSCHOLASTIC COACHES

According to the coaching certification survey just cited, 35 states require that either all coaches or a majority of coaches hold valid teaching certificates. But, as mentioned earlier in this chapter, the demographics of the coaching profession are rapidly changing; in short, the demand for coaches currently exceeds the supply. Therefore, public school administrators are often forced to seek exceptions to state regulations when hiring coaches.

In addition, under the legal doctrine of **vicarious liability**, local boards of education are liable for the negligence of their teachers or other employees (see chapter 12). In this respect, school districts' practice of recruiting and assigning coaches in interscholastic athletics has been described as a "time-bomb ticking away the minutes to disaster" (Clear & Bagley, 1982).

Conversely, school boards that hire only certified personnel demonstrate their desire to provide competent supervision. In a tort suit, however, the question of responsibility is not likely to be determined by the employee's credentials but in terms of whether the board did all that it could to prevent the injury.

Moreover, local school districts have a duty to exercise due care in the selection of coaches and, in so doing, to protect athletes from reasonably foreseeable risks and dangers. The duty to protect athletes extends beyond using due care in selecting coaches; it will be satisfied only if coaches are not negligent in the performance of their duties (*Welch v. Dunsmuir*, 1958).

To prevent needless injuries and subsequent lawsuits from arising, a board should be sure to comply with both the letter and the intent of the appropriate state certification or service requirements. In addition, Clear and Bagley (1982) recommend that the board observe the following precautions:

1. Assign no one to coach unless they have completed systematic in-service.
2. Place all coaches under the direct supervision of an athletic director whose position holds minimum qualifications

of advanced professional study in coaching competencies.
3. Require all coaches to engage annually in formal in-service training to update skills in their coaching areas.
4. Develop and carefully enforce rules regarding length of practice, warm-up activities, and appropriate practice activities.
5. Provide ongoing in-service experiences with regard to the treatment of athletic injuries that are specific to the sport.
6. Permit no one to assist in practices or contests without proper orientation.
7. Cancel or delay the start of a sports season rather than use an untrained coach.

INTERCOLLEGIATE COACHES

The National Collegiate Athletic Association (NCAA) recently adopted procedures for certifying coaches from Division I institutions (NCAA, 1992). As of August 1, 1992, coaches of Division I sports must pass a timed, open-book examination before contacting prospective student-athletes. (Division II and III institutions must also administer certification procedures for coaches of sports that compete in Division I.) Participants are permitted to use copies of the *NCAA Manual* and other reference materials when taking the exam. Three separate exams with multiple-choice and true-false formats have been designed for basketball, football, and all other sports combined. A minimum passing score of 80% has been established to ascertain the coaches' knowledge of such topics as recruitment of prospective student-athletes and other eligibility issues.

VOLUNTEER COACHES

Approximately 20 million youngsters participate in both recreational and competitive nonschool sports throughout the U.S. (Micheli, 1990). Much of the time, however, these young athletes are being instructed by parents whose only exposure to sports was as young athletes themselves, perhaps decades ago. Although the experience of having played the sport is a valuable asset, other coaching skills such as patience, empathy, and enthusiasm are also desirable. The prevailing notion that the only qualification for being a coach is having played the sport is a myth (Martens, 1978).

Furthermore, volunteer coaches seldom receive formal training that would help them both communicate and demonstrate the skills that young athletes require to participate safely or to deal effectively with injuries that may occur in the course of practice or competition. Although well intentioned, these coaches may be exposing their athletes to serious injuries and themselves to subsequent lawsuits (see Case 9.1).

The obvious response therefore is to provide volunteer coaches with basic training in first aid, CPR, and general coaching concepts. Prior attempts to mandate this training, however, have been unsuccessful for both political and economic reasons. Despite the potential benefits of having trained volunteers, the factors inhibiting coaching certification are complex.

As early as the mid-1970s, youth sport educators were bemoaning the lack of an effective nationwide system for educating volunteer coaches and calling for the U.S. Congress to allocate resources to fund this effort (Martens, 1978). Unlike the Canadian National Certification Program, which was effective, the mechanism for both training and credentialing volunteer coaches in the U.S. was inadequate. Ten years later it seemed that little progress had been made,

for within that time, probably fewer than 20% of volunteer coaches had received any formal training (Kimiecik, 1988).

The difficulty with developing a nationwide coaching certification program is not only financial but logistical as well. There are over 3 million adults who volunteer to coach and administer youth sports programs in the U.S. For many of these individuals, the primary motivation for coaching is to spend time with their own children. As these young athletes advance through the recreational leagues, however, so do their parents. This pattern creates a substantial annual turnover rate (approximately 25%-40%) within youth sport programs. This explains, in part, why it has been so difficult to implement coaching education nationwide.

Despite these obstacles, some experts are convinced that certification will become mandatory in most states by the year 2000 (Micheli, 1990). Whether or not that happens, it is clear that, based on recent trends, legal questions regarding the performance and qualifications of volunteer coaches will continue to arise.

The Role of State Legislatures in Volunteer Coaching Certification and Liability

The U.S. Consumer Products Safety Commission reports that over 4 million children seek treatment for sports injuries in hospital emergency rooms every year. Although the number of injuries has been increasing (due in part to more children participating), prior to the 1980s, such injuries rarely resulted in lawsuits against volunteer coaches. Although injured victims retained the legal right to sue, volunteer coaches were perceived as "good people" who provided an important community service and therefore were seldom sued for negligence.

In the 1980s, however, attitudes began to change. Volunteer coaches were being accused of negligence for injuries sustained by their athletes. The resultant impact of these lawsuits on volunteerism and on the ability of youth sports leagues to obtain adequate insurance was devastating.

According to the Nonprofits' Risk Management & Insurance Institute (1990), "Premiums rose dramatically, coverage exclusions increased, and several types of coverage became unavailable. . . . As publicity about the lawsuits and insurance crunch raised volunteers' apprehension, their willingness to serve waned. . . . Many organizations suffered board resignations and volunteer recruitment difficulties."

State legislatures throughout the U.S. responded to the legal liability crisis and skyrocketing insurance costs by enacting civil immunity laws—laws that provide protection from lawsuits for both individuals and their volunteer organizations (Feigley & Heinzmann, 1988). The process of drafting these laws, however, often involves evaluating and balancing a number of competing interests. State legislatures must consider not only the personal liability concerns of volunteer coaches but also the rights of innocent victims who may become permanently disabled by a coach's negligence. Certain states have addressed this dilemma by immunizing only those volunteers whose organizations carry adequate insurance. Other states have established liability only when a coach is found to have acted in a manner that was significantly below the recognized minimum standard (for example, gross negligence or willful and wanton misconduct).

The state of New Jersey enacted the first such law for volunteer coaches—commonly referred to as the Little League Law—in May 1986. This legislation was initiated after four Little League coaches were sued by the parents of one of their injured players. (The case was eventually settled out of court for $75,000.) The interesting feature of the New Jersey law is that the civil immunity protection is tied to attendance at a safety orientation program. This educational requirement, however, should not be construed to be equivalent to teacher certification. Whereas in New Jersey, certification to teach is a regulatory function mandated by law and administered by the state, "certification" for volunteer coaches is nongovernmental and merely offers a measure of protection for those individuals who have attended safety training programs.

Moreover, state certification has nothing to do with one's eligibility for civil immunity. In fact, the New Jersey statute somewhat paradoxically excludes public and private school teachers from immunity unless they are acting in the capacity of a volunteer coach for a nonprofit organization or for a team affiliated with a county or municipal recreation department.

Finally, civil immunity protection for volunteer coaches varies considerably around the nation. The prevalence of these laws, however, has misled many volunteer coaches into believing that they are immune from suit; they are not. Volunteer coaches are still accountable for their actions.

MANAGEMENT GUIDELINES:

PROTECTING VOLUNTEER COACHES

Lawsuits arise even in states where volunteer coaches have civil immunity. The mere existence of a law does not preclude someone from bringing a suit. Furthermore, even though the volunteer has immunity, the organization may still be liable under the doctrine of vicarious liability. Therefore, administrators should focus on the following five basic responsibilities to minimize liability (van der Smissen, 1990):

1. Utilize only competent volunteers, and assign them to functions within their capabilities.
2. Establish rules and regulations and develop a system for communicating and enforcing them.
3. Develop detailed emergency procedures and train coaches to recognize and treat common sports injuries.
4. Provide instruction to coaches about proper supervision.
5. Respond to maintenance concerns and hazards.

ATHLETIC TRAINERS

According to Hossler (1991), only about 10% of the 24,000 high schools in the U.S. have athletic trainers who minister to the health care problems of student-athletes. Assuming that there are 5.6 million student-athletes, this amounts to about one trainer for every 5,500 individuals. In actuality, athletic trainers may be certified, licensed, or **registered** (see Table 9.2). Of the three mechanisms for credentialing practitioners, registration is the least restrictive form and requires that individuals merely file their name, address, and qualifications with a state agency before practicing the occupation.

To attain certification as an athletic trainer from the **National Athletic Trainers Association (NATA)** Board of Certification, a candidate must satisfy "BASIC Requirements" (including passing a three-part exam) and "SECTION Requirements" (academic and experience requirements).

The BASIC Requirements include

1. possessing a high school degree;
2. submitting an official college transcript at the baccalaureate level from an accredited U.S. college or university;

Table 9.2 National Athletic Trainers' Association Credentialing Requirements Listed by State

State	Type of Credential		
	Licensed	Registered	Certified
Delaware	X		
Georgia	X		
Idaho		X	
Illinois		X	
Kentucky			X
Louisiana			X
Massachusetts	X		
Mississippi	X		
Missouri		X	
Nebraska	X		
New Jersey		X	
New Mexico	X		
North Dakota	X		
Ohio	X		
Oklahoma	X		
Pennsylvania			X
Rhode Island	X		
South Carolina			X
South Dakota	X		
Tennessee			X
Texas	X		

3. proving current American National Red Cross Standard First Aid Certification and current Basic CPR (ARC or American Heart Association);
4. verifying that at least 25% of athletic training experience was attained in actual (on location) practice and/or game coverage in certain recognized sports; and
5. having the certification application endorsed by a NATA-certified athletic trainer.

The SECTION Requirements include obtaining athletic training experience under the supervision of a NATA-certified athletic trainer via one of the following two routes:

1. Curriculum—graduate from a NATA-approved athletic training education program (which includes 800 hours of supervised experience)
2. Internship—present documentation of having attained at least 1,500 hours of experience

In addition, effective January 1, 1993, each applicant must complete formal course work in health (including nutrition and substance abuse), human anatomy, physiology, kinesiology/biomechanics, and other subjects.

The NATA Board of Certification (1991) defines a certified athletic trainer as "an allied health professional who has a bachelor's degree from an accredited college/university, has fulfilled the requirements for certification . . . and has passed the NATA certification examination."

The six domains of athletic training are

1. prevention of athletic injuries;
2. recognition and evaluation of athletic injuries;
3. management, treatment, and disposition of athletic injuries;
4. rehabilitation of athletic injuries;
5. organization and administration of athletic training program; and
6. education and counseling of athletes.

RECREATION AND LEISURE SERVICE PERSONNEL

The **National Recreation and Park Association (NRPA)** offers three classifications of certification for recreation and leisure service personnel through its National Certification Board. The standards for these classification levels are as follows:

1. Professional: Certified Leisure Professional (CLP) who possesses a baccalaureate degree and has had at least 2 years of experience following the degree in a recreation, park resources, and leisure service position (Additional experience is required if the institution or program is not NRPA accredited.)
2. Provisional professional: individuals with educational qualifications but insufficient experience to qualify for the CLP classification
3. Technician: Certified Leisure Technician (CLT) who possesses an associate (2-year) degree in recreation from a regionally accredited educational institution (Additional experience is required if the associate degree is not in recreation or if the individual has only a high school diploma.)

After meeting the prescribed education and experience requirements, the individual must submit a $100 examination fee and then pass the CLP exam to receive full certification. Thereafter, professionals must renew their certification by attending professional continuing education workshops within each 24-month period from the date of initial certification or continuing certification.

SPECIALIZED ACTIVITIES

In recent years a number of nontraditional physical activities have become popular in sport and recreational settings: among them, aerobics, cross-country and downhill skiing, orienteering, racquetball, in-line skating, backpacking, rock climbing, canoeing, scuba diving, martial arts, sailing, and equestrian activities. In keeping with the risk management focus of this textbook, administrators should ensure that these activities are also taught by individuals who have had specific formal preparation. Several recognized professional agencies currently provide comprehensive preparation or certification programs in a wide variety of activities. Among them are the Professional Ski Instructors Association for skiing programs; the YMCA and the American Red Cross for aquatics programs such as water safety instructor, lifeguarding, sailing, canoeing; and the National Association for Underwater Instructors and the Professional Association of Diving Instructors for scuba programs.

Sport Instructors

Those who are knowledgeable about programs of sport and physical activity recognize that injuries are a potential consequence and that participants should generally assume an element of risk. That fact alone does not relieve the sponsoring agency from the responsibility of using qualified instructors. Consumers expect their instructors to be knowledgeable, to understand how to minimize the risk of injuries, and to properly treat injuries that occur. Because injury victims are becoming increasingly willing to seek compensation through the legal system, individuals who administer sport and recreation programs must be familiar with the mechanisms for credentialing practitioners.

Unfortunately there is no comprehensive resource available that lists all of the certifications offered by the **national governing bodies (NGB)** in sport. Efforts are currently under way through the **United States Olympic Committee (USOC)** to compile this data. In the meantime, individuals who are interested in becoming certified in a particular sport or specialized activity should contact the sport's national governing body for more information.

Fitness Instructors

Since the mid-1970s, the fitness industry has expanded into a billion-dollar enterprise with over 20 million participants (Missett, 1987). Nevertheless, by 1988 fewer than 25% of the estimated 100,000 fitness instructors in the United States had received formal training (Parks, 1990).

Concerning the quality of instruction in the fitness industry, which includes aerobic dance and dance exercise, Parks (1990) found that certification of fitness instructors had the potential to solve many problems, including high injury rates, unscrupulous owners/operators, and lack of standards. The value of certification in quality control was also cited in Nash (1985), who states that "certification tells the consumer that the instructor has demonstrated a certain standard of knowledge and competence . . . [and] satisfied nationally accepted criteria for safety awareness, injury prevention, and knowledge of anatomy and exercise physiology." A number of organizations, including the American College of Sports Medicine (ACSM) and the American Council on Exercise (ACE), have developed standards for credentialing practitioners in the fitness industry.

American College of Sports Medicine

According to Howley and Franks (1986), the recent proliferation of exercise videos and books has created an inaccurate public perception that little or no formal training is required to be a fitness instructor. Many physical education professionals have argued, however, that exercise leaders need special preparation to be effective. Although traditional undergraduate training programs in physical education have been aimed at preparing their students to teach in public schools, exercise leaders must be able to work with a variety of populations—young and old, healthy and nonhealthy.

Since 1975, the **American College of Sports Medicine (ACSM)** has been providing leadership in the fitness area by developing minimum competencies for individuals who work in both preventive and rehabilitative programs. In 1986 the ACSM specified the following six different categories of ACSM certification:

1. Health/fitness director
2. Health/fitness instructor
3. Exercise leader
4. Program director
5. Exercise specialist
6. Exercise test technologist

A certified health/fitness instructor, for example, in addition to possessing a baccalaureate degree in an allied health field, must demonstrate competence in designing and executing an exercise program. Due to the specificity and comprehensiveness of the training, ACSM certifications are widely recognized as the standard by many in the fitness and cardiac rehabilitation area (Howley & Franks, 1986).

American Council on Exercise

The **American Council on Exercise (ACE)**, formerly known as the International Dance-Exercise Association Foundation, is the largest not-for-profit fitness certification organization in the world. ACE certification is designed primarily for individuals who are interested in working with healthy adults.

Candidates for ACE certification must be at least 18 years of age and possess current CPR certification. Students are also encouraged to obtain instruction through an accredited training program. Thereafter, a $125 fee is required to take either of two 3-1/2-hour written exams: the Aerobics Certification Exam or the Personal Trainer Certification Exam. Certified individuals must renew their certification every 2 years by accumulating continuing education credits.

CASE STUDIES

Case 9.1

Volunteer Coach Certification

Jeffrey Bochar, age 9, was a catcher for the Waynesville Yankees baseball team. At the time of the incident that gave rise to this lawsuit, Jeffrey was in foul territory, approximately 15 ft from the playing field, warming up his teammate. The rest of the team members were in their assigned positions taking fielding practice with their volunteer coach, Wanda Lewis. No other adult coaches were present.

At the time of his injury, Jeffrey was wearing his protective equipment except for his mask. A practice pitch delivered by his teammate landed in front of Jeffrey, bounced up, and hit him in the left eye. The injury required treatment at a local hospital and extensive reconstructive surgery to the bone structure surrounding the eye. Jeffrey's parents sued Ms. Lewis in the Superior Court of New Jersey for willful, wanton, reckless, and gross negligence.

Given the prevailing New Jersey civil immunity statute for volunteer coaches, for the negligence claim to have been successful, the plaintiff would have needed to prove that Ms. Lewis had completely and recklessly disregarded her responsibilities as a coach. During the trial, however, the defense attorney emphasized Ms. Lewis's dedicated service as a volunteer coach. In fact, there were several corroborating witnesses who testified that Ms. Lewis was a conscientious and caring individual.

The judge relied primarily upon the civil immunity statute and ruled in favor of Ms. Lewis, dismissing the negligence claim against her. Shortly thereafter, however, Jeffrey's attorney resubmitted the case to the appellate court, subsequently arguing that Ms. Lewis was not entitled to the civil immunity protection because she had not taken a "safety training course." Her defense in that regard was that the league had not provided a course and that she had therefore been unable to comply with the statutory requirement.

The appellate court ruled that, even though the league had not provided Ms. Lewis with a course, she was "barred from reliance on the statutory immunity." The intent of the New Jersey state legislature was to grant immunity only to volunteers who had participated in a safety training program. Otherwise leagues could immunize their volunteers without instructing them on matters of safety. The case was remanded to the lower court for further consideration. In the interim, both parties agreed to settle without further litigation, and Ms. Lewis discontinued her duties as a volunteer coach.

This case clearly points to the need for recreation directors and youth sports administrators to be aware of the civil immunity laws in their states. It also demonstrates the importance of providing quality continuing education opportunities for volunteer coaches as a measure of protection against lawsuits and as a means for conducting safe programs.

[Adapted from *Byrne v. Fords-Clara Barton Boys Baseball League, Inc. and Dennis Bonk* N.J. Super. 185, 564 A.2d 1222 (A.D. 1989)]

Case 9.2

Physical Education Teacher Certification

Peter Brinkley was a certified physical education teacher who was hired by the Somerview Board of Education to teach health and also to serve as the school's athletic trainer. After he had been employed in that capacity for 4 years and had acquired tenure, Mr. Brinkley was informed that his position was being eliminated as part of a reduction in force due to declining enrollment and "reasons of economy."

During the following school year, a physical education teacher's position became available when a faculty member suddenly became ill. Mr. Brinkley applied for the position but was not hired. He sued the board of education for offering the position to a first-year teacher instead of to him.

At first glance, this case seems to address the same legal issue that was discussed in the scenario at the beginning of the chapter: namely, that among applicants with equal teaching credentials, the law gives preference to tenured, in-district teachers despite their experiential deficiency (see *Bednar v. Westwood Board of Education*, 1987). The fundamental issue in this case, however, was whether or not Mr. Brinkley's credentials legally entitled him to tenure and thus to preference for the vacant physical education teaching position.

Evidence presented to the judge revealed that, although Mr. Brinkley was hired as an athletic trainer and health teacher, he was certified only as a "teacher of physical education." State regulations specifically require that teachers be competent in their subjects and that they possess an appropriate endorsement for their teaching assignment. The board of education therefore acted illegally in hiring Mr. Brinkley to teach health, a subject for which he was not certified.

Moreover, the judge ruled that because Mr. Brinkley did not possess an "appropriate certificate" to teach health, his service could not be credited toward tenure. Therefore, Mr. Brinkley did not have seniority or preference for the position over the nontenured teacher who was hired. Thus his motion for summary decision was denied, and his petition was dismissed. This judgment, however, was only temporary until such time as the commissioner of education made his decision.

After reviewing the facts of the matter, the commissioner of education rejected the judge's recommendation and directed that Mr. Brinkley fill the vacancy in the physical education department. The Commissioner's decision was based largely on Mr. Brinkley's assertion that, because he was required to hold an appropriate teaching certificate to be the athletic trainer, he was entitled to a measure of security (that is, tenure) as a "teaching staff member."

The state board of education, however, disagreed. In a rather bizarre turn of events, the board, which was the final arbiter in this matter, rejected Mr. Brinkley's argument and concurred with the original decision to dismiss his petition. The board's ruling was based on the fact that there was no recognized position title for "athletic trainer." Under applicable regulations, only the county superintendent was authorized to determine the appropriate certifications, if any, for such positions. Furthermore, the board ruled, to establish requirements in the absence of regulatory authority did not elevate the position of athletic trainer to that of teaching staff member. "To hold otherwise would allow each local board of education to define what is a teaching staff member simply through its own certification requirements."

The implication of this decision for aspiring physical education teachers is to be aware of the specific requirements for being employed in a particular position in the public school systems. Throughout these legal proceedings, each arbiter agreed that only holders of "health education" and "health and physical education" endorsements were authorized to teach health in the public schools. That Peter Brinkley avowed this to his supervisors when he was initially hired "cannot be used to excuse the Petitioner's failure to acquire a health endorsement, and Petitioner's reliance upon such actions in the face of clear regulations to the contrary cannot be regarded as reasonable."

[Adapted from *Jennings v. Board of Education of the Borough of Highland Park, N.J.* OAL Dkt. No. EDU 3646 (A.D. 1988)]

CHAPTER SUMMARY

This chapter introduces the variety of credentialing mechanisms that exist for individuals who are involved in sport and physical activity. Learning these concepts can be challenging, not only because of the variety and large number of different activities involved, but because there are no uniform criteria for credentialing practitioners, even within a given field of study.

For example, with regard to the teaching profession, each state administers the licensing of teachers differently. Whereas one state may require only a bachelor's degree and passage of an exam, another state may require 1 or more years of successful experience before it will issue a permanent certificate.

Another factor that makes it difficult to understand the credentialing process is that quite often the terminology used to describe a given credential is inconsistent. Although we often think of teachers as being certified, the fact that the government has issued the authorization to practice means that they are licensed.

Licensure laws are the most restrictive form of state regulation and are enacted to protect public health, safety, or welfare and to assure the qualifications of new practitioners. Certification is recognition granted by a nongovernmental agency or association to someone who has met predetermined qualifications. Registration is the least restrictive form of regulation and usually requires only that individuals file their names and qualifications with a state agency before practicing the occupation.

More important perhaps than determining the type of credential required for a given occupation is knowing that the individual being hired for the position is competent. One cannot assume that all individuals who possess the minimum requirements are knowledgeable about their field and thoroughly prepared to act responsibly. Moreover, because administrators are often legally accountable for the actions of their coaches and instructors, they should develop and implement regular procedures for evaluating personnel and for providing continuing education opportunities to improve any deficiencies.

KEY TERMS

American Alliance for Health, Physical Education, Recreation and Dance (AAHPERD) (167)
Accreditation (163)
American College of Sports Medicine (ACSM) (173)
American Council on Exercise (ACE) (174)
Certification (163)
License (163)
National Athletic Trainers Association (NATA) (171)
National governing bodies (NGB) (173)
National Recreation and Park Association (NRPA) (172)
Registered (171)
United States Olympic Committee (USOC) (173)
Vicarious liability (168)

QUESTIONS FOR DISCUSSION

1. List three mechanisms that are used to credential practitioners in sport and physical activity.
2. Give four reasons why it has become increasingly difficult to staff interscholastic athletic programs with qualified individuals.
3. Explain why "certified" and "qualified" are not synonymous.

4. What impact did the 1980s legal liability crisis have on volunteerism? How did state legislatures respond?

5. Explain how consumers interested in attending aerobic dance classes can begin to differentiate between health clubs that offer similar programs.

REFERENCES

American College of Sports Medicine. (1986). *Guidelines for exercise testing and prescription* (3rd ed.). Philadelphia: Lea & Febiger.

Appenzeller, H. (1985). *Sports & law: Contemporary issues*. Charlottesville, VA: The Michie Co.

Bednar v. Westwood Board of Education, 221 N.J. Super. 239, 242 (App. Div. 1987).

Black, M. (1990). *Black's law dictionary* (6th ed.). St. Paul: West.

Byrne v. Fords-Clara Barton Boys Baseball League, Inc., N.J. Super., 185, 564 A.2d 122 (A.D. 1989).

Chambers v. Board of Education of the Township of Neptune C. No. 291-85 (Commissioner; September 5, 1985).

Clear, D.K., & Bagley, M. (1982). Coaching athletics: A tort just waiting for a judgment. *NOLPE School Law Journal*, **10**(2), 184-192.

Coley, R.J., & Goertz, M.E. (1990). *Educational standards in the 50 states: 1990*. Princeton, NJ: Educational Testing Service.

Dunklee, D., & Shoop, R.J. (1988). Educator's negligence: What, why, and who's responsible? *Educational Considerations*, **15**(2), 20-22.

Feigley, D.A., & Heinzmann, G.S. (1988, November). Protection for coaches extended to municipal volunteers. *New Jersey Municipalities Magazine*, pp. 14, 38-40.

Hossler, P. (1991). *The high school athletic training program*. Unpublished manuscript.

Howley, E.T., & Franks, B.D. (1986). *Health/fitness instructor's handbook*. Champaign, IL: Human Kinetics.

Jennings v. Board of Education of the Borough of Highland Park N.J. OAL Dkt. No. EDU 3646 (A.D. 1988).

Kimiecik, J.C. (1988). Who needs coaches' education: U.S. coaches do. *The Physician and Sportsmedicine*, **16**(11), 124-136.

Martens, R. (1978). *Joy and sadness in children's sports*. Champaign, IL: Human Kinetics.

McCarthy, M.M., & Cambron, N.N. (1981). Terms and conditions of employment. *Public school law: Teachers' and students' rights*. Needham Heights, MA: Allyn and Bacon.

Micheli, L.J. (1990, October 29). Children and sports. *Newsweek*, p. 12.

Missett, J. (1987). *Aerobic dance-exercise instructor manual*. San Diego: International Dance-Exercise Association (IDEA) Foundation.

Moore v. Board of Educ. of Chidester School Dist. No. 59, 448 F.2d 709 (8th Cir. 1971).

Nash, H.L. (1985). Instructor certification: Making fitness programs safer? *The Physician and Sportsmedicine*, **13**(10), 142-155.

NATA Board of Certification, Inc. (1991). *Credentialing information for entry level eligibility requirements, continuing education policies and disciplinary procedures*. Dallas: National Athletic Trainers Association.

National Collegiate Athletic Association. (1992). Coaches certification procedures distributed. *The NCAA News*, **29**(10), 1, 18.

N.J. Stat. Ann. 2A: 62A-6.

Nonprofits' Risk Management and Insurance Institute. (1990). *State liability laws for charitable organizations and volunteers*. Washington, D.C.: Author.

Parks, J.B. (1990). Directory of fitness certifications. *Journal of Physical Education, Recreation & Dance*, **61**(1), pp. 71-75.

Partlow, K. (April, 1992). Why has higher education abandoned coaching education?

Presentation at the 1992 AAHPERD National Convention. Indianapolis.

Schmid, S. (1988, October). Coping with the coaching shortage. *Athletic Business*, pp. 20-24.

Shimberg, B. (1985). Overview of professional and occupational licensing. In J. Fortune & Assoc. (Ed.), *Understanding testing in occupational licensing* (pp. 1-14). San Francisco: Jossey-Bass.

Sisley, B.L., & Wiese, D.M. (1987). Current status: Requirements for interscholastic coaches. Results of NAGWS/NASPE coaching certification survey. *Journal of Physical Education, Recreation and Dance*, **58**(7), pp. 73-85.

U.S. Department of Health, Education, and Welfare (1971). *Report on licensure and related health personnel credentialing*. DHEW publication 72-11. Washington, D.C.: U.S. Government Printing Office.

van der Smissen, B. (1990). *Legal liability and risk management for public and private entities*. Cincinnati: Anderson.

Welch v. Dunsmuir Joint Union High School Dist. of Cal., 326 P.2d 633 (Cal. 1958).

ADDITIONAL READINGS

American Coaching Effectiveness Program. (1993). *Interscholastic coaching: From accidental occupation to profession*. Champaign, IL: Human Kinetics.

Brinegar, P. (Ed.) (1990). *Occupational and professional regulation in the states: A comprehensive compilation*. Lexington, KY: National Clearinghouse on Licensure, Enforcement and Regulation and Council of State Governments.

Cohen, A. (1992, December). Standard time. *Athletic Business*, pp. 23-28.

Fortune, J. (1985). *Understanding testing in occupational licensing*. San Francisco: Jossey-Bass.

Tryneski, J. (1991). *Requirements for certification of teachers, counselors, librarians, administrators for elementary and secondary schools*. Chicago: University of Chicago Press.

PHOTOPHILE/Tom Tracy

CHAPTER 10

HIRING AND EMPLOYMENT PRACTICES

In 1973 Betty Nelson was hired as an associate professor of physical education at Upstate University. Six years later, Upstate hired a new head coach for men's basketball, Pat Patrick, at a salary of $43,000. Coach Patrick was named assistant professor and spent 75% of his time teaching and 25% coaching. Although Professor Nelson had previously coached tennis and bowling at Upstate, when Coach Patrick was hired she was no longer coaching and spent all of her time in the classroom. Professor Nelson, who earned about $600 less than the newly hired Mr. Patrick, claimed a violation of the federal Equal Pay Act in that her skills were equal to his. The court rejected Ms. Nelson's arguments, stating that the **Equal Pay Act**—the federal law requiring equal pay for equal work—applies to *jobs* requiring equal skills, not to employees who happen to possess equal skills.

Two years before hiring Coach Patrick, Upstate had welcomed Dr. Marie Larkin, who went on to coach women's volleyball, basketball, and track with considerable success. Upstate's volleyball and track teams participated in national finals under her reign. In addition, Dr. Larkin carried a full teaching load, served on various college committees, and was an advisor to students and student teachers. Finally, Dr. Larkin had been responsible for developing several courses, including one required for graduation. Dr. Larkin too claimed that, compared to Coach Patrick's, her salary differential was a clear violation of the Equal Pay Act. At the time her case was tried, Dr. Larkin was coaching volleyball and track, but not basketball. She spent two thirds of her time teaching physical education classes and one third coaching, earning $35,000. The court found that Coach Patrick and Dr. Larkin did perform substantially equal jobs. Under such circumstances, the Court was free to assess damages and injunctive relief to redress the wrongs arising out of a violation of the Equal Pay Act.

LEARNING OBJECTIVES

The student will be able to

1. evaluate the impact of legislation on hiring practices in sport;
2. define the circumstances under which male and female coaches and administrators may be treated differently by employers; and
3. distinguish unlawful discrimination in employment and disparate treatment of employees from lawful selection practices of employers based upon bona fide occupational qualifications.

LAWS GOVERNING EMPLOYMENT

At common law, employees were hired and fired at the will of the employer. That is to say, an employer who chose to hire or fire anyone or no one could and would simply do so, without interference from the government. The growth of the labor union movement, the enactment of the numerous civil rights laws on both federal and state levels, the National Labor Relations Act governing labor practices, and the various state and federal laws regarding labor have collectively created a body of law regarding employers and employees that is, needless to say, much different than the common law.

In addition, the common law doctrine of **employment at will**—the concept that an employer may discharge an employee at any time for any reason or for no reason at all—is being eroded in many jurisdictions across the country. Exceptions abound. Courts in many cases are determining the existence of a **contract of employment** based on their interpretations of various written and unwritten policies promulgated by employers to their employees that form the basis for employees relying upon the word of their employers that if they perform their jobs in a certain manner, they will be retained as employees and not fired at will. Personnel manuals, guides for employees, and written evaluation criteria have all been held to be evidence of contracts that are legally binding on employers. Practitioners should therefore be aware that a contract of employment need not be written on parchment with the words "Contract of Employment" emblazoned in Old English print. In fact, a valid contract of employment may be evidenced by a single page listing various policies and practices that is handed out to employees.

Apart from any civil rights considerations, the current body of law that pertains to hiring and firing is a far cry from the vintage doctrine of employment at will. Some preventive legal work in this area can minimize the possibility of litigation. Therefore it is wise to consult an attorney before hiring or, if you are the prospective employee, before taking the job so that the terms and conditions of employment can be explored and documented and claims avoided. Similarly, at the first sign of any potential problems in hiring or firing employees, it is wise to consult an attorney to determine the rights and liabilities of the parties.

To understand what constitutes unlawful discrimination, you must first understand the common law and statutory bases for employees and would-be employees to claim unlawful hiring and employment practices. The forerunners of modern day civil rights legislation are the Civil Rights Act of 1866, which was enacted on the heels of the demise of slavery, the adoption of the 13th Amendment to the Constitution, and the Civil Rights Act of 1871. The socially conscious 1960s saw the birth of the Equal Pay Act of 1963 and the Civil Rights Act of 1964.

The often litigated Title VII of the Civil Rights Act of 1964 precludes covered employers from discrimination against employees or potential employees on the basis of race, color, sex, religion, or national origin, except in cases of so-called **bona fide occupational qualifications** that are reasonably necessary to conduct the employer's business. "Covered employers" are institutions or individuals who employ 15 or more employees for each working day in each of 20 or more calendar weeks in the current or preceding calendar year.

In addition to the Civil Rights and Equal Pay Acts, Presidents Lyndon Johnson, John F. Kennedy, and others issued executive orders that further prohibit employment discrimination on the basis of race, color, religion, sex, or national origin by employers doing business with the federal government. Table 10.1 summarizes the provisions of major legislation that protects employees under the federal legislative scheme.

THE EQUAL PAY ACT

The federal Equal Pay Act is one of a number of federal and state laws that regulate certain employment practices. The act has had a far-reaching effect on hiring and employment practices of coaches, physical education teachers, and others in sport administration.

The Equal Pay Act makes unlawful discrimination on the basis of sex by paying lower wages to employees of one sex for work requiring equal skill, effort, and responsibility and performed under similar working conditions at the same place. The act has often been raised in the context of male and female coaches who have historically been treated differently at the bargaining table and been given different working conditions on the basis of their sex. Unilke some of the other laws that govern employment discrimination, the Equal Pay Act applies to everyone covered by the minimum wage and overtime laws as set forth in the Fair Labor Standards Act.

To prevail in claiming that an employer has violated the Equal Pay Act, a plaintiff must prove five elements:

1. That the employer is subject to the law
2. That the plaintiff and at least one member of the opposite sex have been employed to perform the same jobs and that those jobs require equal skill, effort, and responsibility, insubstantial differences aside. Under the law, *skill* refers to experience, training, education, and ability to perform the job. If the skill required is the same, there may still be a violation of the Equal Pay Act even if the plaintiff does not exercise his or her skills on the job as much as the coworker of the opposite

Table 10.1 Major Federal Employment Legislation

Legislation	Coverage	Protection provided
5th & 14th Amendments to the U.S. Constitution	All citizens of the U.S./all private and government employers	Due process—no person may be denied life, liberty, or property without due process of law
Civil Rights Act of 1866	All citizens of the U.S./all private and government employers	Proscribes discrimination on the basis of race only
Civil Rights Act of 1871	Public agencies only/state actors	Proscribes persons acting under the color of state law from depriving any person of the privileges or immunities secured by the Constitution in carrying out employment responsibilities in public agencies
Fair Labor Standards Act of 1938	All private and government employers	Deals primarily with wages and salary claims; establishes maximum hour limits and minimum wages and regulates child labor
Executive Order 10925	All government contractors	Requires that all government contractors adhere to affirmative action mandates in hiring employees
Equal Pay Act of 1963	All private and government employers	Proscribes discrimination with regard to salary and compensation; requires that coemployees of the opposite sex be paid equally for work requiring the same skill, effort, and responsibility when performed under similar working conditions
Title VII, Civil Rights Act of 1964 as amended by the Equal Employment Opportunity Act of 1972	All employers who employ 15 or more employees for each working day in each 20 or more calendar weeks in a current or preceding calendar year	Proscribes discrimination on the basis of race, color, sex, religion, or national origin, except where religion, sex, or national origin is a bona fide occupational qualification and is reasonably necessary to the conduct of a particular business
Federal Age Discrimination in Employment Act of 1967 (amended in 1974)	All employers who employ 25 or more employees for each working day in each 20 or more calendar weeks in a current or preceding calendar year	Proscribes discrimination on the basis of age; protects persons 40-70 years old
Vocational Rehabilitation Act of 1973	Federal government contractors	Federal contractors must take affirmative action measures to hire and accommodate otherwise qualified handicapped individuals

sex. The *effort* component refers to the exertion, mental or physical, required for the performance of the job. *Responsibility* relates to the authority delegated to the employee in the performance of the job. Beyond that, if the plaintiff needs to expend greater effort, use more intricate skills, or assume greater responsibility only occasionally, the job may not be "unequal" to that of the coworker of the opposite sex.

3. That the jobs are performed under similar working conditions
4. That the plaintiff's compensation is lower than that of the coworker of the opposite sex
5. That the plaintiff has been paid less because of gender

All elements of the statute must be proven if the plaintiff is to prevail in a claim under the Equal Pay Act. (See Cases 10.1, 10.2, and 10.3.)

The Equal Pay Act is only one of the laws that can assist a coach, teacher, or administrator whose rights are being violated. The development of statutory law with respect to hiring and employment practices has profoundly affected athletic institutions of all sizes, particularly in view of the growth of women's interscholastic and intercollegiate sports. To gain a working knowledge of the current status of the law as it relates to hiring and employment practices in sport, you must briefly consider the background of the law governing employment.

THE ROLE OF THE EQUAL EMPLOYMENT OPPORTUNITY COMMISSION

The United States Equal Employment Opportunity Commission (EEOC) is charged with the responsibility of administering federal legislation governing hiring and employment

practices. To that end, the Equal Employment Opportunity Act of 1972 authorized the EEOC to act as plaintiff in bringing lawsuits to enforce these laws.

Discrimination prohibited by the Civil Rights Act is often based on theories of **disparate treatment** and **adverse impact**. This means either that the employer treats certain employees differently than certain other employees or has established policies that result in differing treatment for affected classes of employees. Employees who allege disparate treatment and adverse impact must be able to show, for example, that they belong to a class of persons against whom discrimination is prohibited, applied for a job for which they were qualified, and were rejected. If the position remained open, the burden shifts to the employer to show lawful reasons for not having hired the prospective employee (*McDonnell Douglas Corp. v. Green*, 1973). Successful plaintiffs can receive back pay, seniority, and court orders directing their employers to reinstate them in their positions or to award them promotions.

Aggrieved parties are entitled to maintain lawsuits in the federal courts and damages are specifically available to successful plaintiffs for violation of civil rights with regard to unlawful employment discrimination. For its part, the EEOC is often called upon when athletic departments of schools and colleges decide that women cannot coach male sports or that they should be paid less for doing exactly what the coach of a male team does. Violations of Title VII may also be enforced by lawsuits brought by the EEOC or by aggrieved individuals. In addition, all but a few states have enacted laws against discriminating on the basis of a person's sex, race, color, religion, or national origin.

Due to the somewhat unique nature of the work performed by coaches and the usual practice of fielding separate teams for males and females, discrimination in the athletic area has often caused the EEOC to flex its litigation muscles in court.

ISSUES OF EQUAL PAY AND EQUAL OPPORTUNITY

One such object of government scrutiny was the Madison, Illinois, School District which, it was alleged, paid its female athletic coaches less than its male coaches for essentially the same assignments. Carol Long, the girls' track coach, was paid "substantially less" than the compensation paid to Coach Steptoe, a male coach of boys' track. Coach Steptoe had two assistants; Coach Long had only one. As a result, Coach Long had to put in as long a day as Coach Steptoe. Likewise, in girls' and boys' tennis, where Coach Long also happened to coach the girls' tennis team and Coach Jakich, a male, the boys' tennis team, Coach Jakich was paid more than Coach Long for the same work.

Coach Carol Cole also received unequal compensation as coach of girls' volleyball, basketball, and softball and as assistant coach of girls' track. The court found that Coach Cole was paid less to serve as head coach of girls' volleyball and basketball for each of those assignments than was the male coach of the boys' soccer team. In fact, as head coach of the girls' basketball team, she received lower pay than Coach Tyus, the male assistant coach of the boys' track team. Coach Cole worked longer hours than Coach Tyus, but other than that the work was substantially the same. Circuit Judge Posner ruled that the defendant, Madison Community Unit School District No. 12, discouraged women from applying to coach boys' teams, concluding that

an employer cannot divide equal work into two job classifications that carry unequal pay, forbid women to compete for one of the classifications, and defend the

resulting inequality in pay between men and women by reference to a 'factor other than [the] sex' of the employees. (*EEOC v. Madison Community School District No. 12*, 1987)

Linda Burkey was employed as a teacher by the Marshall County, West Virginia, public schools in 1970. She acquired tenure after a 3-year probationary period, took her master's degree in physical education from West Virginia University in 1976, and had a permanent teaching certificate from the State of West Virginia. Her second year of employment marked the beginning of the girls' interscholastic basketball program at the Moundsville High School: Burkey established this program and coached the team from its inception in 1971 through the 1975-76 season, compiling a 31-5 record. Her achievements were noted by the Moundsville City Council, who passed a unanimous resolution congratulating her for coaching her girls to a county championship in 1975. Although male teachers in Moundsville were paid a stipend for coaching boys' junior high school sports, it was not until 2 years after Burkey had established her basketball program that female coaches of girls' teams in the district were paid. Even then they were paid only one half the salary their male counterparts received, although two men who coached girls' sports were paid the same salary level as Burkey and her colleagues.

The official policy of the board of education was expressed in written statements and set forth as follows:

1. Only female faculty members could coach girls' athletics.
2. Boys' teams could have an unlimited number of coaches; girls' teams were limited to one coach per sport.
3. Boys had separate teams for each grade level; girls had to be content with one squad for 7th, 8th, and 9th grade students.

4. Girls' junior high teams could compete only against schools from within their own county; boys teams were not restricted.

5. Girls' seasons were limited to a specific number of games; boys' were not.

6. Unlike coaches of the boys' programs, coaches of girls' sports were required to allow every squad member to play in every game.

7. Squad limitations applied to girls' teams but not to boys' teams.

Burkey attempted to correct some of the inequities in the Moundsville athletic program, including the salary inequity. She tried to have her grievance heard in accordance with the school board's policy on grievances. Meetings were held, but her requests were denied.

Not content to walk away empty-handed from these injustices, Burkey filed a charge of unlawful discrimination on the basis of sex with the West Virginia Human Rights Commission and the U.S. EEOC. Six months later Burkey found herself transferred from the school where she had established a successful basketball program and had received several letters of commendation from the principals under whom she had served, and was also removed from her coaching position at the school. She was the only teacher "demoted" to a post of elementary school teacher from a position in a junior high school.

Burkey then filed a second charge with the EEOC alleging that her demotion was a retaliatory action by the school board in return for the initial discrimination charges she had filed.

The following year Burkey filed a third charge with the EEOC after her application to move to the John Marshall High School as a coach and teacher for the 1977-78 school year was rejected.

In one last attempt to use the administrative machinery of the federal government to

right a wrong, Burkey filed a complaint with the U.S. Department of Health, Education, and Welfare (HEW), again alleging that the school board and its officers were discriminating in the conduct of the district's athletic programs against female coaches and students on the basis of their sex, in violation of the U.S. Constitution.

HEW agreed with Burkey and issued a finding that both female employees and students were being illegally discriminated against under Title IX of the Education Amendments Act of 1972. Evidently neither this finding nor the determinations made by the EEOC that unlawful discrimination was occurring made a suitable impression on the defendant school district. As a result, after 5 years of administrative hearings and findings of two federal agencies not only of unlawful sex discrimination but of unlawful retaliatory action by the school district, Burkey on April 6, 1978, brought a lawsuit against the Marshall County Board of Education, seven present and former members of the board, the superintendent and assistant superintendent of schools, and the principal of Moundsville Junior High School.

The United States District Court for the Northern District of West Virginia found that the Marshall County Board of Education had a firm (although unwritten) policy to engage only male coaches for boys' athletic teams. The court, citing Burkey's coaching experience inside and outside the district, her physical education teaching experience, her participation as an athlete, the fact that she had included basketball and track and field units in her physical education classes, and her academic pedigree including her master's degree plus extra course work in physical education, found that she was as qualified if not more qualified than 14 male coaches employed by the Marshall County School District.

In fact, the court said Burkey's responsibilities

required work, skill, effort, and responsibility equal to that required of the male coaches of boys' basketball at Moundsville Junior High School during those years. As were the male coaches of boys' basketball, Mrs. Burkey was responsible for selecting, training and coaching in interscholastic competition a junior high school basketball team. Such responsibilities necessitated a knowledge of the rules of girls' junior high basketball, which were and are identical with the rules of boys' junior high school basketball, as well as a knowledge of the proper techniques of coaching and teaching student athletes. As did the male coaches of the boys' junior high school basketball teams, Mrs. Burkey held daily practice sessions with her team over a basketball season of substantially the same length of time as the boys' season, traveled with her teams to away games, and was responsible for scheduling games for her teams. (*Burkey v. Marshall County Board of Education*, 1981)

The court also found that the salary differential was based solely on Burkey's sex, and not on any other factor. As a result, Burkey was awarded back pay with interest, and the school district was ordered to offer her the next available vacant physical education teaching position in junior high or above and further to offer her the position of head girls' basketball coach at any school where she was offered a teaching position in accordance with the order of the court.

Although Burkey had to run an 8-year legal marathon involving several state and federal agencies and was demoted from two positions and passed over for a third before she was properly vindicated and awarded damages, the case proves that there are a variety of legal remedies available to an employee whose employer engages in unlawful discrimination.

MANAGEMENT GUIDELINES:

FAIR HIRING AND COMPENSATION PRACTICES

Management should make sure that its hiring and compensation practices comply with applicable federal, state, and local laws. Doing so will diminish legal exposure to equal employment opportunity claims and lawsuits brought by employees and would-be employees who feel that they have been treated less than fairly by their employers or potential employers. The maze of statutory, administrative, and case law governing hiring, firing, and promotion practices of employers makes these areas virtual minefields for litigation. Therefore, the alert administrator will seek the advice of counsel (or compliance officer in a larger institution) in establishing and maintaining personnel policies and practices.

Volumes have been written advising employers how to comply with applicable law and to avoid negative consequences of noncompliance or allegations of noncompliance. Such a comprehensive treatment of the topic is beyond the scope of this book. However, administrators should be prepared to operate within the framework of the following precautions:

1. Job descriptions should be carefully formulated with a view toward establishing an appropriate compensation level to the job performed while at the same time clearly defining the employer's expectations as to the work to be accomplished and the manner of accomplishing it.
2. Criteria set forth in postings, notices, and advertisements should match job descriptions.
3. Care should be taken to publicize job openings in such a way that a wide

range of candidates have the opportunity to apply.

4. Advertisement copy should be reviewed to ensure that no objectionable or unlawful criteria are set forth or implied.

5. Similarly, employment applications and written communications from the institution about candidates should be reviewed to prevent requests for information that are legally suspect.

6. Appropriate checklists should be developed with the advice of counsel for evaluating applications and information gleaned from personal interviews.

7. Form letters should be developed, again with the advice of counsel, to acknowledge receipt of written inquiries, offer interviews to candidates, reject the applications of candidates, and invite candidates for second interviews or to submit further information.

8. Careful records should be kept of all job applications and their disposition. Adequate data should be maintained to comply with all laws to which the institution is subject. This does not mean, however, that administrators should amass more data than is necessary to accomplish the purpose for which the data is kept. It has been observed that pointless record keeping, often aided by the use of computers, may subject an employer to the additional burden of producing reams of potentially damaging data in the discovery phase of a lawsuit (Diedrich & Gaus, 1982). Keep records, but keep them under control.

9. Compensation should be based on clearly identifiable and quantifiable criteria, with due regard to the Equal Pay Act where applicable, and other relevant criteria and applicable laws.

10. Performance appraisal guidelines should be firmly established throughout the institution. Performance evaluations should be completed and reviewed on a regular basis for compliance with the established policy of the employer.

11. Avoid (and train staff to avoid) offhand remarks about "great *young* prospects" or "we need to hire several *girls* to work in the office."

12. Personnel manuals, employee handbooks, and all written materials disseminated to staff regarding job performance, personnel policies, compensation, promotion, and discipline should be carefully reviewed by counsel and identified so as not to be misconstrued as constituting an employment contract. The advice of counsel is critical in this area.

CASE STUDIES

Case 10.1

Sex and Age Discrimination in Hiring and Compensation Practices
Eloise Jacobs, 36 years of age, was hired by the College of William and Mary as administrative assistant for intramural sports. Ms. Jacobs was at the time a part-time employee and remained so during the term of her employment with the exception of the fall semester of 1976, when she worked full time but still as a "temporary restricted" employee. In 1975 she became director of women's intramurals for the ensuing school year and coached the women's junior varsity basketball team. Ms. Jacobs also taught in the physical education department. In the 1976–77 and 1977–78 school years, she was promoted to women's varsity basketball coach, remained as director of women's intramurals, and continued to teach bowling. (The prior year she had taught softball and basketball.)

In March of 1978, Ms. Jacobs applied for one of four full-time positions in the women's department of physical education that were announced by the college. She was not hired for any of the positions.

Coach Jacobs brought suit against the college, claiming not only a violation of the Equal Pay Act, but that she had been discriminated against on the basis of her sex and that her civil constitutional rights had been violated.

Ms. Jacobs, who was a former athlete, high school coach, and secondary school teacher with a master's degree in guidance and counseling, compared her wages to those of two male coaches: baseball coach Mr. Jones and basketball coach Mr. Parkhill.

Coach Jones was a 19-year employee of the college and associate professor of physical education, a full-time position. He worked approximately 15 to 17 hours per week in the classroom and had been intramural director since 1965, having overall supervision of about 20 activities on campus. More than 1,200 male students participated in intramurals each year at the college. Coach Jones's salary in the school year 1977-78 was $17,320.00. During baseball season, Mr. Jones testified that he spent about 3 hours a day on the field and also that he had responsibility for maintaining the intramural fields and the gymnasium, which he accomplished by using college employees and graduate assistants working under his supervision. Coach Jones received no additional salary for performing his duties as intramural director or maintaining the fields and gymnasium. He held a master's degree in education and administration.

Coach Parkhill, also a full-time employee, was hired in 1972 as assistant basketball coach and was promoted to head coach in 1977. His salary at that time was approximately $17,000.00. As head coach, he routinely made recruiting trips, which often lasted for a week or two at a time. His duties also included academic counseling. Mr. Parkhill had a master's degree in physical education. He was assisted by two assistant coaches, who each taught about 6 hours a week.

The United States District Court for the Eastern District of Virginia heard Ms. Jacobs's case. The jury awarded Coach Jacobs $51,200.00 on the Equal Pay Claim.

However, Judge Kellam, in ruling on a motion made by the defendant, College of William and Mary, for a new trial on the ground that the jury's verdict was contrary to the law and the evidence, reversed the jury's finding and entered an order dismissing the claim. Judge Kellam stated flatly: "There is a complete absence of any evidence of sex discrimination" (*Jacobs v. College of William and Mary*, 1981, p. 798). Judge Kellam noted that Ms. Jacobs was employed for 9 months only, compared to the year-round employment of Mr. Jones and Mr. Parkhill. As to recruiting responsibilities, even the plaintiff admitted that any recruiting she did was done on her own. Although the men's basketball program was playing in Division I of the NCAA—a condition that required active recruiting, scholarship funds, and the wherewithal to generate revenues by producing a winning team—the women's program, for whatever reason, was not playing in Division I, but rather under Association of Intercollegiate Athletics for Women (AIAW) regulations, which prohibited the college from receiving grants-in-aid or recruiting expenditures of the kind undertaken by Coach Parkhill for women's basketball. Judge Kellam concluded:

> Any attempt to compare equal performance which requires equal skill, effort and responsibility between plaintiff and baseball Coach Jones fails. He teaches full time, while plaintiff does not. This is enough to establish a difference, although there are many others. As to comparison with Parkhill, the men's basketball coach, the differences in skill, effort and responsibility are numerous, as are the duties. A substantial part of Parkhill's position is work, effort and skill in recruitment, requiring extended travel and absence from his home, along with writing and telephoning, while plaintiff's required duties were telephoning, writing or responding to letters; Parkhill's employment extends to full employment twelve months a year, while plaintiff's duties are for nine months and generally limited to three days a week; Parkhill's coaching is in Division I, and plaintiff's is a wholly different type. As to the assistant coaches, they have teaching responsibilities of six hours a week and are annual employees. Further, and of importance, is the fact men's basketball is a revenue-producing sport and women's basketball is not. (*Jacobs v. College of William and Mary*, 1981, pp. 797-798)

Thus the court found that Coach Jacobs failed to show that her job was comparable to that of her male colleague in terms of skill, effort, and responsibility. In fact, all three criteria—skill, effort, and responsibility—were substantially different, as the court pointed out. Therefore, Ms. Jacobs could not prevail in her claim under the Equal Pay Act.

Coach Jacobs also claimed that she was not hired as head coach of women's varsity basketball by reason of being discriminated against due to her age, in violation of the Age Discrimination in Employment Act. Approximately 88 applications were received for the four full-time positions that were advertised by the college in March 1978. A search committee chose 24 names from among those applications and then narrowed the list down to 14. The appointments were to be made upon the selection of the entire department faculty, who reduced the list from 14 to 8 and then to 5. The faculty viewed a chart that set forth the various items of information on each candidate, including athletic experience, coaching experience, teaching experience, and the like. The candidate who was selected for the head basketball coaching position, a female, was the unanimous choice of the department faculty. Noting that three of the five members of the search committee were over 40 years of age, and that Coach Jacobs did not have a master's degree in physical education, which was listed as a requirement, Judge Kellam concluded:

There is no evidence that age was ever mentioned by any member of the selection committee or faculty during the process of grading or discussing the qualifications of applicants for the position of a bsketball coach, or that the issue of age played any part in the selection. (*Jacobs v. College of William and Mary*, 1981, p. 800)

[Adapted from *Jacobs v. College of William and Mary*, 517 F. Supp. 791 (E.D. Va. 1980, *aff'd* Mem. 661 F.2d 922) (4th circuit, 1981), *cert. denied* 454 U.S. 1033, 102 S. Ct. 572, 50 L. Ed.2d 477 (1981)]

Case 10.2

Federal Equal Pay Act Issues

On March 11, 1974, Mary Institute, a corporation that operated an elementary school, a middle school, and a high school that collectively spanned grades K through 12, hired Arlene Horner as a part-time instructor of physical education in the middle and upper schools. Her undergraduate degree was in physical education, and she had completed some graduate credit courses. She had taught for 2 years part-time and one full-time summer session at the time she was hired but was not a certified teacher. Ms. Horner's starting salary was $7,500.00.

Two other teachers were hired about the same time as Ms. Horner: Dan Casey, also at a salary of $7,500.00, and another female physical education teacher, Carol Diggs, at a salary of $6,500.00. All three teachers were hired as middle and upper school instructors. The following year, Cynthia Gill was hired as a physical education teacher at a salary of $7,700.00.

In her first year, Ms. Horner was given the task of implementing a gymnastics program and coaching junior varsity field hockey and varsity tennis, supervising recess, and assisting in extracurricular activities.

After hiring Coaches Horner, Casey, and Diggs, the headmaster of the schools learned that there would be another vacancy in the physical education department. A search was begun for a physical education teacher who would be able to construct a curriculum and handle administrative duties such as ordering equipment for the physical education department. In June of the same year, Ralph Thorne, a certified physical education teacher with 2 years of full-time experience, was hired at a starting salary of $9,000.00. In his first year, Mr. Thorne taught physical education, set up a new curriculum, and coached junior varsity basketball. Mr. Thorne also participated in the parents' day convocation by reporting to parents on the physical education programs, administered the president's physical fitness test, and instituted intramural activities.

At the end of his first year, Mr. Thorne's salary was raised to $10,400.00. This increase was meant to reward Mr. Thorne's work and presumably to keep him as an employee, because he had received an offer to return to his previous job to teach and become a head coach.

At the same time, Ms. Horner was offered a $600.00 raise, bringing her salary to $8,100.00. Although Ms. Horner, like Mr. Thorne, had established extracurricular activities, the headmaster felt that Coach Horner did not enthusiastically support the schools' athletic teams and that she left school during her free periods. Nevertheless, the headmaster's testimony revealed that he had not communicated any dissatisfaction to Ms. Horner when the two met to discuss her compensation for her second year at the school.

Over the next two years, 1977–78 and 1978–79, Mr. Thorne received raises that were $200 to $300 higher than those Ms. Horner received. During those school years, both Ms. Horner and Mr. Thorne initiated and supervised various intramural programs and after-school activities, served as faculty advisors to a number of students, and served on school committees. In addition, in the 1978–79 school year, Coach Thorne established and served as head coach of the varsity teams in soccer and cross-country.

Ms. Horner sued her employer, the Mary Institute, in the U.S. District Court for the Eastern District of Missouri. After a 3-day trial, Judge Meredith found for the defendant school, indicating that the plaintiff "was not a particularly innovative teacher," whereas Ralph Thorne, the male teacher who was making a higher salary, "was a credit to the school and outstanding on the faculty" (*Horner v. Mary Institute*, 1980).

On appeal, the Circuit Court of Appeals found that

Thorne's job was not substantially equal to Horner's in terms of "skill" or "responsibility." Thorne was to develop and implement a physical education curriculum for children in grades K–4. Horner, by contrast, was to teach courses selected by someone else. . . . The Court could conclude that Thorne's job required more experience, training, and ability, all of which are factors to consider in determining whether jobs require substantially equal "skill" under the Equal Pay Act. . . .

There was also evidence to find that Thorne's job was not substantially equal to Horner's in terms of "responsibility." Thorne reported directly to his school head and to parents on his physical education programs. The District Court was entitled to conclude that his job differed from Horner's in terms of degree of accountability and the importance of job obligation. . . . There is evidence to find that [Headmaster] Stearns met Thorne's demand not because Thorne was male but because Thorne's experience and ability made him the best person available for the job and because a higher salary was necessary to hire him. The differential was based on a factor other than sex. . . .

Because Horner failed to establish that her job was substantially equal to that of Thorne, the amount by which Thorne's salary exceeded hers is not relevant under the Equal Pay Act. (*Id.* at 714-714.)

[Adapted from *Horner v. Mary Institute*, 613 F.2d 706 (8th circuit, 1980)]

Case 10.3   **Differences in Compensation Practices for Coaching Boys' and Girls' Teams**

Barbara Wallace and Ann Leopold were each paid $324 per year to coach both the varsity and junior varsity girls' high school basketball teams at their respective high schools. The high schools where Barbara and Ann teach are in the White Valley School District, which has four high schools. Joe Wesley and Robert Stanton were each paid $324 to coach the varsity and junior varsity girls' basketball teams at their respective high schools.

The coaches of the boys' basketball teams in the White Valley School District were paid much more. The varsity coaches of boys' basketball were paid $972—three times the salaries paid to Coaches Wallace, Leopold, Wesley, and Stanton—in their first year, and their salaries were raised to $1,080 for their second year of coaching varsity boys and to $1,296 for the third year. The coaches of the junior varsity boys' teams were paid $756 in their first year, $864 in their second year, and $972 for the third and following years of coaching boys' junior varsity basketball.

Ms. Wallace and Ms. Leopold brought suit in federal court under the Civil Rights Act, claiming that they had to perform more coaching duties than the coaches of the boys' teams because they had to first establish the girls' basketball program (the boys' program was already established), and because each woman coach was assigned to many more players than any of the men who coached the boys' teams.

Barbara and Ann lost their case because they were not discriminated against due to their sex: The male coaches of girls' basketball were paid the same as the female coaches of girls' basketball. The court did not recognize the salary differential to violate the Civil Rights Act; coaches of the same sports were paid differently on the basis of the sex of the sport's participants, and not the sex of the coaches.

[Adapted from *Jackson v. Armstrong School District*, 430 F. Supp. 1050 (1977)].

CHAPTER SUMMARY

A variety of federal and state statutory and administrative remedies are available to coaches, physical education teachers, and athletic administrators who are adversely affected by unlawful discrimination in hiring, compensation practices, or working conditions. Civil rights legislation empowers both federal and state governments to bring legal proceedings against employers charged with unlawful discrimination and employment practices. The victims of these practices can maintain their own lawsuits for money damages, equitable relief, and reinstatement to positions.

In the athletic and physical activity areas, unlawful discrimination is most frequently found to exist on the basis of sex. Conflicts between male and female coaches with respect to compensation, allocation of resources, and working conditions related to disparities between male and female teams are frequently the subject of civil rights litigation. Unlawful employment discrimination is generally predicated on disparate treatment or adverse impact on employees of one sex and is not based on the sex of the participants in the activities that the employees are coaching or supervising.

KEY TERMS

Adverse impact (185)
Bona fide occupational qualifications (183)
Contract of employment (182)
Disparate treatment (185)
Employment at will (182)
Equal Pay Act (181)

QUESTIONS FOR DISCUSSION

1. What are the factors that make an employer who pays different wages to employees of different sexes liable under the Equal Pay Act?
2. Identify some ways in which the courts and the legislative arm of government have weakened the doctrine of employment at will.
3. Name four forms of unlawful discrimination practiced by employers in hiring, retaining, or promoting employees. Name three forms of lawful discrimination in hiring.
4. What precautions should every employer take before publishing an employee handbook?

REFERENCES

5th and 14th Amendments U.S. Constitution
Burkey v. Marshall County Bd. of Educ., 513 F. Supp. 1084 (N.D. W. Va. 1981).
Civil Rights Act of 1866. 42 U.S.C. s. 1981.
Civil Rights Act of 1871. 42 U.S.C. s. 1983.
Civil Rights Act of 1964. 42 U.S.C. s. 1981, 1983, & 1985.
Diedrich, W.L., Jr., & Gaus, W. (1982). *Defense of equal employment claims.* New York: McGraw-Hill.
Equal Employment Opportunity Commission v. Madison Community School District No. 12, 818 F.2d 577 (7th Cir. 1987).
Equal Pay Act. 29 U.S.C. s. 206 (d)(1)(1963).
Exec. Order No. 10925, 29 Fed. Reg. 1977 (1961).
Fair Labor Standards Act of 1938.
Federal Age Discrimination in Employment Act of 1967 (Amended in 1974) 29 U.S.C. 623
Horner v. Mary Institute, 613 F.2d 706 (8th Cir. 1980).
Jackson v. Armstrong School District, 430 F. Supp. 1050 (1977).
Jacobs v. College of William and Mary, 517 F. Supp. 791 (E.D. Va. 1980), *aff'd*, 661 F.2d 922 (4th Cir. 1981), *cert. denied*, 454 U.S. 1033 (1981).
McDonnell Douglas Corp. v. Green, 411 U.S. 792 (1973).
Vocational Rehabilitation Act of 1973 29 U.S.C. 1988 Sec 701 et seq.

ADDITIONAL READINGS

Kite v. Marshall, 661 F.2d 1027 (5th Cir. 1981), *cert. denied*, 454 U.S. 1120 (1981).
Modjeska, L.M. (1988). *Employment discrimination law.* Rochester, NY: The Lawyers Co-operative Publishing Company.
Price v. Cohen, 715 F.2d 87 (3d Cir. 1983), *cert. denied*, 465 U.S. 1032 (1983).
Richey, C.R. (1988). *Manual on employment discrimination and civil rights/actions in the federal courts.* Charlottesville, VA: The Michie Co.
Sidle v. Majors, 264 Ind. 206, 341 N.E.2d 763 (1976).
Spector, H.A., & Finkin, M.W. (1989). *Individual employment law and litigation.* Charlottesville, VA: The Michie Co.

CHAPTER 11

THE ROLE OF GOVERNING BODIES

rofessor Jerry Tarkanian became tenured in 1977—4 years after being hired as head mens' basketball coach at the University of Nevada, Las Vegas (UNLV). UNLV is a publicly funded institution and a member of the National Collegiate Athletic Association (NCAA). Several years earlier, the NCAA Committee on Infractions had notified UNLV's president of an "inquiry" into charges that the university had committed violations of NCAA rules regarding recruitment. Following the direction of the NCAA, UNLV launched its own investigation and enlisted the aid of its attorneys and the attorney general of Nevada to do so. In the fall of 1976, UNLV had concluded its investigation and exonerated Tarkanian and the university.

Following its procedures for dealing with such allegations, the NCAA Committee on Infractions conducted 4 days of hearings that resulted in a finding of 38 violations of NCAA rules, 10 of which were attributed to Coach Tarkanian.

Under NCAA rules, the Committee on Infractions, after conducting its investigation and hearings, made a recommendation to the NCAA Council, who is empowered to accept or reject the Committee on Infractions' recommendations. Almost 5 years after UNLV was first informed of the investigation, the NCAA Council adopted the recommendations of the Committee on Infractions. A 2-year period of probation, including exclusion from postseason play and television appearances, was imposed. Coach Tarkanian expected to be suspended during the probation period because the NCAA Council had threatened more severe sanctions for the university if the suspension was not carried out.

As a result, UNLV did impose the suspension. Tarkanian sued the university in the courts of the State of Nevada, claiming that he had been deprived of property and liberty without due process. The trial judge agreed with Tarkanian and issued an injunction preventing UNLV from taking the action against Tarkanian.

The NCAA, which was not sued, filed papers in court, appearing as *amicus curiae*: a "friend of the court"—that is, a party "with strong interest in or views of the subject matter of an action, but not a party to the action . . . [who] may petition the court for permission to file a brief, ostensibly on behalf of a party, but actually to suggest a rationale consistent with its own views" (*Black's Law Dictionary*, 1990). The NCAA took the position that its disciplinary proceeding was being undermined by the court's action and that as a result the NCAA should be permitted to appear in the action. The NCAA argued that, in any event, Mr. Tarkanian was neither denied due process nor treated in any way inconsistent with UNLV's obligation to him. The Supreme Court of Nevada agreed with the NCAA that the association was indeed a necessary party to the lawsuit and reversed the decision of the trial court. Subsequently, the coach brought another lawsuit, this time against both his employer and the NCAA.

Mr. Tarkanian won his trial 4 years later in the Nevada courts. Deciding that the NCAA was engaged in state action and had denied the coach due process of law, the trial court once again ordered that no suspension was to be imposed on Jerry Tarkanian. In addition, the court ordered that there were to be no further proceedings against or penalties imposed on UNLV.

The NCAA appealed to the Supreme Court of Nevada. The court found that the NCAA was indeed a state actor (acting, albeit indirectly, in the place of the government) and that Mr. Tarkanian had not been afforded due process of law in the proceedings that culminated in the recommendation of a 2-year suspension.

However, on December 12, 1988, in a decision that sent substantial shock waves through the sports law community, the U.S. Supreme Court in *National Collegiate Athletic Association v. Tarkanian* (1988) reversed the judgment of the Nevada Supreme Court, declining to rule the NCAA's role in the penalty meted out to Mr. Tarkanian as state action. Justice Stevens wrote for the court:

Neither UNLV's decision to adopt the NCAA's standards nor its minor role in their formulation is a sufficient reason for concluding that the NCAA was acting under color of Nevada law when it promulgated standards governing athlete recruitment, eligibility, and academic performance. . . . UNLV delegated no power to the NCAA to take specific action against any University employee. The commitment by UNLV to adhere to NCAA enforcement procedures was enforceable only by sanctions that the NCAA might impose on UNLV itself (*NCAA v. Tarkanian*, 1988).

LEARNING OBJECTIVES

The student will be able to

1. distinguish between voluntary associations and governing bodies mandated by law;
2. define the limits of legal authority granted to governing bodies imposed by statute and case law;
3. determine if and when governing bodies will be held to constitutional standards of due process of law;
4. articulate the legal significance of a governing body's internal rules and regulations;
5. trace the steps necessary to mount a successful legal challenge to a disciplinary action taken by a governing body; and
6. identify the actions of governing bodies that are most likely to inspire legislative reform.

WHO GOVERNS SPORT?

Amateur sport in the U.S. is regulated and controlled by a broad spectrum of organizations that include the following:

- Associations
- Committees
- Voluntary, government-sponsored, and legislatively authorized national governing bodies
- Groups advocating the advancement of a particular sport
- Groups associated with regulating participation in sport for particular institutions such as schools, colleges, and international competitive sport recreational facilities

These organizations range from the local Little League to the mammoth NCAA, whose $168.7 million budget and far-reaching tentacles envelop the major colleges and universities throughout the U.S., causing it to be described by the Supreme Court of Kansas as a "plump fowl with tempting luxurious plummage" (*NCAA v. Kansas Department of Revenue*, 1989).

How do these groups derive their authority, and how do they affect practitioners? What role does the legal system play in defining the limits of their power? And finally, what do today's practitioners need to know about their rights and responsibilities in dealing with governing bodies?

The Governing Bodies and Their Authority

Amateur sport for school and college athletes is subject to the pervasive influence of two national organizations: the NCAA and the National Federation of State High School Associations. These are the "plump fowl" that, together with their related subgroups, chapters, conferences, affiliated state organizations, and the like, affect the majority of amateur athletes and would-be athletes in the U.S. These two institutions and a dozen or so smaller, unrelated organizations such as the National Association of Intercollegiate Athletics, National Little College Athletic Association, National Christian College Athletic Association, and National Junior College Athletic Association are, legally speaking, "voluntary associations" that are created by and made up of constituent members that are, for the most part, educational and academic institutions.

Still other organizations exercise their authority along geographical or participant classification lines. These include, among many others, the Southwest Conference, the Pacific Ten Conference, Pop Warner Football, Little League Baseball, Inc., and the American Amateur Racquetball Association.

Finally, federal and other legislation have recognized the existence of so-called "national governing bodies" whose focus is sport-specific and whose authority takes up where the academic institutions and lower-level competition groups leave off. Examples are The Athletic Congress of the U.S.A., the U.S. Gymnastics Federation, and the Amateur Basketball Association of the USA.

A seemingly infinite number of college and high school conferences and leagues are superimposed across the national structure of the various governing bodies that embrace and regulate competition among high schools and colleges. Some of these conferences and leagues govern a broad spectrum of sport activity, whereas memberships in others is optional.

How the Governing Bodies Affect Practitioners

Legally speaking, these conferences and leagues are another layer of voluntary associations that academic institutions may choose to affiliate with for any number of reasons,

not the least of which is the prestige associated with being a member of a certain conference or league. Other membership privileges may include access to a specially selected officiating staff, the certainty and predictability of scheduling competition, and the ability to exert greater control over the conditions of competition than mere membership in one of the national associations permits. This control most often takes the form of academic requirements for eligibility, playing rule modifications, and, particularly at the college level, financial requirements.

Limits of Power

In practice, each of these conferences and leagues constitutes its own form of governing body that regulates the athletes enrolled in the institution and is itself subject to be sued and can sue where legal rights are being asserted.

Nevertheless, the nature of the dominion exercised by the national associations requires that the rules of the local and regional conferences and leagues be no less restrictive than their own. Otherwise member institutions would be in violation of the by-laws or regulations of the national bodies to which they belong and have agreed to subscribe.

Rights and Responsibilities of Practitioners

What this means in practical terms for the student athlete and the member institution is that the most restrictive rule of any organization to which the institution belongs will be applied. Athletic administrators, coaches, and athletes must therefore be aware not only of the rules, regulations, and by-laws of the groups to which their schools belong, but also to the procedures by which rules are enforced. For it is often in the enforcement that the denial of procedural due process or violation of the contract rights of the athlete or institution will invalidate what would otherwise be an enforceable rule, regulation, or by-law. Therefore, it is as important for you to be familiar with the by-laws and related regulations of all conferences and associations to which your institution belongs as it is for coaches to be well versed in the playing rules of their sports.

"State action" is by no means an absolute prerequisite for aggrieved parties to vindicate their rights in court when associations fail to live by their own rules in imposing sanctions or penalties. Similarly, when an association's rules run afoul of the concept of conscionability, enforcement will be denied.

But the power to regulate sports depends on the sport and the level. By law, organizations that are **state actors,** that is to say, that take action akin to government action, must afford due process and equal protection safeguards that are expressed in the 5th and 14th Amendments to the U.S. Constitution (see chapter 7). Therefore, even voluntary, private associations of schools and colleges are often state actors and are therefore bound by the due process and equal protection amendments to the Constitution (see Cases 11.3 and 11.4).

Both administrators and officials of governing bodies should therefore encourage adherence to both procedural and substantive due process in their administrative proceedings as an added safeguard against costly and unproductive litigation. Conversely, practitioners who are able to make justified claims that organizations did not afford due process will be able to assert their rights effectively.

Keep in mind, however, that constitutional rights are only one area in which the courts can and will intervene when a governing body becomes involved in a serious dispute with a member or nonmember school or athlete or with another governing body or organization. In addition, where membership in a particular organization is a virtual prerequisite for economic reasons, courts are more likely to intervene in the internal affairs of such an association to prevent one from being wrongly excluded or penalized. For example, for a football referee, membership in the State Football Officials' Association might be required if the official is to receive any engagements to officiate. Therefore membership is not voluntary but, rather, mandatory in the context of that particular member's rights to participate and earn income. In such cases, courts will intervene to prevent or remedy an injustice when the internal rules of such a governing body are disregarded by that body.

This example shows the importance of knowing the legal relationship between participants and governing bodies. When a question arises concerning legal rights and liabilities, look first to the rules or by-laws of the governing body. Finally, you should recognize that constitutional, legislative, and case-made precedent may all limit the authority that governing bodies and would-be governing bodies are able to exercise in all areas of amateur sports and physical activity. Theories of recovery available to an aggrieved party may include remedies based upon violations of an organization's by-laws; the U.S. Constitution; federal, state, and local legislation; and contract theories.

In some cases, major sports governing bodies take the legal form of a corporation governed by a set of internal rules known as **by-laws.** These rules delineate the rights and responsibilities of the members of the body and frequently provide the mechanism for dealing with violations. Unincorporated associations have similar sets of rules, by-laws, or constitutions by which they and their members are bound. Those who become part of an association through membership, whether they are individual persons or other constituent associations, are said under the law to have entered into a contract with the association of which they are members. By the terms of this **contract,** all parties—both the members and their association—agree to abide by the association's rules. For this reason, even in cases where state action is not present because the association is a private organization that is not sufficiently involved with state governmental institutions or functions, courts have enforced rights of both members and associations when by-laws have been violated (see Case 11.1).

Although the U.S. Supreme Court ruled in *NCAA v. Tarkanian* that the NCAA was not a state actor, courts most often rule that state high school associations for athletics and other activities such as the members of the National Federation of State High School Associations (see the next section) *are* engaged in state action within the meaning of the Equal Protection clause of the Constitution. Student athletes, coaches, athletic directors, and member schools that seek to use the legal system to challenge the action of a state actor often include a violation of the U.S. Constitution in their complaints. If the plaintiff alleges that her activities are protected under some part of the Constitution, the court must determine whether the activity is a fundamental right under constitutional law—that is, a right guaranteed by the U.S. Constitution (*Prince v. Cohen*, 1983; *Sidle v. Majors*, 1976). To be enforceable, the denial of one of these fundamental rights by a state actor must be able to withstand the test of **strict scrutiny**. The strict scrutiny test requires that the association prove to the court that the step taken to prohibit or limit the activity (a) was necessary to carry out a **compelling state interest** of the state involved and (b) was the minimum step necessary to carry out the compelling interest of the state.

Conversely, the strict scrutiny test does not apply if a student athlete, coach, administrator, or member school claims that the action of a state actor caused the denial of a right that is *not* protected by the Constitution and is therefore not a fundamental right. In such cases the association need only show that

there was a **rational basis** for the association action that affected the right, interest, or status of the plaintiff (*Kite v. Marshall*, 1981; *NAACP v. Button*, 1963).

Fundamental rights undoubtedly extend to freedom of speech, freedom of religion, and freedom of assembly. Fundamental rights also include the right to be free of sanctions predicated on **suspect classifications**. Examples of suspect classifications are race, religion, and national origin.

Practitioners who work in the area of high school sports should note that, for all the arguments advanced by disgruntled athletes who have run afoul of state high school athletic association rules regarding eligibility; freedom of association, travel, transfer, and residency; nonschool activities; and the like, courts generally do not characterize participation in interscholastic athletics as a fundamental right protected by the Constitution (see Case 11.2). In fact, the U.S. Supreme Court has specifically rejected even the concept of education as a fundamental right (*Goss v. Lopez*, 1975).

Regardless of whether and to what extent the action of a governing body such as a state high school athletic association impinges on a fundamental right, courts will generally not support an association that does not follow its own rules and regulations in taking action against an athlete or member institution. For, constitutional rights aside, the obligations of member schools or organizations—and of the athletes who carry the banners of those organizations—are grounded in the fact that the athletes or organizations made legally binding agreements to abide by the rules of the governing body at the time they joined it.

Similarly, the governing bodies are likewise bound by the rules they make. Therefore, a practitioner's best hope of defeating a governing body in court is to prove that the body failed to follow the rules contained in its own constitution, by-laws, or other materials.

Although courts are generally reluctant to interfere in the internal affairs of associations, they will take action if a right is lost because an association has disregarded its own rules. Even though such lapses may not be grounded in constitutional law, they nevertheless can spell the difference between a governing body that is able to enforce its actions and one that weakens itself by making rules and breaking them.

Courts generally require that an aggrieved party exhaust an association's procedures for redressing a wrong or appealing an unfavorable decision before bringing suit. Even so, you should seek the advice of counsel even before beginning to appeal an association's decision through its appeals and review process, particularly if its rules are extensive or complex. The constitution, by-laws, and rules and regulations of the New Jersey State Interscholastic Athletic Association, for example, span about 130 pages and encompass regulations running the gamut of activities from all-star games through the use of artificial limbs in athletic competition.

Hearings for violations of rules and regulations are typically conducted by the association's attorney, and various court-like formalities, such as the stenographic recording of the proceedings by an official court reporter, are commonplace. In these hearings, anything you say can and will be used against you. Therefore, you should know when to seek professional help in exercising or defending your rights.

Like their college counterparts, high schools also participate in local and regional conferences, leagues, and alliances that may legally enforce stricter rules for competition, eligibility, and restrictions on athletes than national organizations. All of these local and regional organizations must be considered as part of the governing process.

MAJOR GOVERNING BODIES

The governing bodies described in this chapter have many forms. Some governing bodies exert a profound influence over an almost innumerable number of participants that transcends geographical, sport-specific, and even demographic boundaries. Three such organizations—the National Federation of State High School Associations, the NCAA, and the United States Olympic Committee—are explored in the sections that follow.

National Federation of State High School Associations

Interscholastic athletics in North America are principally governed by the 66-member National Federation of State High School Associations, headquartered in Kansas City, Missouri. The federation began in 1920 as the Mid-west Federation of State High School Athletic Associations, composed of the Illinois, Indiana, Iowa, Michigan, and Wisconsin state association representatives. It has grown to an organization that serves about 20,000 high schools and literally millions of participants.

The day-to-day governing of interscholastic athletic competition resides with the 66 state and foreign high school federation associations. These state high school athletic associations, which include 10 Canadian institutional members and 5 foreign associations, serve as governing bodies for high school athletics in their respective jurisdictions, promulgating rules for competition, eligibility, equal opportunity for male and female athletes, coaching and officiating standards and qualifications, conference and postseason championship arrangements, academic standards that affect eligibility, and many related items. The associations range in size from the Philippine Secondary Schools Athletic Association with 5 member schools to the giant Texas University Interscholastic League, which serves 1,178 schools and has 33 full-time employees.

Conspicuously absent from the name of the federation is the term "athletics." In addition to promulgating rules and training vehicles in 15 sports, the federation embraces other high school activities such as speech and debate, music, programs dealing with drug abuse, and school spirit workshops.

Historically associations such as these have been legally termed **voluntary associations** because they are, for the most part, private and not public entities and because the decision to join them resides with individual school boards. In addition, it is not uncommon for association membership to be open to private and parochial schools as well as public schools.

State high school athletic associations typically have purposes such as those set forth in the constitution of the New Jersey State Interscholastic Athletic Association (NJSIAA), which are as follows:

Section 1. To foster and develop amateur athletics among the secondary schools of the State.

Section 2. To equalize athletic opportunities by standardizing rules of eligibility for individuals, and classifying for competitive purposes the institutions which are members of the Association.

Section 3. To supplement the physical education program of the secondary schools of New Jersey by making a practical application of the theories of physical activity.

Section 4. To promote uniformity in the arrangement and control of contests.

Section 5. To protect the mutual interests of the members of the Association through the cultivation of ideals of clean sports in their relation to the development of character and good citizenship. (*NJSIAA By-laws*, 1991)

Given both the purposes for which most state high school athletic associations are formed and the composition of their membership, it is no surprise that our courts have repeatedly called such associations state actors for purposes of constitutional law.

In some states, legislatures have enacted laws specifically granting authority to school boards to join such an association and making the association answerable to a state official, such as the commissioner of education. For example, a New Jersey statute enacted in 1979 provides that

a Board of Education may join one or more voluntary associations which regulate the conduct of student activities between and among their members, whose membership may include private and public schools. Any such membership shall be by resolution of the Board of Education, adopted annually. No such voluntary association shall be operative without approval of its charter, constitution, by-laws, and rules and regulations by the Commissioner of Education. Upon the adoption of said resolution the Board, its facility, and students shall be governed by the rules and regulations of that association. (New Jersey Statutes Annotated, 1979)

In New Jersey, if the commissioner of education disapproves a rule passed by the NJSIAA, the rule cannot take effect.

State public agencies also govern interscholastic athletics in other states. In some cases regions, counties, or other geographical areas maintain their own associations, which oversee the athletic competition of high schools within their exclusive jurisdiction.

The high school athletic director, coach, or administrator should recognize that associations that oversee scholastic athletics are by and large state actors in the constitutional sense, regardless of whether they are public or private. As such, they must comply with the 5th and 14th Amendments to the Constitution when these associations flex their disciplinary muscles.

As has been discussed, courts generally decline to interfere in the internal dealings of these associations unless an association takes action in conflict with its by-laws or violates the due process and equal protection clauses embodied in the Constitution. In other words, courts are most likely to interfere with a state interscholastic athletic association's decisions if the association either violates its own rules or takes action or maintains rules that have the effect of denying a participant either due process of law or equal treatment with fellow participants under the law.

The legal remedies for perceived abuses by state interscholastic athletic associations depend somewhat on the legal authority under which the association derives its existence. In New Jersey, for example, the state legislature has enacted a law specifically permitting a board of education to join a voluntary private association whose purpose is to regulate the conduct of student activities. The same law prescribes the following pecking order for enforcing the voluntary association's rules and regulations:

The said rules and regulations shall be deemed to be the policy of the Board of Education and enforced first by the internal procedures of the association. In matters involving only public school districts and students, faculty, administrators and boards thereof, appeals shall be to the Commissioner and thereafter the Superior Court. In all other matters, appeals shall be made directly to the Superior Court. The Commissioner shall have authority to direct the association to conduct an inquiry by hearing or otherwise on a particular matter or alternatively, direct that particular matter be heard directly by him. The association shall be a party to any proceeding before the Commissioner or in any court. (New Jersey Statutes Annotated, 1979)

This New Jersey law makes a statutory distinction between an alleged deprivation of rights involving only public schools and a similar situation involving a private school as a party. In all cases, the association's procedure for grievances and dispute resolution must be followed. However, if the dispute involves only public school matters and persons associated with public schools, the appeals from the decision of the state high school association must be made to the commissioner of education, a state government official. Only after the appeal is made to the commissioner may a dissatisfied party go to court to seek relief. In matters involving a private school or persons connected with a private school, a party appealing the decision of the association cannot be made to the commissioner of education but must be made directly to the courts.

Although not all state high school athletic associations are tied legislatively to a state agency, the majority of states whose courts have considered the question of whether or not state high school athletic associations are engaged in state action have found that they are and that they must, therefore, afford affected parties due process of law and equal protection as guaranteed by the U.S. Constitution.

Nevertheless, it is interesting to note the disparity with which some courts treat the issue. For example, the Appellate Division of the Superior Court of New Jersey states without comment or explanation that "the activities of the [State High School] Athletic Association in sponsoring, administering, regulating and supervising interscholastic athletics constitute state action" (*B.C. v. Cumberland Regional School District*, 1987). Chief Judge Lay, writing for the Eighth Circuit Federal Court of Appeals, expresses the same sentiment in considering a case involving the Missouri State High School Activities Association: "Because MSHSAA is an association comprised primarily of public schools, its rules are state action governed by the fourteenth amendment" (In Re U.S. EX REL, 1982). Similarly, the Court of Appeals of Texas, in upholding the University Interscholastic League of Texas's rule restricting eligibility for soccer players, assumed without commenting that the University Interscholastic League, which is composed of virtually all public schools in the state of Texas, according to the court, was a state actor. The court then determined that the equal protection guarantees created by the Constitution had not been violated (*University Interscholastic League v. North Dallas Chamber of Commerce Soccer Association*, 1985).

Some reported cases in which disciplinary actions taken by a state high school athletic association have been challenged in court do not mention deprivation of constitutional rights. The Oklahoma case of John Mozingo and Mark Neighbors is an example. These two young men were denied "hardship exceptions" to an Oklahoma Secondary Schools Activities Association by-law that required that students, to be eligible for sports, cannot participate at any school other than the public high school of the district where their parents reside. Mozingo and Neighbors claimed that the application of this "transfer rule" to them was arbitrary and capricious, and that because they were not recruited by a school outside their residence district (the evil the rule was meant to eliminate), the rule did not accomplish its intended purpose. Therefore, they reasoned, they qualified for an exemption from the rule. The court, taking no note of any claim that neither boy was deprived of his constitutional rights, simply recounted that the high school athletic association was voluntary and that

> As a general rule, courts should not interfere with the internal affairs of voluntary associations. . . . In the absence of mistake, fraud, collusion, or arbitrariness, the decisions of the governing body

of an association should be accepted by the courts as conclusive. . . . The courts will not substitute their interpretation of the by-laws of a voluntary association for the interpretation placed upon those by-laws by the voluntary association itself so long as that interpretation is fair [and] reasonable. (*Mozingo v. Oklahoma Secondary School Activities Association*, 1978)

A history teacher admonished her students that "the one thing you can learn from history is that you can learn nothing from history." Likewise, those who study sport law may learn nothing from court decisions involving state high school athletic associations— except that such associations must follow their own rules and that they are likely to be considered state actors; as such, they are liable in the event of disagreements to afford affected parties with equal protection and due process.

National Collegiate Athletic Association

The premier governing body for collegiate sports in the U.S. is, of course, the behemoth 1,056-member NCAA. The 1991-92 *NCAA Division I Operating Manual*, nearly 300 pages in length, "includes only those operating by-laws . . . considered essential in the day-to-day operation of an institution's athletic program" (p. vii). Each division of the NCAA has its own division operating manual, which deals with the following topics:

- Ethical conduct
- Conduct and employment of athletic personnel
- Amateurism
- Recruiting
- Eligibility: academic and general requirements
- Financial aid

- Awards, benefits, and expenses for enrolled student-athletes
- Playing and practice seasons

These are only a few of the areas that NCAA rules address. The complete set of NCAA rules and regulations is published in the multivolume NCAA *Master Manual*, which contains both a constitution and by-laws. The constitution consists of the following articles:

- Name, purposes, and fundamental policy
- Principles for conduct of intercollegiate athletics
- NCAA membership
- Organization
- Legislative authority and process
- Institutional control

You must also consult each of the three divisions' own operating manuals. These tomes, read together with the master manual, yield a complete though confusing picture of the operational structure of this giant governing body.

To give an idea of the breadth and depth of such an organization, items covered in the *Division I Operating Manual* range from the definition of an "award" ("an item given in recognition of athletics participation or performance," p. 121) to providing that a member institution may fund housing and transportation expenses for parents or legal guardians and the spouse of a student athlete and a student athlete's teammates to be present where the athlete suffers a life threatening injury or illness or, in the event of a student athlete's death, to provide these expenses in conjunction with funeral arrangements. (*NCAA Division I Operating Manual*, p. 130.)

Whether the governing body is large or small, whether the procedure for dealing with a violation of its by-laws is a simple voice vote hearing or reference to an intricate and complex manual consisting of hundreds of pages of procedure, case examples, and administrative layering, it is clear that a governing body must follow its own rules in taking action that affects its membership, particularly if membership in an association is an economic necessity for the member or if the association is engaged in state action. But if a governing body's rules are so complex and its procedures so convoluted that it takes several hundred pages of text to describe them, implementation is fraught with the danger of litigation.

As to enforcement of its rules, the NCAA places a significant burden on member institutions to investigate and penalize various violations. Thirteen enforcement representatives with a budget of $2.2 million police violations of NCAA rules (Johnson, 1992). In recent years, the NCAA has devised programs such as "Project Intercept" to glean information on potential recruiting violations from athletes who have already been recruited by a number of schools. Other programs aimed at gathering information provide grist for the NCAA enforcement mill and, in the process, much fodder for litigation.

With information in hand, the enforcement staff may proceed to institute a "preliminary inquiry," which communicates suspected violations to the member institution. If the charges are more grievous, an "official inquiry" may commence. An official inquiry directs the member college to reply to the charge. If a coach is involved, the coach is supposed to be informed of the charges; whether the association observes this practice is open to question.

NCAA by-laws give the NCAA Committee on Infractions power to grant immunity from discipline under the NCAA system to student athletes who are willing to disclose information in exchange for such immunity. In theory, as an investigation takes shape, both the member institution and the enforcement staff are afforded time to gather information in preparation for prehearing conferences and then formal hearings. After the hearings, the committee (paying heed to a complex structure of procedural and substantive rules) has the option of imposing various penalties ranging from minor sanctions aimed to correct what may be technical violations to the so-called "death penalty," which is reserved for major violations that are repeated within a 5-year period and which cancels some or all competition in the sport involved for a 1- to 2-year period.

When coaches are found in violation, both the coaches and their member institutions are targeted for corrective action. The NCAA makes penalty decisions and corrective actions for coaches and members public.

All in all, the controversy over the NCAA's disciplinary machinery began long before Congress held hearings in the House of Representatives Subcommittee on Oversight and Investigations in the late 1970s. Lawsuits brought against the NCAA have ranged from charges that it had violated federal antitrust laws (laws designed to prevent monopolistic business enterprises from interfering with free competition in the marketplace) by contracting with television networks to control broadcasts of college football to charges that it had deprived coaches of their livelihood.

So dreaded is the specter of NCAA enforcement action, which can deprive a member institution of literally millions of dollars in emoluments from national television, tournament play, and related income, that several state legislatures have enacted laws regulating NCAA procedures. These laws not only declare the NCAA to be a state actor for constitutional purposes, but require in minute detail a number of procedural and constitutional safeguards by which the NCAA is required to conduct its investigative and enforcement processes. Not surprisingly, the states that enacted such legislation did so after major educational institutions

in their states had been heavily penalized by the association.

The requirements of these laws range from obligating the NCAA to conduct hearings utilizing the state code of evidence to allowing full and detailed pretrial discovery and disclosure. One state goes so far as to accord those accused of violating NCAA by-laws the right to disclosure that is given to criminal defendants under state penal statutes. Federal legislation (H.R. 2157, 1991) to the same effect has been introduced as well.

The four state laws, in imposing specific restrictions on the power of the NCAA to take action against any institution, coach, or athlete, leave little to the imagination. Each of these four states—Florida, Illinois, Nebraska, and Nevada—has apparently witnessed a groundswell of legislative sentiment to curtail what are perceived as abuses of power on the part of the NCAA.

The Nebraska College Athletic Association Procedures Act (1990 Neb. Laws 397) simply and flatly requires the NCAA—by name—to apply due process of law guarantees contained in Nebraska state law and the Nebraska constitution to "every stage and facet of all proceedings of a collegiate athletic association, college or university that may result in the imposition of a penalty for violation of such association's rule or legislation" (*Id.*) The Florida and Illinois Collegiate Athletic Association Compliance Enforcement Procedures Acts of 1991 (1991 Fla. Laws ch. 91-260; Ill. Public Act 87-462 [1991]) contain lists of various procedures that organizations such as the NCAA must follow in conducting investigations and disciplinary proceedings. Both statutes forbid a collegiate athletic association from imposing any penalty, or requiring a college or university to impose any penalty on a student or employee, unless it complies with the act and holds a formal hearing. These laws specifically list various due process safeguards such as the following:

Any individual employee or student who is charged with misconduct must be notified, in writing, at least two months prior to the hearing of the specific charges against that individual, that a hearing will be held at a specific date and time to determine the truth of the charges, and that a finding that the misconduct occurred may result in penalties imposed on the institution or imposed by the institution on the individual. The institution shall also be notified in writing on the hearing of the charges. . . .

Any such person or institution has a right to have counsel present, to interrogate and cross-examine witnesses, and present a complete defense. (Collegiate Athletic Association Compliance Enforcement Procedures Act, Illinois *supra*, 1991)

What's more, "clear and convincing evidence" is required for action to be taken by an association. If anyone charged with a violation requests, the association must supply a transcript of any hearing without charge. Penalties must be reasonable for the violation and reasonable in relation to penalties applied in the past for similar violations. Time limits are provided for the filing of charges and the conduct of a hearing. There are even rules that specify the procedure an investigator must use to interrogate the possible subject of an investigation.

The Nevada statute, though less detailed, is strikingly similar in scope and purpose. The Nebraska statute leaves it to the court to determine whether the NCAA has observed due process under Nebraska law.

All four statutes do the following:

1. They either specifically name the NCAA as the subject of the law or define "collegiate athletic association" as an organization of colleges and universities that exists to promote and regulate college athletics, that has at least 200 member institutions in at least 40 states, and further that the member institutions collectively receive at least $2 million annually in revenue from broadcasting rights. The Nevada statute defines such an association as "a group of institutions in 40 or more states who are governed by the rules of the association relating to athletic competition." (Nev. Rev. Stat. s. 398. 055, 1991, p. 387)
2. They specifically authorize judicial review of NCAA action—in other words, grant access to the court to overturn an NCAA decision if a party suffers a loss because the NCAA has not complied with the law.
3. They provide for damages amounting to all financial losses suffered (and possibly litigation expenses and attorney's fees if a party wins the case against the NCAA).
4. They make the remedies contained in the laws cumulative, that is, in addition to, and not exclusive of, other lawsuits and actions an aggrieved party may pursue.
5. They forbid an association from taking retaliatory action against an individual or institution who seeks redress under the law. For example, the NCAA may not expel an institution for suing it under the law (Illinois and Florida), or impose a penalty against any member college or university because a student or employee of the college or university brings a lawsuit under the law (Illinois and Florida).

One of the most comprehensive statements of the justification in the minds of the legislators for the enactment of such laws is in the preamble of the Illinois act, a virtual laundry list of the reasons why NCAA procedures should be subject to the controls of government:

The State has a duty to protect citizens, institutions of higher learning, and others in enforcement of contract disputes, especially where one party to a contract (the NCAA) is a virtual monopoly and, as a result, the parties do not have equal bargaining power. Since all major colleges need to be members of the NCAA, there is little choice but for colleges and universities to join and remain as members of the NCAA and subscribe to NCAA rules and regulations.

National major college sports brings recognition, pride and loyalty to the college, encourages alumni and other contributions, and candidly, the legislature admits, ". . . participation in national sports brings in revenue to the university that helps to fund its various programs."

Illinois colleges and universities must belong to a National Collegiate Athletic Association composed of schools of a similar size and standing to those colleges and universities in the State in order for Illinois colleges and universities to compete on a national level in major college sports.

These associations have rules governing admissions, eligibility, academic status and financial aide. All colleges must abide by those rules.

Enforcement procedures are highly significant and must be fair to the accused.

State institutions that are regulated by collegiate athletic associations are engaged in state action due the collegiate athletic associations in regulating those institutions.

Disciplinary procedures in collegiate athletic associations are a matter of public interest and the public policy of the State of Illinois mandates that procedures be fair to the university or college,

its employees, its students and the communities involved.

The personal and professional lives and aspirations of students and those involved in administering athletic programs on behalf of the universities are at risk when collegiate athletic associations prosecute violations or alleged violations of rules.

Disruption of a university or college athletic program may have serious consequences including affecting the amount of taxpayer support that must be provided to the institution. In addition, an institution's reputation is a source of pride to the State and the State has a profound interest in protecting that reputation.

Arbitrary and caprious penalties may result if fairness and due process are not utilized in association proceedings. As a result, the unwarranted destruction of reputations of not only institutions but individuals in the State may occur.

The revenue derived by various communities in the State generated by college athletic programs is an interest which the State has a policy to protect.

And, last, but definitely not least, in the words of the Illinois legislature:

The present procedures of collegiate athletic associations do not reflect the principle that one is innocent until proven guilty. Because of such potentially serious and far-reaching consequences, the procedures used to determine whether a violation of substantive association rules has occurred should reflect greater fairness and due process considerations than now apply and should provide for a speedier determination than at present of whether a violation of association rules has occurred (Collegiate Athletic

Association Compliance Enforcement Procedures Act, Illinois, 1991).

Now that four states have enacted legislation limiting the power of the NCAA and several more states are preparing to do so, the future of the NCAA's power structure is uncertain. To be sure, the association will challenge these statutes and others that may be passed into law in the courts. The battle cry has already been sounded by the Knight Foundation Commission on Intercollegiate Athletics, which stated that

four states already have enacted legislation to lay aside existing NCAA enforcement rules; comparable legislation is pending in six others. Their immediate effect, within each of the various states, is to virtually forbid the NCAA from enforcing any of its rules without court action. Left unchallenged, these measures threaten to kill nationwide collegiate competition.

Although these statutes appear to involve narrow issues of compliance or legislative support for local institutions, they go right to the heart of what athletic competition—Little League, intercollegiate, or professional— is all about. . . .

In this regard, a fundamental obligation of sports administration is maintaining oversight of the rules, changing them as participants agree, and enforcing compliance in the event of violation. If national governing bodies for intercollegiate athletics cannot ensure fair play through common compliance procedures across 50 states and the District of Columbia, nationwide intercollegiate competition as we have known it will not survive. (*Report of the Knight Foundation Commission on Intercollegiate Athletics*, March 1992)

United States Olympic Committee and National Governing Bodies

On a national and, in a sense, international scale lies the ultimate governing body: the United States Olympic Committee (USOC). The International Olympic Committee (IOC) coordinates the efforts of the USOC and all other member nations' Olympic organizations to provide a framework for Olympic competition. In addition, the IOC recognizes more than two dozen international "federations," each of which exercises control and publishes rules for various sports played on the Olympic level.

In 1978, amateur athletics in the U.S. were the beneficiaries of an active Congress, which enacted legislation popularly known as The Amateur Sports Act of 1978. The act gave legal recognition to the concept of **international amateur athletic competition**: defined as any amateur athletic competition between U.S. athletes and athletes representing any foreign country. The act went on to recognize the **national governing bodies** (NGB), as they are designated by the USOC, thereby giving each NGB its statutory niche in establishing rules and regulations for fostering competition.

According to this law each NGB is charged with nine specific duties, which are as follows:

1. "to develop interest and participation throughout the United States and be responsible to the persons and amateur sports organizations it represents";
2. to coordinate with other organizations to minimize scheduling conflicts;
3. to take into account the opinions of amateur athletes in rendering policy decisions and keep the athletes informed of those policy decisions;

4. to promptly review requests of amateur sports organizations or other persons for sanctions to hold or sponsor competitions, within or outside the U.S.;
5. to allow athletes to compete in international amateur athletic competition conducted by the NGB;
6. to "provide equitable support and encouragement for participation by women where separate programs for male and female athletes are conducted on a national basis";
7. to encourage and support amateur sports for individuals with disabilities and to expand opportunities for those individuals to participate in all athletic competition;
8. to render technical information on physical training, equipment design, coaching, and performance analysis; and
9. to "encourage and support research, development, and dissemination of information in the areas of sports medicine and sports safety" (The Amateur Sports Act of 1978).

In short, the act gave the USOC, through the force of law, exclusive jurisdiction over all matters pertaining to U.S. participation in the Olympic Games and in the Pan American Games. Coupled with this power was the authority to resolve disputes and foster equal opportunity for all to participate. For their part, organizations selected to be NGBs are given more or less exclusive positions because there is only one recognized NGB for each Olympic sport. The law specifically requires an NGB to

1. have as its purpose the advancement of amateur athletic competition and, to that end, be incorporated as a nonprofit corporation and maintain the wherewithal to fulfill its purposes;

2. submit a copy of its corporate charter and by-laws and such additional information as the USOC may require;
3. submit to arbitration any disputes as to eligibility of any athlete, coach, trainer, manager, administrator, or official or any disputes regarding its recognition as a governing body;
4. be a member of not more than one international sports federation that governs a sport played in the Olympic or Pan American Games and that exercises independent control over its sport;
5. demonstrate that membership is open to any individual or amateur sports organization in the sport governed;
6. refrain from discrimination on the basis of race, color, religion, age, sex, or national origin to provide equal opportunity to participate;
7. provide fair notice and opportunity for a hearing to any party before declaring him or her ineligible to participate;
8. be governed by persons who are selected to govern without regard to race, color, religion, national origin, or sex;
9. demonstrate that no less than 20% of the voting members of its governing board of directors are either actively engaged in amateur competition in the particular sport or have represented the U.S. in international athletic competition in the sport within the preceding 10 years;
10. provide for reasonable direct representation on its board that reflects "the nature, scope, quality, and strength of the programs and competitions of such amateur sports organizations in relation to all other programs and competitions in such sport in the United States" (36 U.S.C. 391);
11. demonstrate that none of its officers are also officers of any other NGB;
12. provide procedures for prompt and equitable dispute resolution;

13. have eligibility criteria relating to amateur status that are no more restrictive than criteria utilized by the corresponding international sports federation; and

14. demonstrate that it can meet all responsibilities imposed on NGBs by the law.

The significance of the act for the practitioner is, quite simply, that the authority of the NGBs is no longer grounded in any voluntarily or consensual milieu, but rather that it has become a creature of statute. The Amateur Sports Act has survived numerous challenges in the courts throughout the federal circuits.

CASE STUDIES

Case 11.1

Amateurism

Ron Behagan, a former Minnesota All-American basketball player, went on to a professional career in the National Basketball Association. After several seasons, he traveled to Italy where, although paid for his skills on the hardwood, he played for an "amateur" league, in accordance with the rules of the international basketball governing body, Federation International de Basketball Amateur (FIBA).

The FIBA rules govern U.S. amateur basketball players, who are bound by their NGB, the Amateur Basketball Association of the United States of America (ABA/USA). ABA/USA is the United States' delegate to FIBA; therefore Ron's participation was governed by the rules established by both these governing bodies.

One of those rules provides that U.S. players playing in foreign countries must qualify as amateurs. This qualification involves obtaining an ABA/USA travel permit and a license issued by FIBA. Although FIBA rules permitted U.S. professional basketball players to reinstate their amateur status once, but not more than once, in a lifetime, Mr. Behagan was apparently ignorant of the rule. After he played one season as a paid "amateur" in Italy, Mr. Behagan returned to the U.S. and played for the Washington Bullets in the spring of 1980.

Thereafter, Ron returned to Italy, signed a contract with the Italian team for which he had played the prior season, but failed to apply for reinstatement. When FIBA advised the Italian basketball team that their U.S. star was ineligible because he had violated FIBA rules, the team in turn told Ron that they would not honor his contract for the forthcoming season.

Ron was unable to change FIBA's mind and brought suit in the U.S. District Court for the District of Colorado, charging that FIBA and ABA/USA violated federal antitrust laws, interfered with his contract of employment, and caused him to lose his job without due process.

Federal and state antitrust laws date back to the Sherman Anti-Trust Act (1890), a federal law that made illegal contracts, combinations, and conspiracies that restrain trade. Professional sports organizations are exposed to antitrust laws on a much broader scale (see *Amateur Softball Association of America v. United States*, 1972; *Board of Regents, University of Oklahoma v. NCAA*, 1983; and *Association for Intercollegiate Athletics for Women v. NCAA*, 1984).

Ron Behagan won his case against ABA/USA and its executive director, William Wall, after settling out of court with FIBA. But, the Tenth Circuit Court of Appeals reversed the judgment and dismissed the lawsuit against the governing body. In its ruling, the court rejected Ron Behagan's claim that the defendants violated federal antitrust laws by monopolizing competition because, as the court stated:

> The Act also makes clear that Congress intended an NGB to exercise monolithic control over its particular amateur sport, including coordinating with appropriate international sports federations and controlling amateur eligibility for Americans that participate in that sport. . . . Although the Amateur Sports Act does not contain an explicit statement exempting action taken under its direction from the federal antitrust laws . . . we find that *the directives* of the Act make the intent of Congress sufficiently clear.

> The Supreme Court has stated that the Amateur Sports Act was intended to correct the disorganization and the serious factional disputes that seemed to plague amateur sports in the United States. . . . Behagan complains of exactly that action which the Act directs—the monolithic control of an amateur sport by the NGB for the sport and by the appropriate international sports federation of which the NGB is a member. This truth is underscored by the fact that the ABA/USA could not be authorized under the Act unless it maintained exactly that degree of control over its sport that Behagan alleges as an antitrust violation (*Behagan v. Amateur Basketball Association of the United States of America*, 1989).

Perhaps more importantly, the Circuit Court of Appeals, following *San Francisco Arts & Athletics* (1987), held that the U.S. Olympic Committee did not engage in state action such as to trigger the requirement for due process of law in Behagan's case.

[Adapted from *Behagan v. Amateur Basketball Association of the United States of America*, 884 F.2d 524 (C.C.A. 10 1989)]

Case 11.2

Eligibility Dispute Between a National Governing Body and a State High School Athletic Association

Around the time that Ron Behagan's case was being decided (see Case 11.1), three high school students named David Burrows, Kyle Hetman, and Oreluwa Mahoney played high school soccer in Montgomery County, Ohio: David for his public high school team, Kyle for his parochial school team, and Oreluwa for his private school team. All three students also played on independent teams organized through the Ohio South Youth Soccer Association, Inc. This nonprofit organization was a member of the United States Youth Soccer Association, which in turn is a division of the United States Soccer Federation (USSF). USSF, like ABA/USA for basketball, is the national governing body for soccer. This means that amateur soccer not under the control of high school or college governing bodies is governed, for purposes of international competition, by the USSF, under the authority of the Amateur Sports Act.

The Ohio High School Athletic Association, a state interscholastic athletic association composed of public, parochial, and private schools in the state of Ohio and responsible for administering interscholastic athletics in the state, changed its by-laws to make students who had played soccer on an independent team during the spring of 1988 and thereafter ineligible to compete in high school soccer. Suit was brought in the U.S. District Court for the Southern District of Ohio against the Ohio High School Athletic Association, not only in the names of the three high school students, but by the Ohio Youth Soccer Association, Inc., and its related associations on behalf of approximately 15,000 high school students in Ohio who played soccer in 1987.

In this clash between a constituent organization of a national governing body, whose authority was derived from an act of Congress, and a state high school athletic association, a voluntary group composed of public, private, and parochial schools and given the power to regulate the interscholastic athletics of virtually all the public schools and many of the private and parochial schools in the state, the Sixth Circuit Court of Appeals compared the Ohio High School Athletic Association to the NCAA in that both associations have public, parochial, and private scholastic institutions as members, and membership is voluntary. The court also reasoned that "both organizations promulgate and apply rules to promote and protect amateur sports competitions among their respective members" (*Burrows v. Ohio High School Athletic Association*, 1989, p. 125).

Thus, even though the plaintiffs and the defendant in the lawsuit had agreed that the Ohio High School Athletic Association was indeed a state actor for purposes of constitutional law, the court rejected that analysis. Even so, the court said, whether the Ohio High School Athletic Association is a state actor or not, the regulation embodied in the by-law change that the interscholastic association made was certainly a valid exercise of its authority. The court reminded the parties that the state high school association did not prevent the plaintiffs from playing soccer on independent teams, but merely prevents those who have previously played on a high school team regulated by the Ohio High School Athletic Association from again playing on those teams "if, in the interim, they have participated in independent outdoor soccer during the school year" (*Burrows*, p. 126).

Finally, the court rejected the NGB Youth Soccer Association's argument that the Amateur Sports Act prohibited a state high school athletic association from interfering with the authority of a national governing body that was qualified under the federal statute rules and regulations. In rejecting this argument, the court of appeals cited the exclusive jurisdiction, under the Amateur Sports Act, of other amateur sports organizations that restrict participation to a specific class of athletes "such as high school students" (36 U.S.C. Section 396).

[Adapted from *Burrows v. Ohio High School Athletic Association*, 891 F.2d 122 (6th Cir. 1989)]

Case 11.3

An Athletic Conference as a State Actor

Jim Stanley was the head football coach of Oklahoma State University, a member of the Big Eight Conference. The conference is a football league composed of Oklahoma State University and seven other state universities in neighboring states. These institutions are all publicly funded. The conference is in turn a member of the NCAA, another voluntary association consisting of several hundred colleges and universities across the country.

The conference, in joining the NCAA, agreed to be bound by the NCAA's rules and regulations. Member schools are also bound to obey any conference rules and regulations that are more restrictive than the NCAA's rules.

According to conference rules, the head football coach is responsible for any violation of recruiting rules. In June 1982, Coach Stanley was contacted by a representative of the Big Eight Conference and was told that an investigation was in progress concerning the Oklahoma State University football program. No further details of the investigation were given to Coach Stanley. Several months later, the Commissioner of the Big Eight Conference, Charles Nein, prepared a report from information gathered by his representatives and investigators, one of whom had spoken with Coach Stanley several months before. Approximately 50 persons had been interviewed for the report, which contained statements from some of the people interviewed to the effect that Coach Stanley had spent various amounts of money that had been funneled by other persons named in the report to members of the university's football team.

Under the rules of the Big Eight Conference, any member college may be ordered to show cause why it should not be further disciplined in the event of violations of conference or NCAA rules if either governing body maintains that the university did not take sufficient action. Coach Stanley knew that the conference could virtually force additional disciplinary action upon an institution that would prevent a coach from being hired as coach by any member institution in the country. Thus, the effect of disciplinary action imposed by either the conference or the NCAA could well be to blackball a head coach from remaining a head coach or being hired as a head coach of any college or university that is a member of the NCAA.

Without a job in the only career he knew and, worse yet, facing the prospect that he would never be hired to coach college football again,

Jim Stanley sued the Big Eight Conference to prevent the conference from conducting any hearing of charges against him without due process of law.

Because all schools in the conference were publicly funded universities, and because these universities had delegated to the Big Eight Conference the function of supervising their athletic programs, there could be no doubt that the conference was a state actor and that due process protections of the U.S. Constitution applied. Coach Stanley would have his day in court, and instead of a hearing conducted solely on the basis of a "report" containing statements and conclusions of dozens of people whom Coach Stanley would not have had the opportunity to confront in his defense, Coach Stanley would have a hearing with live witnesses whom Mr. Stanley or his attorney could cross-examine.

[*Stanley v. The Big Eight Conference*, No. 78-0891-CV-W-3, W.D. Missouri 1978]

Case 11.4

Athletic Conferences and Due Process
On January 28, 1972, Ron Behagan (see also Case 11.1) was in his junior year at the University of Minnesota. Ron and his teammate, Marvin "Corky" Taylor, become involved in a slight disagreement with Ohio State's Luke Witte during a basketball game, which resulted in the Big Ten Conference suspending Ron Behagan and Marvin Taylor for the remainder of the season. The fight on the basketball court was followed by a second, more genteel battle in the U.S. District Court for the District of Minnesota.

In this case the court recognized the economic value of intercollegiate athletics for those who participate:

In these days when juniors in college are able to suspend their formal educational training in exchange for multi-million dollar contracts to turn professional, this Court takes judicial notice of the fact that, to many, the chance to display their athletic prowess in college stadiums and arenas throughout the country is worth more in economic terms than the chance to get a college education.

It is well recognized that the opportunity to receive an education is an interest of such substantial importance that it cannot be impaired without minimum standards of due process. (*Behagan v. Intercollegiate Conference of Faculty Representatives*, 1972, p. 604)

After criticizing the Big Ten Conference for not having any written procedures to deal with disciplinary situations, Judge Larson found that the investigation that had resulted in the suspension had been conducted in a manner contrary to both procedural due process and substantive due process. The court noted that the handbook did provide for the athletic directors imposing the penalty to appear in person at the meeting at which the commissioner's report is made and for charged athletes to appear to defend themselves. This provision, however, did not provide for due process in the eyes of the court.

Although Big Ten regulations as they existed at the time empowered the commissioner of the conference to promote the conference's general welfare, the court ruled that a temporary suspension of a student athlete must immediately be followed by notice and hearing by the students suspended. In addition, the students must be apprised of the commissioner's report on which the suspension is based and be given an opportunity to defend themselves. Judge Larson concluded:

> This was never done. Any report which was made to the Directors of Athletics at their January 21, 1972, meeting is as yet undisclosed, and it is undisputed that none of the participants were ever appraised [sic] of the meetings, let alone offered an opportunity to speak in their own defense.

> It is elemental that action beyond the scope of a body's own procedural regulations is a violation of due process of law. (*Behagan v. Intercollegiate Conference of Faculty Representatives*, 1972, p. 606)

As a result, the defendant, Big Ten Conference, was given about 3 days to hold a hearing according to various due process guidelines that were set forth by the court. Plaintiffs Ron Behagan and Marvin Taylor were to be given written notice of the time and place of the hearing at least 2 days in advance. The notice was to specify the exact charges against each and the grounds under which they would be penalized. Although the court did not require that the plaintiffs have the right to cross-examine witnesses in the Behagan case, it did require the presentation of testimony and that both sides of the story be heard. Plaintiffs were to be given a list of all the witnesses appearing and were to receive a copy of the athletic director's written report. Finally, the court indicated that the hearing should be tape recorded and that the tapes should be made available to the plaintiffs if they were to appeal, as they were entitled to do according to the Big Ten handbook.

[Adapted from *Behagan v. Intercollegiate Conference of Faculty Representatives*, 346 F. Supp. 602 (D. Minn. 1972)]

CHAPTER SUMMARY

Governing bodies derive their authority in one or both of two ways:

1. With the consent of members of the governing body with the tacit or express imprimateur of government. (Members may be institutional, as in the case of the University of Las Vegas at Nevada's membership in the NCAA, or individual, such as the membership of Florence Griffith-Joyner in The Athletic Congress.)

2. From an enactment of a state legislature or an act of Congress, the most notable example being the Amateur Sports Act of 1978, which vested authority in the U.S. Olympic Committee

and which in turn vested authority in sport-specific national governing bodies whose authority is clearly established by the Act

Litigation frequently arises when

1. individual members of an organization challenge a rule or enforcement proceeding taken against them by their own organizations, either on the ground of deprivation of their legal rights, or on the ground that their organizations did not follow their own rules in imposing a sanction or penalty;
2. individuals challenge rulings or actions of their associations that are mandated by their associations' memberships in a larger association; or
3. individual students enrolled in educational institutions challenge decisions of governing bodies of which their schools or colleges are members.

Although each of these situations presents a different fact pattern, a common issue to all such litigation is the origin of the body's authority and the proper and lawful exercise of that authority. These, then, are the primary questions at the threshold of virtually all court challenges to the authority of governing bodies.

Whatever the reasons, it is abundantly clear that today's administrators, athletic directors, and coaches cannot afford to ignore the increasing interaction of our legal system with the bodies that govern sport. Populations participating in sport and athletic programs are clearly more cognizant of their legal rights and less content to follow, without challenge, the authority of coaches, administrations, and governing bodies. In addition, the universally acknowledged ascension of sports into "big business" precipitates more, not less, government intervention and corresponding interaction with the legal system. Therefore, as a matter of economics and good management, athletic administrators today simply must be aware of the legal consequences of their actions and those of their staffs.

The natural consequence of government intervention, the increased susceptibility to litigation, and the ever-increasing complexity of association, conference, and subgroup affiliations is the possibility of conflict, power struggles, and political maneuvering that require administrators to be fully aware of their legal environments. Finally, the legislative process that has witnessed the proliferation of statutes, the purpose of which is to redress perceived wrongs and allow everyone to participate, has landed full force in the sports arena. The athletic administrator must now be prepared to deal with the legal rights and responsibilities of an ever-increasing superstructure of governing bodies, organizations, chapter groups, sport-specific and special interest spin-offs, and their progeny.

KEY TERMS

By-laws (201)
Compelling state interest (202)
Contract (201)
Fundamental rights (202)
International amateur athletic competition (211)
National governing bodies (211)
Rational basis (202)
State actors (201)
Strict scrutiny (202)
Suspect classifications (202)
Voluntary associations (204)

QUESTIONS FOR DISCUSSION

1. Distinguish between voluntary and legislatively mandated governing bodies and give examples of each.
2. Enumerate the factors that render a governing body a state actor and give examples of the types of governing bodies that are state actors.

3. Discuss how governing bodies, both voluntary and government sponsored, can defend their disciplinary actions in court.

4. Discuss the legal significance of the "contract" into which members of governing bodies enter.

5. What fundamental rights are most frequently associated with litigation against governing bodies?

6. Identify two instances in which courts are likely to interfere in the internal decisions of governing bodies.

7. Describe the relationship between governing bodies for sport-specific activities and educational institutions.

8. Describe the circumstances under which government is most likely to pass laws limiting the power of governing bodies.

9. Identify the set of rules that every governing body must follow so that its actions will be sustained in a court of law.

REFERENCES

Amateur Softball Association of America v. United States, 467 F.2d 312 (10th Cir. 1972).

Amateur Sports Act of 1978, 36 U.S.C. s. 371-396 (1978).

Association for Intercollegiate Athletics for Women v. NCAA, 588 F. Supp. 487, *aff'd*, 735 F.2d 577 (D.C. Cir. 1984).

B.C. v. Cumberland Regional School District, 220 N.J. Super. 214, 531 A.2d 1059 (1987).

Behagen v. Amateur Basketball Association of the United States of America, 884 F.2d 524 (10th Cir. 1989).

Behagen v. Intercollegiate Conference of Faculty Representatives, 346 F. Supp. 602 (D. Minn. 1972).

Black, M. (1990). *Black's law dictionary* (6th ed.). St. Paul: West.

Board of Regents, University of Oklahoma v. NCAA, 561 P.2d 449 (Okla. 1983).

Burrows v. Ohio High School Athletic Association, 891 F.2d 122 (6th Cir. 1989).

Collegiate Athletic Association Compliance Enforcement Procedures Act, Illinois and Florida, c. 260, s. 1 (s. 240.5341 et seq.) (1991).

Goss v. Lopez, 419 U.S. 565 (1975).

In Re United States EX REL Missouri State High School Activities Association, 682 F.2d 147 (8th Cir. 1982).

Johnson, C. (1992, April 13). The rules of the game. *U.S. News and World Report*, pp. 60-62.

Kite v. Marshall, 661 F.2d 1022 (1981).

Mozingo v. Oklahoma Secondary School Activities Association, 575 P.2d 1379 (Okla. 1978).

NAACP v. Button, 371 U.S. 415, 433, 83 S. Ct. 328, 9 L.Ed.2d 405 (1963).

NCAA Division I Operating Manual. (1991). National Collegiate Athletic Association, Overland Park, Kansas, 1991.

NCAA v. Kansas Department of Revenue, 245 Kan. 553, 781 P.2d 726 (1989).

NCAA v. Tarkanian, 488 U.S. 179 (1988).

Nebraska Laws 397 (1990).

Nevada Revised Statutes, s. 398 (1991).

New Jersey Statutes Annotated (1979). 18A: 11-3.

NJSIAA By-laws (1991).

Prince v. Cohen, 715 F.2d, 87, 93 (1983).

Report of the Knight Foundation Commission on Intercollegiate Athletics. (1992, March). Charlotte, NC: Knight Foundation.

Sidle v. Majors, 264 Indiana 206, 341 N.E. 2d 733 (1976).

University Interscholastic League v. North Dallas Chamber of Commerce Soccer Association, 693 S.W. 2d 513 (Tex. Ct. App. 1985).

ADDITIONAL READINGS

Arnold, D.E. (1983). *Legal considerations in the administration of public school physical education and athletic programs*. Springfield, IL: Charles C Thomas.

Johnson, A.T., & Frey, J.H. (1985). *Government and sport*. Totowa, NJ: Rowman & Allanheld.

National Federation Handbook. (1991). Kansas City: National Federation of State High School Associations.

Rapp, J.R. (1984). *Educational law*. New York: Matthew Bender.

Sharp, L.A. (1990). *Sport law*. National Organization on Legal Problems of Education.

Valente, W.D. (1985). *Education law*. St. Paul: West.

Yasser, R., McCurdy, J.R., & Goplerud, C.P. (1990). *Sports law*. Cincinnati: Anderson.

CANADIAN APPLICATIONS FOR PART IV

WHO IS IN CHARGE?

EDUCATIONAL SYSTEM

The legal foundation of the Canadian educational system draws on many sources, which can be divided into three levels of jurisdiction: federal, provincial, and local. Section 93 of the Canada Act, 1982, assigns responsibility for making laws about education matters to the provinces.

Although departments of the federal government have maintained control in certain areas, particularly immigrant training programs and minority language education rights, the ultimate responsibility for most public education in Canada is the provincial government. Provincial authority relies on the statutes enacted by legislatures and the regulations adopted by departments of education. The provincial power to control education includes the prerogative to delegate authority, and all the provinces have used that prerogative to establish local boards, which administer and supervise schools. The powers and duties of these boards are defined in the enabling legislation, for example, Ontario's Education Act (1980) and Alberta's School Act (1970). Boards act as agents of the province and, within the limits of their authority, are the local legislatures in educational matters. As such they can also enact rules and regulations pertaining to schools, both private and public.

Accreditation of teachers is a requirement in each province. However, each province has its own legislation for accreditation. For that reason, there is some limit on portability of accreditation among provinces. Typically, hiring and employment practices are determined by local school boards within the framework of the enabling provincial legislation. Decisions to hire specialist teachers such as those with physical education or coaching qualifications rest entirely with school boards and the individual schools. Obviously, factors such as geographical location, availability of prospective teachers, level of school, school budgets, and school staffing needs affect hiring decisions. Specialists are more likely to be hired to teach physical education due to the specialized nature of the discipline and the dangers inherent in sport and physical activity. The same is not necessarily true in hiring coaches for school systems whose demands and array of coaching activities exceed the capacity of one or two physical education specialists. Schools must depend on the expertise of others, either within the school or in the community, and the nature of that expertise should be seriously considered by the principal.

COLLEGES AND UNIVERSITIES

Colleges and universities are all creatures of statute. Case law (*Douglas/Kwantlen Faculty Association v. Douglas College*, 1990) has suggested that colleges are more closely tied to the government, acting as the government's agent in many internal matters, including employment issues. Nonetheless, in both colleges and universities, the hiring of coaches is a faculty or departmental responsibility within the institution. There are no legislative standards, but almost without exception, coaches hold degrees in a related area (for example, sport psychology, coaching, and sport administration), are experienced, and have earned some level of certification under the National Coaching Certification Program. Provincial and national conference associations for colleges and universities such as the Canadian Intercollegiate Athletic Association are involved only in aspects of intervarsity or national competition and have no bearing on coaches' qualifications.

MECHANISMS FOR CERTIFICATION OF SPORT AND PHYSICAL ACTIVITY PERSONNEL

Awarding credentials to practitioners in coaching, fitness, facility operations, athletic therapy, and recreation is the responsibility of the professional organizations for each of these fields. The following sections provide brief profiles of some certification programs for Canadian sport and physical activity personnel.

Coaching

There are no legislated standards for coaches or coaching in Canada, but there does exist a single, nationwide education and certification program for coaches called the **National Coaching Certification Program, or NCCP.** This program is directed equally toward scholastic, collegiate, and recreational coaches, and although certification is not mandatory at any level, it is seen as desirable by most institutions, organizations, and employers.

The NCCP was launched in the early 1970s by the Coaching Association of Canada and represents a unique model where federal, provincial, and territorial governments, and national and provincial sport bodies have coordinated policies and funding to ensure a consistent approach to coaching education in Canada. For example, in Alberta, coaching theory courses are offered throughout the province by the Alberta Sport Council, an independent body funded through lottery proceeds and some private sector dollars. Practical courses are offered by provincial sport associations. The Coaching Association of Canada, through NCCP, provides the curriculum and course materials, and the provincial government trains and provides the course instructors.

The NCCP offers coaching certification at five levels: Levels I through III are for coaches of developing athletes, and Levels IV and V are for coaches of high-performance athletes—primarily national caliber athletes who are competing internationally. Each level comprises three components: theory, sport-specific technical training, and a practical component consisting of an apprenticeship or internship. Certification at Levels I through III is available for about 60 sports, whereas certification at Levels IV and V is available in 6 and 2 sports, respectively, although certification for 40 additional sports is being piloted or is in development. Since NCCP's inception, over 500,000 coaches have taken its courses; a smaller number, approximately 100,000, have obtained certification.

At the advanced level, the Coaching Association of Canada, in conjunction with five

Canadian Applications for Part IV 225

Canadian universities, offers Coaching Institutes. Participants study for 2 years and obtain Level IV coaching certification and a master's degree. A 1-year version of the program awards Level IV certification and a diploma.

The NCCP program has been successful in providing a consistent approach to coaching training and certification across the country. Coordinated delivery and government funding make the courses both affordable and widely available. Although neither legislated nor mandatory in many settings, certification at the lower levels has become a common requirement for employment in a coaching position. More and more physical education programs at Canadian colleges and universities are incorporating NCCP theoretical and technical content into their curricula, so that graduates obtain lower level certification in addition to a degree. At the elite level of coaching, certification is typically a requirement: For example, all coaches at the Canada Games are required to have Level III certification.

There is currently a strong push in Canada toward professionalization of coaching. As part of this push, the **Minister's Task Force on the Federal Sport Policy (1992)** has recommended establishing an association for coaches that would have among its membership requirements (*Fitness and Amateur Sport*, 1992)

- an educational requirement for a recognized degree as well as technical education through NCCP;
- coaching experience;
- a professional exam; and
- adherence to a coaching code of ethics.

Fitness Leaders

In 1984, the **National Fitness Leadership Advisory Council** established guidelines for the training and certification of fitness leaders in Canada. All of the provinces have fitness leadership programs of one type or another, although not all of them conform to the national guidelines. Although certification requirements for fitness leaders are not legislated, certification has become an industry standard: To work as a fitness leader or instructor, therefore, a certificate is required.

Alberta was the first province to adopt the national guidelines, and the Alberta Fitness Leadership Certification program is perceived to be the most comprehensive in Canada. To obtain certification in Alberta, leaders must undergo

- theoretical training;
- technical training in one of four specialty areas (strengthening and conditioning, aquatic fitness, fitness for the older adult, and aerobic fitness);
- a practicum;
- a practical observation or test; and
- recertification every 2 years.

Certificates are portable between provinces that adhere to national guidelines. However a practical observation or test in the new province is usually required to check a fitness leader's competence.

Additional training is available for individuals who wish to be certified to train fitness leaders. A component of this certification is a recognized university degree.

Fitness professionals may also be certified as fitness appraisers. The first level of certification allows the individual to conduct standardized fitness tests. The second level allows the fitness professional to perform testing and to prescribe exercise programs. Training for the second level involves a week-long course as a supplement to a university degree. As with the fitness leader certificate, these programs are administered by each province in accordance with national guidelines.

Facility Operators

Operators of facilities such as swimming pools, arenas, racquet clubs, leisure centers, and outdoor recreational facilities make up a signficant occupational group in the recreation industry. A number of community colleges in Canada offer 1-year facility operation and management diplomas, whereas associations in each province offer short courses that conform to the guidelines of the **Canadian Recreation Facilities Council**.

The Alberta Association of Recreation Facilities Personnel (AARFP) offers more courses than other provincial associations, and—in Alberta at least—first-level completion of these courses is recognized in the industry as the minimum standard for any full-time employment in a recreation facility. The AARFP awards certificates for completion of Level II courses for operators of pools, arenas, parks, and sports fields and is now piloting an advanced course for facility supervisors.

Athletic Therapists

The **Canadian Athletic Therapists Association** certifies athletic therapists in Canada, most of whom find employment in universities and with professional sports teams. Requirements for certification are a degree or diploma recognized by the association, followed by registration as a certificate candidate. Over a 2-year period, candidates must complete a prescribed number of practical hours on the sports field as well as in a clinical setting, under the direct supervision of a certified therapist. Finally, they must pass both a written and a practical exam. Candidates for certification often complete the required practical hours in voluntary capacities with sports clubs or school teams because few of these organizations are able to afford the services of a certified athletic therapist.

Recreation Leaders

Although there is currently no certification for recreation leaders or coordinators anywhere in Canada, the industry standard for obtaining employment in such a position is a degree or diploma in recreation or physical education and 2 years of experience. There have been discussions about establishing a Western Canada Recreation Management School, which would award a management certificate in recreation. Individual provinces are also discussing certification for recreation professionals; for example, the Alberta Recreation and Parks Association, in conjunction with an Alberta college, is considering implementing a parks management certification program.

HIRING AND EMPLOYMENT PRACTICES

The mechanisms for certification just described are overseen by organizations and associations on both provincial and national levels; legislated bodies such as schools, universities, and colleges; and voluntary private organizations such as provincial and national special-interest groups like the Canadian Coaching Association and the provincial and national sport governing bodies. Taken together, these organizations represent a range of employment situations.

Virtually all employment situations in Canada come under legislative control. There are six categories into which an employment situation can be slotted, and each is governed by a different piece of legislation. The federal and provincial governments each legislate in their own spheres, and each has distinct legislation for the private and public spheres. The **public sphere** is easily identified and is made up of public or civil servants. The **private sphere** refers to employees of private businesses or industries that involve a federal or provincial work, undertaking, or business. The first four categories of employment are thus:

1. federal public,
2. federal private,
3. provincial public, and
4. provincial private.

The main distinguishing feature of these categories is that each is governed by a separate labor statute and administered by a labor board.

A common feature of virtually all labor legislation is the organization of employees into unions (or bargaining units) and the compulsory resort to arbitration to resolve differences arising over the interpretation, application, or operation of collective agreements. Teachers and many college and university instructors fall into the provincial private group and are members of a collective bargaining group. The Ontario Education Act provides three options for teachers in Ontario, including being a part of a bargaining unit under the terms of provincial labor legislation. Employees may also form an association under the terms of the Education Act or join neither and leave the employment relationship to be governed by alternate terms within the Education Act.

The final two categories of employment concern

5. those employees whose employment is governed by a discrete piece of legislation (such as police and armed forces personnel) and
6. all other employees who may not fit into the previous five categories.

This last group, which makes up approximately 65 percent of the workforce, can look to provincial employment standards legislation for minimum standards with respect to employment matters such as wages, hours

of work, age limitations, hiring and firing practices, and pay equity.

Other legislation also affects employment legislation and plays a role in defining employment standards. For example, provincial school legislation in every province requires school-age children to attend school, thus limiting their options for full-time employment, and Canadian immigration regulations stipulate the necessary citizenship requirements to work in Canada. Interestingly, among the few worker groups under this legislation for whom "permanent residency" status is not required to work in Canada are persons engaging in or assisting with the management or administration of athletic or other sporting activities (Canada Immigration Regulations, 1978). A number of provinces and territories including Alberta, Nova Scotia, Prince Edward Island, and the Yukon have equal pay legislation, that is, equal pay for equal or similar work. However, a number of other provinces (Ontario, Quebec, and Manitoba), and the federal government, have implemented pay equity legislation, that is, equal pay for work of equal value. This is somewhat different from the concept of equal pay for similar or equal work. For example, in 1986 the federal government passed the **Employment Equity Act** (1984) in an attempt to redress historical economic discrimination in the workplace and to provide equitable employment opportunities and benefits specifically to women, aboriginal peoples, persons with disabilities, and visible minorities. The legislation applies only to employees in the federal private and public spheres. Finally, both federal and provincial human rights legislation play an important role in protecting the rights of employees, particularly with regard to discrimination in such areas as hiring, promotion, scheduling, benefits, and training. These are just a few examples of the many pieces of legislation that can affect employment standards.

One of the most difficult questions to answer in deciphering an employment law is Who is an employee? Often when an individual enters into a contract for the performance of work, the contract establishes an independent contractor relationship rather than an employment relationship. Four factors are often examined to determine whether a person is an employee or an independent contractor:

1. Control—Who selects, hires, or fires the worker or workers who perform the service?
2. Ownership of tools—Who supplies the materials and tools necessary for the required work? This test may vary depending on the circumstances, but the more items that are supplied by the person contracting the work, the more the relationship will be characterized as an employer/employee relationship.
3. Chance of profit—Has the person financially invested in the enterprise, or is the prospect of gain solely dependent upon work effort? The flow of wages from one person to another is a major indicator of an employment relationship, but it is not necessarily the deciding factor. The person hired to do the work is expected to do it personally. An independent contractor is free to hire others to perform the work.
4. Risk of loss—This is the other side to the chance of profit factor. Provision of tools and materials and hiring others to do the work enhance the risk of loss.

The four factors cannot be treated in isolation from each other. Nonetheless, the essential question is whether individuals can be characterized as working for a superior (employment situation) or as being in business for themselves (independent contractor). This is an important issue because only employees are protected by the provisions of the statutes governing employment and labor situations. Independent contractors are bound by the terms of the contracts they negotiate with the other party.

Employment relationships involving independent contractors are fairly common in sport. For example, many coaches, therapists, fitness leaders, instructors, sport consultants, event and tournament coordinators, and even officials typically enter into agreements as independent contractors and thus would not be covered by any employment or labor legislation.

Nevertheless, the employment situations of the vast majority of persons employed in physical activity and sport are protected by provincial employment standards legislation. Where neither terms of a contract nor the provisions of the legislation address a particular circumstance, common law principles with regard to employment will apply. The common law principles address the economic issues of the employment relationship, including termination, notice of termination, and damages for unlawful termination where the relationship is not defined. In fact, common law principles closely resemble the employment standards legislation.

THE ROLE OF GOVERNING BODIES

The framework or system of sport in Canada is complex. It is made up of organizations deriving authority and jurisdiction from different sources: Some are created by legislation (either federal or provincial), whereas others are private bodies operating at a national, provincial, regional, or local level.

Figure CA4.1 outlines the structure of Canadian sport.

To understand Canada's sport system, it is important to understand where an organization derives its authority to act. We can look at two major sources of this authority: statute

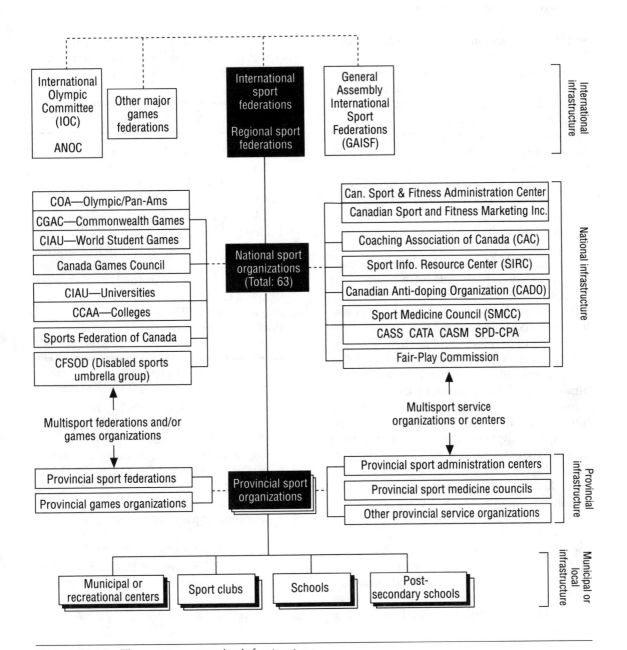

Figure CA4.1   The sport community infrastructure.

Note. From *Sport: The Way Ahead* (p. 32) by the Minister's Task Force on Federal Sport Policy, 1992, Ottawa: Minister of State Fitness and Amateur Sport. Copyright 1992 by Minister of Supply and Services Canada. Adapted with authorization from Sport Canada. ANOC = Association of National Olympic Committees; COA = Canadian Olympic Association; CGAC = Commonwealth Games Association of Canada; CIAU = Canadian Intercollegiate Athletic Union; CCAA = Canadian Colleges Athletic Association; CFSOD = Canadian Federation of Sports Organizations for the Disabled; CASS = Canadian Association of Sport Sciences; CATA = Canadian Athletic Therapists Association; CASM = Canadian Association of Sports Medicine; SPD-CPA = Sport Physiotherapy Division of the Canadian Physiotherapy Association.

and the organization itself, through its constitution and by-laws.

For example, organizations such as schools, colleges, municipalities, and government departments that deal directly with the delivery of sport and recreation programs are created by legislation. Their actions and behaviors are dictated by this legislation and by rights enactments such as the Canadian Charter of Rights and Freedoms, which ensures that the substantive and procedural rights enshrined in the Canadian Constitution are respected in all activities that can be perceived as government action.

On the other hand, private sports organizations derive their authority from their constitutions and by-laws, which form a private contract between the organization and its members. This contract sets out substantive rights of members and participants. The common law is quite clear on what form this contract should take and on how it is legally binding on the activities of the organizations. In a sense, these private entities are like "a law unto themselves": Their memberships comprise the electorate, their boards of directors comprise the legislative body, their executives comprise the cabinet, and their selection/discipline and ethics committees comprise a judiciary. However, there is an overriding legal obligation on these organizations (or on any organization for that matter) to be fair in their procedures and practices. Should fairness not prevail, then they cease to be a law unto themselves, and the courts can intervene in their affairs. These sources of authority and their implications for substantive and procedural rights in sport are discussed more fully in the Canadian Applications for Part III.

KEY TERMS

Canadian Athletic Therapists Association (226)

Canadian Recreation Facilities Council (226)

Employment Equity Act (227)

Minister's Task Force on the Federal Sport Policy (1992) (225)

National Coaching Certification Program (NCCP) (224)

National Fitness Leadership Advisory Council (225)

Private sphere (226)

Public sphere (226)

REFERENCES

Canada Act, 1982, U.K., 1982, c. 11.

Canada Immigration Regulations, SOR/78-772 s. 19(1) [re-en SOR/84-849].

Douglas/Kwantlen Faculty Association v. Douglas College, (1990) 3 S.C.R. 570, 77 D.L.R. (4th) 94.

Education Act, R.S.O. 1980, c.129.

Employment Equity Act, S.C. 1984-85-86, c.3.1.

Fitness and Amateur Sport. (1992). *Sport: The way ahead: The report of the Minister's Task Force on Federal Sport Policy*. Ottawa: Government of Canada.

School Act, R.S.A. 1970, c.3.1.

PART V

LEGAL RESPONSIBILITY FOR PARTICIPANT SAFETY

No one can doubt that the potential for litigation has become a serious problem in U.S. sport. Liability insurance is becoming increasingly difficult to obtain, and its cost has risen exponentially in recent years. As a result of this litigious environment, trampolines are now used in only a small number of private programs, diving boards are no longer found on hotel or motel pools, and most schools have eliminated some portion of their physical education or athletics programs because of fears that someone might suffer an injury and subsequently file a lawsuit. Although many changes brought about by the threat of litigation have been positive and have led to safer and better managed programs, others have resulted from knee-jerk reactions that have served only to reduce the breadth and value of the particular program.

This part of the text examines the rights of individuals who have suffered injuries while participating in programs of sport and physical activity to seek compensation for their losses through the legal system. It enumerates and discusses the fundamentals of tort law, the process of litigation, and the nature of the responsibilities of coaches, teachers, officials, and even other participants for the safety of others.

Although the discussion, of necessity, focuses on discrete points of law or programming, you must remember that managing the risks of participation is a fluid process that requires you to draw upon the broadest possible range of legal and professional concepts to minimize the likelihood of participant injury. A risk management process that is both legally sound and professionally thorough will help reduce the potential for personal injury, which is the root cause of most lawsuits. In addition, the organization and documentation inherent in a legally sound program of risk management will greatly increase the options available to an attorney seeking to defend against a claim of negligence brought on behalf of an injured participant.

CHAPTER 12

BASIC PRINCIPLES AND CONCEPTS
OF TORT LIABILITY

ohn was a star pitcher for his high school baseball team. Although he was only a junior, he was already the object of much attention from professional scouts and college recruiters. In the late spring of his junior year the football coach suggested that John's speed, coordination, and height would make him a natural receiver, even though he had never played organized football. John decided to try out for football in the fall.

From the first day of fall practice, John was used exclusively as a wide receiver. To help him develop his offensive skills and techniques, the coaches released him from all defensive drills and provided him instead with extra practice on pass routes and receiving. The lone exception to this procedure occurred during the second week of practice when John and several other players were given a 5-minute explanation of proper tackling technique, after which John made one tackle under the supervision of the coach. Immediately after he had accomplished the tackle, John was once again directed to practice his receiving skills.

As the season progressed, John's skills improved rapidly, and by the third game he was the starting wide receiver as well as a punt and kickoff return specialist. In the fourth quarter of the fifth game of the season, John ran a pass route to the right side of the field. The ball was thrown to the left and was intercepted by a member of the opposing team. John came across the field toward the ball carrier, lowered his head, and made the tackle, preventing a long return.

As the ensuing pileup was cleared, it became obvious that John had suffered an injury. The game was delayed for over 30 minutes as medical personnel carefully ministered to John and moved him to the waiting ambulance. John had suffered a fractured cervical vertebrae with a severance of the spinal column, resulting in permanent quadriplegia. A long period of intensive medical treatment, followed by the need for nearly constant medical care and costly modifications to the family home, resulted in a financial drain far beyond the means of John's family, who ultimately sought the advice of an attorney.

Although in the past John's injury would most probably have been classified as bad luck, this is no longer the case. Athletes and their families are becoming increasingly aware of their legal rights and consequently more willing to seek compensation through the courts. In this case, John's attorney alleged that the coaches, the team trainer, and the company that manufactured John's helmet all failed in their obligations to protect John's safety and therefore should be held liable for his injuries.

After a lengthy process of litigation, the trainer and helmet manufacturer were found not to have been guilty of negligence. The coaches, on the other hand, were found to have been negligent for their failure to prepare John properly for the foreseeable eventuality that he would be required to attempt a tackle. John was awarded compensatory damages in the amount of $4.25 million.

LEARNING OBJECTIVES

The student will be able to

1. enumerate and explain the factors that underlie the recent growth in personal injury litigation in sport;
2. list the elements of negligence and give examples of their application in programs of sport and physical activity;
3. discuss the applications of the various legal defenses and give examples of how each might apply to specific situations;
4. develop effective releases and participation agreements for specific sports or activities; and
5. explain the importance of record keeping and public relations in the legal process.

ROOTS OF THE LIABILITY EXPLOSION

The recent propensity for litigation among North Americans in general and the sporting community in particular has been strongly affected by factors that are mostly beyond the influence of the sport and physical activity profession. These factors include the following:

1. **Insurance shortfalls**. When someone suffers an accidental injury, the medical and hospital insurance available may not cover all of the treatment and rehabilitation costs. When this occurs, the injured party has only two alternatives: She must absorb the financial burden herself or she may seek redress through the courts.

2. **The right to sue**. Under American civil law, any person can sue another person or persons at any time, for practically any reason. Although this simplistic analysis ignores the legal complexities as well as the possible variations in outcome, the fact remains that the right to initiate a lawsuit is, for the most part, guaranteed.

3. **Doctrine of entitlement**. It is not surprising that jurors, typically people untrained in justice issues, tend to view litigation involving an injured person in humanistic terms. They see a person who, through no apparent fault of his own, has suffered a painful and costly injury. They feel, quite understandably, that *someone* should help to bear the financial burden that has resulted. The problem is that the only "someone" currently available is the one being sued. This sense of the need for compensation—in essence a humanitarian desire to help the needy—can to some degree slant the perceptions of otherwise unbiased jurors.

4. **Settlements**. A settlement is a financial agreement to a lawsuit reached between the opposing parties. In agreeing to a settlement, neither party admits guilt or claims victory. They simply agree that it is more desirable to accept negotiated financial arrangements than to pursue the matter any further. The overwhelming majority of all liability suits end in settlements.

It is not difficult to see that the cumulative effect of these factors predisposes us to litigation. An injured person has a financial loss and a legal right to pursue the matter, and realizes that most people who do so gain at least some compensation through a negotiated settlement. In sport and recreation, the problem is further complicated by an additional factor:

5. **The myth of being risk-free**. It is impossible to conduct a program of physical activity that is entirely safe. If you think this is a gross overstatement, consider the following: The usual connotation of the word *safe* involves freedom from risk, harm, or injury. This condition is, however, contrary to the very nature of physical activity. As long as one or more persons are allowed to move, particularly when this movement includes physical contact, competition with others, and perhaps the use of equipment and apparatus, there exists the threat of danger, harm, or loss.

Table 12.1 shows the extent of estimated injuries during 1991 alone in selected areas of sport and physical activity. Although we can and should do everything reasonably in our power to reduce the number and severity of injuries, we must at the same time recognize that, despite our very best efforts, some injuries will occur.

Unfortunately, each injury must be recognized as a potential lawsuit. We've seen that it is impossible to remove all risk from physical activities; and for many participants, the very element of controlled risk (or the perception of risk) is part of the enjoyment of the sporting experience. It probably would be unwise to entirely eliminate every element

Table 12.1   Estimated Sports-Related, Medically Attended Injuries During Calendar Year 1991

Sport	Medically attended injuries
Playgrounds	262,378
Organized football	149,527
Organized baseball	137,753
Organized basketball	120,503
Weight lifting	61,140
Track and field	58,586
Organized soccer	48,148
Wrestling	43,894
Dance	39,257
Golf	38,626
Swimming	34,748
Field hockey	31,145
Tennis	29,936
Organized volleyball	25,629
Exercise equipment	25,258
Ice hockey	23,456
Organized gymnastics	17,272
Cheerleading	11,682
Archery	7,397
Total	1,166,335

Source: U.S. Consumer Products Safety Commission/ National Injury Information Clearinghouse, 1992.

of danger even if it were possible to do so. The remaining activities would be so sterile and unchallenging that no one would bother with them.

This fact is not, however, an excuse for allowing unreasonable or unnecessary risks to exist. The prudent coach or teacher takes all reasonable steps to remove the dangers in any given activity and then answers this question: Does the value of the activity significantly outweigh the risk that remains? When the answer is yes, the risks can be viewed as both reasonable and controlled, and the activity may be conducted. Where the answer

is no, however, the prudent teacher or coach will either make further modifications to the activity or eliminate it entirely.

ELEMENTS OF NEGLIGENCE

A **tort** is a civil wrong for which an individual may seek recompense through the courts. A tort arises when an injury occurs as a result of another person's failure to meet a legal duty or obligation properly. The overwhelming majority of torts involving sport and physical activity focus on the alleged negligence of the person or persons in charge. **Negligence** is essentially either failing to do something that a reasonable, prudent person would have done under the same or similar circumstances or doing something that a reasonable, prudent person would not have done. Negligence may therefore arise from an act of omission or commission. To meet the legal requirements for proving negligence, the plaintiff must show the following elements:

1. **Duty**—Every civil personal injury action must show that the **defendant** (person being sued) owed a duty of care to the **plaintiff** (injured party). If the injured party was an athlete on a team, a student in a class, or a participant in a program, the duty of the coach, teacher, or administrator under whose direction or supervision the program was run is virtually indisputable.

2. **Breach**—This is the act of negligence charged. The yardstick by which the court determines whether a breach existed is the written standards of the profession as applied to the circumstances in question by an expert. For example, a Little League coach would not necessarily be expected to act as an intercollegiate coach would, but would

be expected to act as a competent, prudent Little League coach.

3. **Damages**—The breach must have resulted in damages or losses to the plaintiff's person, property, or interest.

4. **Proximate cause**—The fact that the defendant negligently breached a duty owed to the plaintiff is not sufficient grounds for a successful lawsuit. The plaintiff must prove that the particular injury for which compensation is sought was actually caused or aggravated by the defendant's negligent act (see Cases 12.1 and 12.2).

5. **Foreseeability**—Additionally, there must be proof that the defendant should have been able to predict the possibility of an injury under the circumstances in question. It is not necessary to show that the specific injury suffered by the plaintiff was predictable under the circumstances; simply that a reasonable person should have realized that *someone* might suffer *some type of injury.*

LEGAL DEFENSES AGAINST CLAIMS OF NEGLIGENCE

A number of legal concepts and professional procedures can be used to help formulate a defense against claims of negligence. Although these procedures are of unquestioned importance in the litigation process, their application to the daily activities of coaching and teaching is sometimes overlooked. It must be remembered that these defenses can only be of value to the degree that they are supported by the routine and faithful application of the administrative and instructional procedures upon which they rely.

Releases

A **release** or **waiver** is a type of contract signed by participants or, in the case of minors, by their parents as well. In the release, the participants or their parents absolve the coach or teacher from liability if an injury occurs as a result of the specified activity. Such documents are seldom considered legally valid for absolving a defendant of responsibility for school-related programs or for minors for the following reasons:

1. The courts are generally reluctant to grant individuals pre-event protection from the consequences of their own negligent actions.
2. No person can legally waive the rights of another. Parents therefore cannot waive the rights of their children.
3. Children under the age of legal majority cannot legally enter into contracts to waive their own rights.
4. The requirement that one execute a release to participate in a public program is commonly held to be a violation of public policy and is therefore invalid.

However, a release can be a valuable legal document for programs involving adults, especially those conducted within the private sector, because adults may waive their rights under certain circumstances. Chief among these are the following:

1. Reasonable options are present. In the private sector, adults can usually find a wide variety of program options. Furthermore, because private programs are not supported by their tax dollars, adults have the option not to be involved or not to support them.
2. The adults are aware of, understand, and appreciate their risks and responsibilities for the program or activity.

Participation Agreement

A **participation agreement** is a signed statement indicating that the participant or the participant's parents

- understand and appreciate the risks involved in the activity;
- know the safety rules and procedures, understand their importance, and agree to comply with them; and
- specifically request that the person be allowed to participate in the activity.

To be of legal value, a participation agreement must do the following:

- Be clearly and explicitly worded
- Clearly explain the nature of the activity and the prerequisite skills or level of physical ability
- Identify the rules that must be followed
- State in detail the possible dangers inherent in the activity and the consequences to the participant should an accident occur (This should include the specific types of injuries that may be encountered and, if appropriate, the possibility of paralysis and death.)
- Require the participant to indicate that she possesses the requisite skills and level of physical condition
- Include a statement wherein the participant agrees to assume the risks inherent in the activity

Although a properly designed participation agreement cannot offer absolute protection from a lawsuit, it can help establish contributory or comparative negligence. The draft in Figure 12.1 can form the basis for a participation agreement. Remember that all such documents should be specific to the activity and situation in question and should be reviewed by an attorney.

Contributory and Comparative Negligence

Under the principle of **contributory negligence**, acts or omissions by the plaintiff that fall below the standard of ordinary care and that contribute to the cause or aggravation of the injury complained of may prevent the plaintiff from legally recovering damages from the defendant. In other words, if the negligent actions of the plaintiff in any way helped to cause or aggravate the injury complained of, the plaintiff cannot win the lawsuit regardless of the negligence of the defendant teacher or coach.

For instance, a gymnastics coach might have a rule that forbids any athlete to attempt any skill unless a spotter is present. The coach faithfully enforces this rule and issues reprimands immediately whenever violations are noted. If on a given day one athlete attempts several back handsprings without a spotter and ultimately falls and sustains a serious injury, the principle of contributory negligence would probably prevent the athlete from successfully pursuing a negligence suit. The injured athlete knew, or should have known, that she was acting improperly and in contravention of established rules. She failed to take the ordinary actions reasonably expected of a person in her position and thus must accept the legal responsibility for her own injury.

Most states, however, currently apply the more equitable principle of **comparative negligence**. In a situation involving comparative negligence, the jury is asked to determine the relative degree of responsibility of the plaintiff and the defendant(s). The amount of damages that the plaintiff could recover would then be decreased by her percentage of responsibility. If, for instance, Jane Barnes sued Coach Thompson for $100,000 in compensatory damages, and if Jane was found to be comparatively negligent in the amount of 20%, her maximum award would be 80% of $100,000, or $80,000.

Some states maintain a threshold beyond which the plaintiff is barred from recovery. This threshold, where applied, is usually around 50%. In other words, if Jane Barnes is found to be more responsible for her injury

I realize that _____ is a vigorous physical activity that involves _____
(name of sport)

(Characterize the elements of the activity: e.g., height, flight, and rotation; violent body con-

tact; rapid directional change.) _____

_____

_____

I understand that participation in _____ involves certain inherent risks
(name of sport)
and that, regardless of the precautions taken by _____
(name of organization providing
_____ or the participants, some injuries may occur. These injuries might in-
program)
clude, but are not limited to:

  1. _(Give examples, being sure to_
  2. _include the most common and_
  3. _most severe injuries; e.g., blind-_
  4. _ness, quadriplegia, death.)_

These injuries may result from hazards such as:

  1. _(List circumstances that might bring about the types of injuries cited_
  2. _above. Again, be sure to include the most common hazards; e.g., being_
  3. _struck by a racquet or ball, making initial contact with head while_
  4. _blocking or tackling.)_

The likelihood of such injuries may be lessened by adhering to the following safety
rules:

  1.
  2.
  3.
  4.
  5.

In order to properly protect my own safety and that of my fellow participants, I
agree to follow these rules as well as any others that may be given by my (coach/
instructor). Further, in recognition of the importance of shared responsibility for
safety, I agree to immediately report any noted deviations from the safety rules as
well as any observed hazardous conditions or equipment to my (coach/instructor).

(continued)

Figure 12.1 Agreement to participate.

I further certify that my present level of physical condition is consistent with the demands of active participation in _____. Following is a full and complete
                                             (name of sport)
list of all of my known health conditions that might affect my ability to participate.

_____

_____

_____

_____

I have carefully read the foregoing document. I have had the opportunity to ask questions and have them answered. I am confident that I fully know, understand, and appreciate the risks involved in active participation in _____ and I am
voluntarily requesting permission to participate.   *(name of sport)*

_____   _____
              Signature   *Date*

Figure 12.1   *(continued)*

than Coach Thompson, in some states she would not be eligible for any compensatory damages (see also Case 12.3). Table 12.2 illustrates the application of contributory and comparative negligence to several hypothetical jury awards.

Assumption of Risk

It is often said that persons who take part in vigorous physical activities must recognize the possibility that they could suffer an injury during the course of their participation. They must therefore assume the risk of any injuries that are normally associated with participation in that activity. However, **assumption of risk** has little absolute value as a legal defense (Davis, 1981).

As a general rule, participants cannot be expected to assume a risk of which they are unaware. It is incumbent upon the teacher or coach, therefore, to warn participants of the

Table 12.2   Relative Effects of Contributory and Comparative Negligence on Compensatory Awards for Damages

Plaintiff	Percent of responsibility for own injury	Damages sought	Maximum award if contributory negligence applies	Maximum award if comparative negligence applies
David Strange	15%	$100,000	$0	$ 85,000
Mary Bishop	45%	$750,000	$0	$412,500
Alicia Ames	0%	$250,000	$250,000	$250,000

risks of any activity and to teach them reasonably effective procedures for reducing or eliminating the dangers associated with those risks. If no such warning and instruction is provided, and the participants have no prior independent knowledge of the risks involved, then they assume nothing. If, on the other hand, a participant who had been warned of the dangers and provided with reasonable instruction and feedback to help reduce or eliminate them did something contrary to the learned procedure and thereby suffered an injury despite this preparation, the issue is really one of contributory or comparative negligence. In either case the assumption of risk terminology has no direct value as a separate defense.

Act of God

Certain types of accidents are sometimes referred to as having occurred as a result of an **act of God**. Like assumption of risk, this term has little absolute value as a legal defense.

If, for instance, a golf class was being conducted on a large field and one of the students was struck and badly injured by a bolt of lightning, one might argue that the lightning was an act of God and therefore beyond the reasonable control of the teacher. The real issue, however, is whether or not the accident was foreseeable. Foreseeability is one of the elements defined earlier in this chapter that must be proven to successfully establish a negligence claim.

Therefore, if the accident occurred on an otherwise beautiful day with no warning of an approaching thunderstorm, or if the teacher had curtailed activities and taken reasonable steps to protect the students from a sudden storm, then there would probably be no cause for a claim of negligence. If, on the other hand, the teacher saw lightning and heard thunder but estimated the storm to have been a safe distance away and directed the students to continue practicing for the

few minutes remaining in the class, then a jury might decide that the incident in question was foreseeable and therefore preventable. The issue is whether or not the incident in question was foreseeable. The act of God terminology is really excess verbal baggage.

MANAGEMENT GUIDELINES:

EFFECTIVE RECORD KEEPING IMPROVES DEFENSIBILITY

Although effective documentation and record keeping are certainly not technical legal defenses, they can be of inestimable value in preparing an effective defense against claims of negligence. Effective documentation actually serves a dual function: First, it is an important component of sound program planning and organization that can lead to the development and delivery of safer activities. Second, if routinely and regularly maintained, it provides a written record of procedures followed and actions taken that can refresh recollection of past events and serve as factual evidence in the event of a lawsuit. Lawsuits usually extend over a period of several years, and few people can remember for that length of time the details of any given event or of the events that preceded it to be able to furnish the kind of information likely to be requested by attorneys for both the plaintiff and the defendant. Only a strong commitment to effective record keeping can spare a defendant from an embarrassing series of "I don't know's" and "I don't remember's" at the time of trial.

Written materials commonly requested as evidence in a lawsuit include the following:

1. *Lesson plans* help to provide evidence of thought and preparation prior to the delivery of a given lesson. Well-developed plans are no less valuable for

coaches than for teachers because they can provide clear evidence of how subject matter was organized, what warm-up and safety procedures were included, the learning sequence, and so forth.

2. *Curriculum and unit plans* show how the activity in question fits into the overall instructional unit. They are particularly useful in establishing the validity of any given activity and the sequence of preparatory activities and lead-ups.

3. *Rosters and attendance records* can help establish the plaintiff's experience by documenting her presence at important preliminary classes, meetings, or practices.

4. *Testing and screening results* are valuable tools for establishing the plaintiff's readiness for the activity in question. Careful screening and testing records can provide factual documentation of the plaintiff's previous achievements and thus justify participation at the next reasonable level. At the same time, they provide inferential testimony regarding the level of care exercised by the instructor or coach in determining participant readiness.

5. *Emergency plans* help document a coach or instructor's readiness for foreseeable emergencies and the soundness of the procedures followed. Moreover, they help guarantee appropriate responses when emergencies arise.

6. *Informed consent documents* provide documentary evidence that the plaintiff understood and accepted both the risks of the activity and his obligation to exercise reasonable care.

7. *Maintenance/inspection reports* for both facilities and equipment provide written confirmation of continuing efforts to maintain the level of safety and function that the appropriate professional standards call for.

8. *Incident reports* provide documentary evidence regarding the exact circumstances surrounding an injury, the names and statements of witnesses, emergency procedures followed, and the nature and results of any follow-up. Figure 12.2 is an example of an effective incident report form you may use as a model.

MANAGEMENT GUIDELINES:

PUBLIC RELATIONS HELP REDUCE THE DESIRE TO SUE

Strong, positive public relations is an extremely valuable tool for preventing lawsuits that is often overlooked. Although positive public relations may have little or no impact on the legal outcome of lawsuits once they have been brought, it most certainly helps determine whether or not injured persons or their parents initiate one. As a general rule, people are reluctant to sue a person who they like and care about and who they think likes them and is sincerely concerned about their welfare and satisfaction. Conversely, they are often quick to strike out against people who they do not like or who they think do not like or care about them. It is important, therefore, that all people who administer and deliver programs give parents and participants the impression that they are skilled, caring professionals who are willing to go out of their way to ensure the safety and satisfaction of the participants. This is not a matter of pretense or slick marketing but of honest, open communication. It must begin with the very first introduction and continue well beyond the conclusion of the activity or event. Most importantly, it must not stop when the participant is pulled out of the activity due to accident or illness.

Name of injured athlete: _____

Date of injury: _____   Time of injury: _____

Nature of injury: _____

Describe the accident: (*Include exact location, nature of the activity, sequence of*
activities/events preceding the injury, and all other pertinent facts.)

First aid/medical treatment: (*Describe procedures followed.*)

Names and addresses of witnesses: (*Append written statements from witnesses where*
appropriate.)

Follow-up: (*Medical diagnosis, visitation, etc.*)

Comments: (*This is an appropriate place to include any statement by the injured party*
that indicated his or her own careless or wrongful actions. In completing the form, how-
ever, report only facts and direct statements, not your opinions or those of other
observers.)

Date of report: _____   Signature: _____

Figure 12.2   Incident report.

CASE STUDIES

Case 12.1   **Proximate Cause**

JoAnn Samuels, age 8, was a member of the Springwood Angels soccer
team. It was raining heavily on the day of her regularly scheduled practice,
so her coach, Alex Wilson, secured permission to use the gymnasium of
Pineville Elementary School. The gymnasium was a typical elementary
facility that measured approximately 50 ft by 90 ft with masonry walls,
a wooden floor, and a stage at one end.

Near the conclusion of the practice, the coach informed the children
that they would have a relay race. The group was divided into four teams,
and the children were told to run the length of the gym, tag the wall,
and return to the starting line where they would tag their teammate. The
starting line was painted on the floor and was 3 ft from the masonry wall.

Although competition and excitement levels were relatively high, the children were well controlled and held to their waiting positions throughout the contest. When JoAnn ran her leg of the relay, her team and one other were competing very closely for the lead. As she completed her leg of the relay and made the tag, she stumbled and fell, striking the end wall and fracturing her shoulder.

Alex Wilson was negligent in the manner in which he planned and conducted the practice session in question. His organization of the relay race was significantly below the accepted standards of practice, and JoAnn Samuels was seriously injured as a result. The jury, in finding Wilson negligent, discounted his argument that JoAnn should have exercised greater care for her own welfare by slowing down before she reached the finish line and awarded full compensatory damages to the plaintiff.

This case illustrates the problems associated with rainy day activities that have not been carefully planned in advance. Although Coach Wilson was well prepared for his scheduled outdoor activity, he had not thought out the modifications that might be necessary if the weather forced a move indoors. Like many individuals forced into similar positions, he elected to play a few simple games and lead-up activities.

Perhaps if Mr. Wilson had realized that games have been found to be one of the leading sources of negligence suits (Dougherty, 1988)—ahead of such activities as soccer, basketball, softball, and football—he would have exercised more care in the planning process. Like many others, however, Mr. Wilson fell into the trap of taking a simple activity for granted. He combined a relatively safe relay with an otherwise safe facility in a manner that created an improper and easily avoidable risk of harm to the participants. The result was a painful injury and a costly negligence suit.

Because he was unprepared for the possibility of a rainout, Alex Wilson had not thought carefully about the nature and organization of the games he conducted on the date of the accident. He therefore ignored the normal provisions for safety zones and the avoidance of walls and other potentially hazardous obstructions. Instead he directed the children to run into a wall at one end of the gym and to complete the race at a line 3 ft away from the wall at the other end. Certainly he should have been able to anticipate the fact that, especially in a competitive event, the children would be running at or near full speed when they reached each of the walls. It would, in fact, be illogical to expect that a child would slow down prior to the finish line and thus risk losing the race and incurring the wrath of her peers. The risk of injury was not only foreseeable but probable.

The professional impropriety of the decision to utilize the Pineville facility in the manner described is compounded by the fact that it was easily avoidable. The simplest and most commonly employed alternative would have been to shorten the race by 15 to 20 ft and to place traffic cones, tape marks, or some other designators at the new stopping and turning points. The athletes would then have had a safe turning radius and a reasonable distance after the designated finish line in which to decelerate and regain their equilibrium. Providing the necessary margin of safety in this way would not have detracted significantly from the nature or value of the game.

[Based on a case adjudicated in the lower courts]

Case 12.2

Proximate Cause

Stephen Latley is a physical education teacher in Carson Elementary School. He has been teaching at Carson for 12 years and is thoroughly familiar with the school and the students in it. The gymnasium in which he teaches is 78 ft in length, with a stage at one end and a solid tile wall at the other.

Mr. Latley knows from long experience that many of the children in his classes will seize any opportunity they can to run to the stage and do a sliding dive along the smoothly polished stage floor. This is especially true of the fifth and sixth grade boys who find the chest-high stage ideal for a running takeoff from the gymnasium floor. For this reason, Mr. Latley exercises great care to keep his students a safe distance from the stage throughout the course of his class activities.

Six months ago he was conducting a relay race for the fourth graders. He placed a tape line on the floor 16 ft from the stage to serve as the starting point. The children were directed to run to the far wall, tag it, and return to tag the next person on their team, who was to be waiting at the starting line with one foot on the taped line. The students were reminded of the hazardous nature of running into the stage and were warned of the possibility of injury if they did so. Further, Mr. Latley told them that they were to walk to the rear of their team after the tag and immediately assume a seated position away from the stage. Failure to comply with this rule would result in disqualification.

As Jimmy Morton completed his leg of the relay, he tagged his teammate and continued running at full speed directly toward the stage. He timed his jump incorrectly and struck the edge of the stage, suffering serious injury. Jimmy's father instituted a lawsuit, naming Stephen Latley as a defendant. Mr. Latley was understandably quite concerned about this suit and wondered whether there was anything more he could or should have done to prevent the injury.

This case is very similar to *Samuels v. Wilson* (Case 12.1). Like JoAnn Samuels in the earlier case, Jimmy Morton was injured when he struck a major obstruction at the conclusion of a relay race. Mr. Latley, like Coach Wilson in the Samuels case, failed to meet the standard of care expected of a prudent professional in the same or similar circumstances. Unlike Coach Wilson, however, Mr. Latley was not held legally responsible for the injuries sustained by the child entrusted to his care. The essential difference between these two cases brings the concept of proximate cause into focus.

Mr. Latley directed his students to race to the far wall of the gymnasium, tag it, and return to the starting point. This was entirely improper and fell significantly below accepted standards. Simply put, walls are not intended to be turning or stopping points. The risk of injury is far too great to be acceptable because it can be avoided easily (Dougherty, 1987). However, Mr. Latley was fortunate that none of his students were injured while approaching or turning at the far wall.

Jimmy Morton was injured at the conclusion of the race. Mr. Latley had provided thorough instruction and warnings about the dangers of running into the stage. Moreover he had provided an ample amount of space between the start/finish line and the stage. In this regard, his actions were fully in compliance with the best practices in the field. There was in fact nothing more that he could or should have done to ensure his students' safety at that end of the floor.

Mr. Latley improperly directed his students to run into a wall, but because that act did not cause or aggravate the injury sustained by Jimmy Morton, he was not held liable for damages arising from the incident. If, however, someone had been injured at the turning point, the results would almost surely have been quite different.

[Based on a case adjudicated in the lower courts]

Case 12.3

Contributory and Comparative Negligence

Mary Wells was a 14-year-old student in the eighth grade at Marsten Junior High School. At the time of the incident that gave rise to this lawsuit, Mary was participating in a required physical education class under the direction of George Bailey, a certified teacher. The class of approximately 25 boys and girls had been divided into four teams, and two whiffleball games were being conducted. Each game used one half of the gymnasium, which measured approximately 85 ft by 100 ft. Mr. Bailey was dividing his attention between the two games by alternately facing and focusing on each game.

One of Mary's teammates was at bat, and Mary and another student were chatting as they awaited their turns at bat. Mary was standing approximately 6 ft behind home plate in the 8 o'clock position. As the batter swung at a pitched ball, the bat slipped from his hands and struck Mary in the eye, causing serious injury. At the time of the accident, Mr. Bailey was on the opposite side of the gymnasium with his back toward the game in which Mary Wells was participating. Mr. Bailey testified, however, that all students had been warned to stand against the gymnasium wall (approximately 20 ft from home plate) while waiting for their turns at bat. He stated that, in his opinion, Mary would not have been injured if she had simply followed these directions. The jury found Mr. Bailey negligent but decreased Mary's award by 30% based on her comparative negligence.

The fundamental causative factors in this injury are those of improper supervision and organization of the class in question. Mr. Bailey's failure to organize and control both segments of his class effectively was entirely improper and precipitated this unnecessary injury.

The importance of proper supervision and class organization as tools for reducing student injuries and the responsibilities of teachers in that regard have been well documented in the professional literature and have been a fundamental component of teacher education programs for many years. The failure to provide for effective supervision and organization is therefore a deviation from the standard of care that one would expect from a reasonable teacher.

Mr. Bailey should have positioned himself so that he could see all of the players and provide effective general supervision. By alternately giving his full attention to one game at a time, he was also alternately ignoring one half of the students for whom he was responsible. Coaches and teachers must position themselves in locations that allow them to see all the participants and should maintain this visual contact as they move through the area. Generally this would mean moving around the perimeter of the playing area and trying to stay in close proximity to the areas of greatest danger.

Mary Wells was standing in an inappropriate area. Her location was far too close to the batter and clearly at variance with the position Mr. Bailey had set in his rules. Moreover, while Mary was chatting with a classmate, it is unlikely that she was attentive enough to react to a sudden hazard such as a slipped or thrown bat. If Mr. Bailey had seen Mary's position, he would have (or at least should have) taken corrective action that would have prevented this injury. Because he was looking in the opposite direction, he neither saw nor corrected the problem, and Mary Wells was injured as a result.

The jury's decision to assign comparative negligence to Mary was due to her violation of Mr. Bailey's rule regarding appropriate waiting positions. Mr. Bailey had emphasized the dangers of standing too near the batter and had set safe guidelines for where students should stand. This was a critical factor in determining comparative negligence and reduced George Bailey's responsibility in proportion to the jury's perception of Mary's responsibility.

[Based on a case adjudicated in the lower courts]

CHAPTER SUMMARY

The threat of a lawsuit arising from an injury suffered by a participant has had a major impact on sport and physical activity programs. Although it is practically impossible to completely eliminate risk, you can reduce the likelihood of lawsuits and improve your chances of winning those that cannot be prevented by understanding the legal requirements to support a negligence claim, the legal defenses available, and the nature and importance of record keeping and public relations.

KEY TERMS

Act of God (241)
Assumption of risk (240)

Breach (236)
Comparative negligence (238)
Contributory negligence (238)
Damages (237)
Defendant (236)
Doctrine of entitlement (235)
Duty (236)
Foreseeability (237)
Insurance shortfalls (235)
Myth of being risk-free (235)
Negligence (236)
Participation agreement (237)
Plaintiff (236)
Proximate cause (237)
Release (237)
The right to sue (235)
Settlements (235)
Tort (236)
Waiver (237)

QUESTIONS FOR DISCUSSION

1. Many of the factors that underlie the so-called "liability explosion" are beyond the control of those involved in the development and delivery of sport and physical activity programs. However, actions can be taken to reduce insurance shortfalls, reduce the desire of injured participants to pursue legal action, and increase one's ability to defend against claims that may be brought. Discuss alternative strategies to achieve these ends and include appropriate activity-specific examples.
2. Name and explain the five basic elements that a plaintiff must prove to win a negligence suit.
3. Develop activity-specific examples of informed consent documents and incident reports. Review those developed by your classmates and share suggestions for modification and improvement.
4. For each of the following circumstances, give three practical examples of an accident or injury situation.
   a. There was a breach of duty but no proximate cause.
   b. There was a breach of duty and comparative negligence.
   c. The incident was not foreseeable.

REFERENCES

Davis, V.J. (1981). Sports liability: Blowing the whistle on the referees. *Pacific Law Journal*, **12**, 937-964.

Dougherty, N.J. (1988). Learning from the mistakes of others. *Athletic Business*, **12**(8), 59-62.

Dougherty, N.J. (Ed.) (1987). *Principles of safety in physical education and sport*. Reston, VA: AAHPERD Publications.

ADDITIONAL READINGS

Appenzeller, H. (1975). *Athletics and the law*. Charlottesville, VA: The Michie Co.

Clement, A. (1988). *Law in sport and physical activity*. Indianapolis: Benchmark Press.

Kaiser, R.A. (1986). *Liability and law in recreation and sport*. Englewood Cliffs, NJ: Prentice-Hall.

Peterson, J.A. (1987). *Risk management for park, recreation and leisure services*. Champaign, IL: Management Learning Laboratories.

Schubert, G.W., Smith, R.K., & Trentadue, J.C. (1986). *Sports law*. St. Paul: West.

van der Smissen, B. (1990). *Legal liability and risk management for public and private entities* (Vols. I-II). Cincinnati: Anderson.

CHAPTER 13

THE STANDARD OF CARE IN SPORTS AND PHYSICAL ACTIVITIES

Melissa Herman, a sophomore member of the cheerleading squad at Southernmost High School, is suing for injuries she sustained while performing a two-person mount at a soccer game. The skill in question, a step-up to a shoulder straddle, had been taught by the coach, Jane Quinn, and was part of the only routine that the cheerleaders had been directed to perform that day.

On the date the injury occurred, considerable rain had fallen, and the start of the game had been delayed. Ms. Quinn sent the cheerleading squad to the field but she did not attend. No instructions or warnings were provided regarding precautions or modifications appropriate for wet ground surfaces. At approximately 4:30 p.m., the cheerleaders began their first stunt of the day. As Melissa Herman was negotiating the step-up to the straddle position, her partner slipped on the wet grass. Both girls fell to the ground, and Melissa fractured her left arm.

The key issues in determining Coach Quinn's potential liability with regard to the injuries sustained by Melissa Herman are: What is the standard of care expected of a reasonably prudent cheerleading supervisor? and Did Coach Quinn fall below this standard? The American Association of Cheerleading coaches and advisers (AACCA) has published the *AACCA Cheerleading Safety Manual* (George, 1990), which clearly outlines the responsibilities of cheerleading coaches and supervisors for the development and delivery of safe and productive activities. Portions of the text that apply directly to this case spell out in detail the requirements for adequate supervision and a safe performing environment and the obligation of the supervisor to make activity modifications when inclement weather causes the element of risk to rise above normal limits. This text would be a persuasive piece of documentary evidence at the time of trial.

The alleged actions of Jane Quinn in connection with this incident fell significantly below the articulated standard. Through her failure to effectively supervise and direct the girls for whom she was responsible, an activity was conducted that exposed the cheerleaders to an improper and otherwise avoidable risk. If Ms. Quinn had properly executed her duties, it is reasonable to assume that she would have noted the danger and modified or eliminated the activity. Under such circumstances, her actions would have been in compliance with AACCA guidelines, and Melissa Herman probably would not have been injured. Moreover, if Ms. Quinn had complied with the standards and, despite her best efforts, Melissa Herman had still suffered an injury, the same standards that were used to condemn her would have become her strongest defense argument.

LEARNING OBJECTIVES

The student will be able to

1. define the nature and importance of effective supervision, appropriate selection and conduct of activities, and safe environmental conditions;
2. differentiate between general and specific supervision and give examples of each; and
3. enumerate guidelines to reduce the risk of injuries attributable to faulty supervision, inappropriate selection or conduct of the activities, and unsafe facilities, and provide activity-specific examples of their application.

MAJOR AREAS OF RESPONSIBILITY

Most sport-related lawsuits allege that the defendant teacher or coach breached the standard of care by failing to fulfill his or her professional duties in one or more of the following three major areas:

1. The responsibility to provide effective supervision
2. The responsibility to provide appropriate and well-conducted activities
3. The responsibility to provide safe and appropriate environmental conditions

A survey of over 400 recent lawsuits (Table 13.1) found that 24% of the plaintiffs had argued that the primary cause of their injuries was faulty supervision on the part of the defendant, 40% alleged that there had been inappropriate selection or conduct of the activities, and 36% claimed that their injuries were the result of unsafe environmental conditions. Note that these results have been generalized across all levels of activity and that the relative likelihood of a lawsuit in each of the three primary areas of responsibility appears to vary depending upon whether the activity is recreational, instructional, or an organized competitive sport. Table 13.1 illustrates the differences in the results when these levels of activity are viewed separately.

For purposes of the survey, the following operational definitions were used:

- Instructional programs are those with an assigned teacher or leader. These programs could occur in a school, club, or any other setting.
- Teams are situations in which athletes are under the structured control of a coach. This includes interscholastic and intercollegiate sports, organized clubs, and private groups. It does not include the more informally structured intramural or recreational teams in which a

player may assume some role in organizational leadership.
- Recreational activities refer to all of the less-structured circumstances not covered in the other two categories. They include children on a playground, participants at a racquet or health club who are not involved in an instructional event, and players in most adult softball leagues.

By examining Table 13.1, you can see that the condition of the environment is the largest source of negligence claims in recreational programs, and that proper selection and conduct of the activity is the primary concern in instructional and team activities. Finally, it is important to recognize that, regardless of the level of activity, it is possible to identify virtually all controllable injury-causing factors by carefully analyzing the areas of supervision, selection and conduct of the activity, and environmental conditions.

SUPERVISION

Because careful supervision can prevent many needless injuries, failure to fulfill one's supervisory responsibilities properly is alleged to

Table 13.1   Survey of Lawsuits by Activity Level

| Responsibility allegedly breached | Levels of activity | | | | |
	Recreation	Instruction	Teams	Number of cases	Percentage
Supervision	58	32	19	109	24%
Selection and conduct of activities	32	113	38	183	40%
Failure to provide a safe environment	125	30	12	167	36%
Total number of cases	215	175	69	459	
Percentage	47%	38%	15%		

be at least a contributing factor in most negligence suits. **Supervision** can be defined as the quality and quantity of control exerted by teachers or coaches over the individuals for whom they are responsible. Therefore the number of supervisory personnel assigned to a group must be sufficient to effectively control the group in question, and the supervisors must have the training and skills necessary to fulfill their assigned duties.

The issue of **qualitative supervision** is of far greater legal concern to administrative personnel than to those directly involved in delivering programs and services. Although greater levels of training and certification are likely to provide teachers or coaches with the skills and knowledge necessary to conduct a safer program or activity, they would not protect them from the legal results of their own negligence. For example, if an athlete is injured due to the coach's failure to fulfill his legal responsibilities for her care, the coach will probably be found guilty of negligence regardless of his credentials.

The potential liability of the coach's employer or supervisor, however, is a different matter that relates to the civil law concept known as *respondeat superior* whereby employers or supervisors may be held legally responsible for their employees' actions to the degree that they may have been able to exert some reasonable degree of control in the matter. Therefore, the supervisors of a relatively untrained coach who is accused of negligence may well face legal action due to their failure to employ a properly trained person who, in theory, would have known better than to commit the negligent act. In this situation the employers face a form of **vicarious liability** whereby their legal responsibilities to supervise and, within reason, to control the actions of their employees places them in the position of being to some degree indirectly responsible for an incident over which they had no direct control.

Consider two identical gymnastics classes, each with 25 students and one instructor. The instructor for Class A is a certified teacher with extensive experience as a gymnastics instructor who received safety training and certification from the U.S. Gymnastics Federation. The instructor for Class B is a former national collegiate gymnastics champion who has had no specific training as a coach or teacher. In each class a student attempted to perform a very difficult skill several times without the aid of mats or spotters. The instructors either ignored or did not see these violations of approved safety procedure. Not surprisingly, the students each suffered serious injury.

In each instance, the instructors were negligent, and the differences in their credentials and qualifications did not affect the outcome of the lawsuit against them. In each case, however, the program administrator was also named as a defendant. Because both administrators performed all other aspects of their duties properly, only the administrator responsible for Class B was found negligent. The plaintiff successfully argued that the administrator in charge of Class B should have realized that an instructor who lacked the training appropriate for the assigned responsibilities would be far more likely to make an otherwise avoidable error that could foreseeably result in an injury than an instructor with proper training. (See also chapter 9 for a discussion of professional credentialing.)

The issue of **quantitative supervision** is different from that of qualitative supervision. Certainly the question of the number and assignment of supervisors is a purely administrative matter, but it is seldom the source of a lawsuit in and of itself. Most activities lack specific guidelines regarding the appropriate instructor/student ratio. Regardless of the activity, most administrators tend to do their best to provide a reasonable number of supervisory personnel. Improper quantitative supervision is of greater concern for the individual teacher or coach. The issue for them is not necessarily one of absolute numbers, however, but of the relative degree of attention and effectiveness exhibited by the supervisor.

The individual teacher or coach is responsible for two types of supervision: general and specific. **General supervision** requires an overview of the entire group. The supervisor must keep all of the participants within sight, be alert for dangers or deviations from accepted procedure, and be ready to intervene quickly and resolve any problems noted.

When problems or dangers are noted, the supervisor must shift to **specific supervision**. Specific supervision is the term applied to the direct interaction between the teacher or coach and one or more individual students. Specific supervision is required when a deviation from prescribed procedures is noted or when a student demonstrates a need for additional assistance or attention.

It is important to recognize, however, that the need to move to specific supervision does not remove the obligation to maintain general supervisory control over the remainder of the group. The supervisor cannot (as in Figure 13.1) become so engrossed in meeting the needs of one or two students that he fails to detect and eliminate a hazardous situation that has arisen in another area of the gym.

The question of how much specific supervision may be required for any given group is a function of the participants' ages and skill levels and their ability to understand and appreciate the risks and consequences of their own actions. Generally, as the participants' ages and abilities increase, it is reasonable to expect longer periods of productive activity with only general supervision.

Figure 13.1   Although this coach is providing excellent specific supervision for one athlete, he is neglecting his duty to provide general supervision for all.

and subsequent lawsuits associated with supervisory shortcomings.

1. Take all reasonable steps to keep supervisory/instructional skills and certifications at the highest possible level (see chapter 9 for more information). Keep abreast of the best practices in the field to reduce the chance of risk or harm to the participants and to provide clear evidence of your readiness to teach, coach, or supervise the activity.

2. Organize the participants to facilitate effective supervision. Move about the area to maximize contact with individual participants, being careful to minimize instances in which some person

MANAGEMENT GUIDELINES:
SUPERVISION

Routine observance of the following guidelines and principles can help prevent injuries

or persons may be out of your direct line of vision.

3. Do not leave individuals or groups unsupervised. You cannot solve problems or eliminate hazards you don't see because you are taking a telephone call in the office or gathering equipment from a closet.

4. Establish, post, explain, and enforce general behavioral and safety rules for the gymnasia, fields, locker rooms, and all areas where activities may be conducted. Figure 13.2 shows an effective set of rules posted in a fitness center.

5. Secure facilities and equipment that are not being used. If the facilities are open and the equipment is accessible, people can be expected to enter and use them.

It is also reasonable to predict that if these facilities and equipment are used in the absence of proper supervision and guidance, the likelihood of an accidental injury will increase greatly (see Case 13.1).

6. Be prepared to render immediate and effective first aid when necessary. In the event of an emergency, the supervisor must take the appropriate actions to sustain life and/or prevent further harm until emergency personnel (trainer, nurse, doctor) arrive and take over (see Case 13.4).

7. Develop emergency procedures to be followed in the event of an accident or injury. Specific guidelines prepared for each group and area in question should

Figure 13.2 Clearly worded and posted safety rules help prevent accidents and increase the legal responsibility of the participants.

include protocols for who contacts whom, when, and how; the actions expected of the rest of the participants; the supervisory backup to be provided; and the usual follow-up procedures.

8. Remember that supervisors must maintain control of their classes or teams at all times to guide their actions and to detect and correct inappropriate behaviors. Never allow the actions of one individual or one group to endanger others or to detract from the effectiveness of the learning environment.

SELECTION AND CONDUCT OF THE ACTIVITIES

Regardless of the nature or level of the program, teachers, recreation leaders, and coaches are expected to select or allow activities that are reasonable for the ability levels of the individuals involved. Courts generally recognize and accept the concept that, with few exceptions, no activity is inherently unsafe in and of itself.

The question then is whether or not the participant was physically, mentally, and emotionally ready for the demands of the activity so that she should have been able to execute it safely. In the event of an injury, therefore, one question that is frequently asked is whether or not it was reasonable to allow the injured person to attempt the particular skill involved.

This question is relevant only to the person who was injured; the fact that the rest of the team could perform the skill or that it was a generally accepted activity for individuals at the grade level in question will not suffice (see Case 13.2). The supervisor must be prepared through appropriate forms of skill testing and successful lead-up activities to document the fact that the injured participant was indeed equal to the demands of the activity that resulted in the injury.

That was certainly not the case in Mr. Dolan's sixth grade physical education class a few years ago. The class had been practicing for a gymnastics exhibition for 6 weeks. Part of the show involved simple vaults performed in rapid-fire fashion by each member of the class. Mr. Dolan's students had all been performing the vaults for some time and had spent 2 weeks working up to the rapid-fire routine.

Mary Worth and her family had just moved into town, and she was enrolled in Mr. Dolan's class 2 weeks before the show. Mr. Dolan, who was preoccupied with preparations for the show, welcomed Mary to his class and told her to join the group activities. After conducting a brief warm-up, the students moved to the horse, where they began with a squat vault.

When her turn came, Mary, who had never before attempted a vault, struck the horse and suffered a serious knee injury. Although the squat vault was a safe and proper activity for Mr. Dolan's class, it was not appropriate for Mary Worth. In his haste, Mr. Dolan neglected to ascertain her readiness and failed to provide the kind of instruction that might have enabled her to succeed at the vault. If Mary Worth's parents elect to seek compensation through the courts, there is every reason to expect that they will be successful.

In addition to selecting appropriate activities, the teacher or coach is expected to provide **instruction** that is both accurate in its detail and that is presented in a manner that maximizes the likelihood of the participants' success. This instruction should include not only information regarding the techniques of successful performance but warnings regarding any potentially hazardous elements of the activity and specific guidelines for minimizing these risks.

To be effective, however, these instructions must be augmented by accurate and detailed **feedback**. The simple act of telling a person how to perform a physical skill in no way guarantees success. Successful performance requires practice supplemented by accurate feedback and remediation. Without these elements, athletes may perform to the best of their ability and may believe that they have been successful, even though the actual performance may have been lacking in one or more respects. Performance discrepancies that are perpetuated can retard progress and, in some cases, pose a risk of injury. Eliminating such problems through a continuous process of evaluation and feedback is essential to the development of a safe and successful program and to legal defensibility.

Even athletes who are physically capable of performing the skills necessary for success may still face unnecessary and improper risk of injury if they are mismatched with their opponents. A **mismatch** is an inequity in the size, strength, or ability of the competitors that, if not properly controlled, can increase the risk of injury to the undermatched athlete. Teams and classes should be organized to minimize the risks associated with mismatching in activities involving physical contact (see Case 13.3).

Remember, however, that mismatching is a function of size, strength, and ability, not sex. With the advent of Title IX (see chapter 4), some professionals became concerned with what they perceived as the inevitable mismatching of boys and girls. This concern has no basis in law or professional logic. A 100-lb girl who is injured in a collision with a 160-lb boy is no more or less mismatched than a 100-lb boy who is injured when he collides with a 160-lb girl. The 60-lb mismatch in the preceding two examples is entirely unrelated to the sex of the participants, and the requirement for equitable and safe balancing of the competitors existed long before Title IX was instituted.

A further means of reducing the risk and the potential severity of injuries is through the provision of appropriate **protective measures**. These measures include the use of spotters for safety in gymnastics and weight training and the use of protective devices and apparatus designed to protect the participants in many sports, including catchers' masks, landing mats, and shin pads. Protective measures such as these are essential to safe participation, and failure to use them within a program of instruction or competition would constitute a violation of proper professional procedure that could result in a lawsuit if that failure is shown to have caused an injury.

MANAGEMENT GUIDELINES:

SELECTION AND CONDUCT OF THE ACTIVITIES

Observing the following general guidelines and principles will help reduce the incidence of unnecessary risks and the likelihood of lawsuits related to negligence.

1. Utilize or allow only activities that are within the reasonable ability levels of the participants.
2. Learning and performance readiness varies greatly from one individual to the next. Implementing and documenting screening and pretesting procedures and providing individualized progressions and lead-ups therefore greatly increase both learning and safety.
3. Thorough planning of lessons and practices is essential both to success in learning skills and to legal defensibility in the event of a lawsuit. Written plans can provide documentary evidence of sequential learning experiences, attention to critical safety factors, and organizational details as well as the nature and extent of warnings provided.
4. All activities should contribute to the educational objectives of the program.

Too many injuries occur in activities that are implemented simply to fill time or that bear no relationship to the goals of the program. Such injuries are both unnecessary and difficult to justify.

5. Prepare alternative plans for activities that are subject to weather conditions or frequent uncontrollable modifications. Regardless of how well you have planned for an outdoor lesson, if rain forces the activity indoors, the only real issue of concern will be how well you have planned for the indoor activity that you are now forced to conduct.

6. Develop routine procedures for excusing students or athletes from class or practice for medical complaints or injuries. Equally important are procedures for resuming participation after an injury or extended illness. As a general rule, persons who have been seen by a doctor or who have missed several practices for medical reasons should not be readmitted without medical clearance (see Case 13.5).

7. If a participant expresses strong fear, insecurity, or reluctance to participate, do not force the issue. The role of the teacher or coach is to help the participant develop confidence, which is predicated upon successful experiences that are most likely to occur when the participant believes that he can succeed. Moreover, when a participant says "I cannot do this" or "I'm afraid to try," the supervisor has just been informed by the best expert imaginable that the participant is not equal to the task. If the supervisor forces the participant to try, and he suffers an injury, the supervisor must be prepared to shoulder both the moral responsibility and the legal consequences.

8. Provide any and all protective measures and devices appropriate to the activity and require their routine use. If adequate and appropriate safety measures cannot be provided for some reason, then make plans to reduce the hazard by modifying the activity (see Case 13.6).

9. In contact sports, carefully organize the group to reduce the likelihood and extent of mismatch situations. Perhaps the worst form of mismatch is when the supervisor participates with the athletes. To be effective, demonstrations should be done at reduced speed and under controlled circumstances. Moreover, it is virtually impossible to play and supervise the entire group simultaneously. Given these facts, playing with the individuals you are supposed to be supervising can only be viewed as a breach of professional responsibility.

10. Not all risks can be eliminated. The role of the program deliverer, therefore, is to carefully examine all elements of the program, to take all reasonable steps to remove or control the identifiable risks, and to make a conscious judgment as to whether or not the value of the activity significantly outweighs the risk that remains. If the identified values significantly outweigh the risks that cannot be controlled, the activity can and probably should be conducted. If this is not the case, however, the activity must be modified or discontinued.

ENVIRONMENTAL CONDITIONS

Even a well-designed and carefully supervised activity can prove unsafe if you fail to properly control factors related to the

environmental conditions: the facilities and equipment involved. A teacher or coach is expected to gain **constructive notice** of defects in the environment by routinely inspecting the facilities and the equipment before use. When a defect has been reported or otherwise brought to the teacher's or coach's attention she is said to have **actual notice**. In either case, she is clearly responsible for correcting the defect or reducing the risk of injury by other means such as modifying the activity or applying protective measures.

Before using any given facility or piece of equipment, the teacher or coach should carefully inspect it to be sure that it is free of observable defects or hazards. If problems exist, appropriate remedial actions should be taken. If a coach or teacher fails to fulfill this duty and an injury occurs as a result of an environmental defect that proper inspection would have disclosed, an unpleasant lawsuit may ensue.

Although most teachers and coaches exercise reasonable care in terms of preactivity inspections, too many carelessly create additional hazards by the manner in which they use otherwise safe facilities. Jane Samuels, for instance, directed her third grade class to run a short race across the gym. The finish line was a painted line on the floor 4 ft from the wall. The class was told that the first three finishers would represent the third grade in the 40-yd dash to be conducted at the upcoming school field day.

Jimmy Tomkins was first across the finish line, but he broke both wrists when he slammed into the wall. The gym was not unsafe in and of itself. Certainly a short sprint is not a particularly hazardous activity either. The problem is that in conducting the activity Ms. Samuels failed to consider the critical importance of a buffer, or safety area between the designated finish line and the wall, in which her students could decelerate and stop. Other examples of environmental hazards

created by those who are responsible for conducting activities include

- relay races in which running lanes and turning directions are not clearly identified,
- the use of equipment that requires a level of skill beyond that of the participants (e.g., high beams and bars for beginning gymnasts), and
- the use of improper substitute equipment (e.g., stones, candy wrappers, and trees as bases).

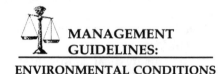

MANAGEMENT GUIDELINES:
ENVIRONMENTAL CONDITIONS

Here are some principles and guidelines for reducing the likelihood of injuries caused by unsafe environmental conditions.

1. Begin each day with an inspection of the facilities and equipment to be used. Note and correct any hazards or deficiencies. Pay particular attention to surface irregularities, slipperiness, and the presence of inappropriate or dangerous materials, and the function and security of all components and fittings. Remember: There is little that can be said to justify an injury that occurs as a result of an environmental hazard that could and probably would have been uncovered through a reasonably conscientious inspection. Conditions such as those found in Figure 13.3 should not be tolerated.
2. If environmental hazards are detected but cannot be immediately corrected, take actions to isolate the area or equipment until repairs can be completed. Put the damaged equipment away, mark off the unsafe area to warn participants,

Figure 13.3   The careless placement of equipment, tables, or chairs presents a hazardous situation that could result in a painful injury and a costly lawsuit.

modify the activity, or do whatever else may be necessary to provide a safe environment.

3. Teach the participants to perform basic safety inspections of the equipment they will be using and require them to do so as part of their daily routine. This procedure should supplement rather than take the place of inspections by the person in charge and should virtually eliminate the dangers and the potential liability associated with equipment failure.

4. Do not allow running activities to be conducted on a slippery or badly uneven surface. Similarly, be sure that all participants have footwear that is appropriate to the activity and the surface conditions (see Case 13.7).

5. When selecting equipment or playing areas, be sure that they meet or exceed applicable safety standards. Keep in mind that size and weight guidelines for many facilities and equipment are meant to promote uniformity, not safety. Therefore it is not necessarily dangerous or improper to shorten a playing field or to use a larger or smaller ball. Shortening the area of unobstructed space between a sideline and the nearest obstruction, on the other hand, may very well increase the risk of injury and thus should be avoided (see Case 13.8).

CASE STUDIES

Case 13.1

Supervision After Practice

Tom Clark was a member of the track team at Douglass High School. After practice, Tom and several of his teammates were in the gymnasium awaiting their rides home. While waiting, the boys began playing on mats that had been left on the floor of the gym. The boys had been engaging in general horseplay and friendly wrestling for approximately 20 minutes without supervision at the time of the accident in question. Tom was being chased by several boys and ran out of the gym and into an adjacent hallway. While running toward an exterior door, Tom extended his hand, which slipped off the opening bar and through a glass panel. He has instituted a lawsuit against his coaches for damages resulting from the injuries he sustained.

Tom Clark's injury was the direct and easily avoidable result of the improper supervision provided by his coaches. Their failure to meet their responsibility to provide effective supervision and to control the behavior of their athletes not only allowed but invited horseplay. This is especially the case in light of the presence of a wrestling mat. Such equipment, when not properly secured or supervised, serves as an open invitation to roughhousing and horseplay. The need for effective supervision increases significantly in the presence of mats, weights, gymnastic equipment, or other inviting paraphernalia that tend to be dangerous if used improperly and not controlled.

All teachers, coaches, and administrators must wrestle with the question of how best to deal with students or athletes who are dropped off early or picked up late or who simply wait for their friends before or after a scheduled activity. Although there is no single best solution, here are some guidelines for minimizing the dangers and maximizing your legal defensibility in the event of a lawsuit.

1. Provide ongoing general supervision for all participants.
2. Notify the parents and the participants in writing of the times during which supervision will be provided.
3. Extend actual scheduling of supervisors at least 15 minutes before and after the announced times to allow time to deal with early arrivals and late pick-ups. For example, if parents have been told that practice will conclude at 4:30 p.m. and that no supervisors will be present after 5:00 p.m., schedule supervisors to be on duty until at least 5:15 p.m. so that, if a problem arises outside of the posted hours, it will be clear that the staff went beyond their acknowledged responsibilities and that the students and/or their parents failed to meet theirs.
4. Secure all equipment when not in use.

5. Establish and enforce rules of conduct for locker rooms and waiting areas.

Remember that the legal and moral responsibility to supervise and control students or athletes is not restricted to the time limits of the actual class or practice. Failure to recognize and account for that fact may result in a lawsuit similar to the one brought against Tom Clark's coaches.

[Based on a case adjudicated in the lower courts]

Case 13.2

Participant Readiness and Protective Measures

Victor Lindsay was a fourth grade student in Holmes Elementary School who was participating in a physical education class conducted by Vivian Hansen. Ms. Hansen had set up several stations throughout the gymnasium, including two balance beams, a vaulting box, a mat station for tumbling, and parallel bars. Ms. Hansen provided instruction and demonstration for the entire class at the parallel bars and then divided the class among all of the stations. Victor went to the vaulting box. When he attempted to jump over it, he stumbled and fell, suffering a fractured arm.

Victor's mother contacted an attorney, who immediately discussed the case with an expert in gymnastics safety. The expert requested the following additional information:

1. What was the nature and extent of previous instruction and/or screening with regard to vaulting?
2. What kind of spotting was provided?
3. What kind of matting was provided?
4. What was the teacher doing at the time of the incident?

During the course of the discovery process, the attorney learned the following:

1. The class had received its first introduction to vaulting on the previous day. The teacher taught and demonstrated the approach, the squat-on-jump-off, and the squat. After the group instruction, Ms. Hansen remained at the box while the students rotated among the stations. During this time she spotted and provided individual assistance.
2. Ms. Hansen has no recollection of whether or not Victor or his group got to the box on that day, nor does she have any recollection of whether or not she had ever seen Victor vault prior to his injury.
3. Although the initial instruction regarding vaulting included a statement indicating the importance of spotting, no one was spotting at the vaulting station at the time of the accident.
4. The landing area at the vaulting station was covered with a 1-1/2-in. folding mat.

Vaulting is an accepted component of a gymnastics program and is commonly taught in schools and clubs throughout North America. As with any skill involving height and flight, however, it can be dangerous if it is not conducted properly. Ms. Hansen ignored several essential safety factors in the conduct of the class in question. To the degree that some or all of these factors are seen as having caused or aggravated Victor Lindsay's injury, she will probably be found liable for the damages that ensued.

The primary reference point for the establishment of standards appropriate to the teaching of gymnastics is the *USGF Gymnastics Safety Manual* (George, 1990). This source and several other authoritative references clearly indicate the critical importance of learning skills slowly and in a progressive manner. The background and readiness of the performer are critical to learning.

Ms. Hansen had little if any knowledge of Victor's ability. She had provided only the most minimal instruction with regard to the specific vaults in question, and (at least insofar as the evidence shows) she had not provided any planned experiences to develop body awareness, landing techniques, or falling skills. Her students were, it appears, unprepared to cope with the physical tasks she placed before them. This situation would be expected to increase the likelihood of falls among the students.

Despite the increased likelihood of falls, however, Ms. Hansen provided only a basic tumbling mat in the landing area. This is well below the standards for competition and ignores the reasonable guidelines of the profession that underscore the importance of soft training mats for providing a safe learning environment for beginners.

Further, although she claims to have told the children that spotters were important to their safety in vaulting, there appears to have been little if any specific training in the techniques and procedures involved, and at least during the 5 to 10 minutes preceding Victor's injury, she failed to notice and correct the fact that no one was spotting at the vaulting station. Surely if she had been providing effective general supervision, she should have noticed and remedied this lapse, which was not a simple and sudden one-time omission but a consistent behavior pattern exhibited over a time period that was more than sufficient to allow instructional intervention and correction.

In summary, Vivian Hansen created a situation in which underprepared fourth graders were allowed to perform activities involving height and flight without the benefit of the safety matting and spotting normally required. It would be difficult to create a scenario more conducive to injury. An otherwise safe and valuable educational experience was allowed to degenerate into a high-risk situation that ultimately caused a costly negligence claim.

[Based on a case adjudicated in the lower courts]

Case 13.3

Activity Selection and Proximate Cause

Richard Banding, a high school sophomore, was injured while participating in an introductory wrestling unit conducted by his physical education teacher, Paul Adams. After three classes of instruction and practice on basic skills, the students were divided into weight classes, and an in-class double elimination tournament was conducted. The tournament was concluded after five classes, by which time each student had wrestled at least twice.

On the ninth class day, Mr. Adams announced that the class would begin a tag-team wrestling tournament. In this contest two wrestlers would be paired off in the center of the mat. From this point they would attempt to force their opponent toward their team's side of the mat so that a teammate could be tagged. The tagged teammate would then replace the person who tagged him and continue the contest against the adversary, who would remain on the mat until he tagged one of his own teammates or was pinned.

Richard Banding was wrestling for the Blue team. His opponent, Anthony Carmino, had worked him over to the Red team's side of the mat. When Anthony tagged his teammate, several others piled on top of the two wrestlers and Richard suffered an injury.

This case is particularly interesting because, although there may have been negligence in the selection and conduct of the activity, the negligence does not appear to be the proximate cause of Richard Banding's injury.

Tag-team wrestling is used in the professional arena. It has no valid association with the sport of amateur wrestling as it is properly taught and practiced in the public schools. Worse, neither the lesson plans nor the curriculum guide supplied by Paul Adams, the teacher, made any reference to tag-team wrestling. Both call for instruction and practice followed by a class tournament. It would appear therefore that the activity was unplanned and instituted to fill at least one of the remaining two days in the two-week unit.

The tag-team activity carries a number of risks not normally associated with the wrestling activity. Most notable among these is the potential for a mismatch. Instead of pairings based on size and skill, this activity pairs participants based on which person one of the wrestlers tags. To be successful, the wrestler should try to tag someone who is far superior to his present opponent. The possible catastrophic results of such a situation should be fairly obvious to even the most naive observer.

In this case, the risk of the activity itself was compounded by the failure to provide sufficient instructional and practice time to develop the skills and techniques necessary to engage safely in competitive wrestling. Even a cursory perusal of any of the accepted resources on wrestling or wrestling safety (Parker, 1993) would indicate that match wrestling requires a level of skill and understanding that simply could not be developed in three class periods.

The most interesting aspect of this case, however, is that although these are valid points that represent an unusual risk of injury and are negligent acts, they do not appear to be the cause of the injury. Richard Banding was injured when several wrestlers jumped on him and his opponent. As inappropriate as tag-team wrestling may have been, there is no indication that group pile-ons was part of the design and no evidence to indicate that such behavior had ever before occurred or been tolerated by the teacher. Therefore, the injury would appear to be the result of a sudden, one-time event that may have been beyond the reasonable prediction or control of the teacher.

If the jury accepts this premise, then it must accept that the teacher's specific acts of negligence did not cause the injuries; therefore Paul Adams should not be held liable for damages. If, on the other hand, student witnesses testify that horseplay and piling on was common during the activity or that Mr. Adams failed to clearly define the tag/exchange procedure and they therefore thought that more than one wrestler could simultaneously enter the contest, then a causal relationship could be established.

A further point that could be stressed eloquently and that could therefore prove quite persuasive in this case is the nature of the contest itself. The only referent the students would have had for tag-team wrestling beyond what their teacher told them is what they had seen in the professional arena. The level of stylized violence and exaggerated disregard for the rules exhibited at that level make it difficult to consider professional wrestling as a sport. Given that background, it should be expected that, unless the strictest rules and closest supervisory control are applied, a tag-team contest among high school students would almost certainly begin to degenerate to the behavioral example set at the professional level. Therefore, although the specific piling-on incident that caused Richard Banding's injury may not have been predictable, it would have been only a matter of time before some form of unsafe behavior were demonstrated.

Choosing such a pointless activity, even though there may be a reasonable technical defense, opens both the choice of activity and the general level of professionalism to such strong attack that, in the eyes of a jury, the defendant would be held responsible for any damages that resulted. It was precisely this point that contributed to the defense's decision to offer a relatively large pretrial settlement in this case.

[Based on a case settled prior to trial]

Case 13.4

Injury Identification and Care

Margaret Downing suffered an injury to her hand and fingers during the final minutes of a junior varsity basketball game—her hand and fingers were very painful, and one finger appeared slightly displaced. Margaret's coach, Rick Westman, acknowledged the injury and directed Margaret to sit on the bench. No first aid was provided, and no medical assistance was summoned.

The game resumed with a substitute filling Margaret's position. But with less than a minute to play and the outcome of the game still very much in doubt, Mr. Westman directed Margaret to reenter the game. On the ensuing play the ball was thrown to Margaret; she attempted to catch it and suffered further damage to her injured hand.

After the game the parent of a teammate noticed Margaret's fingers, which were by this time more noticeably displaced and bleeding slightly. The parent suggested medical examination to the coach. Mr. Westman, however, was preparing to supervise the varsity game, scheduled to begin in a few minutes. Margaret waited unattended and without first aid throughout the varsity game, after which she was transported back to the school parking lot and dismissed with the team. When she arrived home her parents saw the injury and transported Margaret to a hospital emergency room, where a compound fracture was diagnosed and treated. Margaret's enraged parents initiated a lawsuit almost immediately.

This is one of the most callous and blatant examples of a coach's neglect for player welfare and safety that one could hope to find. All coaches are expected to know basic first aid procedures for injuries common to their sports. Furthermore, every coach should have established procedures for obtaining medical assistance for injured team members, both at home and away.

When Margaret Downing initially suffered her injury, her coach should have at the least provided immobilization and the application of cold and sought proper medical attention. Under no circumstances should she have been allowed to reenter the game.

Whether Rick Westman's action in returning Margaret to play was the result of a lapse of attention in the heat of a close contest, a misdiagnosis of her injury, or a conscious decision to run the risk in an attempt to win the game, the consequence was the same. The injury was exacerbated, and Margaret's parents were understandably infuriated.

This parental anger is noteworthy, because it frequently results in legal action that otherwise might not have been taken. Also worthy of note is the relative ease with which the question of proximate cause could be handled. This is often not the case in first aid–related lawsuits. When an individual is injured, there is some level of initial damage. To win a lawsuit alleging improper first aid, it is necessary to prove that the actions or inactions of the defendant caused the initial injury to worsen. This medical question is often difficult and highly disputable. Coach Westman, however, put Margaret back into the game, and the first pass thrown to her changed slightly displaced fingers to a compound fracture. The failure to properly react to an initial injury very clearly resulted in a worsening of her condition. Little could be done to defend the coach's actions from either a legal or a moral standpoint.

Coaches or teachers must be sure to stay current and confident in their first aid skills. They must also be sure that their team or organization has an effective set of procedures for the routine management of accidents, whether in practice or contests, at home or on the road. As with everything a coach or teacher does, these procedures should clearly state and demonstrate the attitude that "when in doubt as to which course of action to pursue, the well-being of the child must always be given precedence."

[Based on a case adjudicated in the lower courts]

Case 13.5

Readiness: Return From Injury

Donna Marino was a high school student who had been under a doctor's care for recurring knee problems. During the course of her freshman and sophomore years she had been under the care of a doctor who pursued conservative treatments. The doctor had written a letter to the school requesting that Donna be excused from all physical activity for a 2-month period during her sophomore year and had thereafter directed her to refrain from any activities that placed excessive strain on her knee. On three occasions after the 2-month excuse period, the school nurse excused Donna from physical education classes because of pain and swelling in her knee.

In mid-April of her sophomore year, Donna once again experienced pain and swelling in her knee and was extremely reluctant to participant in her scheduled physical education class. She related these facts to her teacher, Jeanne Lewis, who told her to dress for activity. After getting dressed, Donna again told Ms. Lewis that she felt her knee was too weak and painful to participate, but Ms. Lewis told her that unless she performed the activity of the day, she would not pass physical education.

The activity of the day was a shuttle run that was being timed for grading purposes. Shortly before she was to perform the run, Donna again reminded Ms. Lewis, who had been her teacher throughout the year, of her knee problem and asked to be excused. Ms. Lewis again refused, indicating the need for documented grading data. Donna reluctantly attempted the shuttle run and fell during one of the turns when her knee gave out. Later that evening she underwent reconstructive knee surgery. Some time later her parents filed suit on her behalf against her teacher, Jeanne Lewis.

It is theoretically conceivable that Donna's knee problem would have required surgery under any circumstances. It is even possible that the surgery should not have been put off as long as it was and that the shuttle run did little to exacerbate the already existing injury. In fact, these are theories that the defendant asked the jury to consider.

However, the jury also considered the facts with which they were confronted. Donna had a clear history of knee problems. Throughout the year both her own physician and the school nurse had frequently excused her from physical education, often for extended periods, to aid in her recovery and to avoid exacerbating the problem. Jeanne Lewis was aware of Donna's problem, and Donna had addressed her several times on the date in question and asked to be excused. A shuttle run is a vigorous running activity requiring explosive starts, stops, and directional changes.

This particular event was being conducted and timed under the pressure of a grade. Given these facts and the irrefutable presence of a severe injury, the swift and generous award that Donna received is not difficult to understand.

Many programs have well-developed guidelines for considering excuses from activity. The best of these routinely send all students who ask to be excused to the school nurse, who examines them and determines whether to excuse them for the day. A note is sent to the parents informing them of the problem and suggesting that they be alert to the possible need for medical attention if it continues. Persistent problems or those that extend beyond a few days require referral to a physician. This policy displays clear concern for the students' welfare and avoids unjustified excuses by alerting parents to the fact that their children are missing important educational experiences.

Unfortunately, no policy of any kind was in effect at the time of Donna Marino's injury. Instead, her teacher took upon herself the role of medical diagnostician and concluded that Donna should participate in the shuttle run.

In forcing Donna Marino to participate in an activity that clearly placed great strain on her knee, against her will and despite her complaints of knee pain and swelling, Ms. Lewis displayed both a lack of sound professional judgment and a total disregard for the welfare of a student entrusted to her care. Such behavior is diametrically opposed to accepted standards of professional conduct and must be expected to result in needless injuries and costly legal actions.

[Based on a case adjudicated in the lower courts]

Case 13.6

Protective Measures

Tina Fraser was a 16-year-old member of the junior varsity softball team at Bathgate Regional High School. She and her teammates were taking batting practice with the aid of an automatic pitching machine. The coach, Ellen Ames, directed Tina to feed balls into the machine, which was pitching balls to a batter at the plate. The fielders were shagging the balls and throwing them to another player, who stood about 15 ft from Tina and was flipping Tina the balls to load into the machine. The school had a safety screen for use with the machine, but Coach Ames had elected not to use it. In fact, when the other equipment was being brought to the field, one of the players asked whether the screen should be brought out as well. The coach answered that it would not be necessary. During the course of the batting practice, one of the batters hit a line drive that struck Tina on the nose, fracturing the nasal spine and causing profuse bleeding. Several surgeries were required to correct the damage caused by the injury.

This injury was the direct and easily avoidable result of Coach Ames's deliberate disregard for the necessary provisions of safety. When she assigned Tina Fraser the task of feeding balls into the pitching machine, she placed her in one of the most dangerous positions on the field. Tina was required to divide her attention among the tasks of feeding balls into the machine, receiving balls returned from the field, and protecting herself from batted balls. The latter responsibility, however, could and should have been eliminated by the presence of an appropriate protective screen.

The risk of injury from a line drive back to the pitcher's mound, especially during batting practice, and the necessity of protecting players from this hazard have been well documented in professional literature. Screens are commonly employed during batting practice to protect the person on the mound from the possibility of being struck by a batted ball. They can be purchased commercially or locally manufactured for use with machine or player pitching. Although such a screen was available at Bathgate Regional High School on the date in question, Coach Ames had elected not to use it.

Coaches are obligated to anticipate the hazards involved in an activity and to take any and all reasonable precautions necessary to ensure the safety and well-being of their athletes. Consequently, it is virtually impossible to justify this injury as an unforeseeable accident. This was not a simple error of omission: Coach Ames made a conscious decision to omit the use of an important safety device that was readily available.

In fact, Ellen Ames would have been no less responsible for the safety of her athletes if no screen had been available. She would have been expected to structure and organize the drill in a manner that eliminated or at least minimized the risk to the person or persons on the mound. But the failure to utilize an effective and readily available safety device is virtually indefensible.

Remember that teachers or coaches should provide safety equipment and require its use. Post reminders for the staff as well as for the participants to make sure they are aware of the importance of protective equipment and that they use it routinely. Such measures serve a dual purpose: They help reduce the risk of injuries, and they help establish the shared responsibility of the participant to adhere to reasonable safety procedures.

[Based on a case settled before trial]

Case 13.7

Field Conditions

Carl Flynn was in the seventh grade at Millwick Junior High School. On October 15, as part of his regularly assigned physical education class, Carl was directed to take part in a game of touch football. After a brief warm-up indoors, teams were selected and the class was led outdoors.

This was the first day on which the football activity was conducted. No instructions were given, the rules were not explained, and no warnings or safety provisions were discussed.

The game was played on a poorly maintained field located behind the school that was strewn with stones and glass. The grass in many areas of the field was worn away, leaving bare ground, and erosion from water runoff had caused even greater surface irregularities. The condition of the field on the date in question was worsened by the weather, which was cloudy and damp, producing muddy conditions and general slipperiness. During the game, Carl attempted to tag an offensive player, lost his footing, and fell, suffering serious injury to his knee.

Although the failure to provide adequate instruction and warnings and some reasonable discussion of safety provisions deviates from proper professional practice, it is not the focus of this particular lawsuit. Carl Flynn was not injured due to these factors. The condition of the playing field on October 15 is the only factor that can be shown to have directly caused or aggravated the injury that Carl Flynn sustained on that date. His attorney therefore based his claim on the alleged failure of the teacher and the school to provide a safe playing environment. But had Carl or some other student suffered an injury due to a lack of skill or understanding that might have been prevented by proper instruction, then the focus of the primary complaint would have been readjusted to reflect the results of the additional areas of negligence.

There is little question that the field behind Millwick Junior High School was unsuitable for the conduct of a vigorous running activity such as touch football. The surface irregularities were sufficient in and of themselves to expose the students to unnecessary risk of injury. When these preexisting surface problems are compounded by the addition of surface moisture, the resultant mud and slippery grass clearly invite falls and injuries like Carl Flynn's.

This case illustrates the problems that can arise when a teacher, coach, or administrative authority fails to demonstrate adequate concern for the quality and safety of the playing surface on which running activities are conducted. It should also serve as a warning to anyone who might be under the mistaken impression that a lower standard of safety can be applied to fields used for instructional classes than for those used by varsity teams. Although the level of amenities such as bleachers, benches, painted lines, and official goalposts can definitely be lowered for instructional classes, the same cannot be said for the level of safety.

All participants, regardless of the level of their involvement, have a right to expect that the facilities they use will be as safe as reasonably possible at the time of their use. If, as in the case of Carl Flynn, a substandard facility is found to be the cause of an injury, the individuals responsible for that occurrence must recognize the very real possibility that they will be held liable for the resultant damages. In this case, generous settlements were reached on behalf of the defendant teacher and school district prior to trial.

[Based on a case settled before trial]

Case 13.8

Buffer Zones

John Sanderson was seriously injured while playing in an intramural basketball game at Morrisville High School when he ran into an unpadded cinderblock wall after a driving lay-up. Although there was a regulation basketball court in the center of the gymnasium, intramurals were conducted on three smaller courts that ran across the gym and perpendicular to the long axis of the regulation court. The backboard involved in this particular incident was 4 ft from the cinderblock wall.

This case brings up the conflict between the valid and commendable desire to maximize participation and the necessity to provide a safe playing environment. On the one hand, the individuals in charge recognized that using the large regulation basketball court would greatly limit the number of games possible in a given time period. They decided that intramural games could be conducted on courts that were both shorter and narrower than the prescribed minimum for varsity sports. In this decision they were entirely correct: There is absolutely nothing wrong with reducing the size of a playing area for practice, instruction, or less formal games provided that safety is not unreasonably compromised. Shortening the length and width of the basketball court for intramurals would therefore be a sound decision provided the reductions were not so drastic as to result in overcrowding, an unlikely though not impossible scenario.

In this case, however, important safety factors were also drastically reduced. All guidelines for basketball safety indicate the importance of a reasonable amount of unobstructed space between the backboard and the nearest obstruction. Although the exact amount of space recommended varies depending upon the source and the level of activity, 4 ft is well below even the most minimal standard. Moreover, most sources recommend padding walls located behind a basket. This would be particularly important in a case such as this one, in which the distance between the backboard or end line and the wall was already substandard.

When laying out courts and fields, it is perfectly reasonable and often more productive to modify the size of the playing area. But unless the game itself is modified, the need will remain for safety zones between the playing areas and around their perimeter that are wide enough to prevent injury to the players. On the other hand, if a safe buffer zone cannot be provided, the only reasonable option would be to find another playing area or to modify the game itself.

Because the intramural supervisors at Morrisville High School failed to provide a reasonable safety area at the end of the court on which John Sanderson was injured, they were found guilty of negligence and ordered to compensate John for his losses.

[Based on a case adjudicated in the lower courts]

CHAPTER SUMMARY

The professional responsibility to provide an appropriate standard of care for participants in sport and physical activity encompasses three general areas: the provision of adequate supervision, proper selection and conduct of the activities, and safe environmental conditions. This chapter presents specific behavioral guidelines that can effectively reduce the risks associated with these areas regardless of the specific nature and level of the activity involved. To be most effective however, the guidelines must be considered in the context of the published standards and recommendations that apply to the specific activity in question. Thus general recommendations for a buffer zone, for instance, can be translated into the 25 ft of space recommended between a baseline and the nearest obstruction on a softball field.

KEY TERMS

Actual notice (258)
Constructive notice (258)
Environmental conditions (258)
Feedback (255)
General supervision (253)
Instruction (255)
Mismatch (256)
Protective measures (256)
Qualitative supervision (252)
Quantitative supervision (252)
Respondeat superior (252)
Specific supervision (253)
Supervision (252)
Vicarious liability (252)

QUESTIONS FOR DISCUSSION

1. Name and define the three primary areas of responsibility with regard to the standard of care in sport and physical activity.
2. Give activity-specific examples to illustrate negligence associated with the following concepts:
   a. general vs. specific supervision
   b. *respondeat superior*
   c. inadequate instruction or feedback

   d. mismatch
   e. unsafe environmental condition
   f. actual notice
3. In each example given above, change one factor other than the occurrence of the injury itself so that, although an injury still occurs, it is unlikely that the person in charge would lose a negligence suit.
4. Given a particular activity, develop a series of specific guidelines in checklist form to reduce the risk of injuries due to faulty supervision, inappropriate selection and/or conduct of the activity, and unsafe facilities.
5. Modify the facts of Case 13.2 so that the teacher, Vivian Hansen, is not negligent.

REFERENCES

George, G.S. (Ed.) (1990). *AACCA cheerleading safety manual*. Memphis: The UCA Publications Department, p. 25.
George, G.S. (1990). *USGF gymnastics safety manual*. Indianapolis: USGF Publications.
Parker, D. (1993). Wrestling. In N.J. Dougherty (Ed.), *Principles of safety in physical education and sport*. Reston, VA: AAHPERD Publications.

ADDITIONAL READINGS

NOTE: One essential source of information is the official rule book of the particular sport in question. The rules provide both directives and recommendations, many of which are essential to safe play and legal defensibility.

The following sources also will be of great value in seeking to identify standards and guidelines for the safe conduct of specific sports and activities:

Adams, S., Adrian, M., & Bayless, M.A. (1987). *Catastrophic injuries in sports:*

Avoidance strategies. Indianapolis: Benchmark Press.

Dougherty, N.J. (Ed.) (1993). *Principles of safety in physical education and sport*. Reston, VA: AAHPERD.

English, J.W. (1986). *Liability aspects of bikeway designation*. Washington, DC: Bicycle Federation of America.

Flynn, R.B. (Ed.) (1993). *Facility planning for physical education, recreation and athletics*. Reston, VA: AAHPERD Publications.

Gabriel, J.L. (Ed.) (1990). *U.S. diving safety manual*. Indianapolis: U.S. Diving Publications.

Gabrielsen, M. (Ed.) (1987). *Swimming pools—A guide to their planning, design, and operation* (4th ed.). Champaign, IL: Human Kinetics.

George, G.S. (Ed.) (1990). *AACCA cheerleading safety manual*. Memphis: The UCA Publications Department.

George, G.S. (1990). *USGF gymnastics safety manual*. Indianapolis: USGF Publications.

Herbert, D.L., & Herbert, W.G. (1984). *Legal aspects of preventive and rehabilitative exercise programs*. Canton, OH: Professional and Executive Reports and Publications.

Management of risks and emergencies—A workbook for program administrators. (1983). Kansas City, MO: Camp Fire.

McIntyre, S., Goltsman, S.M., & Kline, L. (1989). *Safety first checklist*. Berkeley, CA: MIG Communications (distributed by National Safety Council, Chicago, Illinois).

Official special olympics sports rules. (1985, rev. ed.). Washington, DC: Special Olympics.

Sol, N., & Foster, C. (Eds.) (1992). *ACSM's health/fitness facility standards and guidelines*. Champaign, IL: Human Kinetics.

U.S. Consumer Products Safety Commission. *A handbook for public playground safety*. Washington, DC: Author.

Van Rossen, D.P. (Ed.) (1983). *Pool/spa operators handbook*. San Antonio, TX: The National Swimming Pool Foundation.

Webster, S.E. (1989). *Project Adventure Inc. ropes course safety manual*. Dubuque, IA: Kendall/Hunt.

CHAPTER 14

RESPONSIBILITIES OF GAME OFFICIALS

C lampett field was the best high school baseball facility in the county. It was generally well designed and well maintained and was the site of all home games for the high school baseball team. Last year the Clampett High School softball team reached the finals of the state championships and was asked to host the final game. It was decided that, due to the quality of the field and the large permanent seating capacity, Clampett field would be adapted for softball play. The basepaths were shortened from the 90-ft standard used in high school baseball to the 60 ft required for softball play.

In the bottom of the second inning, a short pop fly was hit down the right field line. As the first baseman pursued the ball, she appeared to stumble and fall. She had stepped into the hole surrounding the fixed anchor for the first base used by the baseball team. No caps or covers had been applied when the base was removed; as a result, when she stepped in the hole, her foot caught and twisted between the anchoring stake and the ground, and she suffered a severely fractured ankle.

The injured athlete, through her parents, sued Clampett Township and its agents for maintaining the field in a condition that she claimed was improper and unsafe. She also sued the umpires who were officiating the game in question. Citing the American Softball Association rule that makes the plate umpire responsible for determining the fitness of the grounds for the game, the plaintiff argued that the umpire should have examined the field, noted the hazardous condition, and disallowed play until the problem was corrected.

LEARNING OBJECTIVES

The student will be able to

1. explain the duty of a game official to an athlete through application of the concepts of contractual duty of care and duty to control;
2. explain how the courts would seek to determine whether an injury was the foreseeable result of a breach in the reasonably expected standard of care;
3. describe the application of the but-for test in determining the proximate cause of an injury sustained by an athlete as the alleged result of a referee's negligence; and
4. give specific examples of situations that could give rise to claims of negligence due to an official's actions or omissions with regard to environmental conditions, inappropriate activities, and inadequate supervision.

THE OFFICIAL AS DEFENDANT

Although there is little case precedence on which to base a discussion of the potential liability of sports officials, there is a growing trend toward seeking tort recovery from third parties who are involved, such as officials (Davis, 1981). Sports officials clearly may be liable if they fail to properly execute their duties to control or supervise an athletic event (Davis; Narol & Dedopoulos, 1980). The potential liability of officials can best be understood when examined in the context of the basic aspects of tort law: duty, standard of care, foreseeability, and proximate cause.

DUTY

The duty of an official to a participating athlete rests largely on two legal concepts: **contractual duty of care** and the **duty to control**. When a contractual duty is performed negligently, and damages result, tort action for recovery of the damages is possible. Although participating athletes do not generally share in the process of contracting for referees and officials, their safety and welfare is clearly recognized as the **end or aim** of the contract. Therefore, the contractual relationship between officials and hiring authorities is seen as establishing a legal foundation for liability in the event that the officials should fail to effectively fulfill their prescribed duties to protect the participants' safety.

In addition to the responsibilities imposed by a formal contract, the rules of most sports place officials in a position of authority over the coaches and athletes. For instance, the official is often responsible for ascertaining the playability of the field, penalizing identified violations of the rules or unsafe behaviors, and ejecting athletes and coaches from the game if their conduct flagrantly deviates from the prescribed limits. Because the officials are able to exert a degree of control over the actions and conduct of the athletes, they may bear a legal obligation to do so.

STANDARD OF CARE

Having established that officials have a duty to exercise reasonable care in the control of an athletic contest and its participants, a court must next establish the standards of performance that they must meet in fulfilling this duty. The standard of care is the standard that a reasonably prudent individual would be expected to follow under the same or similar circumstances. In making this determination, the courts give special consideration to training and qualifications beyond the ordinary and the effect that they might be expected to have on the official's actions. Therefore, the yardstick they use to assess the performance of an official is not simply a person of ordinary prudence but a reasonably prudent *official* who must act in a specialized and skillful manner according to the rules of the sport (see Figure 14.1).

Sports officials are almost universally given responsibility for ensuring that the rules and regulations of the sport, the sanctioning body, or the league are enforced. These rules and regulations are key elements in establishing the standard of care required of the official. A distinction should be made, however, between **rule enforcement** and **rule enactment**. Although referees are without question responsible for enforcing the rules and regulations of the contest, they have little or no direct control over the design and enactment of those rules and are therefore bound to uphold the standards as designed.

One notable exception is in games for which local ground rules are instituted. If a local ground rule creates an unreasonable risk of injury to the athletes, and if the official accepts and enforces this unsafe modification

Figure 14.1   The rules of most sports enable the official to exert a degree of control over players' actions and conduct. They may be liable for injuries that result from their failure to provide that standard of care.

without question or correction, then the official must be prepared to share in the potential liability for injuries.

FORESEEABILITY

Before an individual can be held responsible for the damages suffered by another, the possibility of harm must be shown to have been reasonably predictable. All sports have rules that have been instituted for the protection of the participants. Rules regarding spearing and clipping in football, for instance, were enacted to reduce the risk of serious injury to the players. If these rules are not enforced diligently, it is reasonable to assume that the frequency of spearing and clipping will increase and along with it the risk that a player will suffer an injury as a result of these practices. Although specific injury to a particular athlete may not have been foreseeable, the likelihood of *an* injury to *some* player most certainly was. The yardstick by which foreseeability is judged, therefore, is not whether the specific accident or injury was foreseeable but whether or not the possibility of an injury should have been apparent to a prudent official acting under the same or similar circumstances.

PROXIMATE CAUSE

A fourth issue that must be resolved before an official can be held legally responsible for the harm suffered by an athlete is that the official's negligent actions must be the proximate cause of the injury. Although volumes have been written on the concept of determining proximate cause, for purposes of this discussion, it can be reduced to the simple question: Did the negligence of the defendant cause or aggravate the injury in question? If the answer to this question is no, then the injured athlete cannot recover damages from the official even if the official was negligent.

This question is often complicated in the case of an injured player suing a referee, however, by the intervention and actions of a third party, such as another athlete. In such cases, the issue of proximate cause revolves around the question of whether the actions of the player who caused the injury could reasonably have been controlled by the official.

One method of formulating an answer to this question is to use the **but-for test**: that is, to hold all factors of the incident constant

except for the alleged negligence to determine whether, but for the negligence of the official, the injury would have occurred. For example, consider a football game. The quarterback drops back and throws a pass that is completed. The defensive tackle delivers a vicious blow to the quarterback well after the completion, causing serious injury. Because the officials were all concentrating on the completion and the subsequent touchdown run, no penalty was called for the late hit. The officials were remiss in their failure to penalize the actions of the tackle. But had they seen and penalized the infraction, the quarterback still would have been injured. It is unlikely, therefore, that their failure to see and react to the safety violation could be held to be the proximate cause of the injury.

If, on the other hand, the defensive tackle had been delivering late hits throughout the game, and few if any had been penalized, the scenario would be considerably different. Given the proper action of diligent enforcement and, if necessary, ejection, the likelihood of the dangerous act would decrease greatly. If the official had acted properly in this case, the athlete might not have been injured. Therefore, the official's negligence can be held as the proximate cause of the injury.

EMPLOYMENT STATUS OF OFFICIALS

Officials are generally viewed as **independent contractors** rather than as employees of the schools or leagues that contract for their services. This is an important distinction because it greatly restricts the extent to which the school or league can be held responsible for the negligent actions of an official under the concept of *respondeat superior* (see chapter 13).

The single most compelling feature in determining whether or not a given person is an employee or an independent contractor is the degree of control that the employer is able to exert over the person's actions. In an employer/employee relationship, the *employer* usually maintains control over both the employee's products or services and over the process by which they are achieved. However, the more the *employee* controls the services (such as officiating a game or providing medical care for a team) and uses discretion in determining how to accomplish them (for example, positioning players on the field during the game or choosing the appropriate techniques for assessing the health of the athletes), the more likely the individual is to be seen as an independent contractor.

There are a number of other factors that affect the legal nature of any given employment relationship. Among them are the following:

- What the employer and the employee believed to be the case when they agreed to the relationship
- Whether the task or occupation in question is generally considered an independent trade
- The skill level required for the task (In general, higher and more specialized skills are required of independent contractors.)
- The degree to which the employee provides his or her own equipment or tools (Independent contractors generally provide more of their own equipment or tools than employees.)
- The length of the employment and terms of payment (Independent contractors tend to be employed for specific periods of time, such as a game, season, or semester, and are often paid a flat fee for the total task rather than an hourly wage.) (Clement, 1988)

It is possible to consider game officials as employees, and even to do so for some purposes (such as taxation) but not others (Goldberger, 1984). However, for purposes of tort liability, officials are normally viewed as independent contractors, and they, rather than their employers, therefore bear individual responsibility for their negligent actions.

RESPONSIBILITIES OF OFFICIALS

Like teachers and coaches, meet officials are responsible for ensuring the safety of the facilities and equipment and the appropriateness of the activities and for providing effective supervision. The key difference is that the officials' specific responsibilities are, for the most part, limited to the time frame of the actual contest or game.

Facilities and Equipment

The rules and policies of most sports charge officials with the responsibility for ensuring the safety and appropriateness of the facilities and equipment used in a contest. This might entail ensuring that the equipment adheres to appropriate specifications and standards, that the physical layout of the area is appropriate, and that the surface is playable and remains safe throughout the contest. A gymnastics judge, for instance, would be expected to note and correct a situation involving inadequate matting; a softball umpire would be expected to take corrective action if a base path were badly eroded or equipment had been left in the playing area; and a football referee should note and correct the absence of protective equipment and safe field-marking devices (see Cases 14.1 and 14.2).

Like coaches and teachers, officials are expected to respond to both actual and constructive notice. Actual notice might include complaints from coaches or athletes about the facilities or equipment; constructive notice of reasonably obvious deficiencies could be obtained by performing an appropriate pregame inspection. In either case the official would have a clear responsibility to take immediate and appropriate actions to safeguard the athletes involved.

Appropriate Activities

Like coaches, officials may be expected to shoulder some of the responsibility for ensuring that the individual skills of the athletes are appropriate for the activities they attempt. Officials control many elements of play during the game. If they overlook unsafe or improper behaviors, it is reasonable to assume that those behaviors will continue and perhaps increase.

In football, for instance, the act of making primary contact with the head is both unsafe and against the rules. A player who does this, whether by intent or by accident, and is not injured or penalized will probably do it again. If one player appears to get away with a violation, others can be expected to try. Such oversights obviously reduce both the safety of the players and the quality of the contest. It is equally obvious that the official's failure to control the actions of the players to the degree that the rules allow can result in legal action if and when an injury occurs as a result of inappropriate or unsafe techniques or actions.

Supervision

Officials are expected to maintain reasonable control of the environmental conditions and the activities of contests by exercising effective general and specific supervision. To do so, they must place themselves in the field of play where they can have the best possible view of the action both on and away from the ball.

Consider, for example, a field hockey match in which an altercation started when two opposing players collided while attempting to gain control of a loose ball. It continued after the ball had moved downfield and degenerated into a bench-clearing brawl in which an athlete was injured. The officials were focusing their full attention on the ball and neither saw nor attempted to stop the problem until after the brawl had begun. The focus of the ensuing lawsuit was on the time span between the initiation of the altercation and the injury and, correspondingly, the failed opportunity of the officials to initiate reasonable corrective action in time to prevent the injury.

SOMETIMES THE RULES AREN'T ENOUGH

What should officials do when their personal judgment for preserving the players' safety in a particular situation does not precisely follow the letter of the written rules? Although in many ways this question is more a moral issue than a legal one, it is no less important. The critical point is that, regardless of the potential for a lawsuit, the health and safety of the athletes must be the most important factor to be weighed in the decision-making process. If the likelihood of an injury is very remote or the potential severity is very minor, then other factors such as the flow of the contest or the desires of the athletes or the coaches should be considered. As the potential likelihood and severity of injuries increases, however, so must the primacy of the safety issues. An official who must choose between an angry coach and a seriously injured athlete really has no choice. Disagreeing with the coach may cause annoyance or embarrassment, but failure to protect the safety of the athletes may result in a serious injury and costly litigation, as Case 14.1 illustrates.

CASE STUDIES

Case 14.1

A Questionable Ground Rule

Derbeyville High School was preparing to play a varsity football game against Gantley Township on the Derbeyville Memorial Field. Prior to the start of the game, the referee informed both coaches that a trench that had been dug in preparation for the installation of a sprinkler violated the rules for field design and constituted a safety hazard. The trench was approximately 1 ft deep, 2 ft wide, and 20 ft long. It ran away from the field on a perpendicular course from the 25-yd line, beginning at a point about 3 ft outside the sidelines.

Rather than postpone the game, however, the coaches and the referee agreed that the Derbeyville coach would place someone near the trench to prevent anyone from stepping into the hole, and that all plays in that area of the field would be initiated from either the middle of the field or the hash mark on the opposite side.

During the second half of the game, a punt sailed deep into Derbeyville territory toward the trench. The receiver took the ball on a dead run toward the sidelines. He was hit almost immediately by a Gantley player, and their momentum carried them directly toward the trench.

A uniformed Derbeyville player had been stationed near the trench in accordance with the pregame agreement. However, when he tried to keep the athletes from falling into the pit, he himself was knocked in and suffered serious damage to his knee that required hospitalization and surgery.

In a subsequent lawsuit, the injured athlete cited the impropriety of the trench and the responsibilities of the Derbeyville administrators and coaches to avoid such hazards. He also named the officials who had, according to the testimonial evidence, recognized the hazard and agreed to what the athlete claimed was an improper ground rule that had placed him in undue physical danger. All parties agreed to a generous pretrial settlement.

[Based on a case settled before trial]

Case 14.2

Field Condition as Proximate Cause

The Baywood Bombers were playing the Shorefront Sharks in the opening game of an adult softball league. During the bottom half of the first inning, a Baywood player hit a long fly ball to left center field. John and Bill, the Shorefront left and center fielders, both pursued the ball and collided with one another as they tried to make the catch. John suffered serious head and facial injuries as a result of the collision and instituted a lawsuit accusing both the league and the umpire involved in the game of negligence. It seems that the grass in the outfield ranged between 4 in. and 8 in. in height and had scattered clumps and bare spots throughout the area. John, through his expert witness, alleged that the umpire deviated from reasonable standards when he

1. failed to inspect the playing field as specified in the rules of the American Softball Association, and
2. failed to invoke his authority under the rules of play and to cancel the game because of the hazardous condition of the outfield.

The expert for the defense had to concede that the field was indeed unfit for play at the time of the incident. Moreover, the plaintiff's expert was entirely correct in his assessment of the umpire's responsibility for ensuring the safety and playability of the field. The umpire did owe a duty to the plaintiff, and he did fall short of acceptable standards in performing that duty. Moreover, it was reasonably foreseeable that an outfield in the condition described could lead to player injuries. Fortunately for the umpire, however, the issue of proximate cause was not so clear cut.

The defense expert pointed out that there was no testimony to indicate that this collision was, in fact, related to the condition of the playing surface. Neither player claimed to have slipped, tripped, or in any way been impeded by the grass. They simply failed to see and effectively react to one another. Given that, the uneven grass was just as likely to have slowed the runners and reduced the force of their impact as it was to have contributed to it. The case was ultimately settled for a nominal sum.

The umpire was indeed fortunate. He had clearly fallen short in performing his duties. It just so happened that the particular injury in question was not directly attributable to his negligence. If it had been, the end result would almost certainly have been quite different. More importantly, if he had fulfilled his obligation to control the playability of the field, he probably would not have been named in the suit and could have avoided even a nominal settlement.

[Based on a case settled before trial]

CHAPTER SUMMARY

This chapter focuses on sports officials' potential liability for injuries that are allegedly related to the manner in which they fulfill their responsibilities for ensuring the safety of the participants. Officials have a legal responsibility to exercise due care to eliminate foreseeable hazards in the conduct of the game and to assure the safety of the environmental conditions under which it is played. This responsibility is derived from both the specific rules of the sport and the officials' general authority to control the flow of the game itself.

KEY TERMS

But-for test (276)
Contractual duty of care (274)
Duty to control (274)
End or aim (274)
Independent contractors (276)

Rule enactment (275)
Rule enforcement (275)

QUESTIONS FOR DISCUSSION

1. What gives an athlete the right to sue an official for violating a contractual obligation, even though the athlete did not sign, agree to, or even read the contract in question?

2. Explain the application of the but-for test in ascertaining proximate cause in cases involving game officials. Give activity-specific examples in which one or more officials would be held liable for the injuries that result. Modify one or more factors so that, although the injury would still occur, the action or inaction of the official would no longer be a proximately causative factor.

3. Create sport-specific scenarios in which either the rules of the game or the nature of the situation require game officials to intervene to reduce the potential for an injury. Explain the actions that should be taken and outline the specific legal claims that might be lodged if an injury occurred as a result of the officials' failure to act.

REFERENCES

Clement, A. (1988). *Law in sport and physical activity*. Indianapolis: Benchmark Pess.

Davis, V.J. (1981). Sports liability: Blowing the whistle on the referees. *Pacific Law Journal, 12*, 937-964.

Goldberger, A.S. (1984). *Sports officiating: A legal guide*. New York: Leisure Press.

Narol, M.S., & Dedopoulos, S. (1980, March). Potential liability—A guide to referees' rights. *Trial*, pp. 18-21.

ADDITIONAL READINGS

Dougherty, N.J., & Feigley, D.A. (1983, Nov.-Dec.). Liability: Who judges the judges? *USGF Gymnastics*, pp. 10-12.

Goldberger, A.S. (1984). *Sports officiating: A legal guide*. New York: Leisure Press.

CHAPTER 15

CIVIL REDRESS FOR VIOLENCE ON THE PLAYING FIELD

Barleycorn High and Parkside Tech, two ardent crosstown rivals, were contesting a varsity field hockey game. With approximately 3 minutes remaining in the second half and the score tied, a Barleycorn player, Jane Sharp, received a pass and was tripped by Ann Nelson, a defender from Parkside. The referee immediately signaled the penalty. As Jane sat on the ground immediately after the referee's whistle, Ann Nelson, whose momentum had carried her out of the penalty area, returned and kicked Jane in the side of the head, causing serious injury.

Jane and her parents have instituted a lawsuit against Ann for what they argued was a negligent deviation from reasonable and prudent standards of behavior. Specifically, they allege that Ann failed to provide due care for Jane's safety and welfare and failed to properly control her own emotions when she deliberately, willfully, and recklessly kicked Ann after completing the play. Ann Nelson claims that she was acting out of frustration and did not intend to harm Jane. Such suits are becoming increasingly common in the world of competitive sport.

LEARNING OBJECTIVES

The student will be able to

1. recognize the nature and importance of the Nabozny case;
2. articulate the three alternative player conduct standards and the legal problems and issues associated with each; and
3. identify situations in which a coach may be held legally responsible for a player's violent acts.

THE PLAYER AS A DEFENDANT

Julian Nabozny was the goalkeeper for his soccer team in Winnetka, Illinois. Witnesses testified that Nabozny was standing within the penalty area when he went down onto one knee to receive a pass from a teammate. David Barnhill, a forward on the opposing team, pursued the ball into the penalty area and kicked Nabozny in the side of the head, causing permanent skull and brain damage. All the witnesses agreed that Barnhill had sufficient opportunity to avoid contact with the plaintiff and that Nabozny had remained within the penalty area throughout the encounter. The Federation Internationale de Football Association (FIFA) rules under which the game was played prohibit all players from making contact with the goalkeepers when they have possession of the ball within the penalty area. Nabozny, a minor, brought suit through his father against David Barnhill who he alleged had negligently caused his injuries (*Nabozny v. Barnhill*, 1975).

Although the theoretical liability of athletes who commit *intentional* acts is relatively obvious, their legal responsibility for acts of *negligence* (unintentional omissions or commissions) was far less clear at the time of the Nabozny case. In that case, the trial court granted the defendant's motion for a **directed verdict**, in which the judge awards the case to the defendant as a matter of law. The trial court ruled that Nabozny had assumed the risks inherent in the game of soccer. The court of appeals, however, reversed the decision of the lower court and remanded the case for a trial by jury. In so doing, the court concluded that

the law should not place unreasonable burdens on the free and vigorous participation in sports by our youth. However, we also believe that organized athletic competition does not exist in a vacuum. Rather some of the restraints of civilization must accompany every athlete onto the playing field. One of the educational benefits of organized athletic competition to our youth is the development of discipline and self-control.

Individual sports are advanced and competition enhanced by a comprehensive set of rules. Some rules secure the better playing of the game as a test of skill. Other rules are primarily designed to protect participants from serious injury.

It is our opinion that a player is liable for injury in a tort action if his conduct is such that it is either deliberate, willful or with a reckless disregard for the safety of the other player so as to cause injury to that player, the same being a question of fact to be decided by a jury. (*Nabozny v. Barnhill*, 1975)

The Nabozny decision makes it clear that reckless and deliberate acts of violence will not be condoned by the court and, in fact, that when they occur and an injury results, the injured party can seek compensation through the legal system. Some experts have argued, however, that the manner in which the appellate decision was stated leaves some question as to the exact type of circumstances under which a defendant player may be held liable (Goldstein, 1976). Furthermore, athletes' natural reluctance to sue other athletes and their willingness to accept many violently induced injuries as the "breaks of the game" tend to hold down the number of cases of this type, making a consistent body of case law slow in developing. Therefore, the alternative standards for judging the actions of a defendant player, described in the next sections, will be clarified as the body of case law grows and the standards of conduct to which the players will be held become more explicitly defined.

ORDINARY NEGLIGENCE STANDARD

Under an **ordinary negligence standard** athletes would be expected to refrain from unsafe conduct that is prohibited by safety rules. This standard is onerous, and the courts are therefore unlikely to follow it. Carried to the extreme, it would subject any athletes who violate safety rules (for example, clipping, unnecessary roughness, high sticking) to potential lawsuits if their adversaries suffered injuries as a result. Such a stringent standard would be nearly impossible for athletes to meet and would probably cause even the best players to fear the possibility of spending more time in court than on the playing field.

WILLFUL OR WANTON STANDARD

Under a **willful or wanton standard** players would be held liable if their actions indicated willful or wanton disregard for the welfare of others. Willful and wanton acts are more serious than simple negligent errors of omission or commission. At the risk of oversimplification, **wanton acts** are those in which individuals know that their actions or failures to act may very well result in injuries to others, but they go ahead and do it anyway. Although they do not really intend to hurt anyone, they know that it is a distinct possibility and make no reasonable attempt to prevent it.

Willful acts entail more of an intention. For example, athletes who deliberately make late hits to instill fear in their opponents or to take them out of the game are committing willful acts. Obviously the distinction between willful and wanton acts requires some assessment of the defendant's state of mind at the time of the alleged violation. It is therefore difficult to prove willful and wanton behavior in court, especially months or years after the incident, when even defendant athletes may not accurately recollect what was going through their minds at the time of the actions.

RECKLESS DISREGARD STANDARD

Based on the cases that have been brought since the Nabozny decision, the standard of care required of an athlete appears to be moving toward a combination of the ordinary negligence and willful or wanton standards previously discussed. That is, athletes would be required to refrain from behavior that would constitute a **reckless or willful disregard** for the safety of other players as prescribed by the rules of the game (*Bourque v.*

Duplechin, 1976; *Ross v. Clouser*, 1982). This standard appears to be fair and reasonable and within the athlete's reasonable control. It does, however, open the door to some interesting issues that will need to be addressed in the course of future litigation.

The Level of Organization

The reckless or willful disregard standard obviously applies to activities involving structured coaching and organized teams, but what about less structured activities such as intramurals and sandlot games? Although the same standards for civil behavior would seem to apply in both an unstructured game and one with coaches and paid officials, an uncoached athlete's knowledge of safety rules and regulations can almost certainly be expected to be lower than that of a well coached individual. Therefore, if a suit for negligence involving uncoached athletes were allowed at all, the standard of behavior expected would almost certainly be that of a reasonable individual of similar skill and knowledge rather than the higher level of a trained athlete (see Case 15.1).

The Presence of Officials

Regardless of the skill and training of the athletes, how will these principles be applied to games in which no officials are used? If the game was organized by some authoritative body, as unofficiated intramurals and school activities are, it is at least theoretically possible that injured athletes could sue the organizers under the contention that the presence of effective officiating would have significantly reduced the likelihood of reckless and unsafe behavior.

But what of the offending athletes? Is there no recourse unless their actions are so blatant that they fall into the willful battery category and thus move beyond civil negligence and into the realm of criminal law? In theory, it would seem that individuals who participate in unstructured games and contests should be expected to show the same level of care and concern for the safety and welfare of their opponents as formally trained athletes would. Their behavior on the field should conform to societal norms and the rules of the game as it is being played at the time. However, the degree to which the legal system will be able to adjudicate alleged breaches of this standard effectively is not yet entirely clear.

Behaviors Not Covered by Specific Rules

What about those behaviors that do not necessarily violate a safety rule but that are so violent or vicious that they may reasonably be argued to show at least willful disregard for the safety of an opponent? We have all seen a tackle applied to a receiver immediately after a catch or a body check to an unsuspecting person that appeared far more vicious than necessary. If such an action was to result in an injury, would it be actionable in court? Once again, the issue may hinge so heavily on the state of mind of the defendant as to be beyond the scope of law in any but the most extreme cases.

THE COACH AS INSTIGATOR

A final issue focuses not on the athletes themselves but on their coaches. What is the liability of coaches who teach and encourage intense aggressive play from their athletes if any of their players go beyond the rules and spirit of the game and cause injury to their opponents?

The case of *Nydegger v. Don Bosco Prep High School* (1985) is an example of just such a situation. Kevin Nydegger was a high school soccer player in New Jersey. He filed a suit against the opposing coach and school for injuries that he suffered during a game. Nydegger alleged that the opposing coach taught his players to compete in an "aggressive and intense manner" and that he engendered an attitude in which winning was all-important. During the trial, however, Nydegger failed to prove that the defendant coach had ever instructed his players to injure an opponent. In ruling in favor of the coach, the court put forth a conclusion that succinctly summarizes both the level of risk that athletes can reasonably be expected to accept and the point at which coaches must assume responsibility for pushing their players beyond reasonable aggressiveness.

> Those who participate in a sport such as soccer expect that there will be physical contact as a result of 22 young men running around a field 50 by 100 yards. Physical contact is not prohibited by the rules of soccer. Injuries do result. Those who participate are trained to play hard and aggressive. . . .
>
> A coach cannot be held responsible for the wrongful acts of his players unless he teaches them to do the wrongful act or instructs them to commit the act. . . .
>
> Teaching players to be intense and aggressive is an attribute. All sports and many adult activities require aggressiveness and intensity. (*Nydegger v. Don Bosco Prep High School*, 1985)

Clearly coaches, no matter how careful and well intentioned, cannot guarantee that none of their players will go beyond reasonable aggressiveness and improperly cause injuries to their opponents. If such an event occurs and if the behavior of the athlete is determined to be so flagrant as to exhibit a reckless or willful disregard for the safety of others, then the offending athlete may very well become the target of a negligence suit. If, on the other hand, it can be proved that the coach taught or encouraged his athletes to go beyond the bounds of reasonable aggression and to use dangerous or illegal tactics, then the coach may be liable for the resultant injuries.

Although aggression and intensity are normal and often laudable by-products of athletic participation, the courts will not tolerate deliberate and willful behavior that defies the letter and the spirit of the rules or that is intended to cause injury to an opponent. If such behavior occurs, the injured player can, depending on the specific circumstances, bring suit against the player who caused the injury, that player's coach, or both.

CASE STUDIES

Case 15.1

Sliding Player Accused of Negligence

Diane Black, age 19, was a catcher on the Bad News Bombers, a recreational softball team in Drayton Township. The league consisted of eight coed teams that played according to modified slow-pitch rules, which required four female players on the field at all times and allowed sliding. Diane Black was approximately 5 ft 5 in. tall and weighed about 148 lb.

On May 13, Diane was playing in her first league game of the season. During the fifth inning Sam Nolan batted first and safely reached second base. The next batter hit a long fly ball to left center field, and Sam attempted to score. Sam was proceeding down the third base line when

Diane received the throw from the outfield. She estimates that he was approximately 20 ft from her when she gained possession of the ball. Sam continued his approach and attempted to slide. In the course of his slide, some portion of Sam's body struck Diane, who fell to the ground and suffered what was eventually diagnosed as a fractured fibula.

Diane has instituted suit against Sam, alleging through her attorney and his expert witness that Sam

1. failed to exercise good judgment and control of his emotions in the interest of safety;
2. willfully, negligently, and recklessly injured Diane by sliding even though she had gained possession of the ball approximately 20 ft before the point of contact;
3. failed to comply with the meaning and spirit of the rules by purposely and willfully running into Diane in an attempt to score a run;
4. failed to realize that he was physically larger than Diane and that a collision with her would cause injury; and
5. failed to fulfill his duty to avoid collisions with defensive players while running the bases.

This type of scenario in many ways tends to fuel the fires of paranoia with regard to the so-called ''litigation explosion.'' Viewed from the defendant's perspective we see an instantaneous decision to slide rather than a deliberate decision to either run into the catcher or try to stop and turn back toward third while already running at full speed toward home. Because of this decision, the athlete is now embroiled in a time-consuming and emotionally draining lawsuit.

From the plaintiff's perspective, on the other hand, the injury caused a financial drain from both time lost from work and expenses for subsequent medical treatment and required her to give up her part-time graduate study. She certainly never expected any of these complications to arise when she agreed to spend a few hours a week playing softball.

Perhaps the most disconcerting viewpoint, however, is that of the average teacher or coach who sees a relatively commonplace occurrence that an attorney and an expert have portrayed as being willful, dangerous, and negligent and that is now the subject of a major lawsuit. They are likely to fear that if lawsuits are allowed to continue springing up from this sort of incident, there simply will be no one left who is willing to run the risk of either playing in or conducting programs of sport.

It is important to recognize, however, that bringing a lawsuit and winning it are two distinctly different issues. If restrictions were imposed on the right to bring suits, they would stop valid suits as well as those of less merit. On the other hand, if defendants and the insurance companies that represent them successfully defend those cases where there does not appear to be negligence involved, then neither plaintiffs nor their attorneys gain from suing and ultimately realize that undertaking weak cases is too risky. This seems to be the best and fairest way to control the threat of a continued "litigation explosion."

The court ruled that Diane Black's injury was caused by playing errors and/or skill deficiencies that she and/or Sam Nolan committed. There was no evidence to support her allegations that Mr. Nolan's actions had been willful and deliberate. Ms. Black in fact testified during the course of her deposition that she did not believe that Sam had intentionally collided with her. Further, because sliding is a legitimate evasive technique that falls within both the letter and spirit of the rules, it is difficult to question its use in this particular situation.

Sam attempted to avoid a tag and to score a run by executing a slide. Diane attempted to avoid a run by standing within the basepath to apply the tag on the base runner. This is a simple matter of two relatively unskilled players executing complex motor skills in a very imprecise manner. Collisions such as the one described are not entirely uncommon among even highly skilled players but are even more likely to occur among recreational players. Although this fact argues strongly for the wisdom of no-sliding rules instituted by professionals who organize and supervise recreational leagues, it in no way imposes the burden of negligence upon unskilled participants who execute less than perfect slides.

[Based on a case adjudicated in the lower courts]

CHAPTER SUMMARY

Recent case law has made it clear that an athlete who has been injured by an opponent during the course of a game or contest can seek compensation through the courts. Yet to be fully determined, however, is the question of the standard of behavior against which a defendant player's actions are to be measured. It appears that the reckless disregard standard will emerge as the best compromise between the desire to encourage vigorous athletic competition and the rights of an athlete who has been injured by the allegedly wrongful actions of another player. It must also be recognized that coaches who encourage wrongful acts of aggression by their players may be held liable for the results of their players' actions.

KEY TERMS

Directed verdict (284)
Ordinary negligence standard (285)
Reckless or willful disregard (285)
Wanton acts (285)
Willful acts (285)
Willful or wanton standard (285)

QUESTIONS FOR DISCUSSION

1. Discuss and expand upon the following statement: Although the Nabozny decision clearly articulated the right of athletes to sue each other for injuries sustained as a result of their alleged negligence, it failed to define the specific types of behaviors that could reasonably precipitate such a lawsuit.

2. Give activity-specific examples of situations that could reasonably constitute breaches of the reckless disregard standard.
3. Give activity-specific examples of situations in which one athlete is injured by the aggressive or violent act of another but a successful lawsuit is unlikely to result.
4. Devise a scenario whereby someone other than the offending athlete might reasonably be held liable for injuries resulting from player violence.
5. Change some facts in Case 15.1 so that Sam Nolan may indeed be held liable for Diane Black's injury.

REFERENCES

Bourque v. Duplechin, 331 So.2d 40 (La. app 1976).

Goldstein, L.A. (1976). Participant's liability for injury to a fellow participant in an organized athletic event. *Chicago-Kent Law Review*, **53**, 97-108.

Nabozny v. Barnhill, 31 Ill. App.3d 212, 334 N.E.2d 258 (1975).

Nydegger v. Don Bosco Prep High School, 202 NJ Super. 535 (1985).

Ross v. Clouser, 637 S.W.2d 11 (Mo. 1982).

ADDITIONAL READINGS

Goldstein, L.A. (1976). Participant's liability for injury to a fellow participant in an organized athletic event. *Chicago-Kent Law Review*, **53**, 97-108.

Horrow, R. (1985). Legislating against violence in sports. In H. Appenzeller (Ed.), *Sports and law: Contemporary issues* (pp. 53-60). Charlottesville, VA: The Michie Co.

Narol, M. (1991). Sports participation with limited litigation: The emerging Reckless Disregard Standard. *Seton Hall Journal of Sport Law*, **1**, pp. 29-40.

LEGAL RESPONSIBILITY FOR PARTICIPANT SAFETY

ROOTS OF THE LIABILITY EXPLOSION

In the province of Ontario one half of all school-related injuries are the result of athletic activity. More generally, 1.3 million injuries related to sports participation occurred in 1986 in Ontario alone (Saunders & Stewart, 1991). Obviously not all of these involved negligence, but the statistic does show the magnitude of the potential for injury in the sport and recreation setting.

In Canada, medical care and rehabilitation costs are typically covered by a universal health care system, but injuries may bring about expenses well beyond these immediate costs. For example, an injured party may suffer lost earnings, both present and future. Serious injuries may require changes in lifestyle, including modifications to one's home or vehicle. Retraining costs, loss of life expectancy, future care, and other expenses can place an unmanageable financial burden on the injured party. If the person has insurance coverage for personal injury, many of these expenses may be paid out by the insurance company. But in such instances, the insurance company has the right of subrogation,

that is, a right to sue the party responsible for the injury in the name of the injured party to recover what it has had to pay out.

RIGHT TO SUE ANOTHER PARTY

Because lawsuits can be very costly and time-consuming, some injuries that result from negligence may simply not warrant or allow such a course of action. Most personal injury lawsuits are done on a contingency basis, wherein the lawyer takes a percentage of the final award. But under most contingency agreements, the client is expected to pay disbursements, that is, the law firm's out-of-pocket expenses for such items as doctors' reports, courier charges, and document filing charges. These costs can add up quite quickly, making a lawsuit financially prohibitive for many people.

DOCTRINE OF ENTITLEMENT

The plaintiff decides whether to have a matter tried by a judge and jury or before a judge alone. Cases that involve complicated technical or legal arguments are better heard by a judge alone. Cases in which the emotional element is a stronger factor are better directed toward a judge and jury. But even in cases where the jury feels sympathy for the plaintiff, it is the jury's duty to determine the legal issue of negligence and to ensure that, on the balance of probabilities, all the components of negligence are satisfied before it renders a decision. Once the issue of liability has been established, the issue of damages can then be addressed, but only if the injured party can justify the damages.

SETTLEMENT

As noted in the Canadian Applications for Part I, most lawsuits are settled before trial. The provincial Rules of Court are intended to promote **settlement** and to penalize unreasonable offers or positions by either party. As the evidence becomes clear during the course of the lawsuit's discovery phase, the liability of the defendant and plaintiff may become quite apparent and may lead the parties toward settlement.

THE MYTH OF RISK-FREE PROGRAMS

Risk is an inherent part of all physical activity. The challenge for instructors of physical activity is to control or manage the risk to the greatest extent possible. Being sued is always a possibility, but perhaps a more effective approach to take with issues of liability and negligence is one of proactive risk management. Ensuring that your own behavior and the conduct of your program meets an acceptable standard of care will reduce the possibility of lawsuits.

ELEMENTS OF NEGLIGENCE

An action must meet the following four criteria to be considered negligent:

1. A duty of care was owed to another.
2. The standard of care imposed by that duty was breached.
3. Some injury or damage occurred.
4. There is a causal connection between the injury or damage and the breach of the standard of care.

Duty

If it is foreseeable that your actions will affect another party, you are said to have a **duty of care** to that other party. Some examples of such relationships are as follows:

- Teacher to student
- Coach to athlete
- Trainer to athlete
- Volunteer to program participant
- Board of directors of sport organization to participant
- Facility manager to participant

Certain statutes impose a duty on one party toward another. For example, most school legislation outlines the duties of teachers toward their students. For instance, Section 13 of the Alberta School Act (1970) states that, among other things, a teacher "has a duty to provide instruction competently to students" and to "maintain, under the direction of the principal, proper order and discipline in the school, on the school grounds and at any activity sponsored or approved by the Board." In addition, all provinces in Canada have passed occupiers' liability statutes. This legislation outlines the duty and standard of care of facility owners and operators toward participants or occupants of their facilities.

Standard of Care

The duty described above imposes the standard of care one has towards those to whom one owes a duty. A breach of that standard will meet the second criterion towards a finding of negligence. The standard is not perfection, however. Not every risk needs to be eliminated, and accidents will always happen. To determine what the **standard of care** is under various circumstances, you should look at and rely on the following resources:

- The internal written standards of the organization
- Any external standards that are available; for example, government legislation such as the occupiers' liability legislation discussed above, industry standards, and standards of national or parent organizations
- Previous case law, which often shows how the courts expect one to act
- Your own common sense

Damages

The third criterion for a finding of negligence is that some loss or injury resulted from the accident. Judgments or settlements are intended to compensate injured parties for their losses and to put them back in the position they were in prior to the injury by restoring what was lost as a result of the accident. Obviously some losses simply cannot be restored. In such cases the courts try to compensate the loss through a financial award—the only real tool available to them. The sorts of compensable damage or loss for which the courts award compensation are listed in the Canadian Applications for Part I.

Causation

The final criterion for a negligence finding is that the breach of the standard of care actually caused or significantly influenced the injured party's condition. In general, people are considered responsible for the probable consequences of their actions even though the actual injuries that occurred may not have been foreseeable. In *School Division of Assiniboine South No. 3 v. Hoffer et al.* (1971), the Supreme Court of Canada apportioned damages between a 14-year-old youth, his father, and the Greater Winnipeg Gas Company when the youth negligently lost control of his father's snowmobile and hit an unprotected gas riser pipe. Escaping gas entered a nearby school, causing a massive explosion. Mr. Justice Dickson set out the test for **causation**:

> It is enough to fix liability if one could foresee in a general way the sort of thing that happened. *The extent of the damage and its manner of incidence need not be foreseeable if the physical damage of the kind which in fact ensues is foreseeable* [italics added]. (*Assiniboine v. Hoffer*, 1971, p. 752)

It is important to note that all four criteria must be present and met for negligence to be established. Figure CA5.1 depicts the line of reasoning that must be followed in a bona fide case of negligence.

DEFENSES FOR NEGLIGENCE

One defense available to a defendant in a liability case is to prove **voluntary assumption of risk** (*volenti nonfit injuria*). If the defendant can show that the plaintiff voluntarily assumed the risk, this will act as a complete defense barring the plaintiff from any recovery for damages. It is essential that the defendant show that the plaintiff understood what the risk or risks were, had an appreciation for the risks, and consented to assume the risks. This refers to both the physical risks inherent in the activity *and* the legal risk (i.e., the risk of negligence).

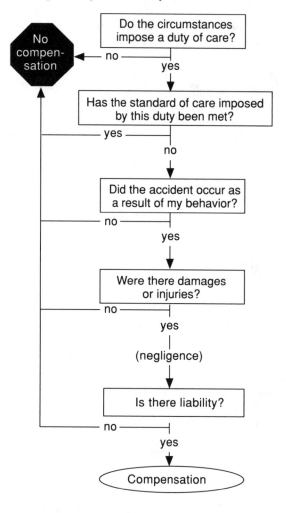

Figure CA5.1　Determining negligence and liability.

Note. Reprinted with permission of Sport Networking, Inc.

Just exactly what risks is the plaintiff accepting under the circumstances? In very common sports such as ice hockey and soccer, it is implicitly understood that the participant accepts a certain amount of incidental physical contact that will take place during the activity and assumes the risks arising from such contact. It is generally accepted that, although not part of the rules, a certain

amount of incidental contact will occur and that it is an obvious and necessary part of the game. The extent of physical contact accepted by the participants has long been an issue in the area of violence in sport. Does the participant accept the risk of physical contact after the whistle has blown and, if so, for what period after the whistle has blown? Are fights an accepted part of the risks?

In less familiar activities or ones of very high risk, it is essential that the defendant be able to prove that the participant knew and understood the risks. A well-drafted **informed consent document** that clearly outlines the potential risks and their consequences goes a long way toward meeting this requirement.

It has been argued that by signing a waiver, participants not only accept the physical risks of the activity but also waive their legal rights to take any legal action in conjunction with an accident. In light of the court's definition of voluntary assumption of risk, however, the waiver must, among other things, fully set out the risks the participants would be assuming, including the risk that program officials or instructors may behave negligently. It is also necessary that the waiver set out the consequences of assuming such risks, including being precluded from any legal action against the negligence of the other party. The following factors should be considered when drafting and executing waivers.

1. **Drafting**: Both parties must clearly understand the terms of the waiver. Therefore, wording must be completely clear and unambiguous.
2. **Scope**: The waiver must state explicitly that it covers all parties (directors, employees, agents, contractors, officials, sponsors, operators, volunteers, and so forth). The waiver must also state specifically what it is protecting the parties against, namely, responsibility for the consequences of accident, harm, injury, or death caused by risks inherent in

the activity, whether foreseeable or not foreseeable (both should be identified if possible), and specifically legal charges of negligence.

3. **Comprehensiveness**: The waiver must cover all aspects of the activity, which may include preprogram and postprogram activity and transportation to and from the program site. Any prerequisites for participation, such as a medical certificate or a skill level, should be identified in the waiver. The waiver should also require participants to acknowledge that they will adhere to the rules of the activity and the organization.

4. **Execution**: The person signing the waiver must understand what rights he or she is giving up. The waiver should contain a clause in which the participant acknowledges having read and understood the waiver. A waiver cannot be signed by a minor or by someone who does not have the mental capacity to sign a contract, such as an intoxicated person or a person with a mental disability. All waivers must be in writing and should be witnessed. The advantage of having waivers witnessed is that it helps to establish that the waiver was properly executed.

5. **Suitability**: Finally, the waiver must be appropriate from an ethical perspective for the organization, program, or client group. Consider whether there are alternatives to a waiver, such as an informed consent agreement.

CONTRIBUTORY NEGLIGENCE

According to common law, **contributory negligence** on the part of the plaintiff completely barred the plaintiff from any claim. Now that apportionment legislation has been passed in virtually every province, liability can be distributed between the plaintiff and the defendant, and the plaintiff's claim can be reduced in proportion to the plaintiff's degree of assessed negligence or contribution to the negligence.

The defense of contributory negligence is not considered until the negligence of the defendant has been established. In other words, finding the plaintiff even partially responsible for his or her injuries will not absolve the defendant of negligence and ensuing liability.

The contributory negligence of a child acting as plaintiff is determined on a slightly different basis than that of an adult. Generally speaking, children under the age of 6 are immune from charges of contributory negligence, whereas older children are judged against the behavior of reasonable children of like age, intelligence, and experience under similar circumstances.

VIOLENCE IN SPORT

In many sports, physical contact is such an accepted part of the game that it is often accepted as an implicit part of the rules. When does acceptable physical contact cross the line and become unacceptable? Or more to the point, Is violence on the playing field different from violence elsewhere in society, and should it be treated differently?

Generally, sport organizations (both professional and amateur) attempt to deal with the issue of violence internally. A good example is the National Hockey League, which has debated the merits and drawbacks of fighting for several years. The issue has not been fully resolved, in part because some fans of professional hockey like the fighting. When sport organizations' internal efforts to deal with such issues have not been successful, the trend has increasingly been toward dealing with violence in sport—particularly the more serious instances—through the criminal courts.

CRIMINAL ACTION FOR ASSAULT

Under the criminal law, violence falls within the assault sections of the Criminal Code of Canada (1985). Two types of assault are defined in the Code. Basic or **common assault** is defined in Section 265 as follows:

(1) A person commits an assault when

    (a) without the consent of another person, he applies force intentionally to that person, directly or indirectly;

    (b) he attempts or threatens, by an act or gesture, to apply force to another person, if he has, or causes that other person to believe upon reasonable grounds that he has, present ability to effect his purpose;

    (c) while openly wearing or carrying a weapon or an imitation thereof, he accosts or impedes another person or begs.

A more serious form of assault, **assault with a weapon** or assault causing bodily harm, is defined in Section 267 as follows:

(1) Everyone who, in committing an assault,

    (a) carries, uses or threatens to use a weapon or an imitation thereof, or

    (b) causes bodily harm to the complainant, is guilty of an indictable offence and liable to imprisonment for a term not exceeding ten years.

(2) For the purposes of this section and sections 269 and 272, ''bodily harm''

means any hurt or injury to the complainant that interferes with the health or comfort of the complainant and that is more than merely transient or trifling in nature.

As Section 265 of the Criminal Code states, there are two main criteria for a forceful act against another person to be considered an assault: intention to inflict the force and lack of consent to the force. The element of **intention** is what distinguishes assault from negligence. In assaults, the aggressors must be shown to have intended their actions, whereas in negligence cases, the fact that the negligent parties did not intend the consequences of their actions is not relevant; the very fact that they acted without reasonable care is usually sufficient for findings of negligence, assuming that the other criteria for negligence are also met.

Defenses for Assault

In sport, the first criteria for assault can usually be met because there is typically an intention to exert some force. The more difficult aspect to determine in the sport situation is whether or not the injured party consented to the force. For this reason, a common defense to a charge of assault in sport is that the other party consented to the force. In rare cases, however, aggressors may claim that they lacked the intention to inflict force and instead may use as their defense that their actions were the result of involuntary reflex. Finally, a third defense to a charge of assault is self-defense. Each of these defenses is examined in the sections that follow.

Consent

The case law has focused on three main ways of determining whether there has been **consent to the infliction of force**. These are

1. consent implied by participation in the game;
2. consent implied by specific acts during the game; and
3. public policy limitations on the ability to consent (White, 1986, p. 1038).

Consent Implied by Participation. Some may suggest that a player consents to whatever occurs during the course of a game simply by participating in it. In fact, the courts generally accept that players are presumed to consent to conduct incidental to, or inherent in, the game or reasonably related to it. Although this standard is reasonable in theory, in practice it provides little assistance in determining consent to specific acts of force or violence during the game. Some courts have tried to narrow the test somewhat by applying the notion of *fair play* to incidental conduct, including fighting. For example, fighting with hands only, as opposed to with a stick or other piece of equipment, may be considered within the bounds of fair play and thus reasonably consented to (*R. v. Henderson*, 1976).

The courts have been more successful in defining conduct to which consent is *not* given. The passage most frequently quoted in this regard comes from the case of *Agar v. Canning* (1966): "Injuries inflicted in circumstances which show a definite resolve to cause serious injury to another, even when there is provocation and in the heat of the game, should not fall within the scope of complied consent" (*Agar v. Canning*, 1966, p. 304). On this issue, and in extreme cases, the courts have been consistent and clear in their decisions.

R. v. Henderson (1976) involved an attack on a hockey player who could be described as an "innocent bystander." The victim and attacker had no contact throughout the game. The victim was looking away from his assailant at the time of the blow and was merely standing by waiting for play to resume following an altercation between two other players. The blow by his attacker knocked him to the ice unconscious and resulted in a serious laceration. He had clearly not consented to any such conduct.

In *R. v. Gray* (1981), also a hockey case in which the incident took place during an altercation, the assailant came off the bench, skated straight toward an uninvolved player, struck him in the face and neck, and then veered off to head for a fight in progress about 10 to 15 ft away. As in *R. v. Henderson* (1976), the victim was oblivious to the impending attack and, in fact, had moved away from the ongoing altercation, clearly indicating his intention to disassociate himself from it.

These are fairly clear examples in which it is not difficult to determine the issue of consent. Unfortunately, the courts have given little direction for less extreme instances of violence. Clearly, players in contact sports consent to a variety of minor body contacts but it is difficult to draw the line between what is criminally sanctioned and what is not. That difficulty is one of the reasons charges of common assault in sport are likely to fail as opposed to the more serious assault causing bodily harm.

Consent Implied by Specific Acts. Although consent implied by specific acts is not usually discussed apart from consent implied by general participation, it emerges as an important aspect in the case law. In *R. v. Watson* (1976), the courts noted two acts by the victim involved in a hockey incident that might suggest implied consent. First, the victim was involved in a minor scuffle just prior to the alleged assault. Second, the victim dropped his gloves and stick immediately before the altercation.

A similar analysis of the victim's behavior is evident in a number of other cases. In *R. v. St. Croix* (1979), at p. 24, for example, the courts recognized that most athletes consent to "the normal risks of the game and to a foreseeable amount and type of assaults." This would suggest that the only basis for any implied consent was participation in the game generally. But the fact that the court noted in detail the actions of the victim just prior to the assault suggests that it also considered that specific acts of the victim could be construed as implied consent to certain acts of force.

In *R. v. Ciccarelli* (1990), the court set out the following four factors to be considered when assessing the scope of implied consent:

1. The nature of the game played
2. The nature of the particular act and its surrounding circumstances
3. The degree of risk of injury
4. The state of mind of the accused

The courts used this analysis in *R. v. Krzysztofik* (1992), another hockey checking incident. The court stated that the force employed near the boards was unnecessarily violent, entailed a high degree of risk of injury, and was not associated with or related to any play at hand, concluding that the check "would be denounced as falling outside the parameters of any acceptable standard by which the game is played."

Consent Limited by Public Policy.   There are legal limits to the consent a person can give, regardless of what they imply or express. The courts have long confirmed the principle that one cannot do by agreement what the law states shall not be done. Public policy simply does not permit consent to some types of assault, particularly those constituting vicious attacks and those that result in death.

Lack of Intention

Where there is **lack of intention**, that is, no intention to inflict force, there can be no assault. It has been argued that in the emotionally charged atmosphere of competition, some responses are of a reflexive or automatic nature rather than deliberate acts. In such cases, the courts will consider whether the act was reasonable, given the circumstances: that is, whether a reasonable person under similar circumstances would have acted in a similar manner.

Self-Defense

Individuals are allowed to defend themselves against the threat of violence, but there are certain limits to the defense of **self-defense** that restrict its usefulness in athletic competition. Only the amount of force necessary to avoid bodily harm is permissible, and even then only for as long as there is an immediate threat. Once the immediate threat has been defended, the athlete can almost always move away from the situation. The courts will accept acts of defense and self-protection but not acts of retaliation or aggression. Therefore, if there is a significant delay between the initial threat and the so-called act of self-defense, the defense will probably fail.

In addition to examining whether a person is justified in the act of self-defense, the courts will also consider the amount of force used. In *R. v. Maki* (1970), the court found Maki, a National Hockey League player, justified in using force to defend himself and, considering the second element of the defense, said that, although the force used caused serious injury, Maki simply had misjudged the degree of force necessary to ward off the attack. The court did not consider the act retaliatory or intentionally excessive.

Provocation in and of itself is not a defense but may be considered justification for an act of self-defense if it is so extreme that the other party actually fears for his or her safety. To succeed, such a defense would have to meet the threshold criteria for self-defense just noted.

CIVIL ACTION FOR ASSAULT

The preceding discussion of defenses is directed toward those who must either bring, or defend themselves against, criminal charges of assault. But it is also possible to bring a civil action in assault cases. The difference between a criminal charge of assault and a civil action for assault is that the former is tried in the criminal courts. Charges are brought by the state against the defendant who, if found guilty, may face criminal sanctions ranging from a fine to jail. In a civil action, the plaintiff, or victim of an assault, files a suit just as he would in a negligence action. The suit follows the same course as that described in the Canadian Applications for Part I and, if the defendant is found liable or responsible for the assault, he may have to pay damages to the plaintiff. The criteria for assault in a civil suit and its defenses are virtually the same as those for criminal charges.

CASE STUDIES

Case CA5.1

Contributory Negligence, Voluntary Assumption of Risk, and Waiver Enforceability

Crocker v. Sundance Resorts Ltd. (1983) is an important and fairly recent decision of the Supreme Court of Canada. In this case, Sundance, a ski resort, ran as a promotion a fun competition wherein participants slid down a mogul slope on oversize inner tubes. The plaintiff and his friend entered the competition. Over the course of the day, the plaintiff consumed a large quantity of alcohol and became very drunk. The defendant recognized the plaintiff's inebriated state and suggested that he should not compete in the race. Despite his condition, however, the plaintiff did compete in the race. During one of his runs, his inner tube was upset, and the plaintiff suffered a neck injury that resulted in quadriplegia.

While the plaintiff was found 25% contributorily negligent for his injuries, the Court found the resort had a positive duty to take steps to prevent a visibly intoxicated person from putting him- or herself at risk by competing in the event. The policy behind this decision of the court can be understood from the following comment made by the Chief Justice: "One is under a duty not to place another person in a position where it is foreseeable that that person could suffer injury. The plaintiff's inability to handle the situation in which he or she has been placed—either through youth, intoxication or other incapacity—is an element in determining how foreseeable the injury is" (*Crocker v. Sundance*, 1983, p. 328).

The defendants put forth the defense of *volenti nonfit injuria* (voluntary assumption of risk), that is, that Mr. Crocker, the plaintiff, voluntarily assumed the risk when he engaged in the activity. The Court prefaced its decision on this issue with the following comment: "Since the *volenti* defense is a complete bar to recovery and therefore anomalous in an age of appropriation, the courts have tightly circumscribed its scope. It only applies in situations where the plaintiff has assumed both the physical and the legal risk involved in the activity" (*Crocker v. Sundance*, 1983, p. 332).

The Court questioned whether Mr. Crocker in his inebriated state had consciously consented to the physical risk, notwithstanding the fact that he did indeed participate in the event. With regard to waiving his legal rights, the Court held that the very act of sliding down the slope on the inner tube could not be construed as a waiver of those rights.

Finally, the Court addressed the issue of the validity of the combination waiver and entry form Mr. Crocker had signed 2 days prior to the day of the accident. The trial judge found that Mr. Crocker had not read the form, and that the waiver portion of it was not brought to his attention. He concluded that Mr. Crocker did not understand it to be a waiver but merely an application form. The Supreme Court of Canada upheld this view.

The decision in this case is in contrast to the Court's decision to uphold the waiver in *Dyck v. The Manitoba Snowmobiling Association* (1981), a decision of the Manitoba Court of Appeal. The Court in *Crocker* referred to the *Dyck* decision but distinguished the circumstances under which the waiver had been signed. In that case, as a condition of entering the race, Mr. Dyck, a snowmobile racer, was required to sign a waiver. Mr. Dyck had entered over five other races that season, acknowledged having read the form on each occasion, and had at least scanned the form for this particular race. At trial, Mr. Dyck claimed that he did not know what the words meant—that it was all "mumbo-jumbo." He signed because he had to in order to race. As far as he was concerned, "These things were something he ignored, and that he regarded them as something used to avoid hassles and to frighten people off from suing" (*Dyck v. Manitoba*, p. 102).

The trial judge found that, although Mr. Dyck may not have understood the precise legal meaning of the waiver, he was aware that the form related to the responsibility of the defendant, Manitoba Snowmobiling Association, to him. He termed the plaintiff's state of mind more one of attitude than ignorance, holding that the waiver had been properly inserted into the entry form and that Mr. Dyck had been notified of it. The trial court's decision was upheld by the Manitoba Court of Appeal.

[*Crocker v. Sundance Resorts Ltd.* (1983), 150 D.L.R. (3d) 478 Rev'd [1985] 20 D.L.R. (4d) 552 (Ont. C.A.) Rev'd 44 C.C.L.T. 225 (S.C.C.)]

Case CA5.2

Waivers

The deceased plaintiff, Mr. Delaney, was a paying customer on a whitewater rafting excursion conducted by the defendant, Cascade River Holidays Ltd. During the excursion, the raft in which Mr. Delaney was traveling overturned, and the life jackets Mr. Delaney and his fellow passengers were wearing failed to keep a number of them afloat. Mr. Delaney was one of several who did not survive the accident. The evidence at trial clearly showed that the defendant knew that the life jackets were inadequate and that other local operators were using better life jackets. (It should be noted that the defendant's life jackets did meet federal government standards but were nevertheless clearly inadequate under the circumstances.)

The Court determined that the less-than-adequate jackets increased the risk of drowning and materially contributed to the death of Mr. Delaney. It said that Cascade owed a duty to its passengers to take reasonable care by providing the best available jackets, particularly at that time of year, when the river was high and turbulent.

In spite of the defendant's negligence in its conduct towards the plaintiff, the Court found that the waiver signed by the deceased before the trip was a valid waiver. The Court found that the deceased knew it was necessary for him to sign the release to participate in the trip. Given the hazardous nature of the trip, the Court held that the use of a waiver under these circumstances was not unreasonable. Further, the waiver was complete in its scope, covering the defendant, its employees, and agents during travel to the trip location, just prior to the trip, during the trip itself, and the period after. It was clear and explicit in what it covered and who it covered. It clearly relieved the defendant's agents and employees of liability for any reason, including negligence. Finally, the deceased had the opportunity to read the waiver, understand what it said, and appreciate the risks involved.

[*Delaney v. Cascade River Holidays Ltd.* (1983), 24 C.C.L.T. 6 (B.C.C.A.)]

Case CA5.3	**Appropriate Standard of Care**

This case involved a 24-year-old novice who signed up for a course in parachute jumping. The course consisted of a 4-hour theory session on the ground followed by a jump from the air.

A parachute canopy is usually steered by pulling on different ropes. As the students made their first jumps, a person on the ground helped them steer by pointing a large arrow indicating which rope to pull. During her initial jump, the plaintiff became confused about how to control her parachute and could not orient herself. She drifted dangerously toward a group of trees but was able to make an emergency landing in the upper branches of one tree. (This had been taught during the course.) Unfortunately, however, the branches snapped and she fell to the ground, where she initially landed properly, feet first, but then fell backward over a log, breaking her back.

The Court had no difficulty with the issue of causation, declaring that the accident was caused by the plaintiff's inability to control the chute. The real issue for the Court was the content and method of instruction. The plaintiff maintained that she had not been taught the method of controlling the direction of the parachute in such a way that she could do it properly in descent.

The Court depended heavily on the evidence of experts, who testified about the content and duration of the course. Although the Court found the content appropriate for preparing a person for a first jump and the

4-hour length not unreasonable given the amount of content, it found that the instructor had a duty, either through questioning or a written test, to ensure that the students had grasped the elements that were essential to a successful jump.

The Court accepted the evidence of the experts that stress can inhibit both recall and performance. The instructor had a duty to ensure that each student was in a proper physical and emotional state to be able to exercise clear and quick judgment during the jump. In this, the Court found that the instructor had failed in his duty.

Further, although the theory part of the course was satisfactory, the Court said that too many elements of the actual jump were left undiscussed, so that the plaintiff did not know what she would encounter during the actual jump. Again, unfamiliarity heightens stress, which in turn inhibits performance.

The plaintiff was not found completely blameless for the accident. The Court deemed her 30% contributorily negligent because she had shared in the decision that she should jump despite her emotional uncertainty.

This case also points out one of the critical factors that can invalidate a waiver or exculpatory agreement. Unfortunately for the defendants, their waiver was poorly drafted. The waiver covered injury caused by fortuitous accident such as equipment failure, but nowhere did it refer to any potential negligence on the part of the defendant. To protect the defendant from its own negligence, a waiver must clearly refer to the action of the defendant, whether negligent or not. Here the defendant neglected to do the very thing it had contracted to do—to use reasonable care to teach the plaintiff how to jump safely. The waiver simply did not cover this negligence.

[*Smith v. Horizon Aero Sport Ltd.* (1981), 130 D.L.R. (3d) 91, 19 C.C.L.T. 89 (B.C.S.C.)]

Case CA5.4

Activity Selection and Supervision

Although this case was decided in 1975, it remains a landmark decision regarding physical education instruction in the schools. Mr. Thornton, the plaintiff, was a 15-year-old boy who was injured during a gymnastics class. The students were doing somersaults by jumping off a springboard and landing on a pile of rubber chunks held together in a net. With the permission of their instructor, the boys placed a box horse in such a way that they could jump from it to the springboard to get a better takeoff for the somersault.

Although the boys had received some preliminary instruction in basic skills, none of them had ever attempted this particular stunt. They received no instruction about the somersault nor warnings about its hazards. During the entire class the instructor sat at a table completing report cards.

Part way through the class, one of the students missed his landing and broke his wrist, but still the instructor gave no warning, although additional foam mats were placed around the existing foam. The boys were allowed to continue with their activity. While attempting a somersault, the plaintiff landed on his head on the floor and suffered a severe spinal injury.

The decision of the Court was influenced significantly by the testimony of experts, who commented on instructional content, supervision, equipment, task difficulty, and related matters. The Court found that the instructor had failed to reach an acceptable standard of care in the following four main areas:

1. The equipment was never intended to be used as it was being used at the time of the accident. The instructor knew or should have known the dangers of allowing students to use the equipment in such a fashion.
2. The first mishap (the broken wrist) should have put the instructor on notice. It was clearly foreseeable that further injury might occur.
3. The instructor failed to adequately supervise the students, particularly in light of their inexperience.
4. The instructor failed to provide adequate preliminary instruction in the skill and to warn the students of the dangers in performing the skill.

Finally, because the instructor was acting within the scope of his employment duties (albeit negligently), his employers were equally liable. In other words, an employer is responsible for all employees under its control as long as those employees are acting within the scope of their duties. Therefore, the school board in this case was also held accountable for the accident.

[*Thornton v. Board of School District No. 57 (Prince George)* (1975), 3 W.W.R. 622; 57 D.L.R. (3d) 438 (B.C.S.C.): (1976) 5 W.W.R. 240; 73 D.L.R. (3d) 35 (C.A.), rev'd in part; (1978) 2 S.C.R. 267; 3 C.C.L.T. 257; (1978) 1 W.W.R. 607; 19 N.R. 552; 83 D.L.R. (3d) 480)]

Case CA5.5

Supervision and Contributory Negligence
In this case, a 15-year-old student was attempting a dismount from the rings during a gymnastics class. There were approximately 30 students in the gym with one teacher supervising the activity. With the permission of the teacher, 6 or 7 of the students, including the plaintiff, moved off to a separate room adjacent to the gym. The students had no additional supervision and in fact were out of sight of the teacher, who remained in the main gym.

The plaintiff attempted a trick on the rings while being spotted by a friend. After the trick was done, the spotter moved away, but the plaintiff decided to try a maneuver he had never done before—a straddle dismount. Unfortunately, the plaintiff missed the dismount and fell to the floor, breaking his neck.

The plaintiff was found 20% contributorily negligent because he knew that the maneuver was dangerous and provided no notice to his spotter that he was going to try it. The instructor was found 80% liable for the accident.

In determining the negligence of the teacher, the Court noted a number of factors that would affect the standard of care required of the instructor. The factors that the court considered most important were as follows:

- Nature of the activity
- Age, skill, and training of the student prior to the activity
- Nature and condition of the equipment
- Competency and capacity of the students
- Number of students being supervised

[*Myers v. Peel County Board of Education* (1981), 2 S.C.R. 21, 17 C.C.L.T. 269, 37 M.R. 227, 123 D.L.R. (3d) 1]

KEY TERMS

Assault with a weapon (296)
Duty of care (292)
Causation (293)
Common assault (296)
Consent to the infliction of force (296)
Contributory negligence (295)
Informed consent document (294)
Intention (296)
Lack of intention (298)
Self-defense (298)
Settlement (292)
Standard of care (293)
Voluntary assumption of risk (293)

REFERENCES

Agar v. Canning (1966), 54 W.W.R. 302 (Man. Q.B.); affd. 55 W.W.R. 384 (C.A.).

Criminal Code of Canada, R.S.C. 1985, c.C-46.

Crocker v. Sundance Resorts Ltd. (1983), 150 D.L.R. (3d) 478 Rev'd [1985] 20 D.L.R. (4d) 552 (Ont. C.A.) Rev'd 44 C.C.L.T. 225 (S.C.C.).

Delaney v. Cascade River Holidays Ltd. (1983), 24 C.C.L.T. 6 (B.C.C.A.).

Dyck v. Manitoba Snowmobiling Association and Wood (1981), 3 W.W.R. 97 (Man. Q.B.); 136 D.L.R. (3d) 11 (Man. A.C.); (1985) 1 S.C.R. 589 (S.C.C.).

Myers v. Peel County Board of Education (1981), 2 S.C.R. 21, 17 C.C.L.T. 269, 37 M.R. 227, 123 D.L.R. (3d) 1.

R. v. Ciccarelli (1990), 54 C.C.C. (3d) 121 (Ont. Dist. Ct.).

R. v. Gray (1981), 6 W.W.R. 654 (Sask. Prov. Ct.).

R. v. Henderson (1976), 5 W.W.R. 119 (B.C. Co. Ct.).

R. v. Krzysztofik (1992), 16 W.C.B. (2d) 7 (Man. Q.B.).

R. v. Maki (1970), 3 O.R. 780. 1 C.C.C. (2d) 333, 14 D.L.R. (3d) 164 (Ont. Prov. Ct.).

R. v. St. Croix (1979), 47 C.C.C. (2d) 122 (Ont. Co. Ct.).

R. v. Watson (1976), 26 C.C.C. (2d) 150 (Ont. Prov. Ct.).

Saunders, L.D., & Stewart, L.M. (Eds.) (1991). Report of the Sport and Recreation Work

Group. *A safer Canada: Year 2000 injury control objectives for Canada.* Proceedings of a national symposium, Edmonton, AB, 29-32.

School Act, R.S.A. 1970, c.S 3.1, ss. 13.

School Division of Assiniboine South No. 3 v. Hoffer et al. (1971), 4 W.W.R. 746; (1971) 21 D.L.R. (3d) 608: (1971) 1 W.W.R.: 4 W.W.R. 746.

Smith v. Horizon Aero Sport Ltd. (1981), 130 D.L.R. (3d) 91, 19 C.C.L.T. 89 (B.C.S.C.).

Thornton v. Board of School District No. 57 (Prince George) (1975), 3 W.W.R. 622; 57 D.L.R. (3d) 438 (B.C.S.C.): (1976) 5 W.W.R. 240; 73 D.L.R. (3d) 35 (C.A.), rev'd in part; (1978) 2 S.C.R. 267; 3 C.C.L.T. 257; (1978) 1 W.W.R. 607; 19 N.R. 552; 83 D.L.R. (3d) 480.

White, D.V. (1986). Sports violence as criminal assault: Development of the doctrine by Canadian courts. *Duke Law Journal,* 1030-1054.

INDEX

Entries that refer to Canadian law are identified as such, except for cases (in italics) and proper names.

ABOUT THE AUTHORS

Neil Dougherty, EdD, is a professor of sport law in the Department of Exercise Science and Sport Studies at Rutgers University in New Brunswick, New Jersey. He has 20 years of experience consulting for attorneys, insurance groups, and professional groups on liability and  safety in sport. Dr. Dougherty is a member of the National Association for Physical Education in Higher Education (NAPEHE) and the American Alliance for Health, Physical Education, Recreation and Dance (AAHPERD). He is the editor of *Principles of Safety in Physical Education and Sport*.

David Auxter, EdD, is a research consultant for Special Olympics International with a broad background in adapted physical education. He has served as legislative chairperson for the National Consortium on Physical Education and Recreation for the Handi-  capped and is the author of *Principles and Methods of Adapted Physical Education*. Dr. Auxter is a member of AAHPERD.

Alan Goldberger, JD, is a practicing attorney in sport law representing sport organizations, insurance carriers, and athletic officials. Mr. Goldberger is the author of *Sports Officiating: A Legal Guide* and a member of AAHPERD. He serves as the chair of the National  Association for Girls and Women in Sport's (NAGWS) Committee on Legal Issues and as the chair of the Constitution Committee of the International Association of Approved Basketball Officials. He is an active basketball, baseball, and football official.

Hilary A. Findlay, PhD, LLB, is an attorney practicing in Edmonton, Alberta. She also lectures on sport and the law at the University of Alberta. Dr. Findlay is a member of the Canadian Bar Association and the Law Society of Alberta.

Gregg Heinzmann, EdM, is the administrator of the Rutgers Youth Sports Research Council, where he develops and disseminates safety education training to coaches and administrators. He is a member of the National Association for Sport and Physical Education (NASPE) and AAHPERD.